Windows® XP Hacks & Mods For Dummies®

Cheat Sheet

Getting the Most from Your Music

Music companies make enormous piles of money. Microsoft and Apple both want a piece of the action. But what's best for them may not be best for you, or for consumers in general. Here's what every electronic-music consumer needs to know:

- **File formats count.** You might think that Microsoft's WMA files, Apple's AAC files, and the lowly, decade-old MP3 file format are basically the same. They aren't. The rules get more complicated (and more onerous!) all the time. If you want your music to be free, it has to be MP3.

- **Windows Media Player** *can* **"rip" audio CDs to MP3 files.** Back in the early days of Windows XP, converting audio CDs into unprotected MP3 files was difficult. Now it's easy — if you know the trick (Chapter 20).

- **Your iPod isn't chained to iTunes.** If you have an iPod, you've probably discovered that (1) you can't copy songs from the iPod onto your computer, and (2) your iPod is "married" to one computer. You don't have to live with those restrictions (Chapter 21).

- **Plays For Sure doesn't.** A Microsoft "Plays For Sure" song certainly won't play on an iPod. A Microsoft "Plays For Sure" MP3 player (er, personal audio player) won't play music you buy from the iTunes store. The only music that really "Plays For Sure" is MP3. That's why they call it an MP3 player, eh?

- **Each music store has different rules.** Some stores sell songs that can be played on at most four PCs. Others allow you to burn the songs you buy on at most five CDs. Some stores give you access to millions of songs, but if you can't connect your MP3 player to an anointed PC at the end of the month, all the songs go bye-bye. It's a jungle out there (Chapter 21).

- **Not all music trading is illegal.** *Most* of it is. Not all of it. Some bands encourage no-cost trading: the Grateful Dead blesses the free exchange of fans' concert recordings, for example, and has since the sixties (Chapter 22). What a long, strange trip it's been.

P9-EEJ-017

For Dummies: Bestselling Book Series for Beginners

SHW *Windows* *& Mods For Dummies*®

BESTSELLING BOOK SERIES

Cheat Sheet

Breaking In a New Computer

If your computer's brand-spankin'-new, or if it's never been seriously modded before, follow this check-list from Chapter 3 and take control of your Windows destiny. Hey, it's your computer. You paid for it. Why let the advertisers and scum-meisters gunk it up?

- ❑ **Get Windows up-to-date,** but don't let Microsoft automatically update it for you. *FREE*
- ❑ **Check your firewall** before you do anything else.
- ❑ **Fire your antivirus program** — get a free one that won't beg you for money every time you turn around. *FREE*
- ❑ **Show filename extensions,** overturning one of the dumbest design decisions Microsoft ever made.
- ❑ **Install an aggressive anti-spyware program.**
- ❑ **Change your wallpaper** so you don't look like every other DELL user. *FREE*

- ❑ **Get a cool screensaver** or none at all.
- ❑ **Set up user accounts** that make sense for your situation.
- ❑ **Tame (or dump!) Windows/MSN Messenger.**
- ❑ **Get Firefox** and throw away Internet Explorer. It's free! *FREE*
- ❑ **Use Google's Desktop Search** for industrial-strength searching on your computer. It's free! *FREE*
- ❑ **Install Adobe Acrobat Reader** so you can read PDF files. It's free! *FREE*

What You Need to Do Now to Protect Yourself

- ✔ **Buy, install, update, and religiously use a major antivirus package.** I recommend the free-for-personal-use package called AVG Free from Grisoft (see Chapter 18).
- ✔ **Force Windows to show you filename extensions.** Microsoft's decision to have Windows hide filename extensions is a dangerous design mistake that every Windows user can and should fix (see Chapter 3).
- ✔ **After you can see filename extensions, watch out for suspicious extensions in e-mail attachments.** If you receive a file with one of the doubtful extensions attached to an e-mail message (see the table of filename extensions in Chapter 8) and you double-click the file, it may run immediately, with potentially disastrous results. This is the most common way for viruses to travel via e-mail. And it's 100 percent preventable.
- ✔ **Never open or run a file attached to an e-mail message until you**
  - ✔ Contact the person who sent you the message and verify that he or she specifically sent you the file.
  - ✔ Save the file on your hard drive, update your antivirus software's signature file, and run your antivirus software on the file.
- ✔ **Get Windows Firewall working right.** Check to see if it's doing the job by inviting a Web site that will poke and prod at your machine (Chapter 17).
- ✔ **Clobber scummy programs before they clobber you.** Microsoft's Antispyware, Sunbelt Software's CounterSpy, and Mike Lin's StartupMonitor belong on every PC (Chapter 18).

For Dummies: Bestselling Book Series for Beginners

Windows® XP
Hacks & Mods
FOR
DUMMIES®

Windows® XP
Hacks & Mods
FOR
DUMMIES®

by Woody Leonhard

Wiley Publishing, Inc.

Windows® XP Hacks & Mods For Dummies®

Published by
Wiley Publishing, Inc.
111 River Street
Hoboken, NJ 07030-5774

www.wiley.com

Copyright © 2005 by Wiley Publishing, Inc., Indianapolis, Indiana

Published by Wiley Publishing, Inc., Indianapolis, Indiana

Published simultaneously in Canada

For general information on our other products and services, please contact our Customer Care Department within the U.S. at 800-762-2974, outside the U.S. at 317-572-3993, or fax 317-572-4002.

For technical support, please visit www.wiley.com/techsupport.

Wiley also publishes its books in a variety of electronic formats. Some content that appears in print may not be available in electronic books.

Library of Congress Control Number: 2005927631

ISBN-13: 978-0-471-74897-7

ISBN-10: 0-471-74897-8

Manufactured in the United States of America

10 9 8 7 6 5 4 3 2 1

1O/RZ/QZ/QV/IN

WILEY

About the Author

In the past fifteen years, **Woody Leonhard** has written more than computer books, drawing an unprecedented six Computer Press Association awards and two American Business Press awards. Woody was one of the first Microsoft Consulting Partners and is a charter member of the Microsoft Solutions Provider organization. He's widely quoted — and reviled — on the Redmond campus.

Woody's Web site, `askwoody.com`, keeps an eye on the computer industry, covering the latest shenanigans from Microsoft, the best software for your computer, the worst pitfalls (and patches!) to avoid, updates to his books, and all the other information you need to keep your PC chugging away.

Woody lives just this side of paradise in Phuket, Thailand, along with his most significant other, Add, and his son, Justin. Most mornings, you can find him jogging on Patong Beach with their beagle, Chronos, or sipping a latte at Khun Woody's Bakery. Drop by when you get a chance!

Dedication

To Duangkhae Tongthueng (better known as "Add"), and to Justin, the best parts of my life. Forgive me for all the long hours slaving away on this project.

Author's Acknowledgments

Justin Leonhard contributed numerous ideas, warnings, and hacks to the sections on gaming and the iPod, in particular, and helped with insightful comments in several other parts of the book. Thanks, Justin!

Many thanks, as always, to Claudette Moore and Debbie McKenna at Moore Literary Agency, my guides for nearly 15 years. Thanks, too, to Steve Hayes, Becky Huehls, Colleen Totz, Lee Musick, and all the people at Wiley who made this project work.

What a concept: Windows hacking made accessible to regular Windows users. With your help, I think this book succeeds marvelously.

Publisher's Acknowledgments

We're proud of this book; please send us your comments through our online registration form located at www.dummies.com/register/.

Some of the people who helped bring this book to market include the following:

Acquisitions, Editorial, and Media Development

Project Editor: Rebecca Huehls

Senior Acquisitions Editor: Steven Hayes

Development and Copy Editor: Colleen Totz

Technical Editor: Lee Musick

Editorial Managers: Leah Cameron, Carol Sheehan

Media Development Manager: Laura VanWinkle

Media Development Supervisor: Richard Graves

Editorial Assistant: Amanda Foxworth

Cartoons: Rich Tennant (www.the5thwave.com)

Composition Services

Project Coordinator: Adrienne Martinez

Layout and Graphics: Carl Byers, Andrea Dahl, Lauren Goddard, Joyce Haughey, Julie Trippetti

Proofreaders: TECHBOOKS Production Services, Leeann Harney

Indexer: TECHBOOKS Production Services

Special Help: Andy Hollandbeck

Publishing and Editorial for Technology Dummies

    Richard Swadley, Vice President and Executive Group Publisher

    Andy Cummings, Vice President and Publisher

    Mary Bednarek, Executive Acquisitions Director

    Mary C. Corder, Editorial Director

Publishing for Consumer Dummies

    Diane Graves Steele, Vice President and Publisher

    Joyce Pepple, Acquisitions Director

Composition Services

    Gerry Fahey, Vice President of Production Services

    Debbie Stailey, Director of Composition Services

Contents at a Glance

Table of Contents

Part II: Controlling the Look and Feel of Windows XP ...45

Introduction

*W*indows XP *deserves* to be hacked.

Hey, it's your computer, your copy of Windows, your life. Why settle for the same old stuff that 250,000,000 Windows XP owners take every day? It's time to take control of your computing destiny. Break free from the shackles of mediocrity. Throw away the training wheels and make Windows work the way you want, not the other way around.

You can do it. I show you how.

About This Book

Windows XP Hacks and Mods For Dummies takes you into the belly of the beast, showing you where and how to bend Windows to your way of working. Some of the changes you find in this book use tools built into Windows itself — frequently in ways you might not have considered. Many of the changes require poking and prodding in ways that Windows' designers never imagined. Sometimes you walk in the front door; sometimes you shimmy down the chimney. Whatever it takes, eh?

Back in the not-so-good old days, a Windows "hack" was, by definition, a modification to the Registry that made Windows work better. Or at least it made Windows work differently. Nowadays, it's unusual to find a hack that has to be performed *mano a mano* with the Registry: Third-party programs (including, most notably, TweakUI — which comes from Microsoft) frequently do the heavy work.

The kind of hacks and mods you find in this book allow you to customize and protect your computers, and make your computer work better. I avoid hacks that only offer marginal improvement. Unfortunately, a large percentage of published hacks you'll find on the Internet and in books fall into that category. I warn you about the most-commonly-cited "hacks" that only waste your time or make your system unstable. There's quite a crop of 'em.

Think of it this way. For years, Windows has been biting you. Now it's time to bite back.

Conventions Used in This Book

I keep the typographical conventions to a minimum:

- ✔ The first time a buzzword appears in text, I *italicize* it and define it immediately. That makes it easier for you to glance back and reread the definition.

- ✔ When I want you to type something, I put the letters or key name in **bold**. For example: "Type **Mind Meld** to initiate a Vulcan Mind Meld."

- ✔ Keep on clicking when you see ➪. I like to make instructions short and sweet, so this book avoids high-fallutin' phrases like "on the Windows Explorer menu bar choose Folder Options from the Tools menu, then select the View tab from the top of the resulting Folder Options dialog box." Pretentious fluff. I just say, "Choose Tools➪Folder Options➪View."

- ✔ I set off Web addresses and e-mail addresses, when they need to be set off, in monospace. For example, my e-mail address is woody@AskWoody.com (fact), and my Windows news and help page is at AskWoody.com (another fact).

- ✔ When a Web address gets too long — I particularly dislike typing Microsoft download addresses like www.microsoft.com/downloads/details.aspx?FamilyId=321CD7A2-6A57-4C57-A8BD-DBF62EDA9671&displaylang=en — I use a nifty Web-based program called TinyURL to come up with a short equivalent address, thus reducing the strain on your eyes and fingers. (To see how it works, try typing tinyurl.com/5jhcs into any handy Web browser; you end up at that monstrous download address.) I talk about TinyURL and how to hook it directly into Firefox in Chapter 11.

There's one other convention, though, that I use all the time. I always, absolutely, adamantly include the filename extension — those letters at the end of a filename, like doc or vbs or exe — when talking about a file. Yeah, I know Windows XP hides filename extensions unless you go in and change it. Yeah, I know that Bill G Hisself made the decision to hide them, and he won't back off. (At least, that's the rumor.)

I also know that hundreds — probably thousands — of Microsoft employees passed along the ILOVEYOU virus, primarily because they couldn't see the filename extension that would've warned them. Bah. Bad decision, Bill.

If you haven't yet told Windows XP to show you filename extensions, take a minute right now and hop to Chapter 3. Knock some sense into Windows.

What You're Not to Read

If you have a new PC or one that hasn't been changed much since you first bought it, jump to Chapter 3. Right now. There's so much junk on that PC that you're committing a crime against nature by not getting it cleaned up and running right.

On the other hand, if you're an old hand at the hacking and modding game, take a leisurely stroll through the chapters and try the tricks that tantalize. Bet you'll find more than a few that you haven't seen before — and I bet you'll also find that some of those hacks you read about on the Web aren't such a great idea.

Foolish Assumptions

Assumptions? About you? Well, you're obviously intelligent and discerning. Curious. Adventurous. Perhaps a bit cautious. That's good. Too many people uncritically accept the dubious hacking advice floating around on the Web and then wonder why their machines don't work right after following BillyJoeBob's Patented Registry and Halitosis Cures meticulously. You, however, are more cautious than those people.

There's nothing particularly magical about hacking and modding Windows XP. You can do it, even if you're all thumbs (like me). Just remember to back up all your data files, disinfect your Registry, turn your monitor upside down, play a Beatles CD backward, burn patchouli incense, and chant *"om mani padme hum"* while trying any of the tougher hacks, okay?

I was joking about the incense.

How This Book Is Organized

Windows XP Hacks & Mods For Dummies tackles the top Windows XP changes in seven parts.

Part 1: The Nuts & Bolts of Hacks & Mods

An overview of the good, the bad, and the ugly of Windows XP: what tools you have at your disposal to change it and, most important, a detailed step-by-step description of how to get rid of the garbage on a new (or almost new) computer. If you're still looking at icons you never use, read this part.

Part II: Controlling the Look and Feel of Windows XP

This part takes you through TweakUI, the ultimate hacker's toy; modifications to the Start menu; using the Windows taskbar effectively; and how to make the Windows desktop look (and behave!) the way *you* want, not the way some guy in a lab in Redmond thought might be cool.

Part III: Adjusting Everyday Activities

In this part, you bring Windows Explorer to task, using the keyboard in ways you never dreamed possible. It also covers Google Desktop Search, Firefox, and Trillian (for instant messaging), and offers industrial-strength tips for working with pictures.

Part IV: Modding to Monitor and Manage

This part shows you how to use the built-in Windows tools to see what's going on under the hood, explains how to reverse-engineer your CD key, illustrates how to use Remote Assistance to get help from somebody who knows, and helps you run down your disks and keep the platters spinning.

Part V: Protecting Yourself (And Your PC)

Keep Microsoft's mitts off your machine! This part gets you started using security settings that work in the real world, fighting scumware, and making sure that prying eyes can't spy on you.

Part VI: Entertaining Yourself

Got an iPod? You need this part. Find out how to avoid Microsoft's money-mongering in Media Player; how to buy music and videos; how to trade files with P2P file-sharing programs; and, the toughest technical problem of all, how to get games to work.

Part VII: The Part of Tens

Every *For Dummies* book ends with the Part of Tens, and this book is no different. Check out this part to find ten steps to mastering the Registry and ten hacks that might speed up your computer. (Or maybe not. But at least it's fun to try.)

Icons Used in This Book

Windows XP Hacks & Mods For Dummies absolutely brims with challenging hacks and worthwhile mods that'll turn Windows on its heels. To keep you pointed in the right direction, I use these icons:

Sometimes a hack is so incredibly . . . incredibly . . . *hackalicious* that I can't stand it. (Er, uh, "hackalicious" is a technical term. Yeah. You know, like "Little Endian Double Word." Never mind. You don't want to know.) A few truly rare, utterly fine hackalicious hacks merit SuperHack status, as conveyed by this award-winning icon.

Achtung! Cuidado! Thar be tygers here! Any place you see a Warning icon, you can be sure that I've been burnt — badly — in the past. Mind your fingers. These are really, really mean suckers.

You don't need to memorize the stuff marked with this icon, but you should try to remember that there's something special lurking about.

The Tip icon points out the real gems — the really cool suggestions or a bits of insight you won't find anywhere else.

Where to Go from Here

If you have a new (or nearly new) computer, start with Chapter 3.

Other than that, the world's your oyster, and this book holds the pearls. Read it from front to back or hop around to your heart's content. Have fun!

Part I
The Nuts & Bolts of Hacks & Mods

The 5th Wave   By Rich Tennant

Wanda had the distinct feeling that her husband's new operating system was about to become interactive

In this part . . .

"Why would you *want* to change Windows?" I remember the day a visitor to my Web site asked me that question. After I finished sputtering and pulled myself off the floor, I gave him the best answer I could muster: "Because Windows deserves to be hacked."

If you honestly believe that Windows XP is perfect, right out of the box, you have my undying admiration. Some people aren't interested, or can't be bothered, to whack Windows around a bit. I suspect that most of them are too intimidated to get their hands a trifle dirty, but that's okay. Therapy can help.

This part introduces you to a few of the tools of the trade — picks, Slim-Jims, sledge hammers, RPGs, and the like. Then I show you how to take an ad-infested new machine, get rid of the scum, mash things around a bit, and turn the new PC into an object of pride.

Chapter 1

Windows XP: What's Not to Love?

*L*et's face it. Most Windows users just sit there and take it. If Windows crashes and says it wants to send information to Microsoft, they just let it go. Literally. If their PC vendor put putrid pink wallpaper on the desktop, well, it could be worse, right? If AOL wants to stick its signup icon on the desktop and make it hard to remove, or if Norton keeps advising to send $30 to keep all hell from breaking loose, or if Windows Media Player keeps ripping songs that can't be played on any other machine, well, that's the way the Windows gods set things up, right?

Guess what. The gods are *crazy.*

Well, Perhaps There's Room for Improvement

I'll never forget the day, about ten years ago, when one of my readers wrote to me, castigating me for taking Microsoft to task about one of its truly stupid Windows design decisions (of which there are many). If Windows is so bad, he said, why don't I use some other program? Why do I always assume that key decisions are made simply to line Microsoft's coffers? And if Bill Gates has such lousy products, Woody, tell me this: Why is he so rich?

Indeed.

Several worms have turned in the intervening decade. Bashing Microsoft has replaced baseball as the national pastime, or so it seems. But even though we all love Windows and we hate Windows and we love to hate Windows, an old truth still reverberates: *You don't have to take it*. You can change Windows significantly to make it work the way *you* want.

That's what this book is all about.

Microsoft put Windows XP together to make life easy for beginners and to convince you to spend more money (see, for example, the link to a DoubleClick ad on Microsoft's Start Something New page, shown at the bottom of Figure 1-1). After you use Windows XP for a couple of months, you're no longer a beginner — but it can be infuriatingly difficult to remove the training wheels and dislodge the advertising, and even more of a challenge to get Windows to work more like the way you do, instead of the other way around.

Figure 1-1:
Start
Something
New —
take
Windows by
the horns
and change
it the way
you want.

Hacking and modifying Windows puts you back in the driver's seat, right where you belong.

When to Hack Windows XP — and When to Let It Be

If you read the books and magazine articles and rifle through the Internet, you'll find hundreds — no, *thousands* — of Windows hacks and mods. A large percentage of them don't do anything worthwhile. Some even make your machine unstable. Most simply take a lot of effort and accomplish basically nothing.

You tell me: Why would you spend half an hour trying to shave five seconds off the time it takes Windows to reboot? Take off your shoes, pilgrim; count on your toes; and do the math. If you reboot Windows three times a week, it takes . . . lessssee . . . two and a half *years* to break even. Sure, hacking's fun, but if you're going to devote some time and energy to the pursuit, why not do something worthwhile?

Hacks that don't work

Having seen many hacks come and go over the years, I can tell you that these hacks are largely overrated:

- **Making Registry changes to speed up a computer.** In some very specific cases (which I discuss in Chapter 25), changing the Registry can speed up your computer a little bit. Sometimes. But by and large, spelunking through your Registry looking for a killer bit that'll boost your speed by 10 percent is a fool's game.

  If you *do* find a hack that'll speed up your computer by 10 percent, you'll never even notice the difference. It takes a speed-up of 20 percent or so to be noticeable — and even a 30 percent gain won't seem like much after a day or two. On the other hand, if that speed-up hack makes your computer unstable, believe me, you will notice. Right between the eyes you'll notice.

- **Using any Registry cleanup utility.** There's one born every minute. Software companies have made millions and millions of dollars offering programs that scan and clean your Registry entries. I've never seen a single Registry cleaner that was both *safe* and *effective*. Sure, your Registry gets clogged up with useless entries. Does that make your machine slower? No. "Cleaning" little-known Registry entries can make your machine roll over and die. You're better off using a sledgehammer.

- **Disabling Windows processes.** I've seen a dozen reasons for disabling the Windows programs that automatically launch when Windows starts. (You can see which processes are running on your computer — except the really stealthy ones — by pressing Ctrl+Alt+Del and clicking Processes in the Windows Task Manager, per Figure 1-2). None of the reasons I've seen for disabling processes manually makes any sense. Years ago, a Windows process called UPnP opened a huge security hole in Windows XP. Microsoft fixed the hole, eventually, and for a while it made sense to disable the UPnP process.

  If you have renegade processes, they're symptomatic of another problem — generally a worm, spyware, or some other form of malware. You should treat the problem by zapping out the offending software instead of attacking things piecemeal by manually disabling a running process that you don't understand.

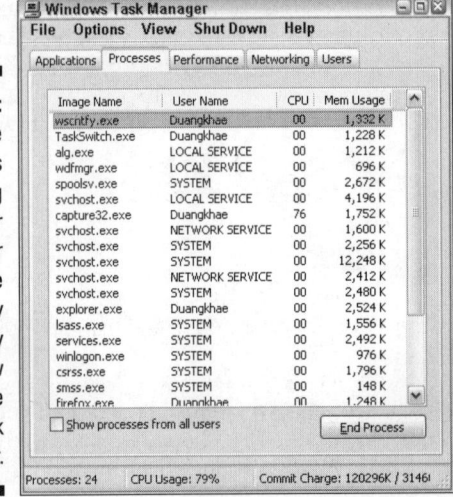

Figure 1-2:
All of the processes running on your computer (except the really sneaky ones) show up in the Task Manager.

✓ **Assigning fancy file access permissions.** Yes, I know you can fine-tune folder and file permissions, even with Windows XP Home, so you can allow certain people to see your files, keep others out, and make others dance like bears before the data comes up. But for most people, it isn't worth the effort. Why? If you really need to set up sophisticated file access permissions — so that John can read a file and Mary can update it — and you aren't willing to use passwords, you need to bite the bullet and install a server, Windows XP Pro, and Active Directory. The half-fast approaches to restricting access in Windows XP Home are doomed to failure simply because the tools aren't all there.

✓ **Doing anything involving DOS.** Okay, there are exceptions. I even talk about one of them in this book (see Chapter 8). But if you aren't conversant with DOS — and few of us are after all these years — you can almost always find a better way to accomplish what you want by using Windows alone or one of the nearly infinite number of free utilities.

✓ **Making parental control software and modifications.** Doomed to failure, no matter how hard you try. Windows doesn't have the tools to properly implement parental control, and the world on the Web changes much too fast. Don't even bother.

Keeping hacks and mods in perspective

You aren't going to turn a sow's ear into a silk purse. And with a little luck, you won't mess things up and turn things the other way around — although I *have* seen fancy systems that look and run like a sow's ear.

The best hacks and mods make Windows do something that you really like — something that will make your day go better or get you home earlier. The worst ones gum up the works and cause no end of problems down the line.

A Quick Look at Some Cool XP Hacks and Mods

Here are my favorite hacks and mods, replacements, and enhancements:

- ✔ Without doubt, **TweakUI** — Microsoft's tool with a checkered past — rates as the premiere hacker's Swiss army knife (Chapter 4). If you want to change the way Windows looks or works, chances are good that making the change takes only a couple of clicks, thanks to this enormously powerful tool.

- ✔ Many people don't realize that they can change the contents of the **Quick Launch Toolbar** — the devilishly clever box of icons to the right of the Start button (Chapter 6). Even those who have discovered Quick Launch don't know the many different shortcuts it can handle or how to customize them.

- ✔ **Google Desktop Search** (Chapter 10) has changed my life. Really. I used to dread having to use Microsoft's enormously buggy search functions, both in Windows and in Office, and after I ran a search through the wringer, I could never be sure if Windows or Office found everything. All that's a thing of the past because I can put my finger on what I want, right now.

- ✔ It may be just as buggy, statistically, as Internet Explorer, but I breathe easier knowing that **Firefox** (Chapter 11) keeps me out of the crosshairs of most of the world's malware miscreants.

- ✔ Working with big photo files drove me nuts until I discovered Microsoft's free **Image Resizer PowerToy** (Chapter 12). Now I can change a giant photo file into a high-quality snapshot with a simple right-click.

- ✔ On the fun side, I just about flipped when I discovered how to use a photo as my **"user picture"** — both on the Windows logon screen and at the top of the Start menu (Chapter 14).

- ✔ I'll never pay for an antivirus product again — or put up with their begging me to part with my hard-earned cash for another update. I use **AVG Free,** and it works just as well as all the expensive programs (Chapter 18).

- ✔ Microsoft wants you to use its proprietary file format for all of your music. Why? Does the phrase "feeeeelthy lucre" mean anything to you? You need to twiddle a setting and know when to stick to your guns (Chapter 20), but using **MP3 files** makes your music-listening experience a whole lot simpler.

✔ And my **iPod.** Oh, my iPod. There's something cool about the little beast — and something comforting in the knowledge that I can hornswoggle Windows into working well with an Apple product (Chapter 21).

✔ I detest **malware,** sleazeware, and all those other pieces of junk floating around. It's personal. Back when the PC was new and Windows was a gleam in Bill Gates's eye, we computer folks hung together, helped each other, and (heaven help us!) believed in The Common Good. All of that's changed, particularly with the commercial success of all that crapware. But there are good, solid ways to fight back, and I talk about them in Chapter 18.

✔ I use the firewall that ships with Windows XP Service Pack 2, and I feel a whole lot better knowing that I can **lock down Windows Firewall** with the click of a single icon (Chapter 17).

Of course, this book abounds with hundreds of hacks, mods, tweaks, and tips, and I urge you to give them all a once-over to see which ones are right for you.

Staying Safe and Sound While You Work

When you hack and slash at the innards of Windows, you need to be prepared for the possibility that something will go bump in the night. Of course, everyone knows that you should back up your data and program settings. Be that as it may, you really *should* back up your data and settings. Know what I mean?

Many folks get confused about the various types of backups that Windows and software manufacturers make available. Not all backups back up the same things. Here's a quick guide to backing up for hackers and modders:

✔ **Data backups** involve making copies of your data files and sticking them someplace where they won't get clobbered. That way, you can copy the originals back if your original data (or hard drive) goes kaput. Hacking Windows rarely disturbs a data file, but if anything should go wrong, you'll be happy to have a pristine copy.

Although your choices for data backup are legion, I've always used a small, reliable program called ZipBackup (www.zipbackup.com), which compresses data and stores everything in zip files. That way, if you need to get your data back, you don't need to hassle with loading a complicated restore program — you just grab a zip and you're on your way. At $29.95 (with a free 30-day trial), I think it's a great deal.

✔ **Registry backups** take the contents of the Windows Registry and write everything out to a data file. In effect, you turn an amorphous glob known as the Registry into a simple (if lengthy) text file, which you can subsequently back up like any other data file. I give you the lowdown on Registry backups in Chapter 24.

✔ When you (or Windows or an application program) establish a **System Restore Point,** Windows creates one big file that includes a full Registry backup, copies of all the users' personalized settings (even the ones that aren't in the Registry), and copies of many key system files.

Note that a System Restore Point doesn't do anything with your data files. You can create a Restore Point, change a gazillion Word documents and spreadsheets, copy a thousand pictures and songs to your PC, and then go back to the Restore Point, and all of your data comes through intact.

Most programs (including Windows updates) and hardware device drivers create restore points before you install them. If something goes wrong, it's relatively easy to "roll back" to the Restore Point and get your system running again. You can roll back to a Restore Point manually by choosing Start⇨All Programs⇨Accessories⇨System Tools⇨System Restore and following the wizard, shown in Figure 1-3. (You can roll back to the last System Restore Point by starting Windows while holding down the F8 key and then choosing Last Known Good Configuration.) For all the key details on System Restore, look at Technique 64 of *Windows XP Timesaving Techniques For Dummies,* 2nd Edition.

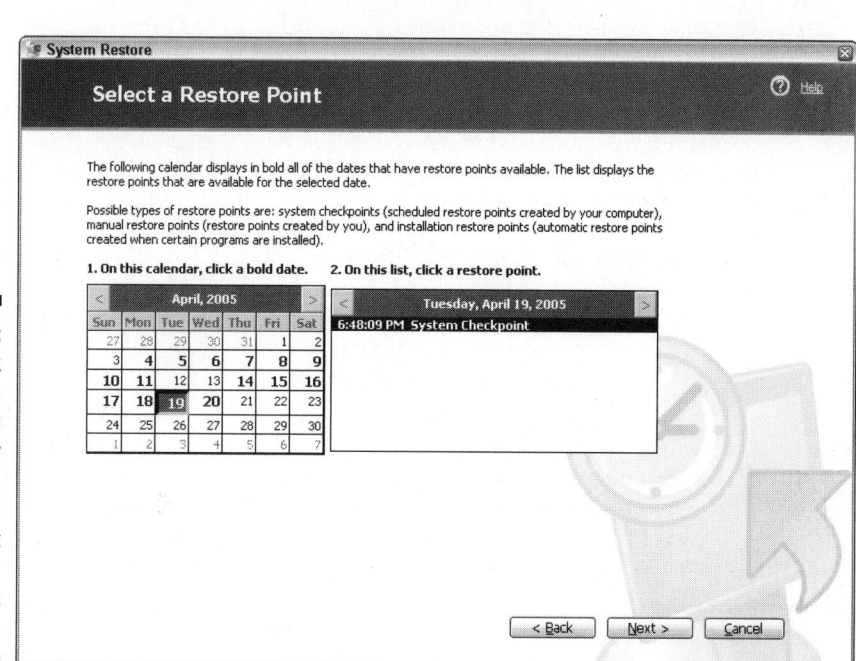

Figure 1-3: Rolling back to a Restore Point takes a few minutes and requires a restart, but the wizard makes it easy.

- ✔ The most thorough backup? **A complete copy (frequently called a *ghost*) of your hard drive.** Running a ghost not only backs up your data files, but also gets your Registry and everything that would go into a Restore Point — and all the other little bits and pieces.

  The archetypal disk ghosting program, Norton Ghost (`www.symantec.com/sabu/ghost`), will set you back $69.95, but it's the most complete and reliable solution to the perennial backup problem.

Personally, I use ZipBackup daily to keep my data backups fresh and Norton Ghost once a month, just in case. I let Windows and the program installers automatically generate System Restore Points. The amount of time and effort involved is minimal, and if I ever get carried away with my hacking, I know that relief is just a few clicks (and maybe a two-hour-long restore!) away.

Windows XP has a built-in backup program called NTBackup, but I don't use it. If you're connected to a Big Corporate Network, you may want to try it, but I don't think it's worth the effort. Windows XP Home users, in particular, have to jump through all sorts of hoops to get NTBackup to work.

Chapter 2

Tools of the Hacking Trade

●●

In This Chapter

▶ Discover what goes on behind the scenes

▶ See how hacks and mods fit into the picture

▶ Find reliable sources of hacking information

▶ Get the best tools, in the right places

●●

> *HACKER [originally, someone who makes furniture with an axe] n. A person who enjoys learning the details of programming systems and how to stretch their capabilities, as opposed to most users, who prefer to learn only the minimum necessary.*
>
> —*The New Hacker's Dictionary*, Eric S. Raymond, MIT Press

Understanding How Windows Hangs Together

*B*efore you go digging under the hood, it would behoove you to understand the beast inside your PC. More than 700,000,000 PCs all over the world run Windows. Or try to.

Scary thought, that.

A world of processes

Windows XP is the most sophisticated computer program ever constructed: 50,000,000 lines of code, and nobody — absolutely nobody — knows how it all works.

I misspoke.

Windows XP isn't a program per se. It's actually hundreds of separate programs, dozens of which are running at any given moment (see Figure 2-1), all banging around like amoebae in what I think of as the Windows Primordial Ooze.

Figure 2-1:
A typical list
of programs
that are
running
when
nothing
interesting
is
happening
in Windows.

To see a similar list of all the programs currently running on your computer:

1. **Hold down the Ctrl and Alt keys simultaneously and then press the Del key.**

   Windows shows you the Task Manager.

2. **Click the Processes tab.**

   You see the list of running processes, as in Figure 2-1.

You can click any column heading in the processes list to sort on that column. For example, click CPU, and Task Manager sorts the list so that the program using the most computer time comes out on top.

If you look at Figure 2-1, you'll see a lot of mystifying entries. Many of them are so-called "system services" — programs that Windows automatically kick-starts when it boots.

Yes, you can tell Windows to not load certain services when it starts. (Click Start➪Run, type `services.msc`, and double-click the service you want to start or stop.) Several Web sites recommend that you knock out a service or two, presumably to make Windows faster or more secure. I say balderdash — it isn't worth your time or sanity to go chasing after services, as I explain in Chapter 1.

What is SvcHost?

Almost everyone has a large number of processes called `svchost.exe`. If you aren't expecting to see a big bunch of SvcHosts, you might think that you're coming down with a virus. Ain't necessarily so.

SvcHost is kind of a cocoon for other programs. More to the point, it's the name that appears on the Processes tab when many different kinds of programs are running. The program being swaddled by SvcHost may be quite benevolent, or it could be a nasty piece of scumware. If you suspect the latter, don't try to monkey around with SvcHost processes — you might clobber an important task. Instead, follow the nostrums in Chapter 18 to get at the root of the problem.

Windows as referee

Windows' first and most pervasive job is to act as referee among all the programs running under Windows — even the pieces of Windows that are running under Windows. Got that?

When Windows starts, it transfers a bunch of programs from your hard drive into memory — thus populating the seminal primordial ooze — and sets the whole apparatus in motion. When a program wants to run (prompted, perhaps, by your incessant insistence on clicking something), the program asks Windows to give it some space in the ooze. Windows obliges, allocates space for the program and the system baggage that goes along with it, and then starts the program by running its first instruction.

You might think that Windows would then rest on its laurels, but noooo . . . You see, other denizens of the ooze want to run, too, from time to time — performing tasks from the mundane ticking of a clock to the hypervigilant monitoring of an antivirus program. It's Windows' job to play traffic cop; to allow each program to run for a slice of time, and then to push the program out of the way and back into the ooze, allowing a different program to take control.

Kind of like the guy who handles the microphone at the Amoeba Karaoke bar.

If you get the idea that Windows' job is kinda simple — just tossing the mike from one amoeba to another — consider this: Every time you press a key, Windows has to figure out which key you pressed and send it to the right program. Every time you move the mouse, Windows has to swing the pointer across the screen. Every time you click, Windows has to figure out where and how you clicked, kick the responsible program into a state in which it's capable of receiving commands, and then pass on the click information.

When you hack into Windows — to set up a hotkey to launch a program, for example — keep in mind that everything you do goes into Windows *before* it goes into the application. You may think you're typing a word in, uh, Word. You aren't. You're pushing a key, and that keystroke gets picked up by Windows and then fed to Word. That's how hotkeys work: They intercept the key combinations while Windows is in control.

Amoebus interruptus

The amoebae in the primordial karaoke bar can be terribly bad mannered. At any given moment, an amoeba can demand to have the mike, and Windows has to figure out a way to get it over to the interrupting amoeba with, at most, mere milliseconds of delay. That kind of "interrupt" takes place when, say, your cable modem needs to shove data into your computer or when you're burning a DVD and the drive can't wait. And, of course, the interrupting amoeba can, itself, be interrupted.

It ain't easy being Windows.

Windows errors, particularly the infamous "Microsoft *<insert program name here>* has encountered a problem and needs to close" errors (see Figure 2-2), frequently reflect squabbling among the amoebae in the primordial ooze. For example, if one amoeba tries to reach over into another amoeba's territory, Windows slaps the offender upside the head and shuts it down.

Figure 2-2:
What happens when one program doesn't get along with the others.

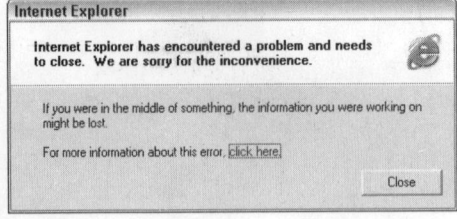

If you change something and suddenly find a lot of programs triggering errors like the one in Figure 2-2, you probably disturbed Windows' ability to referee events in the primordial ooze. Your best bet is to roll back to a previous restore point, as described in Chapter 1.

Programs talk, talk, talk

No organism is an island, and amoebae are no exception.

Windows' second-most-important function involves keeping the lines of communication open among the amoebae floating around in the primordial ooze. In some cases, it's a question of finding out who's calling whom, waking up any programs that are sloughing off, and making sure that the communication goes through. But frequently, Windows' responsibilities go deeper.

Any program — er, amoeba — that wants to talk to Windows has to speak Windows' language, and it has to know which part of Windows to talk to. If a program wants to draw something on the screen, for example, it usually talks to a Windows program known as GDIPlus.exe, and it follows a strict set of rules about what to say and how and when to say it.

The set of rules covering what to say and how and when to say it is called an *Application Program Interface* (known as an API to one and all). In a very real sense, the Windows API defines Windows. Many of the hacks you apply — particularly if they involve installing a new program — work by insinuating themselves into the Windows API, taking over for native Windows functions, or hooking into Windows functions. They must speak the Windows language precisely. When there's the slightest flaw in the hack's ability to conform to Windows' strict rules, instability often results, and you get error messages like that in Figure 2-2, or a Blue Screen of Death, shown in Figure 2-3.

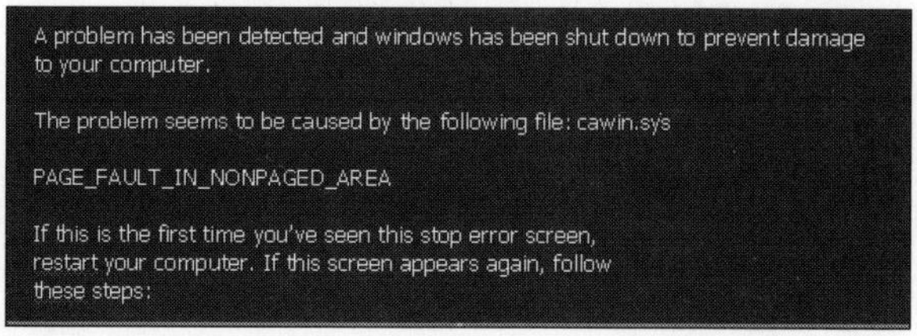

Figure 2-3:
The Blue
Screen of
Death
signifies
that
Windows is
seriously
out to lunch.

A problem has been detected and windows has been shut down to prevent damage to your computer.

The problem seems to be caused by the following file: cawin.sys

PAGE_FAULT_IN_NONPAGED_AREA

If this is the first time you've seen this stop error screen, restart your computer. If this screen appears again, follow these steps:

The Role of the Registry

Most hacks and mods you make to your computer fall into one of two categories:

- ✔ Programs that you install and run, either continuously (such as antivirus software) or sporadically (such as registration key sniffers).

✔ Changes to the Registry, either performed manually (which is rarely necessary), using one of the hooks that are built into Windows, or by using a program that knows which Registry entries to hack.

You probably know that the Registry is Windows' central repository of information. You may not know that, in fact, the Registry is a horrendous mess, poorly organized (in fact, it's a stretch to use the terms *organized* and *Registry* in the same sentence), sprawling, bloated and . . . well, a lot like Windows XP.

The Registry made its debut in Windows 95 (although there was something called the "Registration Information Editor" in Windows 3.0), and it's been devolving ever since. Thousands of programmers have stuck their entries in the big database without coordinating among themselves, and it shows.

The Registry's one great redeeming social value: It's always there. If a programmer needs to save something so it'll be around a week or a day or a second from now, the Registry is the obvious place to put it. In addition, many Registry entries are maintained by Windows on the fly, changing to reflect the current operating environment, who's logged on to the PC, and so on.

The core of the Registry lies in a bunch of files that you can't edit directly — Windows won't let you get into them (you need to use Regedit; see Chapter 24). Most of the files are in `c:\Windows\System32\Config` (see Figure 2-4):

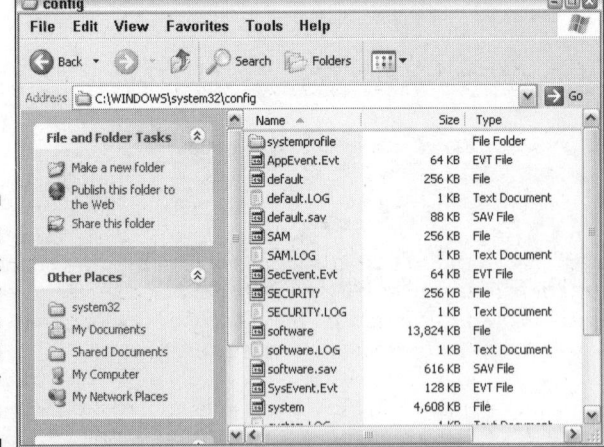

Figure 2-4:
Most
Registry
settings are
stored in
files on your
hard drive.

✔ **Default** stores settings that are applicable to all users.

✔ **SAM** has information from the Security Accounts Manager service. **SECURITY,** as you might imagine, holds security settings. You can't get at SAM or SECURITY with Regedit; you have to use Windows' built-in security programs.

> ✔ **Software** and **System** hold settings for all of your software, including Windows and other Microsoft software, which end up in the HKEY_LOCAL_MACHINE\SOFTWARE and \SYSTEM Registry keys.
>
> ✔ **UserDiff** has data that modifies default settings to form the HKEY_CURRENT_USER key.

Don't be afraid to go into the Registry, but make sure you know what you are going to accomplish before you go in and stick to what you intended to do. Avoid the temptation to poke around and change things just because you think you know what they do.

Or, heck, if you're like me, you can go in and change things just to see what goes "bump". . . er, "dump." I've been playing with the Registry for about a decade now, and it's exceedingly rare to lock up Windows or make changes that can't be readily undone. Still, if you want to make changes to the Registry that push the envelope, make sure that you have a current System Restore Point (see Chapter 1) before you do.

At the same time, I suggest you avoid *Registry cleaners* — packages that you buy to scan your Registry and remove entries — like the plague. I talk about them in Chapter 1. I've never seen a Registry Cleaner that made a big difference in performance. I've seen plenty of screw-ups caused by removed entries that the Cleaner just didn't understand.

I talk about hacking the Registry safely in Chapter 24.

Great Sources for Hacking Tools

The number-one source for Windows hacking tools?

Microsoft.

Are you shocked? You shouldn't be. It's in Microsoft's best interest to provide information and tools to safely modify Windows. TweakUI, discussed in Chapter 4, sets the standard: Hundreds of Registry hacks take only a few clicks, thanks to Microsoft's own (unsupported) program.

There are many, many Windows hack 'n' mod sites on the Internet. As is generally true with all things Internet, some of the sites are great, but many contain advice of . . . shall we say . . . dubious value. I've found the following sites to be particularly useful:

✔ **AskWoody,** my own site at www.AskWoody.com, contains the latest information on all sorts of hacks, mods, pitfalls, and pratfalls in the Windows arena. I specialize in no-nonsense advice on Windows and Office — and in holding Microsoft's feet to the fire.

✔ The **Microsoft Knowledge Base,** www.support.microsoft.com, rates as the definitive source of information — or at least the Microsoft Party Line.

✔ Jim Foley, the **Elder Geek,** www.TheElderGeek.com, always amazes me with his encyclopedic — and down-to-earth — coverage of Windows.

✔ The **Registry Mechanic,** www.winguides.com/registry, contains a lot of useful information, with a twist: They want to sell you a program that makes it easy to perform hacks, but if you want to go in and change the Registry by hand, they show you how to do that, too. The only downside: They'll try to sell you a Registry Cleaning program.

✔ Steve Sinchak's **TweakXP.com,** www.TweakXP.com, packs a bunch of hacks and mods into the exceedingly well-organized site. Steve's the author of *Hacking Windows XP,* from ExtremeTech and Wiley.

I also suggest that you subscribe to an electronic newsletter, the *Windows Secrets Newsletter* from Brian Livingston, that covers all sorts of hacks, mods, and Windows-related gotchas. The basic newsletter is free at www.Windows Secrets.com, or you can subscribe to the paid version — and pay whatever amount you feel is appropriate.

Chapter 3

A Quick XP Makeover

*W*hen you bought your PC, chances are good that it came with all sorts of junk that only gets in your way — offers for services you'll never use, icons that are hard to remove from the desktop, programs (and I won't mention Norton and McAfee by name) that keep pestering you with reminders to spend more money, "features" such as MSN that insinuate themselves into your Internet browser's main page and ooze around the edges of everything you do.

Enough is enough, eh? Here's how to finally turn off MSN Messenger once and for all; how to disable Norton and/or McAfee and replace them with perfectly usable, free alternatives; how to get the latest Service Pack installed (hint: it ain't easy!). In short, this chapter helps you take control of your PC, instead of the other way around.

Do You Need a Makeover?

In a word: Yes.

If you're still looking at wallpaper that says "Dell" or "Vaio," if you have icons on your desktop that advertise products you wouldn't touch with a three-meter pole, if Norton or McAfee come after you every few months demanding obeisance and money, if MSN Messenger (or, worse, Windows Messenger) keeps buzzing around like a mosquito inside your tent, then yep, you're ready to take control.

Whether you have a brand-new computer or you're finally getting around to setting up your old computer in a way that makes sense, here's a handful of easy, quick steps that everyone should take to make Windows work better.

That's what this chapter is all about.

Security Check — NOW

I know it's boring. But before you do anything else, take a few minutes to make sure your system can take care of itself out in the cruel, cruel online world.

Get up-to-date

I *don't* recommend that you tell Windows that it's OK to automatically apply patches as soon Microsoft makes them available. AutoUpdate is a disaster. If you don't yet know the inside story about Microsoft's automatic updates — the Keystone Kops of the Windows biz — you can read all about it in Chapter 17.

I *do*, however, recommend that you apply the patches after Windows consumers have had a chance to put them through the wringer. Let the other guys and gals get the arrows in their backs. Wait a week or two to apply security patches. I keep a running account of the good, the bad, and the very, very ugly on the Microsoft Patch Reliability Ratings page at AskWoody.com.

If you haven't updated Windows lately, do it now:

1. **Check AskWoody.com's Microsoft Patch Reliability Ratings page (shown in Figure 3-1) to see if any recent patches are causing big problems. Write down the "KB" number for any patch that you want to avoid.**

   Dangerous patches are identified with a red stoplight. Ones that have serious side effects you should know about get a yellow light. The six-digit Knowledge Base number will help you identify which patches to avoid.

2. **Choose Start⇨All Programs⇨Windows Update.**

   Windows uses Internet Explorer to take you to the Windows Update site (see Figure 3-2).

   Even if Firefox serves as your browser of choice, Microsoft will only allow you to download and apply updates using Internet Explorer. Go figure.

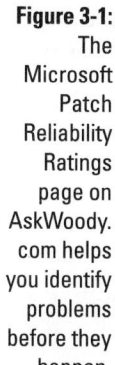

Figure 3-1:
The
Microsoft
Patch
Reliability
Ratings
page on
AskWoody.
com helps
you identify
problems
before they
happen.

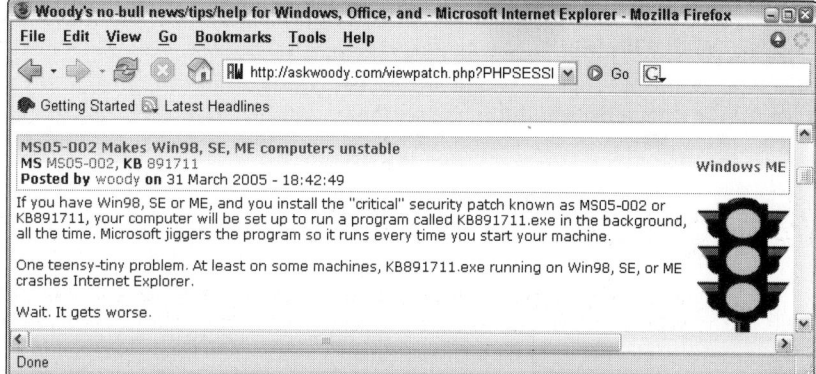

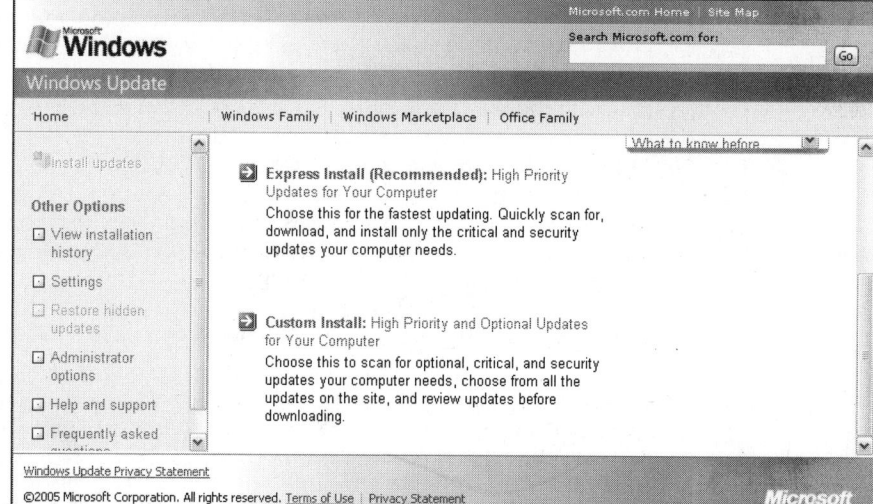

Figure 3-2:
The
Windows
Update site.

3. **If necessary, follow the instructions to install new versions of the Windows Update "sniffer," the download management program, and any other ancillary software.**

   Microsoft changes versions of the update software with alarming regularity. The process can be quite time consuming, but sooner or later you see the choice in Figure 3-2.

4. **Do *not* choose Express Install (Recommended). If you do, your PC will be updated with all the outstanding patches. Instead, click Custom Install.**

   The Windows Update sniffer examines your computer and presents you with a list of all the high-priority patches available for your particular computer (see Figure 3-3).

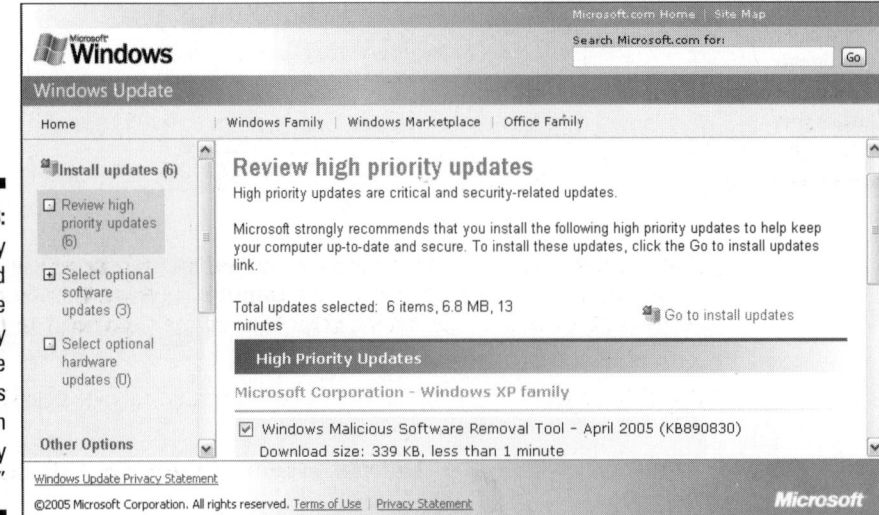

Figure 3-3: Security patches and severe stability patches are listed as "high priority updates."

5. **Uncheck the boxes in front of any patches that you identified in Step 1.**

   Don't worry — the patches will still be there the next time you run Windows Update. With a little luck, the patches may even be fixed in a week or a month.

6. **Click Go to Install Updates and then click the Install button. Depending on the updates involved, you may have enough time to grab a latte. Or ten.**

   If Windows Update tells you that it has to install one patch before it can install others, don't panic. Go ahead and follow the directions.

7. **If any of the updates requires some intervention on your part, accept all the defaults.**

   It's unusual for a security patch to ask for your intervention, but it does happen (for example, the abominable GDI+ patch known as MS 04-028). Usually, you see a window that says Downloading Updates, followed by a window that says Installing Updates, with several rolling progress bars.

8. **Allow Windows Update to restart your computer, if need be.**

   If you need to restart your computer, you should get a warning (see Figure 3-4). Click Restart Now.

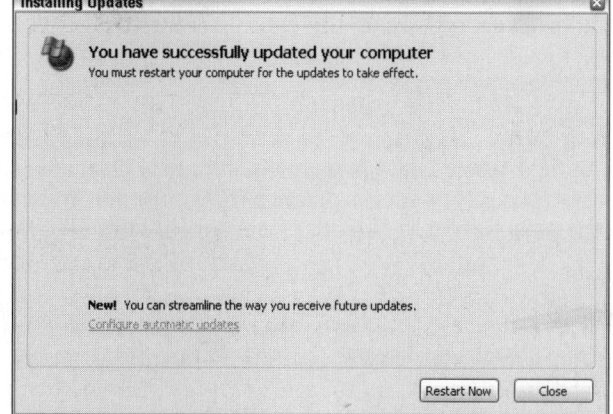

Figure 3-4:
Sometimes
Windows
Update
needs to
restart your
computer.

9. **If Windows Update said it needed to install one patch before it could install others (in Step 6) or if your computer restarted, as soon as you have control of the computer again, immediately go back to the Windows Update site.**

   If Windows doesn't take you there automatically, choose Start⇨ All Programs⇨Windows Update.

10. **Repeat Steps 4 through 9 as many times as necessary to install all the "good" updates.**

   Many people who try to install Windows XP Service Pack 2 go to Windows Update and come away mystified when the site doesn't even offer to install SP 2. There's a good reason why. SP 2 has several bugs in it, and if you try to install SP 2 on a computer that hasn't been properly prepped, you can end up crashing your machine — permanently. Windows Update goes through a two-step process, first downloading and running the patches that are necessary precursors to installing SP 2, forcing you to restart Windows, and then offering SP 2 as an option on the *second* time around. It's important that you repeat Steps 4 through 9 as many times as it takes to get your system completely, totally patched.

   Windows Update pesters you incessantly, trying to get you to turn on Automatic Updates. Make sure that you understand the consequences of your actions, as explained in Chapter 17, before you heed the Update Siren's Song.

11. **Choose File⇨Exit to get out of Internet Explorer.**

   Congratulations. Windows is up-to-date.

As we went to press, Microsoft was attempting to pull all of its updates under one umbrella, so you could get the patches to Office and Media Player and all the other Microsoft products from one location. The early incarnations of "Microsoft Update" were a disaster. If Microsoft doesn't have its act together by the time you read this, remember that you may have to independently apply patches to all of your Microsoft applications — and right now is as good a time as any to bring everything up-to-date.

To get the rest of your system in order:

- ✔ In **Microsoft Office,** click Help⇨Check For Updates. Microsoft has a nasty habit of showing you a page full of (thinly veiled) advertisements in response to your request for patches to its product. You may have to hunt on the page to find the link to Check for Updates (see Figure 3-5).

  Office Update requires you to use Internet Explorer, for no earthly reason I can determine. If you have an alternative browser — such as Firefox — installed as your default browser, you have to start IE manually. Click Start⇨All Programs⇨Internet Explorer, and type this address into the address bar: http://office.microsoft.com/en-us/officeupdate/default.aspx.

- ✔ To update **Windows Media Player,** choose Help⇨Check for Player Updates.

- ✔ To update **Microsoft Works** programs, choose Help⇨Microsoft on the Web⇨Microsoft Works Home Page. Then, at the site, choose the link to Downloads⇨Product Updates.

Check for updates

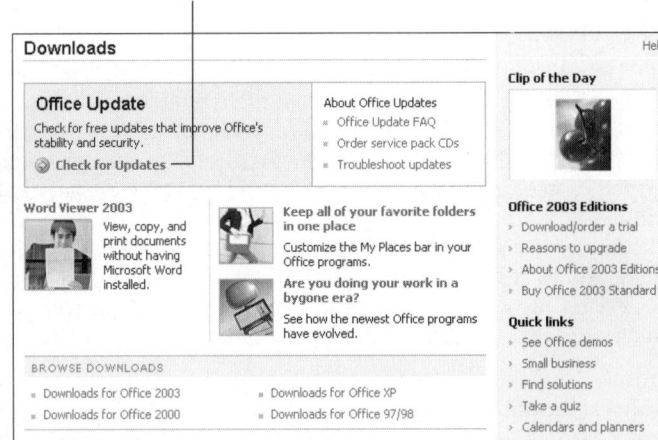

Figure 3-5: Microsoft likes to have you look at lots of advertising before you fix its errors.

Check your firewall

The minute you have your computer up-to-date, you need to make sure that you have a firewall alive and kicking to keep you from getting zapped or zombified via your Internet connection. The Windows firewall is not bad, all things considered, although it has one huge, glaring design flaw. I urge you to read about and consider installing a free alternative called Zone Alarm (see Chapter 17).

If you don't have ZoneAlarm or a good alternative installed, you should check right away and make sure that Windows Firewall is in place and protecting you from the outside world. Here's how:

1. **Click Start➪Control Panel➪Security Center.**

   You see the Windows Security Center, shown in Figure 3-6. The Windows Security Center tells you whether Windows Firewall is working.

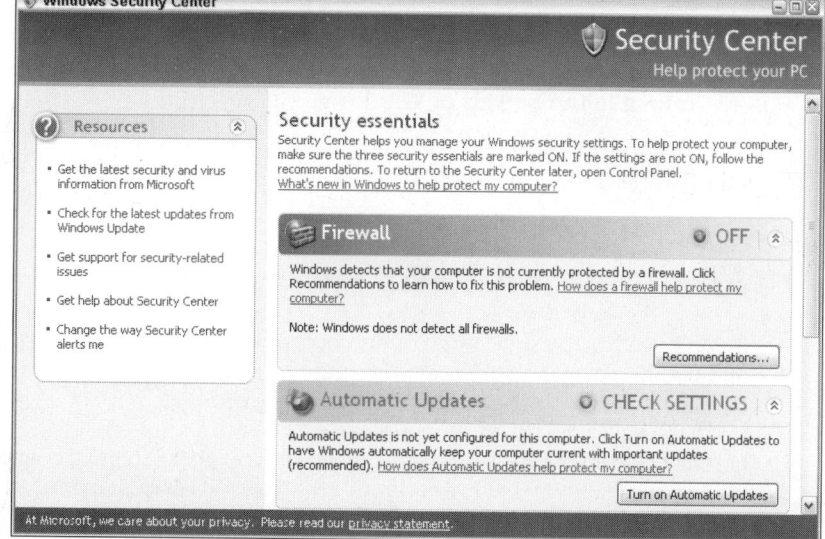

Figure 3-6: The Security Center tells you whether Windows Firewall is working.

If the Security Center tells you that you need to Check Settings for Automatic Updates (at the bottom of Figure 3-6), you have my permission to yawn. Be sure to read Chapter 17 before you let Microsoft patch your system automatically.

2. **If the Security Center shows that your firewall is on, breathe a sigh of relief and go to Step 5.**

3. **If the Security Center shows that your firewall is off, click the button marked Recommendations.**

   An odd little dialog box titled Recommendation appears, admonishing you to Turn on Windows Firewall for All Network Connections.

4. **Click Enable Now.**

   Windows responds with another odd dialog box (see Figure 3-7), telling you that it turned on the firewall.

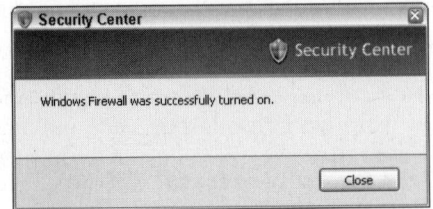

Figure 3-7:
Turning on
the firewall
is a
multistep
process.

5. **Click Close in the Security Center dialog box and then click OK in the Recommendation dialog box to get back to the Windows Security Center.**

   The Security Center should tell you that your firewall is on.

6. **Click "X" in the upper-right corner of the Security Center to let it return to the bowels of Windows.**

   Your firewall has sprung to attention. Check out Chapter 17 to explore the many security options available in Windows.

Fire your antivirus program

If you have Norton or McAfee or one of the other big-name antivirus programs and you like it, make sure that you update the virus signature file frequently; then skip down to the next part of the makeover.

On the other hand, if the antivirus program you got with your computer is driving you nuts, I may have a better alternative: AVG Free. It's free for personal use (businesses and organizations have to pay). The free version doesn't include one-on-one tech support, but I bet you don't need it. Some people have trouble getting through to the update site, but I run updates automatically in the middle of the night and have never hit a snag.

I talk about AVG Free in Chapter 18. If you decide to give your current antivirus program the heave-ho, here's how to safely uninstall the program you have now and get AVG Free working:

1. **Follow the instructions in Chapter 18 to download AVG Free, but don't install it yet.**

2. **Run one last scan of your whole system with your old antivirus program.**

   Each program is different, but you can usually conjure up the devil by double-clicking its icon in the System Tray, down near the clock.

3. **Unplug your computer, both from the Internet and from your local network (if you have one).**

4. **Click Start⇨Control Panel⇨Add or Remove Programs.**

5. **Choose your current antivirus program and click Remove.**

6. **Follow the uninstaller's advice and accept all of the defaults.**

   You may have to restart your machine once or twice.

7. **Follow the instructions in Chapter 18 to install AVG Free.**

8. **Reconnect to your local network and the Internet.**

9. **Go through AVG Free's setup routine (see Chapter 18).**

   Make sure that you get the latest virus signature file and scan your entire computer.

Show filename extensions

This is the single most important step you can take to get some control over your Windows destiny. That's why I recommend you tell Windows to show you filename extensions immediately after you have your security defenses up.

You can read the details in Chapter 8, but the bottom line is quite straight-forward: Some (ahem) genius at Microsoft decided years ago that Windows should refrain from showing you the full names of all your files. So, for example, Windows doesn't tell you that a file is really called `resume.doc`; it tells you the file is called `resume`. Windows puts a picture of Word on the file's icon and tells you the file is "Type: Word document," but it doesn't tell you the simple truth: The file's real name is `resume.doc`. Windows hides the `.doc` — the filename extension.

There are many reasons why you want to be able to see the full name of every file that you work with, but I think one simple incident speaks volumes: Thousands of people inside Microsoft — including a bunch of executives who should know better — got infected by the ILOVEYOU virus because they double-clicked a file, thinking it was a letter, not realizing it was a program. A very infuriating program. Had they seen the full name of the file — `ILOVEYOU.vbs` — many (if not all) of the "Softies who got stung" would've realized that double-clicking the file would run a Visual Basic program.

Anyway, trust me, you want to see the full names of all of your files. Here's how:

1. **Choose Start⇨My Documents.**

2. **Choose Tools⇨Folder Options.**

   The Folder Options dialog box appears.

3. **Select the View tab. Under Advanced Settings, uncheck the box that says Hide Extensions for Known File Types.**

While you're here, click the button that says Show Hidden Files and Folders and uncheck the box that says Hide Protected Operating System Files (Recommended). See Chapter 8 for details.

When you are finished, the Folder Options dialog box should look like Figure 3-8.

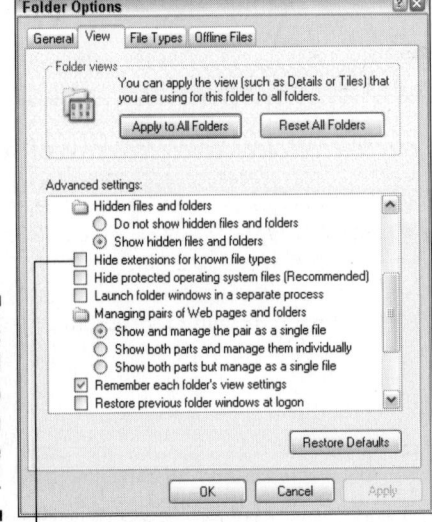

Figure 3-8:
Tell
Windows to
show you
the entire
filename.

Uncheck this box to show file extensions.

4. **Click OK and then close out of the My Documents window.**

From that point on, Windows (and Office and many other applications) will show you the full filename. No more secrets, eh?

Protect against spyware

Every Windows user needs spyware protection. I talk about several products in Chapter 18, but you will be well served if you follow these simple steps:

1. **Start your favorite Web browser. Go to** www.microsoft.com/athome/ security/spyware/software/default.mspx **and click the link to download Microsoft Antispyware.**

2. **Run the downloaded program, take the defaults, and install Antispyware.**

Make sure that you activate all of the Security Agents.

3. Next, go to www.mlin.net/StartupMonitor.shtml. Click to download Mike's StartUpMonitor.

4. Double-click the downloaded file to open it and then double-click StartupMonitor.msi to install it.

   You now have excellent — although not infallible — spyware protection. Free.

Personalize Your eXPerience

Are you the kind of person who never changed the factory recording on her answering machine? Kept the default ringer tone for her mobile phone? Let all the digital clocks in the house flash "12:00" after an extended power outage? Brings a bologna sandwich to work every day because it's safe? Has the days of the week printed neatly on her . . . oh, never mind.

C'mon. Get a life. Show some personality! The following sections get you started.

Change the wallpaper

What, you're still staring at that DELL logo? Sheesh. Kinda low bandwidth, ain't ya?

Seriously, there's no reason in the world to keep the Windows desktop background picture (commonly called *wallpaper*) that you got when you bought your PC. You can download hundreds of thousands of different specially designed pictures by using Google to search for "free Windows wallpaper." Or better yet, you can stick your favorite photo or other picture file on the desktop.

It's remarkably easy:

1. Navigate to the photo or picture that you want to put on the desktop.

   You might choose Start➪My Pictures or you might download a picture from the Internet.

2. Right-click the picture and choose Set As Desktop Background.

   Windows puts the picture on the desktop (see Figure 3-9).

Figure 3-9:
Use a
favorite
snapshot
as your
Windows
wallpaper.

3. **If the picture appears distorted, right-click on the desktop and choose Properties⇨Desktop. In the Position box, choose**

   - **Center** to put one copy of the picture in the middle of the screen.

   - **Tile** to put multiple copies of the picture on the screen (the exact location and number of copies varies depending on the size of the picture).

   - **Stretch** to take a single copy of the picture and stretch it both horizontally and vertically to fit the screen.

4. **Click OK.**

   Your picture replaces DELL's. Now isn't that an improvement?

Set the screensaver

Once upon a time, screensavers served a useful purpose: They kept monitors from getting "burned in" by moving things around a bit on the screen. Nowadays, screensavers are just for fun.

You probably know that you can use Windows' built-in screensavers by right-clicking on the desktop, choosing Properties⇨Screen Saver, and picking one from the drop-down list in the Screen Saver box. But an entire universe of screensaver options awaits.

Here are two of my favorites:

✔ The My Pictures Slideshow — one of the options in the Screen Saver drop-down list when you right-click on the desktop and choose Properties⇨ Screen Saver — lets you show folders (and folders of folders!) of pictures, one at a time. It's a great way to make everything old new again.

✔ The Web abounds with great screensavers, and they won't cost you a penny. Use Google to search for **"free screensaver"**. If you're looking for a particular kind of screensaver, try, for example, **"free aquarium screensaver"** or **"free butterfly screensaver"**.

Align your accounts

If more than one person uses your computer, take the time to set up an account for each user. It will make your life soooooo much simpler if you get into the simple habit of logging on with your own username: Each person's preferences and histories get stored separately, e-mail goes into each individual's inbox, and you spend much less time tussling over the TV remote. At least, from a computer point of view.

Best of all, if each person uses his own account, all of the good stuff happens automatically. You don't have to lift a finger.

To set up a new account:

1. **Click Start⇨Control Panel⇨User Accounts.**

   Windows brings up the User Accounts dialog box.

2. **Click Create a New Account.**

   Windows asks for a name.

3. **Type a new username, click Next, and then click Create Account.**

4. **Click "X" to get out of the User Accounts dialog box.**

   The new username appears on the logon screen or whenever you switch users (Start⇨Log Off⇨Switch Users).

To delete an old account that you don't need anymore:

1. **Click Start⇨Control Panel⇨User Accounts. In the dialog box that appears, click Change an Account.**

2. **Select the name of the user you want to delete.**

3. **Click Delete the Account.**

4. **Click Keep the Files and then Delete the Account. Click "X" in the upper-right corner twice (once in each of the open dialog boxes) to get back to Windows.**

   The old account is gone, but the old user's files are safely stored in a new folder on your desktop.

Eliminate the Obnoxious

Windows has plenty of obnoxious settings, but these stand out, both for the degree of obnoxiousness and for the ease with which they can be circumvented — if you know the tricks.

Tame (or trash!) Messenger

Windows Messenger. MSN Messenger. Two different programs. Two different sources of gray hair. Windows Messenger ships as part of Windows XP. It's a dowdy, stable, corporate-oriented version of the venerable instant messaging program. MSN Messenger, its considerably more lively offspring, comes pre-installed on many machines. It also comes along for the ride sometimes when you install other software.

Some people like MSN Messenger. (I don't think I know anybody who would admit to *liking* Windows Messenger.) Personally, I think both Windows Messenger and MSN Messenger constitute enormous time sinks that, in almost all cases, should be banished from the face of the earth. But that's the subject of a rant in a different part of this book, Chapter 11.

You probably already know whether Windows Messenger or MSN Messenger has taken over your PC, but if you have any doubts, check the System Tray, down near the clock. If you see the Pillsbury Doughboy — er, Winged MSN Messenger of Corpulent Glory — down in the tray, one of Microsoft's Messengers is alive and broadcasting your presence to anyone who knows (or can guess) your Hotmail address.

In Chapter 11, I talk about ways to completely cut both Messengers off at the knees, but as part of a makeover, I suggest you take the kinder, gentler approach:

1. **First, remove MSN Messenger. Choose Start⇨Control Panel⇨Add or Remove Programs.**

   Windows shows you MSN Messenger in the resulting Change or Remove Programs list (see Figure 3-10).

2. **Click once on MSN Messenger and then click Remove.**

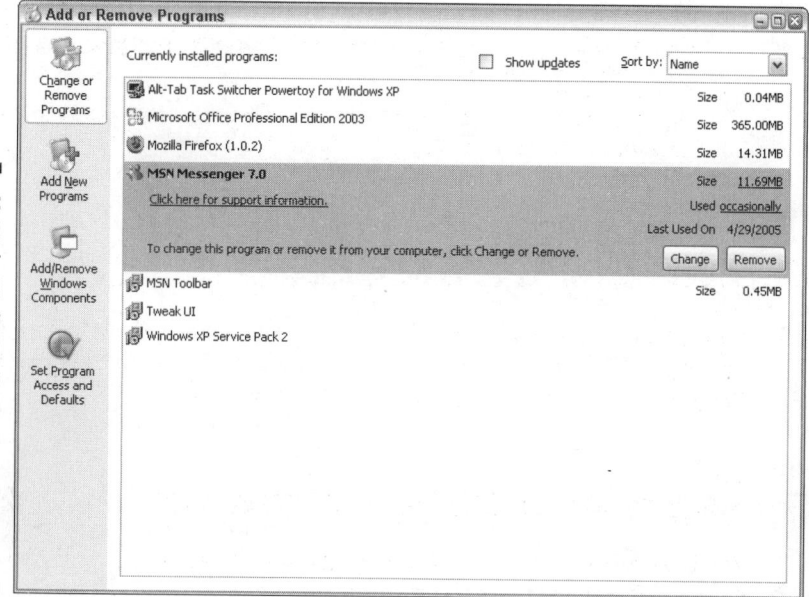

Figure 3-10:
MSN
Messenger
is installed
separately
from
Windows
and should
appear in
the Change
or Remove
Programs
list.

3. **Windows Installer asks if you're sure you want to remove MSN Messenger. Click Yes, Yes, a Thousand Times Yes! (or some similar button).**

   The uninstaller unceremoniously dumps you back in the Add or Remove Programs window, shown in Figure 3-10.

   While you're at it, you might want to remove the MSN Toolbar and any other marketing flotsam and jetsam Microsoft may have left on your system. Click the offensive program, click Remove, and take the defaults to get rid of other junk.

4. **Next, block access to Windows Messenger. On the left side of the Add or Remove Programs window, click Add/Remove Windows Components.**

   Windows brings up the Windows Components Wizard (see Figure 3-11).

5. **Scroll to the bottom of the Components list and uncheck the box in front of Windows Messenger.**

   Microsoft was required to add this component to Windows XP in Service Pack 1 as part of an antitrust agreement. Unchecking the box doesn't completely remove Windows Messenger, but it should keep Messenger from running.

6. **Click Next.**

   Windows goes through a lengthy, complicated process that pulls Windows Messenger from the user interface.

7. When the wizard is done, click Finish.

Windows Messenger should never darken your door again. If it does, look at Chapter 11.

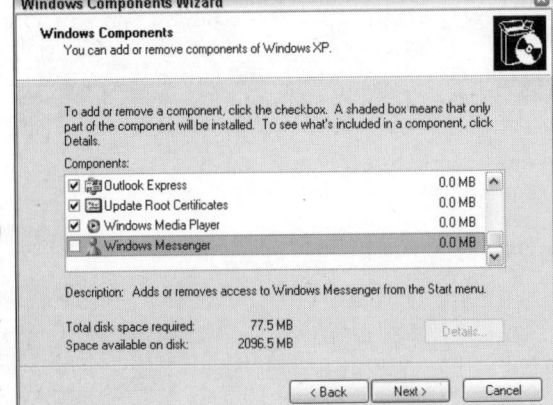

Figure 3-11:
Windows
Messenger
gets the
heave-ho.

Remove the Language Bar

Office XP introduced an obnoxious toolbar called the *Language Bar*. It sits immediately to the left of the < arrow button in the System Tray. If you (or the folks who put together your computer) performed a complete install of Office XP or a custom install of Office 2003, you may have a bar (similar to the one shown here) sitting at the bottom of your screen.

If you use the voice recognition technology built into Office XP or 2003, you have my sympathy and probably should keep those buttons where they sit. But for almost everyone, they simply take up room, mystify the bewilickers out of mere mortals, tempt you to try voice recognition (which doesn't work worth beans), and get in the way — for no good reason.

To get rid of the Language Bar, more or less permanently, right-click any empty spot down on the Windows taskbar, choose Toolbars, and then uncheck the line marked Language Bar.

Get Better (Free!) Software

Some people think that any software from Microsoft is, automatically, superior to any other company's software.

I say bunk. Microsoft works best when it's competing, hard, in a market that's hotly contested. When consumers like you and me choose competing products, we're forcing Microsoft to get off its hind end and innovate. When those competing products are almost as good as Microsoft's products (even better, in some ways), I say go with the competitor. And if the competition's program is free, hey, what are you waiting for?

Dump Microsoft's browser

The browser war rages. Refreshing, isn't it? Not long ago, Netscape curled up its tail and slunk away, whimpering like a kicked dog. Microsoft stole away its market share the old-fashioned way, by playing dirty. Netscape succeeded in court but failed in the marketplace.

Microsoft rested on its laurels, making almost no improvements to Internet Explorer in nearly five years. Then Blake Ross, a scrawny 19-year-old, took the bull by the horns and, with a motley group of gifted designers and programmers, all working *gratis,* built a better browser: Firefox. "People ask how we got it right in Firefox, but doing good requires only that you understand what's bad. We took everything we learned at Netscape and ran in the opposite direction." Ya gotta love it.

I talk about the pros (Firefox) and cons (Internet Explorer) of browsing in Chapter 11. Suffice it to say that I recommend Firefox, in spite of its manifest shortcomings and teething problems.

To get a browser worthy of your respect, hold your nose and point IE at www. mozilla.org. Click to download and install, take all the defaults, and forget about Internet Explorer.

Search like a pro

Rover, the (ahem) Windows Search Companion, can take a hike as far as I'm concerned. If you ever click Start⇨Search and get the Windows Explorer Search Pain again, you deserve it (see Figure 3-12).

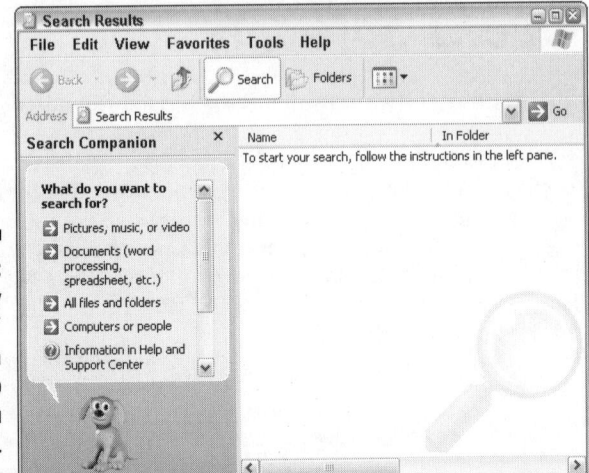

Figure 3-12:
Say
"Goodbye,"
Rover. Lift a
leg for Bob
when you
see him.

I've spent months wading through the innards of Microsoft's various search engines — Windows Search, the old Windows Indexing Service, several Office search engines, MSN Search, and others — and I've come to the inescapable conclusion that they're all bloated, buggy, and slow, slow, slow. Many times, they don't work at all, returning erroneous results or no results whatsoever.

Those days are gone. Now you have many excellent desktop search engines to choose from. Any of the new breed of search programs will scan essentially all items on your computer, index them, and let you look for files' contents in the blink of an eye. I talk about desktop search engines in Chapter 11.

My favorite? Google Desktop Search. It's fast, it works very well, it's free, and most of all, *it ain't Microsoft.* To install:

1. **Wait until you aren't going to use your computer very much.**

   Indexing your computer can take many hours. You can still work while Google Desktop Search is indexing your computer, but you'll find yourself fighting the indexing program, which has a big job to do: The indexer will pause itself if it senses that you're trying to work, but that's a bit like trying to share a chocolate-chip cookie with a four-year-old. Best to wait until you can simply ignore the computer for a few hours, or even overnight.

2. **Point your Web browser at** `http://desktop.google.com`.

   The download page should look like Figure 3-13.

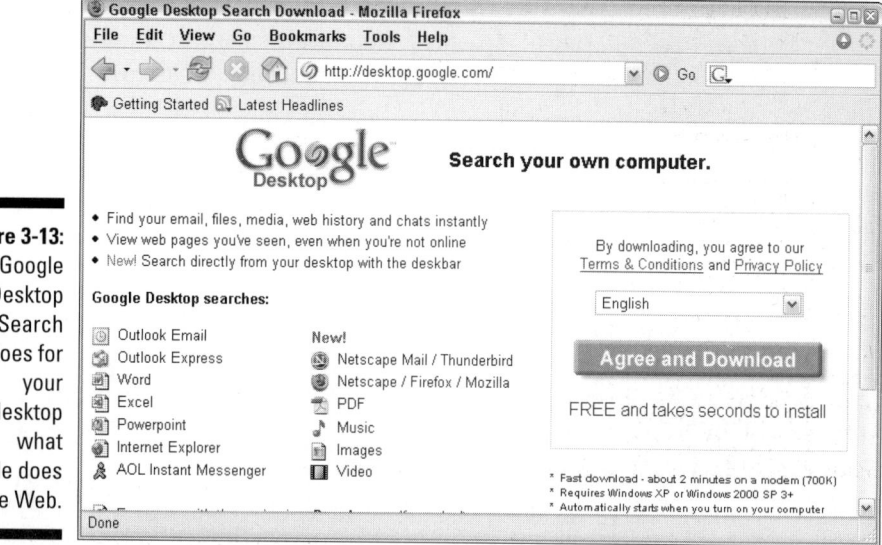

Figure 3-13:
Google
Desktop
Search
does for
your
desktop
what
Google does
for the Web.

3. **Click Agree and Download on the Web page, download the file to your computer, and then run** GoogleDesktopSearchSetup.exe.

   The Setup routine takes a few minutes, and you end up staring at a Web page called Google Desktop Search: Initial Preferences.

4. **Uncheck the box marked Enable Search Over Secure Web Pages. Then click Set Preferences and Continue.**

   Indexing secure Web pages is just asking for trouble.

   Google indexes your computer.

5. **Click the button to Go to the Desktop Search Homepage.**

   Google puts a Desktop Search box down on your Windows taskbar. You're ready to search.

If you ever want to get rid of the Google Desktop Search bar, right-click the Windows taskbar, choose Toolbars, and then uncheck Google Desktop Search.

Read PDFs

No makeover would be complete without an update for Adobe's Acrobat Reader, the program that lets you read PDF files. It's easy:

1. **Point your browser to** www.adobe.com/products/acrobat/ readstep2.html.

2. **Choose your language, operating system, and download speed.**

3. **If you see an offer to download the Adobe Yahoo! Toolbar and the Photoshop Album 2.0 Starter Edition, uncheck the boxes.**

    You can always go back to adobe.com and download them later.

4. **Click Continue and then click Download.**

    Your browser prompts you to save a small file called AdbeRdr70_enu_full.exe (or something similar) to disk.

5. **Save the small file to disk and then run it.**

    That starts the big download of the reader itself (20 MB), which can take quite a bit of time.

6. **When the download finishes, the installer starts automatically. Take all of the defaults.**

7. **When the installer is done, click Finish.**

    You need to restart your computer, after which you can read PDF files.

Part II
Controlling the Look and Feel of Windows XP

The 5th Wave   By Rich Tennant

"Remember – I want the bleeding file server surrounded by flaming workstations with the word 'Motherboard' scrolling underneath."

In this part . . .

In this part, I show you how to turn Windows' plain-Jane face — its interface, if you will — into a work of art. Your art. At the heart of it all sits a program written and distributed (and disavowed) by Microsoft: TweakUI. Chances are good that half of the hacks and mods you've seen on the Web can be handled faster, and infinitely easier, by TweakUI.

But that's just the start. Er, Start. The Start menu holds untold wonders, if you dig into it. And there's an enormously useful piece of screen real-estate, ready to mold to your every whim: The taskbar, down at the bottom of the screen, can dance the boogaloo, if you know its secrets.

The desktop? Don't settle for just changing the wallpaper. Anybody can change the wallpaper. Dig deeper and see how you can change the entire look and feel of your PC. This ain't your father's Windows. . . .

Chapter 4

TweakUI, the Power User's PowerToy

*T*he collection of programs known as Windows PowerToys started as a kind of "skunk works" project back in the early days of Windows 95. The folks who wrote the shell of Windows 95 built a whole lot of capability into the program that never saw the light of day: tweaks and twiddles and (yes) hacks and mods that, thanks to The Powers That Be, never made it into Windows 95's official feature set.

As the Windows 95 effort wound down, a few bored developers spent time perfecting their testing tools — their Power Toys. After Windows 95 hit the stands, some enterprising engineer convinced The Powers That Be to release those internal testing tools, to make it easier for guys in white lab coats (like me!) to dig deeper into the belly of the beast. The programs were unpolished, unsophisticated, hadn't been designed or reviewed by committees, never saw the inside of a Microsoft Usability Lab — and proved wildly popular with the techie crowd.

The Powers That Be asked the engineers for more, and they gladly obliged, in many cases gleefully resurrecting features that TPTB had zapped from the shipping version of Windows 95. That's how TweakUI came into being. The guys and gals who built all these cool capabilities into Windows, only to see them clipped by the Bean Counters, Usability Droids, and Marketing Flaks, got a chance to strut their stuff. And, boy howdy, did they show those Bean Counters a thing or three.

The "UI" in *TweakUI* stands for *User Interface*. If you want to change the way Windows looks or acts, chances are good TweakUI can help. TweakUI is, by far, the most sophisticated of the current crop of PowerToys (see the sidebar "The other PowerToys"). It belongs in every serious Windows user's arsenal.

Microsoft has released "unofficial" versions of TweakUI for every flavor of Windows since Windows 95. Microsoft still refuses to support the PowerToys, even though they're written by Microsoft employees and developed, tested, reviewed, distributed, and recommended by Microsoft. References to the PowerToys abound in the Microsoft Knowledge Base. I've never had any problems with any of the PowerToys. But if something goes wrong, you can't go running to Microsoft for help. As if you would anyway.

Downloading and Installing TweakUI

I refer to TweakUI and the other PowerToys frequently in this book. It's well worth taking a few minutes to download and install them.

TweakUI makes hundreds of otherwise daunting hacks and mods as easy as a couple of clicks. Of all the complicated Windows XP hacks and mods you'll find on the Internet (and in many books), you can handle a large percentage in just a few seconds by using TweakUI. Before you go spelunking through the Registry or bouncing around in some dialog-box backwater, check whether TweakUI can handle the job first.

To get your own copy of TweakUI, make sure you have Windows XP Service Pack 2 installed (see Chapter 3). Then:

1. **If an older version of TweakUI is already installed on your computer, uninstall it.**

   Microsoft has released at least two incompatible versions of Windows XP TweakUI. If in doubt, uninstall whatever version you may have and install the latest version. It's quick and easy.

   To see if you have TweakUI installed, try clicking Start➪All Programs➪ Powertoys for Windows XP➪TweakUI. Can't find it? Great. You don't have TweakUI installed, and you can proceed to Step 2.

   If you find TweakUI on your All Programs list, and you don't recall installing it recently, get rid of it. Microsoft re-released TweakUI in April 2002, and older versions may cause problems. To uninstall TweakUI, click Start➪Control Panel➪Add or Remove Programs. Then scroll down to Tweak UI, click it, click Change/Remove, and follow the instructions.

2. **Crank up your Web browser (Firefox or Internet Explorer) and navigate to www.microsoft.com/windowsxp/downloads/powertoys/ xppowertoys.mspx.**

   You see the Web page shown in Figure 4-1.

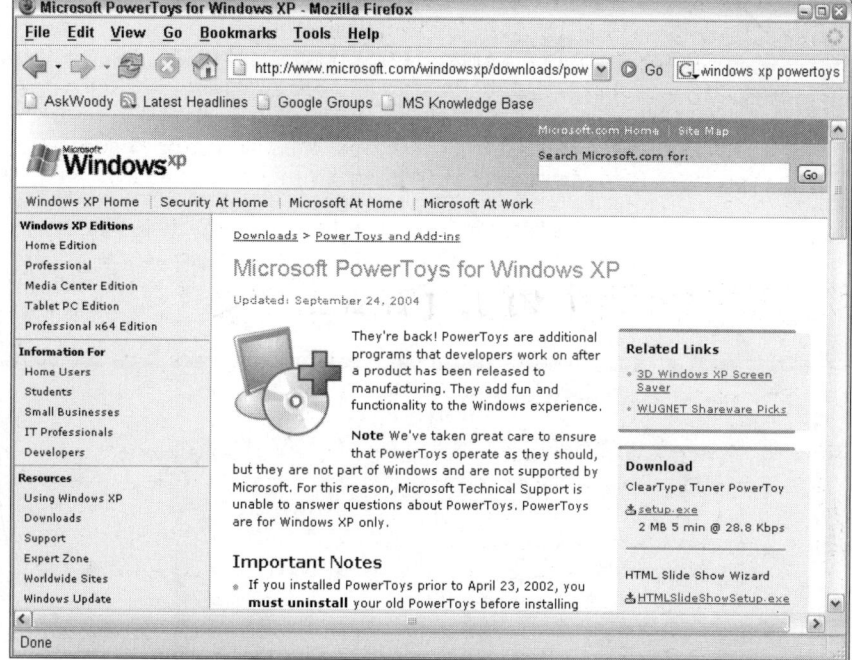

Figure 4-1:
Download
TweakUI
from
Microsoft's
Windows
XP
PowerToys
site.

3. **Scroll down the Web page until you see Tweak UI listed along the right. Click TweakUI.exe.**

   In spite of what the Web page says, you actually download a file called TweakUiPowertoySetup.exe. If your Web browser asks you what to do with the file, save it to disk. Make sure you remember where you saved it!

4. **Click Start and navigate to the downloaded file. Double-click the downloaded file, TweakUiPowertoySetup.exe, to run it.**

   A very simple Setup Wizard takes you through the setup. Follow the instructions and take the defaults.

5. **When the Setup Wizard is done, click Start⇨All Programs⇨Powertoys for Windows XP⇨Tweak UI.**

   TweakUI responds with its main "About" page, shown in Figure 4-2.

6. **To get out of TweakUI, click OK or Cancel.**

The other PowerToys

TweakUI rates as the universal user interface modding tool — kind of like a Windows hacker's Swiss army knife. But it's just one of the PowerToys. While you're downloading TweakUI, you should consider downloading others. My favorites are the ClearType Tuner (which adjusts the appearance of fonts on the screen; see Chapter 7), the Alt+Tab "Coolswitch" Replacement (which shows big icons when you press Alt+Tab to move among running programs; see the "A cooler Coolswitch" sidebar in this chapter), the Power Calculator (a truly full-featured graphing calculator), Image Resizer (for changing the size and resolution of pictures; see Chapter 12), and the Virtual Desktop Manager (which lets you work with four separate desktops; see Chapter 7).

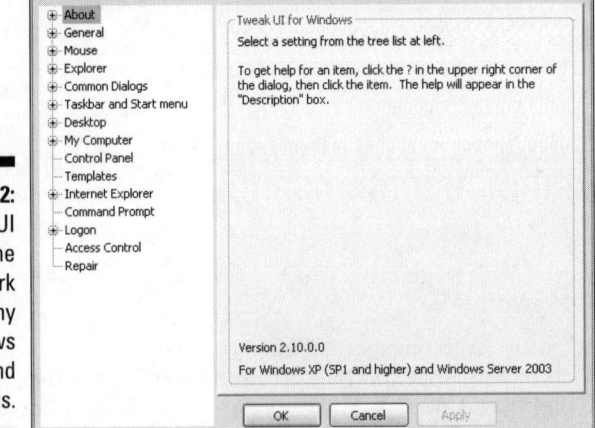

Figure 4-2: TweakUI takes the hard work out of many Windows hacks and mods.

TweakUI from 30,000 Feet

Several of the chapters in this book take you through specific settings in TweakUI. As you wield your vorpal Tweaker's blade, it may help to understand what's going on behind the scenes:

> ✔ **Most (but not all!) of the TweakUI settings go straight into the Windows Registry.** I talk about the Registry in Chapter 24. Although the Registry isn't a snarly, dangerous place, in spite of what you may have heard, walking through the Registry is no stroll in the park. I tend to think of the

Registry as a giant Windows sewer: It's dirty and dark, with incredibly poor organization, but you can pinch your nose and get through it. If you use TweakUI to manage your Registry settings, there's no need to dive down the manhole.

✔ **TweakUI makes registry hacks easier.** In your travels through the Internet and in other publications, if you ever encounter a Windows hack that involves editing the Registry, STOP. Take a minute or two to fire up TweakUI and see if the engineers who built Windows already have the hack covered. Chances are good they do. Even if you found the Registry editing tip in, oh, the Microsoft Knowledge Base!

✔ **Some hacks in TweakUI can be . . . shall we say . . . more than a little bit dangerous.** In particular, if you go into the About⇨Policy section and run the Windows Group Policy Editor, you can get yourself into all sorts of trouble unless you know precisely what you're doing. Come to think of it, you can get yourself into a lot of trouble even if you *do* know what you're doing. Just because you *can* change it doesn't imply that you *should* change it. Knowhatimean?

Knowing the Essential TweakUI Lingo

The people who built TweakUI are computer jocks, and computer jocks talk funny. You'll find a lot of confusing terminology inside TweakUI. Here's my quick translation of the important words — a Dummies TweakUI babelfish, if you will:

✔ When you read about a program *stealing focus,* that means the program suddenly jumps up and forces itself onto the top of your desktop, yanking you away from whatever program you were working on. Most uncivilized.

✔ A *per-user setting* is a setting that can be assigned for each user on a computer. If you have three users on a PC — Woody, Justin, and Duangkhae — each of them can establish his or her own values on per-user settings. The computer has three different settings, one for each user. Contrast this with a *per-machine setting* (also called, confusingly, a *system-wide setting*), which is always the same for all the users on a PC. For example, the Desktop background (also known as Windows wallpaper) is a per-user setting: Each user gets to choose her own wallpaper. But the ability to share printers on a network is a *per-machine* setting.

✔ A *cascading menu* used to be called a fly-out menu. It's the kind of menu that pops out when you hover your mouse over an item in the menu (see Figure 4-3).

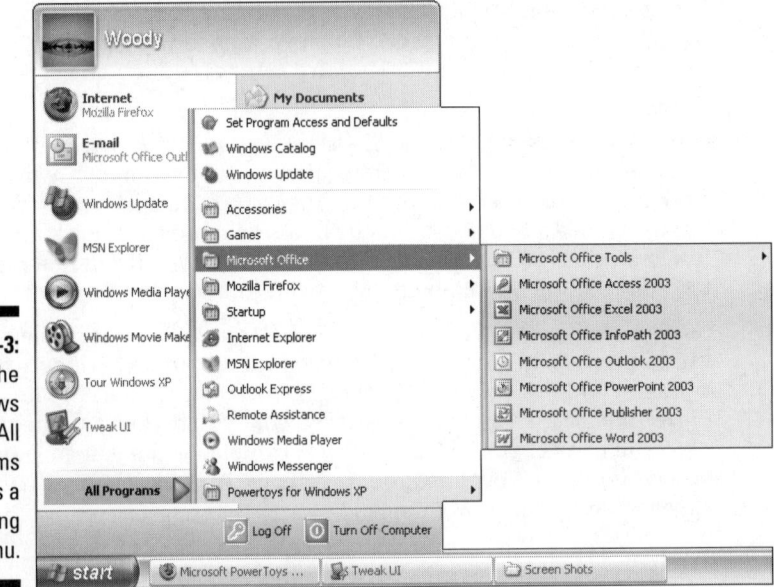

Figure 4-3:
The
Windows
All
Programs
menu is a
cascading
menu.

Squeezing TweakUI

Big parts of TweakUI feature in several chapters throughout this book, often in conjunction with supporting hacks and mods that make the tweaks go farther.

In the remainder of this chapter, I want to tell you about several important parts of TweakUI that aren't covered elsewhere in this book. They're quick and easy, and could make your life with Windows a tad less contentious.

Making your mouse sensitive

If you've worked with Windows for a while, you have no doubt encountered the Mouse applet in your Control Panel (click Start⇨Control Panel⇨Printers and Other Hardware⇨Mouse). Many mouse manufacturers install their own custom versions of the Mouse Properties dialog box (see Figure 4-4), so it's difficult to draw any generalizations. But a few minutes spent poking around in those settings may help you make your mouse behave in a way that feels more comfortable.

TweakUI contains a handful of mouse settings that probably don't appear in your Control Panel's Mouse applet. Here's how to get at them:

1. **Follow the instructions at the beginning of this chapter to install TweakUI and get it running.**

2. On the left, double-click Mouse.

TweakUI shows you its main mouse settings, as shown in Figure 4-5.

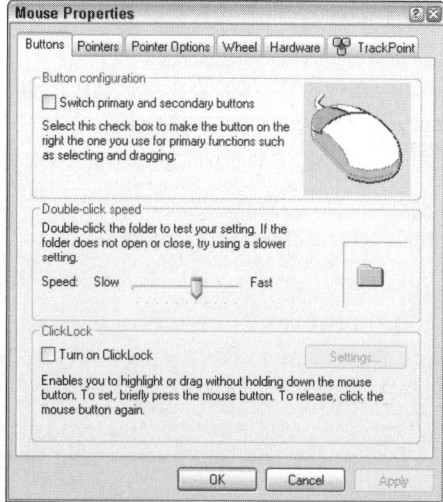

Figure 4-4:
Every mouse manufacturer offers a unique set of Properties that you can set from the Control Panel.

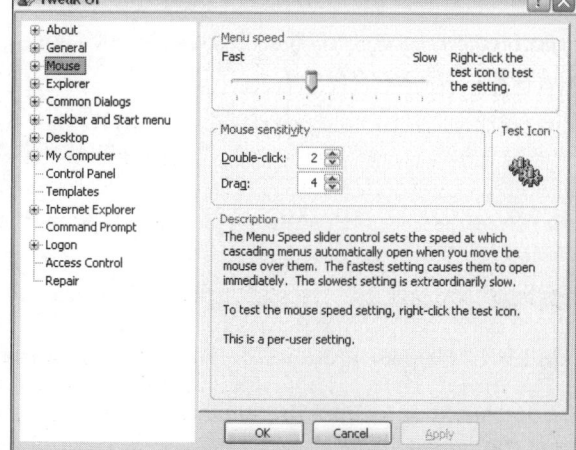

Figure 4-5:
TweakUI's mouse settings probably don't appear in your Control Panel.

There's a reason why TweakUI can offer you settings that your mouse manufacturer may not make available in the Control Panel. TweakUI works directly with Windows — its settings are completely independent of the brand of mouse you're using or the mouse's idiosyncrasies. Where mouse manufacturers tend to stick to Microsoft's officially approved hooks into Windows, TweakUI isn't so constrained. The result: more choices for you with TweakUI.

3. **If you like to see your fly-out menus appear faster (and I do!), move the Menu Speed slider to the left. Then right-click the Test Icon and see if you can stand the change.**

   If you make the Menu Speed too slow, you may have to click a menu item before its fly-out menu appears!

4. **When you feel comfortable with the Menu Speed, click Apply to have Windows adopt the new setting. Then click Start⇨All Programs and play with it a bit.**

   Many people find that working with the Test Icon leads them to chose a speed that's just too fast when working in the "real world" of All Programs.

5. **Repeat Steps 3 and 4 until your mouse feels right.**

   Don't forget to click Apply before moving on to the next setting.

6. **If you have trouble double-clicking icons because your mouse moves between the two clicks (a problem I encounter frequently with tiny laptop-size mice), increase the number in the Double-Click box.**

7. **Again, run tests on the Test Icon, but before you go on to the next setting, click Apply and make sure that the new setting works better for you.**

8. **If you have a laptop (particularly one with a touchpad), and you have problems with icons getting dragged around when you really don't mean to drag them, adjust the number in the Drag box.**

9. **Run tests on the Test Icon and verify your testing by clicking Apply and checking inside Windows itself.**

   I find that this setting comes in handy most often in Windows Explorer, so I test by clicking Start⇨My Documents and clicking files to make sure I don't drag them.

10. **Run through the other TweakUI settings just in case something jumps out at you. Click OK when you're done.**

    Personally, I don't have any problems with "hover" sensitivity — the amount of time I need to leave the mouse pointer over an object before it lights up — but your mileage may vary. Similarly, I like to keep the mouse wheel at its default sensitivity setting, and I wouldn't use X-Mouse activation if my life depended on it. Don't bother.

Changing places

The Windows Places Bar isn't used very much. It shows up on the left side of the dialog box when you try to open or save a file in Paint, Notepad, WordPad, or Outlook Express. The built-in Places Bar includes icons for five locations (see Figure 4-6).

Figure 4-6:
The
Windows
Places Bar
lets you
quickly
move to
different
places on
your
computer.

TweakUI lets you build a custom Places Bar, replacing any or all of the five icons with locations you specify. To change the Places Bar, bring up TweakUI. On the left side of the window, double-click Common Dialogs, click Places Bar, and follow the instructions on the screen.

The Windows Places Bar may look like the Office Places Bar, but there's no interaction between the two. If you want to change the Places Bar in any of the Microsoft Office programs (Word, Excel, and PowerPoint in particular), there are lots of tricks. See my *Office 2003 Timesaving Techniques For Dummies* for the whole nine yards.

Disabling Autoplay

TweakUI's My Computer settings run quite a gamut, but (as you'll see if you look at the individual entries) in many cases it's smarter and easier to make the changes inside Windows itself.

The one exception: Autoplay, the (frequently accursed) willingness of Windows to scan new CDs and DVDs as you insert them into a drive and try to automatically run or play whatever is on the disc.

It's possible to disable Autoplay on your CD or DVD drive by using Windows Explorer to laboriously change the Autoplay action for each type of file, but it's much easier to use TweakUI to simply turn the lousy thing off. Here's how:

1. **If you haven't already, use the steps earlier in this chapter to install TweakUI.**

2. **On the left, double-click My Computer and then double-click AutoPlay. Click the line marked *Types*.**

TweakUI displays the AutoPlay Drive Types box, shown in Figure 4-7.

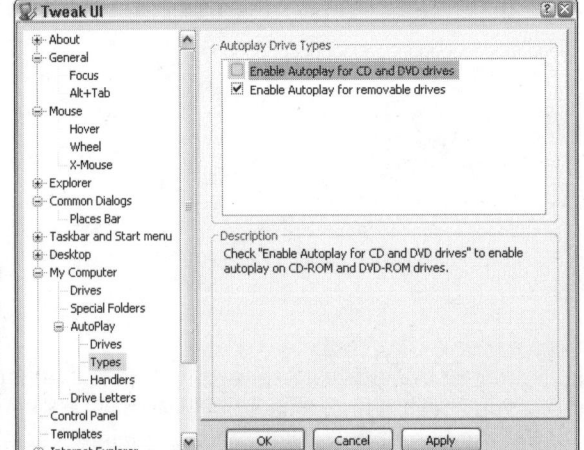

Figure 4-7:
Turn off CD
and DVD
AutoPlay
here.

3. **Uncheck the box marked Enable Autoplay for CD and DVD Drives. Then click Apply or OK.**

Windows will no longer attempt to automatically play or run CDs and DVDs inserted into your drive(s).

I bet you've always wondered how to do that.

A cooler Coolswitch

One of the most colorful (and useful) PowerToys isn't part of TweakUI. You have to download and install it separately. Variously called "Alt-Tab Replacement" and "TaskSwitch," I call it the coolest Coolswitch ever. *Coolswitch* was Microsoft's internal code name for a feature that every Windows user should know: the ability to hold down the Alt key and then hit Tab to cycle among running programs. If you ever get stuck in a game and can't get out, the Coolswitch can make it easy.

To install the souped-up Coolswitch, point your Web browser to the PowerToys home page,

`www.microsoft.com/windowsxp/` `downloads/powertoys/xppowertoys.` `mspx`. Look on the right for "Alt-Tab Replacement" and download the file called `TaskswitchPowertoySetup.exe`. Run it, step through the (overly verbose) Wizard, and choose a Complete setup. When the wizard's done, press Alt+Tab and you'll see large thumbnails of all the programs that are currently running. Press Tab again to cycle through the programs, and release the Alt key when you find the one you want. Repeat after me: Coooooooooooool.

Chapter 5

Pinning Down the Start Menu

In This Chapter

▶ The strength to change the things you can

▶ The serenity to accept the things you can't

▶ The wisdom to know the difference

*T*his chapter tells you everything you need to know to put the Start menu to work. Once you get over the (huge!) conceptual hurdle that you must click Start in order to stop, the rest of it's easy.

Hard to believe, but early versions of Windows managed to survive without a Start button. Start didn't appear until Windows 95, which debuted with the Rolling Stones theme song, *Start Me Up.* (Second verse: "You make a grown man cry.") Windows XP introduced a new, two-column format (see Figure 5-1) with all sorts of advanced capabilities, and the Start menu has never been the same.

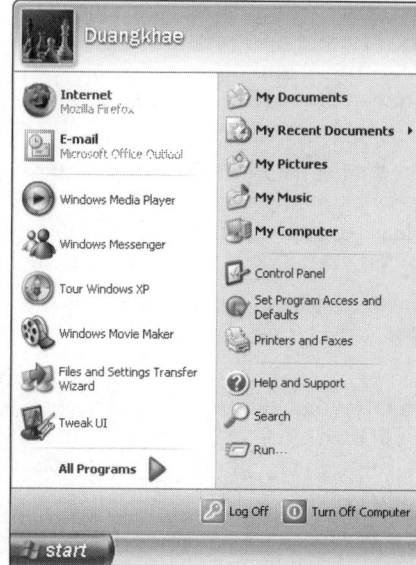

Figure 5-1:
The Windows XP Start menu.

Scoping Out the Start Menu

If you look at the Start menu (refer to Figure 5-1), you see

- ✔ **The name and picture of the user at the top:** You can easily change the name and the picture by following the steps in Chapter 14. Want to be known as Napoleon and use a portrait to match? No problem, *mon ami.*

- ✔ **A block of "pinned" programs in the upper-left corner:** Unless you change things, Windows reserves two slots in the pinned area and puts your Web browser and e-mail program in those slots. You can (and should!) override Windows' choices with ones that suit your purposes. See the next section and "Pinning the Tail on This Donkey," later in this chapter, for details.

- ✔ **Below the pinned programs, a list of programs that you've used recently:** Well, sorta. Microsoft makes some programs more equal than others, giving them a boost on the list, even if you've never used them. See "Controlling the Frequently Used Programs List." later in this chapter.

- ✔ **All Programs:** It isn't really a list of all the programs on your computer, but most well-behaved programs that get installed on your PC add themselves to this list. See "Rearranging All Programs" later in this chapter.

- ✔ **On the top right, a list of locations that you might want to visit:** Microsoft calls these "user locations" because they're different for every user (except for My Computer, anyway). You can easily make many changes to the list. See the section "Advanced Start Tweaks," later in this chapter, for details.

- ✔ **Next on the right, what I call the "Control Group":** icons for Control Panel, Set Program Access, Printers and Faxes, and possibly Network Connections, Administrative Tools, and others. To make changes to these icons, see the "Advanced Start Tweaks" section at the end of this chapter.

  Want to know what's worse than a user interface designed by committee? A "feature" designed by a bunch of lawyers. The Set Program Access and Defaults icon may be the least useful appendage in Window-dom. To get rid of the icon, see "Advanced Start Tweaks" later in this chapter.

- ✔ **At the bottom, Help, Search, and Run:** Unlike the rest of the Start menu, all of these icons are useful and well placed. I suggest you leave them there.

- ✔ **Finally, Log Off and Turn Off:** Log Off lets you switch users without logging off and Turn Off (called Turn Off Computer on some systems) lets you hibernate without, er, turning off. Other than those oxymorons, these buttons work well, too.

Hacking and slashing the Start menu

The Group Policy Editor (shown below) lets you hack and slash the menu like Hannibal Lecter on Mason Verger. Using this tool, you can perform such Hannibal-esque maneuvers as decapitat-ing the user's name and picture from the Start menu or removing the Shut Down button entirely, thereby dooming the user to interminable Windows agony. Something karmic in that.

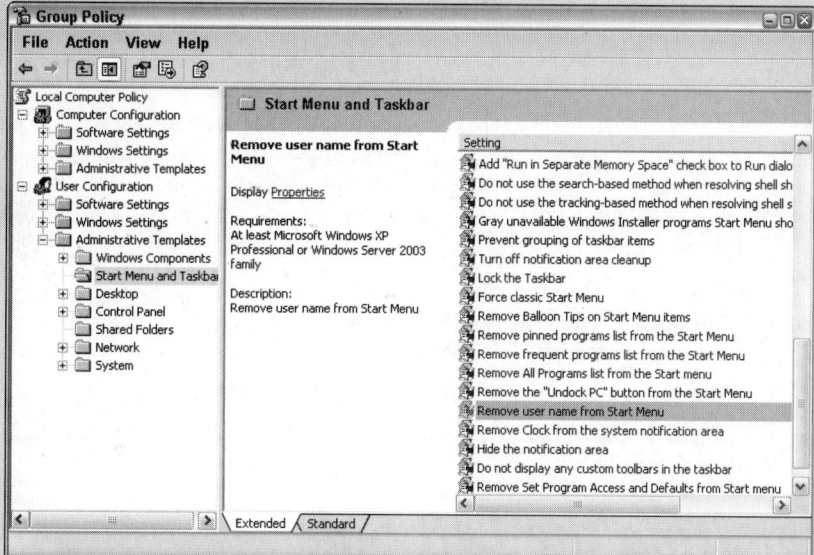

To use the Group Policy Editor:

1. **Choose Start⇨Run, type `gpedit.msc`, and press Enter.**

   The Group Policy Editor appears.

2. **On the left, double-click to navigate down to User Configuration\Administrative Templates\Start Menu and Taskbar.**

You see the Start Menu and Taskbar settings.

3. **To change the way the Start menu works, double-click a setting that looks interesting.**

GPE responds with an action dialog box similar to the one shown in the following figure.

(continued)

(continued)

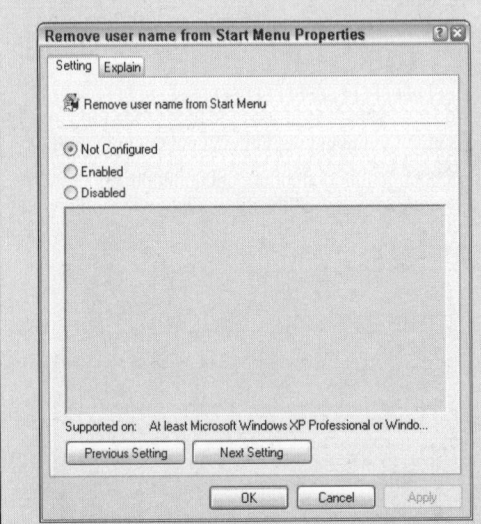

Frequently, the description on the Explain tab doesn't tell you much.

5. **If you're absolutely sure you want to make a change, click the appropriate button and click OK.**

   Usually you have to log off and log back on — or, on occasion, reboot the machine — for the changes to take.

   Warning: Many Group Policy Editor modifications have extreme side effects. That's why Microsoft made it relatively easy to change parts of the Start menu through the Customize Start Menu dialog box (which I cover in the section "Customizing the Left Side of the Start Menu" later in this chapter) but hard to go in through the GPE. Make sure you understand what you're doing before you go hacking. But if you really want to monkey with another monkey's monkey, the GPE lets you grab for a lot of strange bananas.

4. **Make changes cautiously. If in doubt, click the Explain tab and see if GPE offers detailed advice.**

Customizing the Left Side of the Start Menu

It's easy to adjust certain aspects of the left side of the Start menu — just use the Customize Start Menu dialog. To get at it:

1. **Right-click Start, choose Properties, and then click the Start Menu tab.**

   Windows should show you the Taskbar and Start Menu Properties dialog box. If you have Classic Start Menu checked, select the Customize button next to Start Menu, as shown in Figure 5-2.

   Some old-time Windows users prefer the Classic Start menu, which mimics (but doesn't duplicate) the old Windows 2000 Start menu. If you take a few minutes to customize the Windows XP Start menu, as explained here, you'll have all of the benefits of the Classic version, plus a whole bunch of worthwhile new features.

2. **Click the Customize button (the top one).**

   Windows brings up the General tab on the Customize Start Menu dialog box, as in Figure 5-3.

Figure 5-2:
It's easy to
modify the
Windows
XP Start
menu.

Figure 5-3:
The default
settings for
the left side
of the Start
menu.

3. **Take a look at Figure 5-4 and decide if you prefer smaller icons on the left side of your Start menu. If you want to use small icons, click the Small Icons button in the Customize Start Menu dialog box.**

   Although you can pack more items on the left side of your Start menu if you use small icons, many people (present company included) are sloppy mousers and would rather have a larger spot to hit.

   The icon size on the right side of the Start menu is fixed; you get small icons on the right whether you want them or not. This setting only affects the left side.

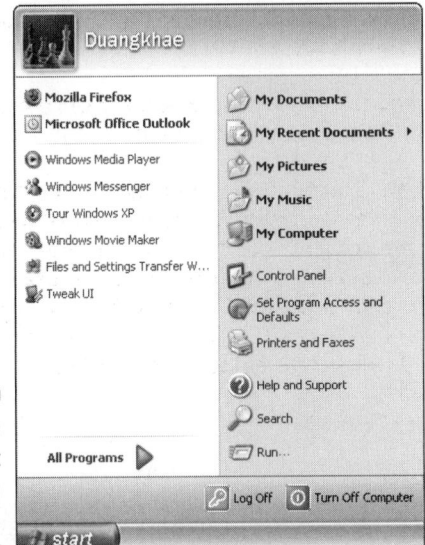

Figure 5-4:
The Start
menu with
small icons.

4. **Leave the Number of Programs on Start Menu spinner where it is.**

   I talk about that strange setting in "Controlling the Frequently Used Programs List," later in this chapter.

5. **Consider whether you want your Web browser and/or e-mail program to appear at the top of the Start menu. If you don't use the Start menu to get at either or both, uncheck the corresponding boxes under Show on Start Menu.**

   Personally, I always use the Quick Launch Toolbar to get at my browser (Firefox, of course) and e-mail program (Outlook), as I describe in Chapter 6. So I uncheck both boxes here, to reserve more room for my favorite programs in the "pinned" part of the Start menu, as described in the next section.

6. **Click OK twice.**

   The Start menu transmogrifies to your expectations.

Pinning the Tail on This Donkey

The upper-left corner of the Start menu contains "pinned" programs. Two of the programs are pinned for you — shortcuts to your Web browser and to your e-mail program. Straight out of the box, Windows puts icons up there for Internet Explorer and Outlook Express. If you install alternative (some would say "superior") programs, such as Mozilla's Firefox or Microsoft Office's Outlook, they're smart enough to replace those entries on the top of the Start menu. Thus, if you look at Duangkhae's Start menu in Figure 5-1, you see that Firefox and Outlook sit at the top of the heap.

I describe an easy way to remove the Web browser and/or the e-mail program from the top of the Start menu in the preceding section.

In fact, you can pin just about anything in that upper-left corner. It's one-click easy to pin programs. Many people don't realize that it's almost as easy to pin folders, Web addresses — even individual files — to the Start menu. If you click a pinned folder, Windows Explorer starts with the folder open. Click a Web address, and your browser starts with the page loaded (or at least *loading,* if your Internet connection ain't so swift). Click the file — say, a .doc Word document — and Word starts with the document loaded.

Pinning a program

Here's how to pin a program in the upper-left corner of the Start menu:

1. **Find the program.**

   The easiest way to find a program, generally, is by choosing Start➪ All Programs and then navigating your way to the program. In Figure 5-5, for example, I get to Word 2003 by choosing Start➪All Programs➪ Microsoft Office.

   You can use just about any method you like to find the program: choose Start➪My Computer and go from there; or run a Start➪Search; or ask your eight-year-old niece where she put it. Windows isn't picky.

2. **Right-click the program and choose Pin to Start Menu.**

   You're done. Windows pins the program to the top of the Start menu (see Figure 5-6).

When to pin?

Windows XP offers many alternatives for getting at your programs, folders, and files quickly. The three most common places to put custom shortcuts are on the Start menu, on your desktop, and in the Quick Launch Toolbar (which I describe in Chapter 6).

As a general rule, I recommend that you not use the Windows desktop for shortcuts. Yes, I know that Microsoft practically invented the desktop for shortcuts, but it's hard to maintain all those tiny icons and hard to find the stuff you want quickly. I recommend that you use the Quick Launch Toolbar for a small handful of programs, folders, and files that you use all the time. If you can look at a Quick Launch icon and tell immediately whether you have the right shortcut or not, it's a good candidate for Quick Launch. But if you have an icon that's hard to identify — or if your Quick Launch list runs to more than a dozen programs — it's best to start pinning on the Start menu.

You can pin programs in your sleep using that simple two-step process.

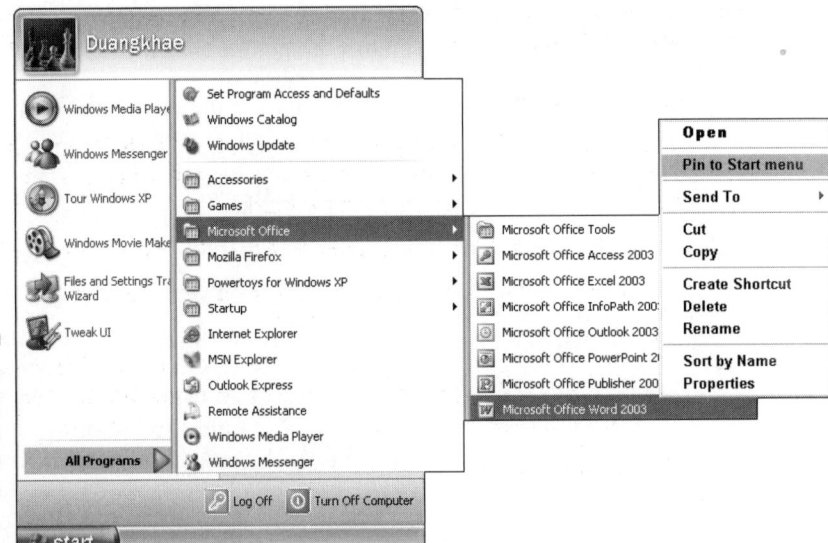

Figure 5-5:
Searching
for a
program to
pin on the
Start menu.

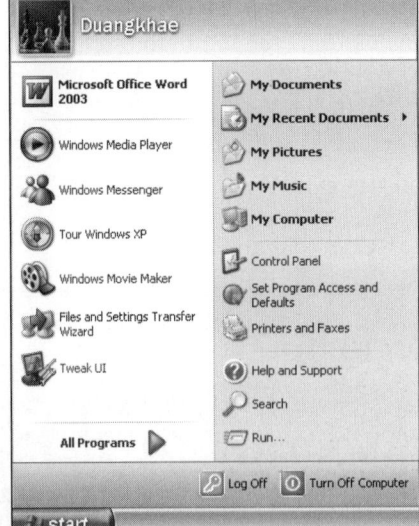

Figure 5-6:
Choose Pin
to Start
Menu, and
Windows
pins a
program in
no time.

Pinning a folder

Pinning folders is almost as easy as pinning programs, in spite of what you may have read. Here's how:

1. **Find the folder.**

   Usually you find folders by going through Start⇨My Documents, Start⇨My Pictures, or Start⇨My Computer, but you can also run a Start⇨Search or go out on your network.

2. **Right-click the folder and choose Send To⇨Desktop (Create Shortcut).**

   Windows sticks a shortcut to the folder on your desktop. Rocket science, eh?

3. **Click the newly created shortcut. Drag it to the Start button and "hover" until the Start menu opens. Then drop the shortcut wherever you want it in the pinned list — in the upper-left corner.**

   Windows pins the folder to the Start menu (see Figure 5-7).

Figure 5-7: Pinning a folder to the Start menu involves a simple three-step process.

Pinning a file

Do you find yourself repeatedly opening the same file? Me, too. Here's how to pin a file to the upper-left corner of the Start menu:

1. **Navigate to the file.**

   You can use Start⇨My Documents, Start⇨My Pictures, Start⇨My Computer, or go through Start⇨Search — any method for finding files that you like.

   Note: I don't know why, but this approach doesn't work if you try to get at the file from inside the Open or Save As dialogs in any of the Microsoft Office applications.

2. **Click on the file. Drag it to the Start button and "hover" until the Start menu opens. Then drop the shortcut wherever you want in the upper-left corner.**

   Hard to believe, but that's all it takes (see Figure 5-8).

Figure 5-8:
Pinning a document to the Start menu couldn't be simpler.

Pinning a Web page

It's only a little harder to pin a Web page — its URL — on the Start menu. You can use this mod with both Internet Explorer and Firefox:

1. **Start your Web browser and navigate to the page you want to pin on the Start menu.**

2. **Click the icon to the left of the address.**

   If you look at Figure 5-9, you can see the icon immediately to the left of the `http://www.dummies.com` address.

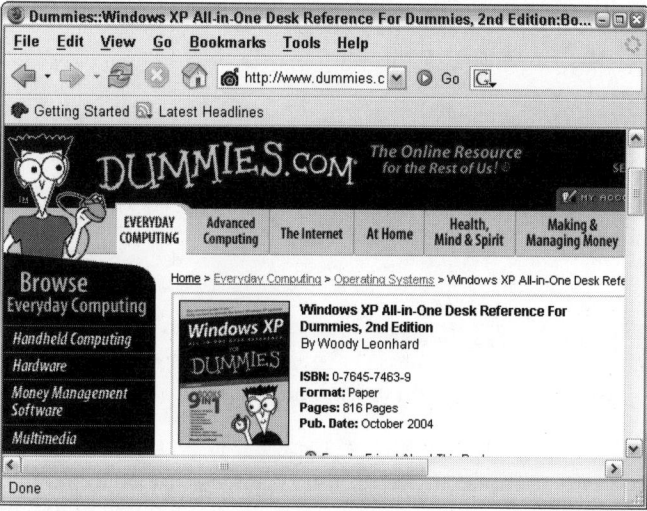

Figure 5-9: The icon that you have to drag is immediately to the left of the Web page's address.

3. **Drag the icon onto the desktop.**

   You may have to drag the icon down to an empty place on the Windows toolbar, "hover" it there for a few seconds, wait for Windows to show you the desktop, and then drop it on the desktop.

4. **Click the newly created shortcut. Drag it to the Start button and "hover" until the Start menu opens. Then drop the shortcut in the upper-left corner.**

   Your Start menu should look something like Figure 5-10.

Figure 5-10:
Duang-
khae's
modified
Start menu,
with the
Web
browser
and e-mail
program
removed
and a
program
(Word),
folder, file,
and Web
page pinned
to the
upper-left
corner.

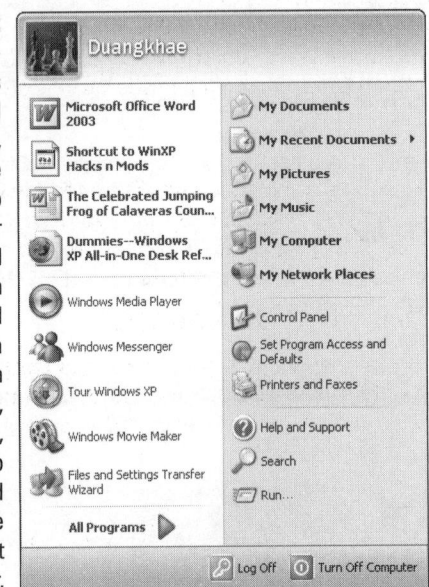

Renaming, moving, and unpinning

After you've pinned a program, folder, file, or Web page to the Start menu, modifying it is easy:

- ✓ To **rename** a pinned shortcut, right-click it, choose Rename, type a new name, and press Enter. Note that changing the name of a pinned program here in the upper-left corner of the Start menu also changes the program's name in the Start⇨All Programs list.

- ✓ To **delete** a pinned shortcut, right-click it and choose Remove From This List.

- ✓ To **move** a pinned shortcut, click it and drag it wherever you like in the upper-left corner of the Start menu. Note that you can move a pinned shortcut onto the Start button's All Programs menu by just "hovering" over All Programs, waiting until Windows opens the list, and then dragging the shortcut onto the All Programs list.

- ✓ It's easy to **change the icon** that appears on the pinned menu next to **folders** and **Web pages.** To do so, right-click the shortcut and choose Properties. If the shortcut goes to a folder, choose Customize and then, at the bottom, click Change Icon, choose a new icon, and click OK twice. If the shortcut goes to a Web page, click Web Document, click Change Icon, pick a new icon, and then click OK twice.

Changing the icon for *programs* pinned to the Start menu is considerably more difficult. Sometimes it's as simple as right-clicking the shortcut pinned to the Start menu and clicking Change Icon. Usually, though, the Change Icon button is grayed out, and you have to go through a much more complex hack:

1. **Find the program.**

   Sometimes that isn't easy. Generally, you can choose Start➪My Computer, double-click the `c:` drive, choose Program Files, and go from there. If you're looking for the Office 2003 programs, for example, you should try `c:\Program Files\Microsoft Office\OFFICE11`.

2. **Right-click the program and choose Create Shortcut.**

   That puts a shortcut to the program in the same folder as the program itself. For example, if you right-click `WINWORD.EXE` (the Word program) and choose Create Shortcut, you see a new file called `Shortcut to WINWORD.EXE`.

3. **Right-click the shortcut and choose Properties.**

   Windows shows you the Shortcut Properties dialog box, as shown in Figure 5-11.

Figure 5-11:
To change a program's icon on the Start menu, you have to create a new shortcut and change the icon in the shortcut.

> **Shortcut to WINWORD.EXE Properties**
>
> General | Shortcut | Compatibility
>
> Shortcut to WINWORD.EXE
>
> Target type: Application
> Target location: OFFICE11
> Target: s\Microsoft Office\OFFICE11\WINWORD.EXE'
>
> Start in: "C:\Program Files\Microsoft Office\OFFICE11"
> Shortcut key: None
> Run: Normal window
> Comment:
>
> Find Target... | Change Icon... | Advanced...
>
> OK | Cancel | Apply

4. **Click Change Icon. In the resulting dialog box, choose the icon you want and then click OK twice.**

   The icon on the shortcut changes to match your choice.

5. **Click the shortcut with the modified icon. Drag it to the Start button and "hover" until the Start menu opens. Then drop the shortcut in the upper-left corner, pinning it on the Start menu.**

   From that point, you can rename the shortcut, change the icon again, move it, unpin it, and so on.

I recommend that you pin programs, folders, files, and Web pages to your Start menu with wild abandon. If you put too many on the Start menu, when you restart your PC, or log off and log back on again, Windows warns you with a catty message. See the next section for details.

Controlling the Frequently Used Programs List

If you follow the hacks and mods in the preceding section to pin your choice of programs on the Start menu, sooner or later you're going to run out of room. Windows itself maintains a list of kinda-frequently-used programs in the lower-left section of the Start menu. When Windows starts to feel the squeeze, it presents you with the really catty "Some Items Cannot Be Shown" message shown in Figure 5-12.

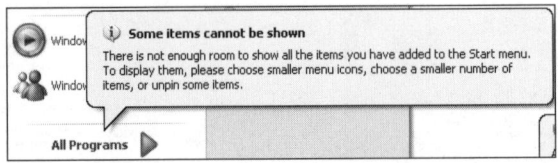

Figure 5-12:
Windows
squawks.

I say "kinda" frequently used programs because Microsoft doesn't play fair with the Most Frequently Used Programs list. Conceptually, if you use a program frequently, it should appear automatically on this list — it's a so-called "adaptive" menu, and the more frequently you use the program, the higher it should rise on the list. In practice, Microsoft uses its own nefarious methods for deciding which programs appear on the list, how high they fly, and how long they remain. In a default Windows installation, Windows Media Player goes at the top of the list. (Care to hazard a guess that Microsoft makes a lot of money from people running Windows Media Player?) Windows Messenger and/or MSN Messenger seem to appear with alarming tenacity. (How do you spell "ka-ching"?) Windows Movie Maker jumps in there, too. Chances are good that your PC manufacturer puts a few items on the list, just to sweeten the(ir) pot.

If you feel like I do and want to limit the number of programs Windows puts on the Most Frequently Used Programs list — mostly so it stops kvetching about all the programs I like to see pinned to the Start menu — here's how to trim it down:

1. **Right-click Start, choose Properties, and then click the Start Menu tab.**

   Windows shows you the Taskbar and Start Menu Properties dialog box, shown previously in Figure 5-2.

2. **Click the Customize button on top.**

   Windows displays the General tab of the Customize Start Menu dialog box.

3. **Run the Number of Programs on Start Menu spinner down.**

   Duangkhae's final Customize Start Menu dialog box is shown in Figure 5-13.

Figure 5-13: Good choices for taking control of your Start menu.

4. **Click OK twice.**

   Your Start menu should be looking pretty good — and Windows will stop bothering you with those catty "I want more room for my advertising" messages.

If you decide that you actually *like* the adaptive menu (*de gustibus non est disputandum,* eh?), there's a little trick that Microsoft stuck into TweakUI that will give you a bit more control over what kinds of programs appear on the menu. Here's how to hack it:

1. **Fire up your Web browser and go to** support.microsoft.com/ ?kbid=282066 **to see how Windows automatically excludes some programs from the Most Frequently Used Programs List.**

   In general, only shortcuts to .exe programs make it onto the list, and any program that installs or uninstalls another program probably won't get on the list.

2. **Follow the directions in Chapter 4 to download and install TweakUI, Microsoft's <nod, nod, wink, wink> "unsupported" Windows-wrenching tool.**

   TweakUI is at www.microsoft.com/windowsxp/downloads/powertoys/ xppowertoys.mspx. If you haven't already installed it, take a look at Chapter 4 for a lot of good reasons why you should.

3. **Choose Start➪All Programs➪Powertoys for Windows XP➪TweakUI to launch TweakUI. On the left side, navigate to Taskbar and Start Menu➪Start Menu.**

   TweakUI constructs a list of all the programs it can find, per Figure 5-14.

Figure 5-14:
TweakUI
allows you
to exclude
specific
programs
from the
Most
Frequently
Used
Programs
list.

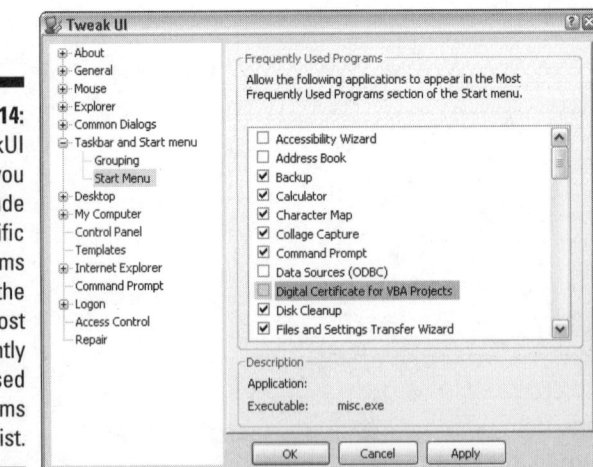

4. **Uncheck the boxes next to any programs that you want to be excluded from consideration in deciding what appears on the Most Frequently Used Programs list.**

   In Figure 5-14, Duangkhae decides that she doesn't particularly want to see the Accessibility Wizard, the Address Book (an ancient Windows application), the ODBC Data Sources program, or the Digital Certificate for VBA Projects program to appear on the MFUP list.

5. **Click OK three times.**

The programs you specified will never darken your Most Frequently Used Programs door.

Rearranging All Programs

It's easy to change the contents of the Start➪All Programs list if you understand how Windows puts together the list.

Entries in the All Programs list fall into two categories: the ones above the line and the ones below the line (see Figure 5-15). Windows assembles both lists on the fly. Every time you choose Start➪All Programs, Windows reaches out to four places to assemble the list.

Figure 5-15:
The All
Programs
menu has
two
different
levels:
above the
line and
below the
line.

✔ Files and folders in the `c:\Documents and Settings\All Users\ Start Menu` folder appear above the line.

✔ Files and folders in the `c:\Documents and Settings\<yourname>\ Start Menu` folder (where *<yourname>* is your username) appear above the line.

✔ Files and folders in the `c:\Documents and Settings\All Users\ Start Menu\Programs` folder appear below the line.

✔ Files and folders in the `c:\Documents and Settings\<yourname>\ Start Menu\Programs` folder (where *<yourname>* is your username) appear below the line.

So, for example, the three entries above the line in Figure 5-17 are all there because corresponding shortcuts sit in `c:\Documents and Settings\All Users\Start Menu`, as demonstrated in Figure 5-16.

Figure 5-16: The three shortcuts that give rise to the three programs above the line in the All Programs list in Figure 5-15.

The All Programs menu is a *cascading menu,* which means that clicking a marked line in the menu brings up a submenu. For example, the All Programs⇨Games menu cascades, as you can see in Figure 5-17.

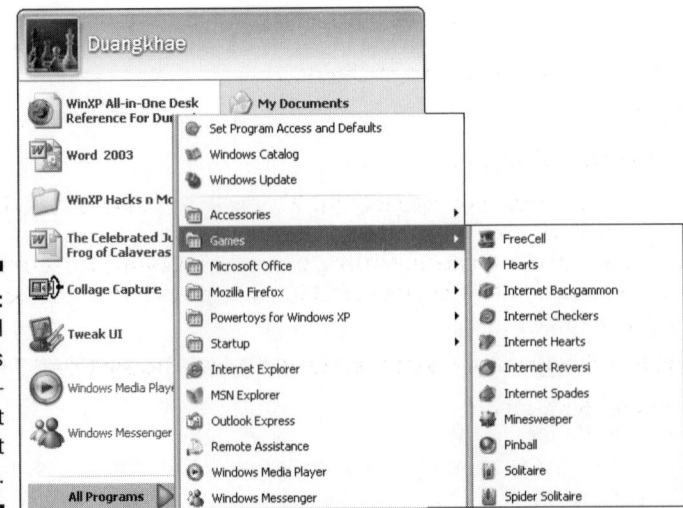

Figure 5-17: Menus in All Programs *cascade* — they roll out one level at a time.

Windows constructs All Programs cascading menus in a remarkably simple way: It turns folders in the four \Start Menu locations into cascading menus, with entries on the menu corresponding to entries inside the folder. So, for example, the All Programs⇨Games menu you see in Figure 5-17 originated with the folder structure from c:\Documents and Settings\All Users\Start Menu\Programs\Games, as shown in Figure 5-18.

Figure 5-18: The Games folder that gives rise to the Games cascading menu.

If you change the contents of any of the folders in the four \Start Menu locations, your changes appear immediately in Start Menu⇨All Programs. To show you how that works, I'll take four tired old Windows programs — Internet Explorer, Outlook Express, MSN Explorer, and Windows Messenger — off the main All Programs menu and stick them under a cascading menu called, oh, Tired Old Windows Programs. Here's how:

1. **Right-click Start and choose Open.**

   That opens c:\Documents and Settings\<*yourname*>\Start Menu.

2. **Double-click Programs.**

   You see one of the two folders that Windows combines to produce the high-level entries on the Start⇨All Programs menu. Figure 5-19 shows the default Windows arrangement, in which shortcuts for Internet Explorer and Outlook Express turn into the IE and OE entries on the All Programs menu.

3. **Right-click any empty space on the right and choose New⇨Folder.**

   A new folder appears.

4. Type Tired Old Windows Programs **and press Enter.**

The new folder gets renamed.

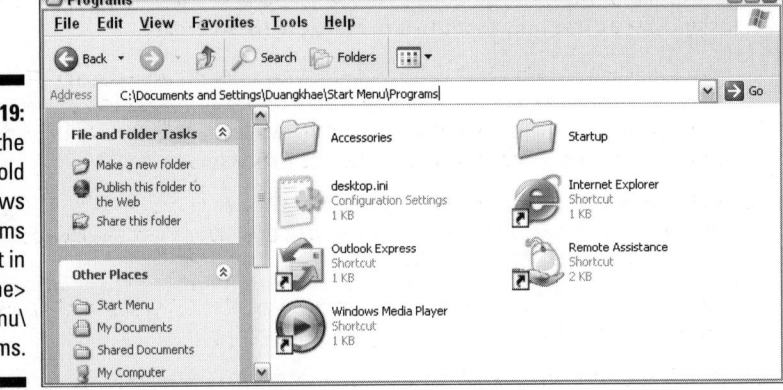

Figure 5-19:
Two of the tired old Windows programs sit in <yourname> \Start Menu\ Programs.

5. Click the Internet Explorer icon and drag it into the new Tired Old Windows Programs folder. Then click the Outlook Express icon and drag it in there, too.

The Programs folder should look like Figure 5-20.

Figure 5-20:
Move the two icons into a new folder called Tired Old Windows Programs.

6. Click the "X" in the upper-right corner of the Programs window to close the window.

Now you're ready to perform a parallel operation on the \All Users branch of the Start Menu folder.

7. **Right-click Start and choose Open All Users. Double-click Programs.**

   You are in the `c:\Documents and Settings\All Users\Start Menu\Programs` folder.

8. **Right-click any empty space on the right and choose New⇨Folder. Type** Tired Old Windows Programs **and press Enter.**

   You have a new folder with precisely the same name as the one in the `<yourname>\Start Menu\Programs` folder. The spelling of the folder names must be identical so that Windows knows to merge the contents of both folders when it creates the All Programs menu.

9. **Click the MSN Explorer icon and drag it into the new Tired Old Windows Programs folder. Then click the Windows Messenger icon and drag it into the same folder.**

10. **Click the "X" in the upper-right corner of the Programs window to close the window.**

11. **Choose Start⇨All Programs⇨Tired Old Windows Programs (see Figure 5-21).**

    All four programs appear to the right of the new line in the menu. Nifty, eh?

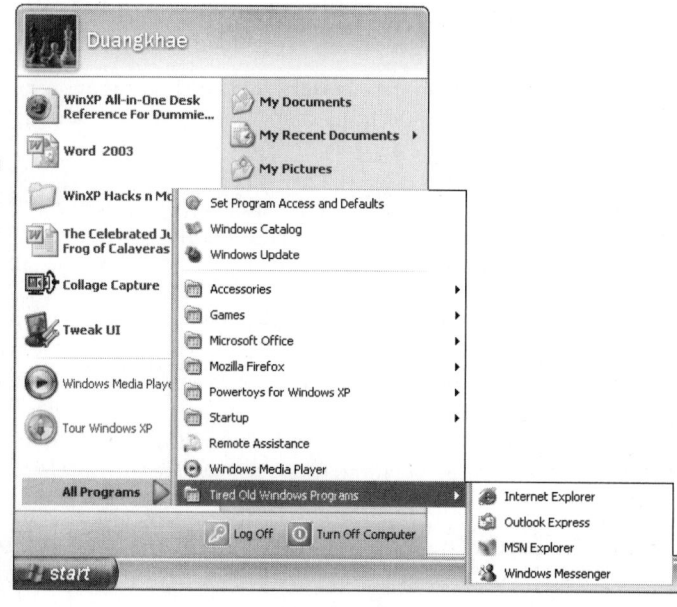

Figure 5-21: Windows combines the contents of the two Tired Old Windows Programs folders and turns them into a single cascading menu.

You might think the All Programs menu would consist, exclusively, of programs. Balderdash. The All Programs menu simply slavishly gathers the contents of those four \Start Menu folders and displays them on the screen. You can put a shortcut to a file or folder or Web page in any of the four folders, and they'll appear in the All Programs menu. The items in the menu work, too: Choose Start⇨All Programs⇨The Jumping Frog of Calaveras County.doc, for example, and Word opens with the document ready to go.

Although modifying the Registry to change the order of entries in the All Programs menu seems possible, I don't recommend it. If you want to move a particular line up or down, click on the line and drag it to its new position. So if you want to move Accessories below Games, say, just click Accessories and drag it down.

Controlling the My Recent Documents List

Depending on which version of Windows XP you have installed, the whims of your hardware manufacturer, and the phase of the moon, you may have an entry near the upper-right corner of the Start menu that says My Recent Documents.

In theory, if My Recent Documents appears on the Start menu, you can choose Start⇨My Recent Documents and immediately pick any of the documents that you recently used.

In practice, Windows frequently doesn't get the list right. Even Microsoft Office programs don't seem to "register" their most recently used documents properly. I'm not sure what's happening, and Microsoft is mum on the subject.

Here's how My Recent Documents really works:

- ✔ When you open a document (even by, for example, double-clicking a document in Windows Explorer), the program that opens the document is supposed to put a shortcut to the document in a hidden folder called C:\Documents and Settings\<yourname>\Recent. In fact, not all programs perform their duties properly, so you can't rely on the \Recent folder being entirely accurate.

- ✔ If My Recent Documents appears on the Start menu, choosing Start⇨My Recent Documents starts a program that goes through the \Recent folder and gathers the 15 newest items in the folder. It then sorts the list alphabetically and shows the result on the cascading menu.

To remove My Recent Documents from your Start menu (or to put it on your Start menu):

1. **Right-click Start and choose Properties.**

   Windows shows you the Customize Start Menu dialog box.

2. **Click Customize and then click the Advanced tab.**

   The Recent Documents box on the Advanced tab controls whether My Recent Documents appears on the Start menu (see Figure 5-22).

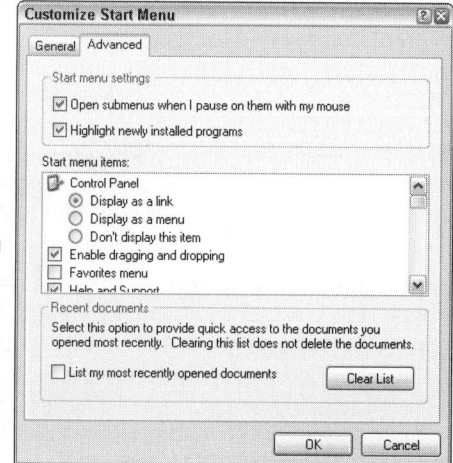

Figure 5-22: The Recent Documents box on the Advanced tab.

3. **To remove My Recent Documents from the Start menu, uncheck the box marked List My Most Recently Opened Documents. Conversely, if you want My Recent Documents to appear on your Start menu, check the box.**

4. **Click OK twice and the Start menu adjusts properly.**

   Note that this check box controls only whether My Recent Documents appears on the Start menu. If someone wants to see what you've opened lately, they only need to look in your \Recent folder.

As you can see, the heart of the matter isn't so much whether My Recent Documents appears on your Start menu. For privacy's sake, it's much more important to control what appears in your \Recent folder. You have three fairly straightforward options:

✔ You can clear all the entries out of the folder, using one of two methods: opening the folder in Windows Explorer, selecting everything in it, holding down the Shift key and pressing Escape; or opening the Customize Start Menu dialog box using the preceding steps and clicking the Clear List button (refer to Figure 5-22).

✔ You can tell Windows to clear out all the entries in the \Recent folder every time you log off. To do so, follow the steps in Chapter 4 to download and install TweakUI. Choose Start➪All Programs➪Powertoys for Windows XP➪TweakUI. On the left side of TweakUI, double-click Explorer. Check the box marked Clear Document History on Exit and then click OK.

✔ If you're really serious, you can tell Windows not to maintain this history log — or any other document history log, for that matter. If you're willing to give up your document history in all the Office programs, among others, you can do it with TweakUI. Follow the instructions in Chapter 4 to download and install TweakUI. Choose Start➪All Programs➪Powertoys for Windows XP➪TweakUI. On the left side of TweakUI, double-click Explorer. Uncheck the box marked Maintain Document History and then click OK. From that point on, Windows doesn't put new shortcuts in the \Recent folder.

After you tell Windows not to maintain a history log of your recent documents, all bets are off. When you start Word, Excel, or PowerPoint and you click File, expecting to see a list of your most-recently-used files at the bottom of the File menu, don't come crying to me if the list disappears. OK? This TweakUI setting packs some powerful mojo. To go back to keeping track of your history, follow the steps in the bullet above, but check the box marked Maintain Document History.

Advanced Start Tweaks

Microsoft bundles a whole bunch of Start menu settings on the Advanced tab of the Customize Start Menu dialog box. To see the dialog box:

1. **Right-click Start and choose Properties.**

2. **Click Customize and then click the Advanced tab.**

   Windows shows you the Advanced Start menu settings shown in Figure 5-23.

3. **Look through the rest of this section to choose which settings you want to change. When you're done, click OK twice.**

   All of your new settings go into effect.

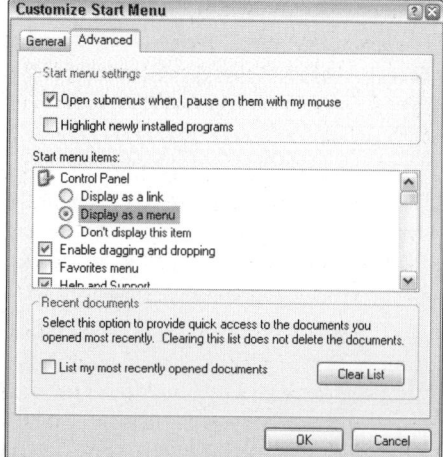

Figure 5-23:
Advanced
Start menu
settings.

I strongly recommend that you uncheck the box marked Highlight Newly Installed Programs at the top of the Advanced tab. That box controls Window's inane insistence on popping up cute notification balloons and highlighting programs immediately after you install them. Follow the logic here. You stick a CD in your computer and spend a few minutes (or, in the case of Microsoft Office, a weekend) installing your new software. After you've gone through all that effort, Windows "helps" by telling you that you've installed new software. Golly gee. Windows' helpfulness doesn't end there. If you don't use the Start⊏> All Programs menu to start the new program, Windows continues to "help" by keeping that inane message and highlighting on the screen for days (weeks? years?). Give it the axe.

The Start Menu Items box in the Advanced tab of the Customize Start Menu dialog box lets you control the appearance and behavior of the lines on the right side of the Start menu. Many of the items in the Start Menu Items box have three options:

- ✔ **Display as a Link.** Although the terminology might throw you for a minute, this is just the normal setting. If you set My Documents to Display as a Link, for example, choosing Start⊏>My Documents brings up the My Documents folder.

- ✔ **Display as a Menu.** This setting turns the item into a cascading menu. See Figure 5-24 for an example of My Computer set to Display as a Menu.

- ✔ **Don't Display this Item.** Click this button and the item is removed from the Start menu.

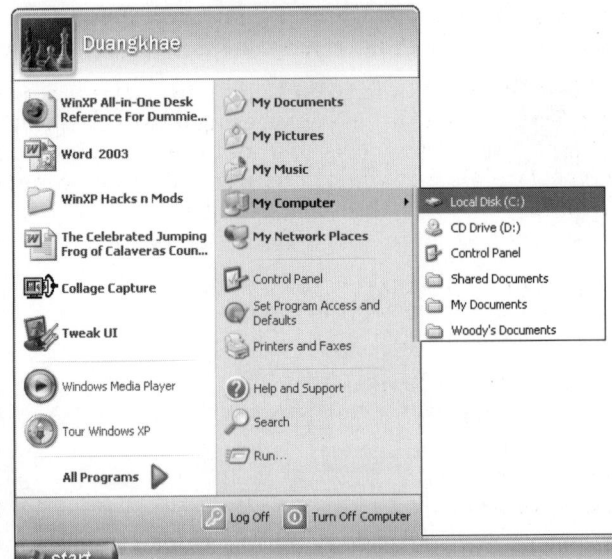

Figure 5-24:
With My
Computer
set to
display as a
menu, all of
your drives
appear in a
fly-out
menu.

Here are my recommended mods to the appearance of items on the right side of the Start menu:

- ✔ **Control Panel.** I like to keep this at the default setting, Display as Link, because I like the "new" method of organizing Control Panel applications into groups. Heaven help me. The Mongolian Horde approach of showing dozens of Control Panel applets popping out of the Start menu — the result of choosing Display as Menu — really hurts my eyes. And my head.

- ✔ **My Computer.** I prefer to Display as a Menu because I find it very handy to be able to jump directly to one of the drives (see Figure 5-25).

- ✔ **My Documents, My Music, My Pictures.** I keep all of these as Display as Link because those folders get really big, and having all of the icons pop up on the screen amounts to a big nuisance.

- ✔ **Network Connections.** I always set this to Display as Connect to Menu because my network connections have a bad habit of going up and down like a ping-pong ball on a roller coaster. If something goes belly-up, I can choose Start⇨Connect To⇨Show All Connections, and the culprit's usually easy to find.

- ✔ **Set Program Access and Defaults.** The icon designed by a bunch of lawyers deserves to get unchecked. This abomination originated back in the summer of 2002 as Microsoft's response to an antitrust judgment. It accomplished nothing at the time and even less now — every Internet browser, e-mail program, and media player knows how to set itself up, thank you very much, and there's no need to change things manually.

✔ **System Administrative Tools.** I always turn this to Display on the All Programs Menu and the Start Menu (see Figure 5-25). While it's true that you can shoot yourself squarely in the foot by monkeying around with some of the Admin Tools, the Event Viewer and Performance Monitor (see Chapter 13) are worth their weight in gold.

Figure 5-25: Some System Administrative Tools can come in very handy.

Chapter 6

Taking On the Taskbar

* *

* *

*T*hat lowly bar at the bottom of your screen rates as the best piece of real estate in Windows. Why? You can always get to it, no sweat, with (at most) a simple swoosh of the mouse. The taskbar shows you everything that's running — the ultimate "adaptive" menu. Drag a file onto a taskbar button, and the associated program opens, ready for the file to be dropped. That little bar packs a whole lotta power.

For some reason I've never understood, Microsoft hides the power of the Windows XP taskbar. Consider the default Windows XP Professional taskbar shown in Figure 6-1. Hard to believe it's a powerhouse trimmed back to look like a wallflower.

Figure 6-1:
The bone-stock taskbar, just waiting to get tricked out.

Customizing the Taskbar

Most of the taskbar's hidden power lies just a few mouse clicks away.

Here's how to unleash the taskbar and make it work for you:

1. **Right-click the taskbar and choose Properties⇨Taskbar.**

   You see the Taskbar and Start Menu Properties dialog box, as shown in Figure 6-2.

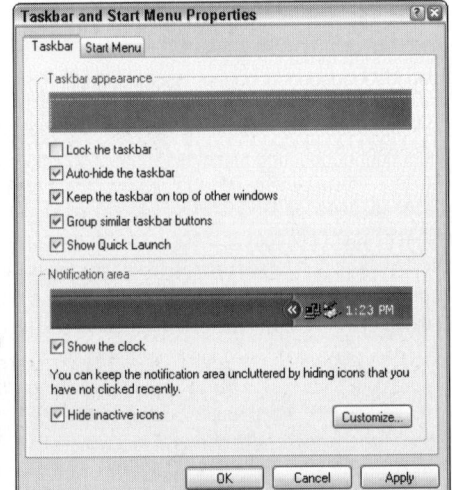

Figure 6-2:
Easy,
powerful
mods await.

2. **Leave the box marked Lock the Taskbar unchecked for the moment and check the other boxes that make sense for you:**

   • **Auto-Hide the Taskbar** makes the taskbar disappear until you move your mouse down to the bottom of the screen. Check this box unless you have a fabulously high-definition monitor and can afford to leave the taskbar sitting at the bottom of the screen all day.

   • Check the **Keep the Taskbar on Top of Other Windows** box. It doesn't make sense to have the taskbar roll underneath other windows.

   • Check **Group Similar Taskbar Buttons** in anticipation of the discussion later in this chapter called "Controlling Groups of Buttons."

   • Check **Show Quick Launch** so you can take advantage of the Quick Launch toolbar, one of Windows' great (frequently hidden!) assets.

3. **Click OK.**

Your newly modified, greatly improved taskbar looks like Figure 6-3.

Quick Launch toolbar

Sizing the Taskbar

In the preceding section, if you unchecked the box marked Lock the Taskbar, you can see little bumps immediately to the right of the Start button. No, it isn't terminal acne. Those bumps signify that the taskbar can be stretched and moved to make more room for the programs you want to run.

Every Windows user who has a screen bigger than a postage stamp needs to make the taskbar bigger. Here's how:

1. **If you can't see the little bumps to the right of the Start button (shown in Figure 6-3), right-click an empty part of the taskbar and clear the check mark in front of Lock the Taskbar.**

   That unlocks the taskbar so you can move it around.

2. **Hover your mouse over the top line of the taskbar.**

   You know you're doing the right thing when the cursor turns into an up-and-down arrow.

3. **Click and drag the top line of the taskbar higher.**

   I recommend that you give the taskbar at least two rows (see Figure 6-4), but you might want to boost that to three.

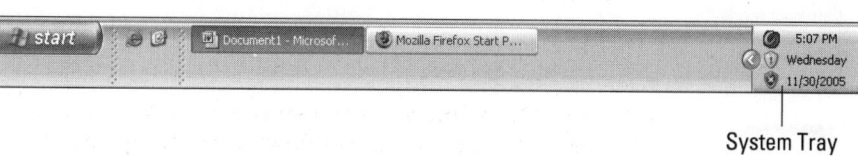

System Tray

4. **Lock down the taskbar by right-clicking any empty space and checking the line marked Lock the Taskbar.**

   This way, you can't inadvertently mess up the taskbar while you're going about your usual Windows business.

Taming the System Tray

The Windows System Tray — er, uh, the Windows *Notification Area* (to use the current politically correct term) — sits down at the lower-right corner of the screen. It includes the time and a whole bunch of icons.

If you follow the steps in the preceding section, your System Tray not only shows you the time, but also shows you the day and date (refer to Figure 6-4).

Some people like having lots of icons in the System Tray. Some people get tired of specific icons always showing up in the tray. And some people want to blow them all away. I tend to be ambivalent on the subject.

To get rid of all the icons in the System Tray:

1. **Follow the steps in Chapter 4 to download and install TweakUI.**

2. **Choose Start⇨All Programs⇨Powertoys for Windows XP⇨TweakUI. Then, on the left, double-click Taskbar and Start Menu.**

   TweakUI shows you the settings in Figure 6-5.

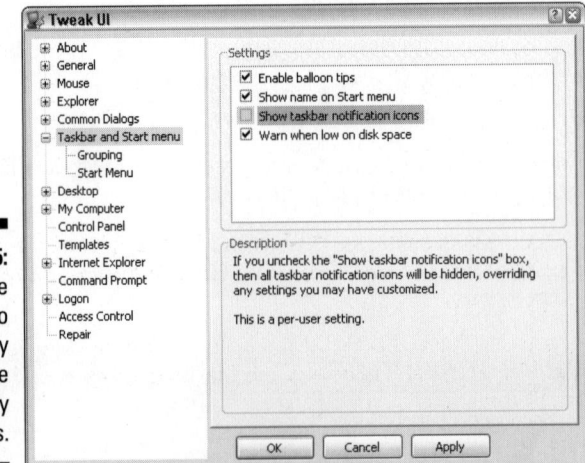

Figure 6-5:
Use
TweakUI to
blast away
all the
System Tray
icons.

3. **Uncheck the box marked Show Taskbar Notification Icons.**

4. **Click OK.**

All the icons are gone.

If you want to see your most-recently-used icons (where Windows determines, rather strangely, what "most-recently-used" means) but hide specific icons that give you the willies (or, uh, won'ties):

1. **Right-click an empty spot on the taskbar and choose Properties⇨ Taskbar.**

You see the Taskbar and Start Menu Properties dialog box (refer to Figure 6-2).

2. **In the Notification Area section of the dialog box, click Customize.**

Windows brings up the Customize Notifications dialog box, shown in Figure 6-6.

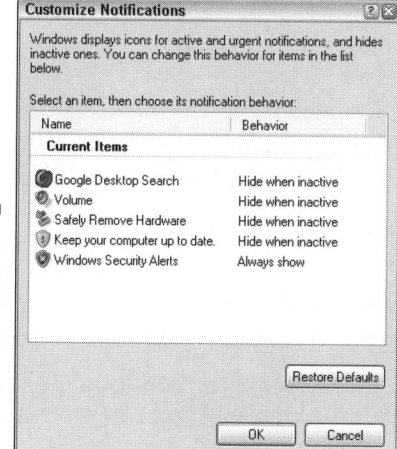

Figure 6-6:
Pick and choose which icons appear and which get hidden.

3. **If you want to choose the way an individual icon appears, click its entry in the Behavior column and choose Hide When Inactive, Always Hide, or Always Show.**

For example, you can make sure that the Volume icon always appears in the System Tray by clicking its Hide When Inactive entry and changing that to Always Show.

4. **Click OK twice.**

The icons you chose to appear show up in the System Tray. To see the hidden icons, you have to click the <, the left wedgie.

Controlling Groups of Buttons

In the normal course of events, Windows is smart enough to group icons in the taskbar. But if you uncheck the box marked Group Similar Taskbar Buttons (see the section "Customizing the Taskbar" earlier in this chapter), Windows reserves smaller and smaller slots as you add more and more buttons (see Figure 6-7).

Figure 6-7:
If Windows doesn't group taskbar buttons, you can't tell one button from another.

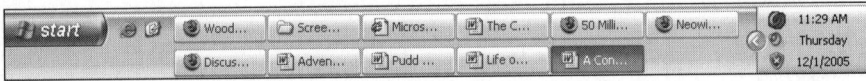

The Taskbar and Start Menu Properties dialog box shown in Figure 6-2 lets you tell Windows whether it should group buttons from the same program, but you have very little control: You can turn the feature on or off.

Windows can handle button grouping in a much more refined way. To get a better handle on taskbar button grouping, you need to use TweakUI:

1. **Follow the steps in Chapter 4 to download and install TweakUI.**

2. **Choose Start➪All Programs➪Powertoys for Windows XP➪TweakUI. Then, on the left, double-click Taskbar and Start Menu➪Grouping.**

   You see the Button Grouping menu in Figure 6-8.

3. **If you commonly open a lot of windows with one program, check the Group Applications with the Most Windows First button.**

   This way, all of the open windows are easy to run through in one click. For example, if you commonly have ten or more Word documents open, and you use the Word Window menu to move among them, choosing this button can make it easy to jump to other programs in the taskbar.

4. **Alternatively, click the button to have Windows group any application that has more than a specific number of windows open.**

   If you run the number up to four or five, you may get many buttons in the taskbar, but eventually Windows coalesces groups of them.

5. **Click OK.**

   Your change takes effect immediately (see Figure 6-9).

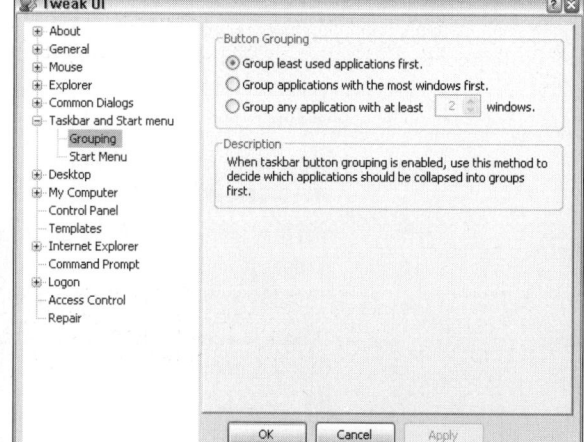

Figure 6-8:
Group
buttons
according
to the way
you work.

Figure 6-9:
The results
of grouping
applications
with the
most
windows
first.

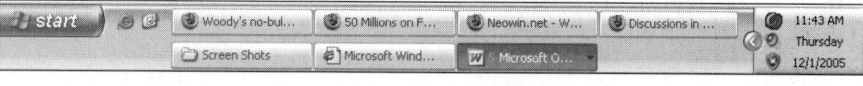

Modifying Quick Launch

The Quick Launch toolbar consists of a bunch of small icons immediately to the right of the Start button, and it rates as one of the most useful features in all of Windows. Yet you might never have used it before — some versions of Windows hide the toolbar unless you specifically bring it out.

You can make the Quick Launch toolbar appear in two easy ways:

✔ Right-click any empty spot on the Windows taskbar and choose Toolbars. Click to check the line that says Quick Launch.

✔ Check the Show Quick Launch box on the Taskbar and Start Menu Properties dialog box, as I describe earlier in this chapter in the section "Customizing the Taskbar."

Restoring the Show Desktop icon

If you accidentally delete the Show Desktop icon from the Quick Launch toolbar, here's how to get it back:

1. **Choose Start⇨All Programs⇨Accessories⇨ Notepad.**

   Notepad springs to life.

2. **Type these lines, precisely, into Notepad:**

   ```
   [Shell]
   Command=2
   IconFile=explorer.exe,3
   [Taskbar]
   Command=ToggleDesktop
   ```

3. **Choose File⇨Exit. Click Yes to save the changes. Save the file on your desktop, and call it** Show Desktop.scf.

You see a new icon on your desktop that looks remarkably like the Show Desktop icon that used to be on your Quick Launch toolbar.

4. **Right-click the new icon on your desktop and drag it to the Quick Launch toolbar.**

   You may have to "hover" your mouse at the bottom of the screen for a few seconds to have the Windows taskbar appear.

5. **Drop the icon wherever you like on the Quick Launch toolbar and choose Move Here.**

If you choose Move Here, Windows automatically deletes the icon from the desktop.

Deleting Quick Launch icons

Depending on who paid your computer manufacturer to plaster your copy of Windows with unnecessary junk, you may have several icons in your Quick Launch toolbar. Fortunately, it's easy to get rid of the ones you don't want: Right-click any offensive icons and then click Delete.

Don't delete the Show Desktop icon — the one that looks more or less like a pencil scribbling on a piece of paper. (I think it looks like an off-center joystick, but art is in the eye of the beholder, eh?) Getting it back isn't too difficult (see the sidebar "Restoring the Show Desktop icon"), but it's much easier to just refrain from deleting it in the first place. That icon can save your bacon at times. If a rogue program takes over your machine and won't let go, the easiest way to switch over to the desktop is via that little icon.

Adding programs to Quick Launch

Putting your own programs on the Quick Launch toolbar couldn't be simpler — but there's an important trick:

1. **Find the program that you want to put on the Quick Launch toolbar.**

   Generally, you choose Start⇨All Programs and go looking from there, but you can also choose Start⇨My Computer⇨c:⇨Program Files or Start⇨My Computer⇨c:⇨Windows and spelunk. Any way you find the program is okay.

2. **Right-click the program file and drag it to the Quick Launch toolbar.**

   Avoid the temptation to left-click the program file. Depending on where you found the file, you may end up removing it from the Start menu or making it totally inoperative! Always right-click when dragging to the Quick Launch toolbar.

   You may need to hover your mouse at the bottom of the screen for a bit until Windows shows you the toolbar.

3. **Drop the icon in the Quick Launch toolbar and choose Copy Here.**

   It's important that you choose Copy Here. One of Windows' worst design faults is in the way it can move programs without any warning — and you hit that design fault square in the jaw when dragging icons to the Quick Launch toolbar.

Adding folders and files to Quick Launch

Many people don't realize that you can put folders and files on the Quick Launch toolbar, too. It's easy. Here's how:

1. **Find the folder or file that you want.**

   You can go the Start⇨My Documents route, if you want, but you can also start in the Open dialog box of any Microsoft Office program or some other programs. You can even use the results of a Google Desktop Search.

2. **Left-click the file and drag it to the Quick Launch toolbar.**

   Again, you may have to hover your mouse at the bottom of the screen and wait for the Windows taskbar to appear.

   It's important that you right-click on a *program* when you drag it to the Quick Launch toolbar: If you left-click on a program, Windows may decide to move the program entirely, and that could prevent the program from running and cause all sorts of havoc. Fortunately, Windows isn't quite so dumb with folders or files. When you left-click and drag a *folder* or *file,* Windows always creates a shortcut to the folder or document and places the shortcut in the Quick Launch toolbar.

Adding Web pages to Quick Launch

Putting a Web page on the Quick Launch toolbar takes only a little more effort:

1. **Start your Web browser and go to the Web page you want to put on the Quick Launch toolbar.**

2. **Click the icon to the left of the address.**

   If you look at Figure 6-10, you can see the icon immediately to the left of the http://www.askwoody.com address.

Click and drag this icon to the Quick Launch toolbar.

Figure 6-10:
The icon
you need
sits
immediately
to the left of
the Web
page's
address.

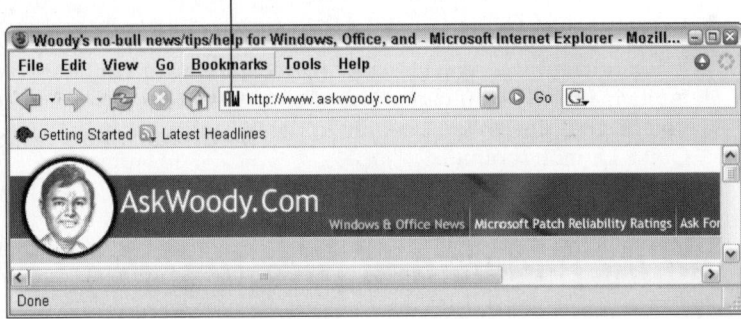

3. **Left-click and drag the icon to the Quick Launch toolbar.**

   Again, you may need to hover your mouse at the bottom of the screen until the Windows taskbar appears.

When it's on the Quick Launch toolbar, clicking a Web page icon launches your Web browser and takes you directly to the page.

Making room for more icons

What? You're running out of space? Not to worry. If you need to make more room for Quick Launch icons, follow these steps:

1. **Right-click an empty spot on the Windows taskbar.**

2. **Uncheck the line marked Lock the Taskbar.**

3. **Drag the dotted line at the right edge of the Quick Launch toolbar farther to the right until you create enough room for all of your icons.**

4. **Right-click an empty spot on the Windows taskbar and check the line marked Lock the Taskbar.**

Changing Quick Launch screen tips

On occasion, Windows does a good job of choosing the screen tip — the text that appears in a yellow box when you hover your mouse over an icon — for Quick Launch icons. Sometimes, though, the verbiage really piles on. If you put Word 2003 in the Quick Launch toolbar, for example, the screen tip reads *Microsoft Office Word 2003 / Create and edit text and graphics in letters, reports, Web pages, or e-mail messages by using Microsoft Office Word.*

In many cases, you can change the text for a screen tip by right-clicking the icon, choosing Rename, and typing your preferred text. But if you try that with any of the Office 2003 programs, among others, you can't get rid of most of the marketing drivel.

Here's how to well and truly change a Quick Launch icon's screen tip:

1. **Right-click the Quick Launch icon and choose Properties⇨General.**

   Figure 6-11 shows the resulting Properties dialog box for Word 2003 — er, Microsoft Office Word 2003.

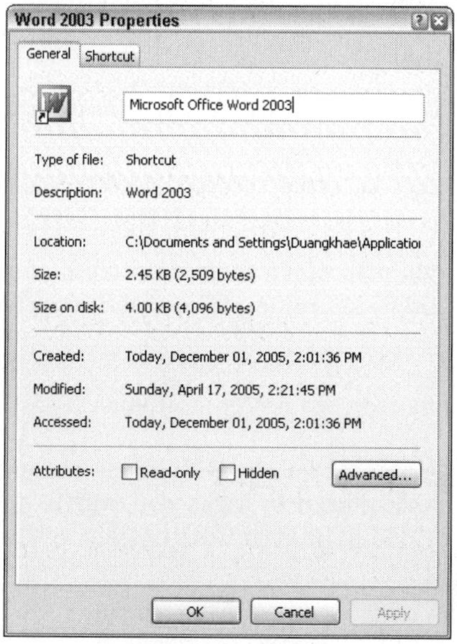

Figure 6-11: The Properties dialog box for Word 2003.

2. **Change the name in the box at the top to something short and sweet.**

   For example, in Figure 6-11, I get rid of the *Microsoft Office Word 2003* claptrap and simply type *Word 2003.*

3. **Click the Shortcut tab.**

   Recognize the text in the Comment box? It's the marketing fluff that appears in the screen tip.

4. **Delete everything in the box marked Comment.**

5. **Click OK.**

   Congratulations. You've reduced screen clutter significantly.

Changing Quick Launch icons

A friend of mine loves to use her Quick Launch toolbar because it's fast and easy to find, and it doesn't take up a lot of room. One problem: She puts four of her favorite folders on the Quick Launch toolbar, and because all of the folders have the same icon, it's hard to tell which one is which.

If you know the trick, it's easy to change icons for folders, files, and Web pages in the Quick Launch toolbar:

1. **Right-click the Quick Launch icon you want to change and choose Properties⇨Shortcut.**

2. **Click the Change Icon button.**

   Windows goes out to a file called She1132.d11. It's renowned for having a large collection of icons.

3. **Choose an icon from the ones on offer, or click Browse and go find your own icon.**

   The Web is full of icons, or you can make them yourself if you have a spare week or two. Run a Google search on **"Free Windows Icons"**.

4. **Click OK twice.**

   The Quick Launch icon changes to whatever icon you chose.

 Most of the time, you can change a program's icon by using the previous steps. Other times, the program manufacturer locks you out. To see whether it's possible, open the Properties dialog box for the program and see if the Change Icon button is grayed out.

Chapter 7

Decking Out the Desktop

You probably spend more time in front of your computer than you do in front of your TV. So why settle for something mundane? The Windows desktop was made to be mangled. With a simple hack here and a mod there, you can turn it into a fun, inviting place.

At least it'll look a whole lot better than your cubicle.

Making Your Desktop Home

The Windows desktop consists of several layers. To change the appearance or the contents of the desktop, you can monkey with items in any of the layers:

- ✔ The bottom layer (which you may never see!) is a **solid color.** You can set the color by right-clicking an empty part of the desktop, choosing Properties⇨Desktop, and changing the Color drop-down list in the lower-right corner (see Figure 7-1).

- ✔ On top of the solid color sits the **background** (which has been known since the dawn of Windows as the *wallpaper*). If the wallpaper is big enough, it hides the solid color behind it. You can choose one of the bone-stock Windows wallpapers from the list in Figure 7-1, or you can right-click any picture file and choose Set as Desktop Background. I talk about this mod and its idiosyncrasies in Chapter 3.

✔ You can put **"active" content** on top of the wallpaper, but I strongly advise you against doing so. Windows gets slow and cranky — and sometimes unstable — when it has to deal with stuff on the desktop that changes all the time. If you insist on playing with the Active Desktop, start with the Display Properties dialog box in Figure 7-1 and then click Customize Desktop➪Web.

✔ On top of the wallpaper sit the **icons,** which can be deposited by programs (typically when they're installed), or you can add icons at will (see the section "Wrangling with Icons," later in this chapter). The desktop is a horrible, cluttered place to stick an icon — putting an icon on your desktop is like cramming another piece of junk into your entry hall closet — and once there, it could take you hours to find the icon you need.

✔ On top of the icons floats the **mouse cursor.** You can easily change the mouse cursor — if you can figure out where Microsoft put the %$#@! dialog box. Try choosing Start➪Control Panel➪Printers and Other Hardware➪Mouse➪Pointers to get to the dialog box in Figure 7-2.

✔ Lurking in the sidelines, ready to take over at any moment, sits the **screensaver,** which takes complete control of the desktop, and its archnemesis, the **monitor power saver,** which fades all the layers to black. I talk about screensavers in Chapter 3.

You can also change the appearance of individual pieces of the desktop — such settings as the font for the heading of message boxes, the color of some buttons, or the spacing of icons on the desktop — by right-clicking any empty part of the desktop, choosing Properties➪Appearance, and clicking the Advanced button.

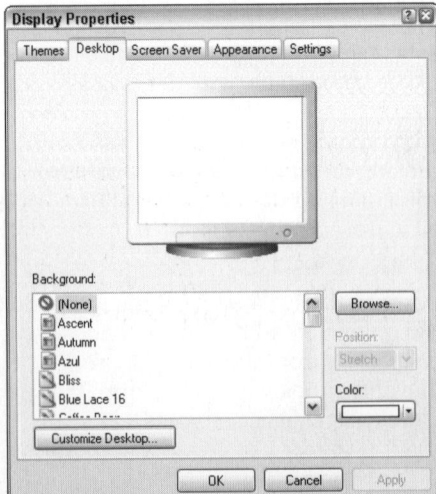

Figure 7-1:
Choose the solid color at the bottom of the desktop in this dialog box.

Figure 7-2:
Change the
mouse
pointer in
the Mouse
Properties
dialog.

These advanced desktop settings are riddled with bugs that have persisted since the earliest days of Windows 3.0. For example, if you change the font for Windows menus, you may (or may not) end up changing fonts in various applications. The side effects of all the settings aren't documented anywhere that I can find. You will probably find that making changes to the advanced settings will have far-reaching consequences that are essentially impossible to predict.

Windows XP lets you save collections of settings — colors, wallpaper, icons, screensaver, and the like — as a package called a *Theme.* I go over Themes in the section "Working with Themes," later in this chapter.

Wrangling with Icons

Microsoft created the Windows desktop as a convenient place to store things — programs, documents, and the like. To some extent, it works well. But the minute you get more than a few dozen icons on your desktop, you'll find yourself bogged down rummaging through them, searching for the icon you need. Compounding the problem: Most programs insist on putting an icon on the desktop when you install them. What a headache!

Use desktop icons sparingly.

Exploring and installing Iconoid

If you're going to work with your desktop icons, consider installing a free program called Iconoid that lets you control myriad aspects of your icons' existence:

- ✔ **Remember the current location of all your icons,** which is particularly helpful if you're going to make mass changes to your icons but want to have an "Ooops/Undo" button.

- ✔ **Remember icons' locations at various screen resolutions,** so if you change from, say, 1024 x 768 to 1280 x 1024, you can control where icons appear at each resolution.

- ✔ **Change the color box behind the icons' text,** making it contrast highly with the desktop or making it transparent.

- ✔ **Hide or display desktop icons, depending on how long your mouse pointer hovers over a window,** so that if you hold the mouse over, say, a Word document that doesn't appear full screen, all the icons on your desktop disappear, so you can concentrate on the document.

Installing Iconoid is a snap. Here's how:

1. **Point your Web browser to www.sillysot.com and click where indicated to download iconoid.zip.**

2. **Double-click iconoid.zip on your computer and run setup.exe. Take all of the defaults.**

3. **Choose Start➪All Programs➪Iconoid➪Iconoid and when the program starts, click the Positions tab.**

   Iconoid's Positions dialog box looks like Figure 7-3.

Figure 7-3:
Iconoid
keeps track
of all your
icons'
locations.

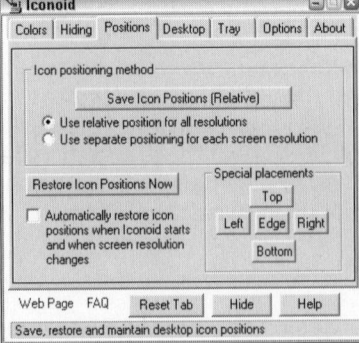

4. **Click the Save Icon Positions (Relative) button.**

   Iconoid remembers the location of all your icons. If you ever want to restore them, click the Restore Icon Positions Now button in this dialog box.

5. **Click the Hiding tab and click the Never Hide button.**

   Iconoid automatically hides your icons if your mouse hovers over an open window for five seconds — disconcerting if you don't expect it.

6. **Click "X" in the upper-right corner to close Iconoid. Then click Exit when asked.**

   If you ever want to get rid of Iconoid, choose Start⇨Control Panel⇨Add or Remove Programs, select Iconoid, and remove it.

"Snapping" icons to Windows' invisible grid

To make the icons "snap to" Windows' invisible grid, right-click an empty part of the desktop, choose Arrange Icons By, and then check the line that says Align to Grid (see Figure 7-4).

Figure 7-4:
You can align icons to Windows' invisible grid by using the Align to Grid option.

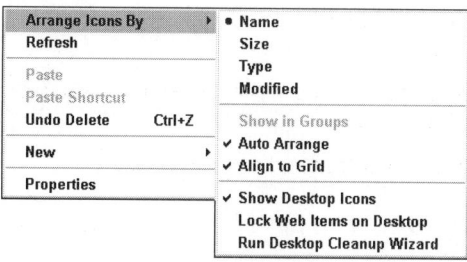

If you don't want Windows to automatically snap icons to its grid, right-click an empty part of the desktop, choose Arrange Icons By, and then remove the check in front of Align to Grid. Rocket science.

Autoarranging icons

Windows says that it will automatically arrange icons by Name (presumably alphabetically), Size, Type, or the Date Modified, but I'll be hanged if I can figure out what it *really* does. If you right-click the Desktop and choose to

Arrange Icons By⇨Name, for example, icons get tossed willy-nilly into their spots in an order that has absolutely nothing to do with the Roman alphabet. Sometimes Windows marches to a different drummer, eh?

If you want to try to Auto Arrange by Name, be sure to install and use Iconoid first, so you can get your icons back in place after Windows messes them up.

Moving all icons to the upper-left corner of the screen

I like to organize my desktop from time to time by moving all of the icons to the upper-left corner of the screen. That frees up room on the right and at the bottom, and makes it easier to see the icons I have. There's no setting (even in TweakUI!) that tells Windows to slide the icons together, but there is a trick. To quickly move all of your icons into the upper-left corner of the screen:

1. **Right-click any open spot on the desktop and choose Properties⇨ Settings.**

2. **Adjust your screen resolution so it's one size smaller than what you have now.**

   For example, if you're running at 1024 x 768, adjust your resolution to 800 x 600.

3. **Click Apply. When Windows asks if you want to keep this resolution, click Yes.**

4. **Once again, right-click any open spot on the desktop and choose Properties⇨Settings.**

5. **Choose your old screen resolution and click Apply.**

6. **When Windows asks if you want to keep this resolution, click Yes.**

   All of your icons will be moved to the upper-left corner of the screen.

Working with Themes

Microsoft created the concept of a Windows desktop "theme" so it could make more money. That probably doesn't surprise you. Starting in the times of Windows 98, Windows Plus! Packs (you may recognize them from the Da Vinci, Nature, or Space Themes) made a few coppers for the coffers. Although a couple of Plus! Packs have shipped for Windows XP, most of the bits on offer from Microsoft aren't very exciting — particularly when free alternatives abound.

A Windows *Theme* may include:

- ✔ Big pictures. Wallpaper — er, a Windows desktop background. A screensaver.

- ✔ Little stuff. Custom advanced desktop settings (such as colors or fonts for all windows), different icons, new mouse cursors, modified colors for buttons.

- ✔ Weird stuff. System sounds. A skin for Windows Media Player. "Visualizations" for the Media Player.

Using a purpose-built installer

Installing a Theme by hand isn't difficult (see the next section), but you may want to pay for a purpose-built Theme installer. If you have a Windows Plus! Pack, you already have a Theme installer. If you don't want to shell out the money for a Plus! Pack, the $15 Theme installer from Left Side Software has a good reputation (`www.lss.com.au/lss/windows/dt/themes.htm`).

A few really scummy companies have taken Themes that individuals posted on the Internet and repackaged them, wrapping them with scumware installers. If you ever try to install a Theme and you hit a warning message like the ones shown in Figures 7-5 and 7-6, click Cancel immediately and get out before your computer gets clobbered.

Figure 7-5:
If you install a Theme and see a screen like this one, click Cancel and get out.

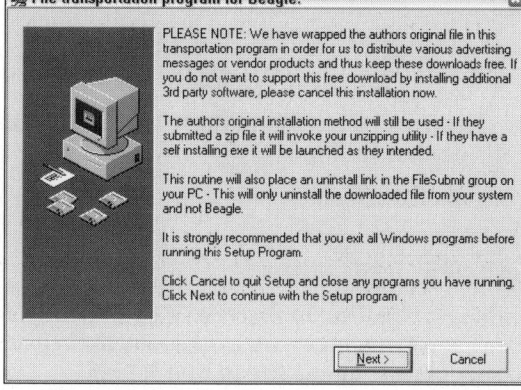

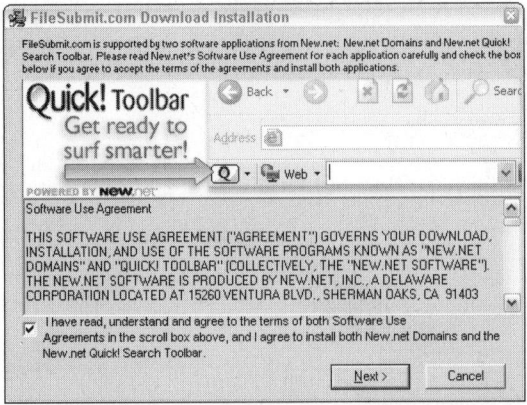

Installing a Theme manually

Here's a way to hack into many freely available Themes on the Internet with-out buying the Plus! Pack or paying for an installer — or worrying about whether that self-installing Theme will install all sorts of junk. The approach (which hasn't been documented before, as best I can tell) is a little tricky, but it should work with any Windows Theme, no matter how dated:

1. **Find a Theme that you want to install and download it.**

   Look for a `.zip` file (`.exe` files have a nasty propensity to include scumware). The best places I've found to search for `.zip` Themes are Tucows Themes (`http://themes.tucows.com`), CNet downloads (`www.download.com/Themes/2001-2319_4-0.html`), and ThemeWorld (`www.themeworld.com`). Other Themes are available all over the Internet. Chances are good that your favorite organization, movie, com-pany, and disease all have custom-made Themes.

   For this example, I download the Windows Me Theme file `beagle.zip` from `http://hkbn.themes.tucows.com/preview/74439.html`.

2. **Double-click the downloaded zip file to open it and then click once on the `.theme` file inside the zip file.**

   In Figure 7-7, I click once on the file called `Beagle.theme`.

   If you don't see a `.theme` file, you can't use this approach — and you should be on the lookout for scumware.

3. **On the left, click Copy This File. In the resulting Copy Items dialog box, navigate to `c:\WINDOWS\Resources\Themes` and click the Copy button to put a copy of the `.theme` file in that folder.**

   Unless you've changed it somehow (possibly by installing an off-brand Theme manager program), Windows XP looks for `.theme` files in that folder.

Figure 7-7:
Your
downloaded
zip should
include a
.theme file.

4. **Choose Start⇨My Computer and navigate to** `c:\WINDOWS\Resources\`
   `Themes`. **Right-click the** `.theme` **file you just copied, and choose Open**
   With⇨Notepad.

   The `Beagle.theme` file looks like Figure 7-8.

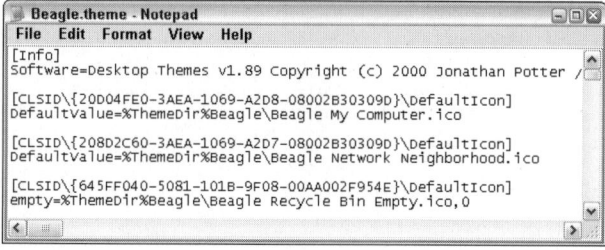

Figure 7-8:
The
.theme file
tells you
where to
unzip all the
other files.

5. **Determine which folder the Theme requires by looking to the right of**
   the `%ThemeDir%` **parameter.**

   In Figure 7-8, `Beagle.theme` repeatedly refers to `%ThemeDir%Beagle`.
   That means this Beagle Theme expects to find its files in a folder called
   `c:\WINDOWS\Resources\Themes\Beagle`.

   Another example: A very popular Theme called Starcraft Terran refers to
   `%ThemeDir%Starcraft Terran`. So you need to put all of the associated
   files in a folder called `c:\WINDOWS\Resources\Themes\Starcraft`
   `Terran`. You get the idea.

   Most Themes expect to have their files stored in a folder under `c:\`
   `WINDOWS\Resources\Themes`. By looking inside the `.theme` file, you
   can see for yourself where the files should go.

6. **Click File⇨Exit to get out of Notepad and then go back to the** `.zip` **file**
   (per Figure 7-7).

7. On the left, click Extract All Files.

Windows brings up the Compressed (Zipped) Folders Extraction Wizard.

8. Click Next.

Windows asks you to select a destination for the unzipped files.

9. Click Browse. In the Select a Destination dialog box, navigate to My Computer⇨c:⇨WINDOWS⇨Resources. Click once on Themes and then click the Make New Folder button.

Windows creates a new folder and lets you type in a new name.

10. Type the name of the folder you found in Step 5.

In Figure 7-9, I type **Beagle**, which is the name of the folder that my new Theme expects.

Figure 7-9:
Make a new folder to house all of the files associated with the Theme.

11. Click OK and then click Next.

Windows extracts all of the files that make up the Theme into the new folder. It then shows you a do-nothing dialog box at the end of the Extraction Wizard.

12. Uncheck the box marked Show Extracted Files, and click Finish.

The Extraction Wizard extricates itself.

13. Click "X" in the upper-right corner of the zip-file dialog box to clear the box (refer to Figure 7-7).

14. Right-click any empty area on the desktop and choose Properties.

You see the Themes tab of the Display Properties dialog box (see Figure 7-10).

Figure 7-10:
Choose your
new Theme
here.

15. **Choose your new Theme from the drop-down list of Themes and then click OK.**

Windows shimmers and shakes for a few seconds and then changes to your new Theme (see Figure 7-11).

Figure 7-11:
The Beagle
Theme's
desktop.

Yes, my Beagle Theme's Recycle Bin looks like a doghouse. Yes, Windows now growls at me, regularly. I just growl back. Yes, my beagle wonders if there's a new mutt in the house.

If you ever want to change back to the standard Windows XP Theme, right-click any empty spot on the desktop, choose Properties, pick Windows XP from the drop-down list of Themes, and click OK.

Getting the Most from ClearType

You probably know that the characters you see on your computer screen are composed of dots. There have been many attempts over the years to make the dots look more like . . . well, characters. Microsoft's approach is called *ClearType*.

If you have an old-fashioned monitor (ah, yes, I'm guaranteed they still exist!), activating ClearType on your computer probably won't do anything but give you a headache. On the other hand, if you have a flat-panel display, or if you're working on a laptop, ClearType may improve what you see — which is to say, turning on ClearType may make the characters on the screen look more like characters and less like bunches of dots.

Understanding ClearType

ClearType takes advantage of one pervasive fact: Flat computer screens don't work with dots. Instead, each pixel — each "dot" that your brain sees — comprises three rectangles, side by side, one each in red, green, and blue. A sufficiently clever computer program can take advantage of that fact to trick your eye into seeing characters that are significantly clearer than those composed of large dots; by manipulating the red, green, and blue rectangles separately, your computer can show you three times as much detail, horizontally.

To see the actual effect, in color, check out Steve Gibson's "How Sub-Pixel Font Rendering Works" at `http://grc.com/ctwhat.htm`.

No doubt you're wondering why anybody with a flat screen wouldn't use ClearType. In fact, some people (including me!) just don't like the effect. Many flat-panel displays these days have automatic image adjustment circuitry — you push a button on the front panel and the picture adjusts itself. I find that a large flat display, properly adjusted, looks better without ClearType. Best for you to give it a try and see what you think.

Modifying ClearType

You can turn ClearType on and off by using the Control Panel's ClearType application (Start⇨Control Panel⇨Appearance and Themes⇨ClearType Tuning, check Turn On ClearType), but you'll be giving ClearType short shrift unless you download the fine-tuning apparatus and give it a run.

Here's how:

1. **Go to the PowerToys download page,** www.microsoft.com/ windowsxp/downloads/powertoys/xppowertoys.mspx

   I talk about TweakUI and the other PowerToys in Chapter 4.

2. **Click** setup.exe **and download the ClearType Tuner PowerToy.**

3. **Run** setup.exe.

   The ClearType Tuning Control Panel Applet installation wizard appears. Take all the defaults.

4. **On the wizard's final panel, check the box marked Launch the Program and then click Finish.**

   The ClearType Settings Wizard starts (see Figure 7-12).

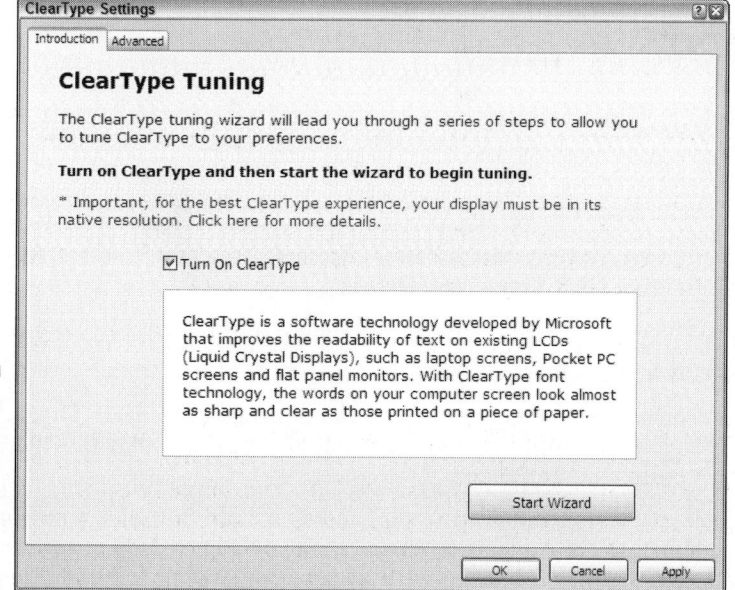

Figure 7-12: Go through the ClearType Tuning Wizard.

5. Check the box marked Turn On ClearType and then click Start Wizard.

The ClearType Settings Wizard takes you through two adjustment steps. At each step, you choose the text that looks best and then click Next.

6. When you get to the final step of the wizard (shown in Figure 7-13), if you're satisfied with the final settings, click Finish. Otherwise, click Back and try again.

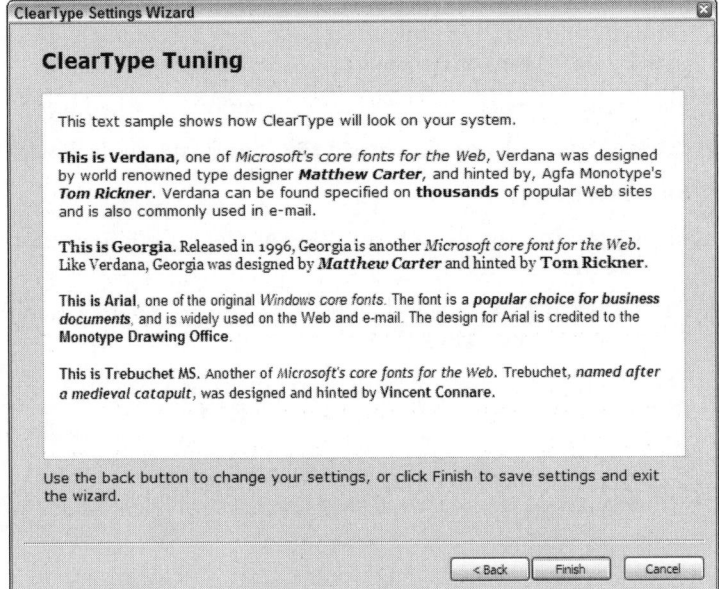

Figure 7-13: Follow the wizard through.

Wait. Even though the wizard's done, you aren't. You can do better.

7. Choose Start➪Control Panel➪Appearances and Themes. At the bottom, click ClearType Tuning.

You see the ClearType Settings Wizard again (refer to Figure 7-12).

8. Click the Advanced tab.

The settings you chose by stepping through the wizard appear here (see Figure 7-14), but you may be able to do better by adjusting the ClearType Contrast Setting slider.

If your monitor has an automatic adjustment button, try moving the slider on the Advanced tab and then clicking the adjustment button on your monitor. Then move the slider again and click the button again. ClearType and the monitor's auto adjustment may work at cross-purposes to each other, so take your time and get it right. Your eyes will thank you.

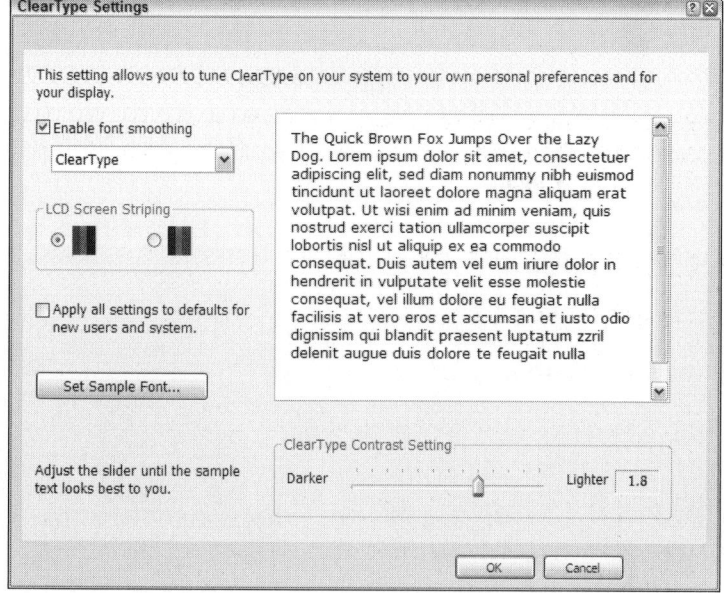

Figure 7-14:
The fine-
tuning
controls are
on the
Advanced
tab.

9. **When you're happy with the results, click OK.**

Don't forget that you can turn off ClearType by unchecking the box marked Enable Font Smoothing.

Part III
Adjusting Everyday Activities

The 5th Wave   By Rich Tennant

"Okay, make sure this is right. 'Looking for caring companion who likes old movies, nature walks and quiet evenings at home. Knowledge of hacking the registry and customizing Windows XP a plus'."

In this part . . .

Do you spend 16 hours a day in front of your computer? Do your glasses have computer screens etched into the lenses? Mine do. Can't even blink without missing a screen refresh.

Face it. Windows Explorer, straight out of the box, is designed to work for a wet-behind-the-ears newbie. I figure most people grow out of the "beginner" stage in less than a month. Why put up with settings that were meant to help people who can barely click a mouse? For that matter, why stick with Microsoft add-ons when free products from other folks work better, faster, and safer?

In this part, I go over hacks and mods for Windows Explorer, and then I dig into the best non-Microsoft alternatives for desktop searching, Web browsing, and instant messaging.

Chapter 8

Reining In Windows Explorer

Most people think of Windows Explorer as that dumb little program that lets you move from folder to folder, file to file. Choose Start⇨My Computer or Start⇨My Documents, and Windows Explorer appears and does your bidding.

Few people realize that Windows Explorer rules the roost when it comes to interacting with your computer — and it's a powerful little beast to boot.

Fixing Key Explorer Settings

Before you even think about using Windows Explorer — heck, before you even think about using Windows, full stop — you really need to fix a couple of stupid design decisions that Microsoft made years ago. And therein lies a story.

How programs start

When you double-click a file or an icon, Windows usually runs a program. You knew that, right? If you double-click a Word document, Windows runs Word and loads up the file. If you double-click a picture, Windows cranks up some sort of graphic program (possibly Paint) and brings in the picture. If you double-click a `.php` file that you received via e-mail, your system turns into a zombie and sends out 2 million pieces of spam.

How does Windows know which program goes with which document? Easy. Windows looks at the last group of letters in the file's name — the letters following the final period — and, based *solely* on those letters, cranks up the program that's registered to take care of files with that name. These letters are called the *filename extension.*

So if you double-click a file called `resume.doc`, Windows looks up `doc`, finds that `.doc` files belong to Word, starts Word, and feeds `resume.doc` to it. If you double-click `Tibet Flag.jpg`, Windows looks to see which program is currently registered to handle `.jpg` files, starts that program, and sends in `Tibet Flag.jpg`.

If you rename the file `Tibet Flag.jpg` to, oh, `Tibet Flag.txt` and then double-click `Tibet Flag.txt`, Windows "knows" that the file is a text file and fires up Notepad, which dutifully opens `Tibet Flag.txt` and shows you the raw gibberish that constitutes a JPEG picture file (see Figure 8-1).

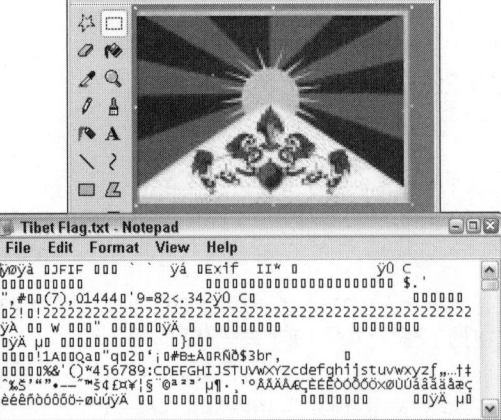

Figure 8-1:
The Tibetan flag, first as a JPEG file and then as a text file.

Unfortunately, somebody at Microsoft made a very stupid decision years ago to hide filename extensions from garden-variety Windows users and thus deprived the unwary of a very important piece of information.

Changing filename extension associations

If you want to see which filename extensions have been registered for your computer or change the program registered to a particular extension, follow these steps:

1. **Start Windows Explorer.**

   The easiest way to do that is to choose Start⇨My Documents, My Pictures, My Music, or My Computer. Doesn't matter which.

2. **Choose Tools⇨Folder Options⇨File Types.**

   Windows Explorer shows you the Folder Options dialog box, as shown in Figure 8-2.

Figure 8-2: Filename extensions are associated with programs in this dialog box.

3. **To see which program is associated with a particular filename extension, click a filename extension in the Extensions list.**

   Figure 8-2 shows that Microsoft Word is associated with the .doc filename extension on this particular computer.

4. **If you want to change the program that's associated with a particular filename extension, click the Change button.**

   Explorer gives you a list of programs to choose from.

5. **If you want to change the default action when you double-click a file or an icon, click the Advanced button.**

   Say you want to change Windows so that double-clicking a Word template (a .dot file) simply opens the template. (Normally, double-clicking a template creates a new document based on the template.) To do so, click the DOT extension and then click Advanced. In the Edit File Type dialog box (shown in Figure 8-3), select Open, click the Set Default button, and then click OK.

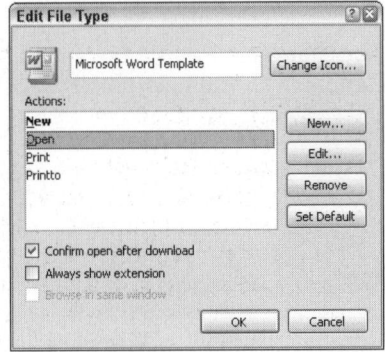

Figure 8-3:
Change the
default
behavior for
double-
clicking DOT
files here.

6. **When you're happy with your new associations and actions, click OK and then "X" out of Windows Explorer.**

   The changes you made take effect immediately.

It's important to understand that Windows' behavior when you double-click a file or an icon depends solely on the filename extension. If Windows doesn't show you the filename extension, you don't stand a Hypothalamus' chance in Hannibal's Hades of predicting what will happen when you double-click a file. Please take a moment and follow the nostrums in the sidebar "Unsafe filename extensions."

Showing filename extensions and hidden/system files

Here is the singularly most important mod in this book: Make Windows show you filename extensions. While you're at it, you should have Windows show you hidden files and all of your system files, too. Here's how:

1. **Bring up Windows Explorer.**

   You can choose Start⇨My Documents, My Pictures, My Music, My Computer, or My What a Beautiful Morning, should you be so inclined.

2. **Choose Tools⇨Folder Options⇨View.**

   Windows Explorer shows you the Folder Options View tab, shown in Figure 8-4.

3. **Under Advanced Settings, uncheck the box that says Hide Extensions for Known File Types.**

   If that box is checked, Windows hides any filename extension listed in the Folder Options File Types dialog box. If you want to see all your filenames in all their glory, uncheck the box.

Unsafe filename extensions

Over the years, many malware authors have taken advantage of Windows' shortsightedness, hiding destructive programs behind innocuous-sounding filenames. You might expect a file called `Gotcha.exe` or `Clobberyourcomputer.doc` to contain some sort of malicious program, but chances are pretty good you'd be surprised to get hit by, oh, `3D Aqaurium.scr` (presumably a screensaver) or `Halcyon Days.ppt` (which looks like a PowerPoint slide show, eh?).

You should treat all the filename extensions in the following table with kid gloves: if you encounter a file with one of the listed filename extensions, and you're not 1,000% certain of its pedigree, make sure you run your antivirus scanner on the file before doing anything with it. Any file with a filename extension on the list could potentially come in and take over your computer, without any warning or opportunity for intervention on your part. Experts may debate the relative danger of the various file types (for example, as of this writing, it's possible to create a `.jpg` picture file that locks up your computer when it's opened, but nobody has yet found a way to zap your computer when you open a `.jpg` file). But each of these types of files has been exploited to nefarious ends.

ade	adp	app	asp	asx	bas
bat	cdr	cer	chm	cmd	com
cpl	crl	crt	csh	doc	dot
exe	fxp	hlp	hta	htm	html
inf	ini	ins	isp	its	jpg
jot	js	jse	ksh	lnk	mad
maf	mag	mam	mapimail	maq	mar
mas	mat	mau	mav	maw	mda
mdb	mdbhtml	mde	mdt	mdw	mdz
mht	mhtml	mpp	msc	msi	msp
mst	ocx	ole	ops	pcd	pif
ppt	ppthtml	prf	prg	pst	reg
scf	scr	sct	shb	shs	tmp
url	vb	vbe	vbs	vsmacros	vss
vst	vsw	ws	wsc	wsf	wsh
xla	xlb	xlc	xld	xlk	xll
xlm	xls	xlshtml	xlt	xlthtml	

Figure 8-4:
Make
Windows
Explorer
show you
complete
filenames.

4. **Directly above the Hide Extensions setting, under Hidden Files and Folders, select Show Hidden Files and Folders option.**

   There's nothing magical about hidden files. You can make a file (or folder) hidden by right-clicking it, choosing Properties, and checking the box marked Hidden. Rocket science.

   Typically, a company that distributes a hidden file (Microsoft being the number-one culprit) is trying to protect you by making it just a teensy-tiny bit difficult to see the file. You're a big kid. Take off the training wheels.

5. **Directly below the Hide Extensions setting, uncheck the box that says Hide Protected Operating System Files (Recommended).**

   More training wheels. You need to be able to see the files that Windows uses in case one goes bump in the night.

6. **Click OK and then "X" out of the Folder Options dialog box.**

   From that point on, Windows (and Office and many other applications) will show you the full filenames. You'll also be able to work with hidden files and Windows' own files.

Starting Explorer on your terms

Most people, most of the time, start Windows Explorer in My Documents (Start⇨My Documents), My Computer, or one of the other "My" folders.

Some people start Windows Explorer in a different folder. In Chapter 5, I explain how to create shortcuts for your desktop and for the Start menu that let you open Windows Explorer in the folder of your choosing. In Chapter 6, I show how to do the same for the Quick Launch toolbar.

With a bit of fancy maneuvering, you can convince Windows Explorer to start in a specific folder and *not* show any folders above the chosen one. You can also tell Explorer to open with the usual file list on the left or to show the Task pane (copy, move, and so on). For an explanation of how to construct shortcuts that turn Explorer on its ear, see `http://support.microsoft.com/kb/130510`.

Setting File Folder Templates

Based on the contents of a folder, Windows decides what kind of "template" to apply to the folder. The available choices are

- ✔ **Documents** should be called "all other," which covers any type of file, including programs

- ✔ **Pictures,** a good choice for folders that contain many picture files, or many folders of picture files, because Windows Explorer opens these folders in Thumbnail view

- ✔ **Photo Album,** which acts much like Pictures, except Explorer opens these folders in Filmstrip view, so you can immediately see large images of individual files

- ✔ **Music,** kind of a hodge-podge designation for audio files

- ✔ **Music Artist** and **Music Album,** which Windows Media Player uses to store information about albums as you rip them — the songs go in a Music Album folder, which goes inside a Music Artist folder

- ✔ **Videos,** used for any kind of video file

Usually Windows does a good job of guessing what kind of folder I want to use, but when it doesn't, life can turn much too difficult. For example, if I accidentally put a couple of text files inside a folder full of pictures, Windows may misidentify the folder as *Documents*. When I double-click the folder, the View menu suddenly loses its ability to show me the files as a filmstrip, and the Task pane on the left no longer lets me view the files as a slide show.

Blechk.

Setting a folder's template

Don't waste your time trying to change the template for My Documents, My Pictures, or My Music. Windows won't let you. For any other folder, here's how to set Windows right:

1. **Navigate to the folder that's been misidentified.**

   In Figure 8-5, I show a folder that should be a Photo Album but that Windows insists is Documents.

Figure 8-5: A folder that has been misbranded with the Documents template.

2. **Right-click any blank area in the folder and choose Customize This Folder.**

   Explorer shows you the Customize tab in the Properties dialog box, shown in Figure 8-6.

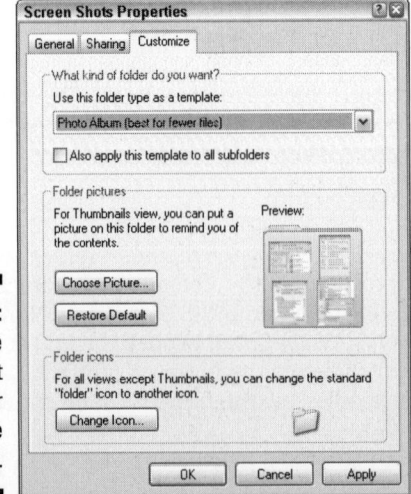

Figure 8-6: Choose the correct folder template here.

3. **In the Use This Folder Type as a Template drop-down box, choose the template that you want to apply.**

   No need to follow Microsoft's descriptions (for example, "best for collections of pre-Greco-Roman manuscripts"). Just get the right type for the effect you want.

4. **Click OK.**

   The folder takes on the template you chose.

Curing template amnesia by setting aside extra memory

Believe it or not, Windows may, quite intentionally, "forget" your choice of folder template. You see, it takes memory to keep track of which folders have which template, and Microsoft's programmers never found a way to set aside enough memory to remember them all. So if you try to set the template for more than 400 folders (which can be easy, if you rip a lot of music with Windows Media Player), Windows Explorer may develop a severe case of amnesia.

Fortunately, it's easy to tell Explorer to set aside enough memory to do its job. All you need is (tell me if you've heard this one before) TweakUI:

1. **Follow the steps in Chapter 4 to download and install TweakUI.**

2. **Choose Start⇨All Programs⇨Powertoys for Windows XP⇨TweakUI. Then, on the left side of the TweakUI dialog box, choose Explorer⇨ Customizations.**

   TweakUI looks like Figure 8-7.

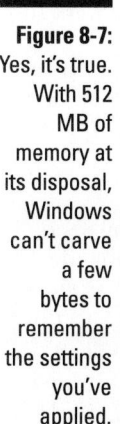

Figure 8-7:
Yes, it's true. With 512 MB of memory at its disposal, Windows can't carve a few bytes to remember the settings you've applied.

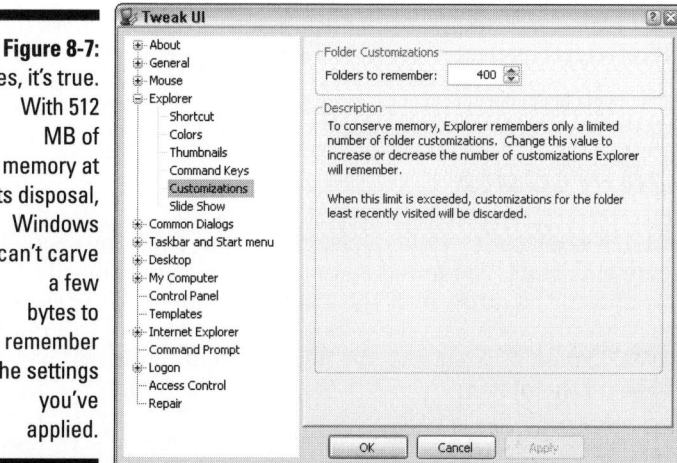

3. **If you're having trouble with folder template amnesia, increase the Folders to Remember setting from 400 to 5000 or so. (Windows XP Service Pack 2 is supposed to set it to 5000 automatically, but TweakUI may show you a different value. It doesn't hurt to manually set it at 5000, whether SP2 performs as advertised or not.)**

   You have my permission to feel a bit miffed that Windows isn't smart enough to adjust itself automatically.

4. **While you're here, click the Slide Show text on the left.**

   TweakUI brings up the Slide Show timer dialog box, shown in Figure 8-8.

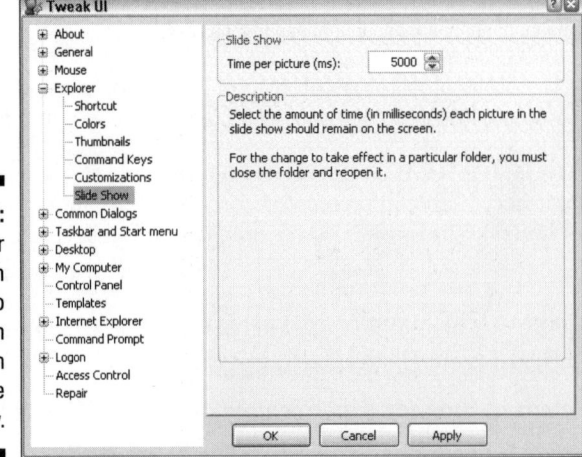

Figure 8-8: Tell Explorer how much time to spend on each slide in a slide show.

5. **Adjust the amount of time you want Explorer to spend on each slide when you choose View as Slide Show.**

6. **Click OK to leave TweakUI.**

   And if you ever experience template amnesia again — or if you want to make your slide shows go faster — you know where to look.

Customizing Shortcuts

When you create a new shortcut by right-clicking a file and choosing Send To➪Desktop (Create Shortcut), Windows Explorer creates an icon for the shortcut by superimposing an arrow over the icon of the object of the shortcut (say, a picture of a Word document if you're creating a shortcut to a document). In most cases, Explorer also names the new shortcut "Shortcut to" followed by the name of the object.

So, for example, if you choose Start⇨My Documents, right-click a document, and choose Send To⇨Desktop (Create Shortcut), you get a new icon on your desktop that looks like a Word document icon with an arrow in the lower-left corner and the text "Shortcut to" followed by the name of the document.

Personally, I like to have the arrow in the lower-left corner, but I *hate* looking at that "Shortcut to" text over and over again. Fortunately, it's easy to change either or both with TweakUI, if you know where to look:

1. **Follow the steps in Chapter 4 to download and install TweakUI.**

2. **Choose Start⇨All Programs⇨Powertoys for Windows XP⇨TweakUI. On the left side of the TweakUI dialog box, double-click Explorer.**

    TweakUI shows you the dialog box in Figure 8-9.

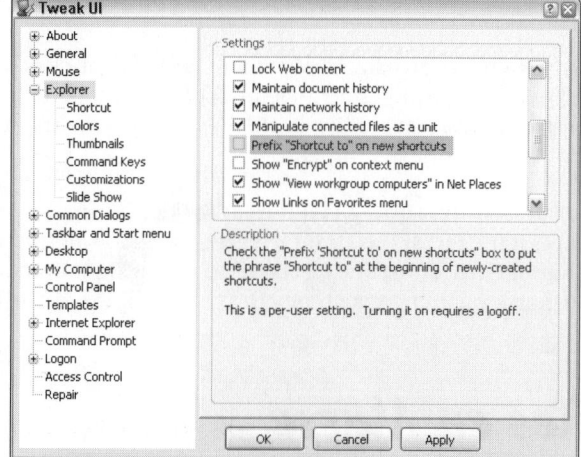

Figure 8-9: You can't customize the "Shortcut to" text, but you can eliminate it.

3. **If you don't want Windows Explorer to put "Shortcut to" at the beginning of new shortcuts, uncheck the box that says Prefix "Shortcut to" on New Shortcuts.**

4. **On the left side of TweakUI, under Explorer, double-click Shortcut.**

    TweakUI allows you to select the arrow (or other, custom graphic) that gets superimposed in the lower-left corner of shortcuts, as in Figure 8-10.

5. **Choose one of the offered arrows to superimpose on new shortcuts, or click Custom and then Change to specify any picture you like.**

    Note that any change you make will affect all shortcuts, even on icons that have already been set up.

6. **Click OK to exit TweakUI.**

    If you turned off the "Shortcut to" text, you may need to log off and log back on for the change to take effect.

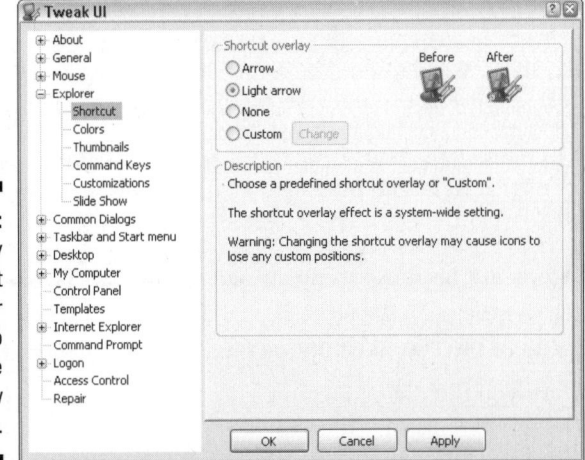

Figure 8-10:
Use any
picture that
strikes your
fancy to
superimpose
on new
shortcuts.

To test my settings, I go back to Start⇨My Documents, right-click A Connecticut Yankee.doc, and choose Send To⇨Desktop (Create Shortcut). The resulting shortcut has a tiny arrow in the lower-left corner, and the (blech!) "Shortcut to" text doesn't appear.

Oddly, the "Shortcut to" text setting is different for every user on the computer, but the superimposed arrow graphic is the same for all the users, all the time. Sounds to me like somebody goofed up the design on this one. Oh, well. It's just another foolish inconsistency that hobgobbles my little mind.

Renaming Files en Masse

Do you have a whole bunch of photos with filenames that look like DSCN1487.JPG or 100_0417.JPG? Man, I do. What a mess.

If you figure out how to use the Windows Scanner and Camera Wizard (see Chapter 12), you shouldn't have problems in the future when you pull pictures off your camera. But what happens when your relatives or friends e-mail you a gazillion files? Sure, you could right-click each one, choose Rename, and type 'til your fingers turn into stunted nubs. Should take about a dozen years.

Fortunately, Windows XP has a built-in group file renaming routine. It isn't as slick as the ones you can buy (go to Google and look for Windows file renaming software), but it'll do in a pinch, and the price is right.

Here's how to use it:

1. **Navigate to the files you want to rename.**

   Typically, you bring up Windows Explorer with Start⇨My Pictures, but you can use a more circuitous route if you like.

2. **Select the files.**

   To select a bunch of files in a row, click the first one, hold down the Shift key, and click the last one. To select one at a time, hold down the Ctrl key while you click away. You can even "lasso" a bunch of files by clicking and dragging around them.

3. **Right-click the first file and choose Rename.**

   Explorer highlights the name.

4. **Type the name you want for the first file in the bunch.**

   Here are a few tricks:

   • Always right-click the first file in the list. Otherwise, Windows' numbering scheme gets a bit dicey.

   • Windows attaches numbers to the end of the filenames, but if you're clever you can start with the number (1), and the rest of the names will follow suit. In Figure 8-11, I give the first file the name Patong Tsunami 2004 12 26 (1).JPG.

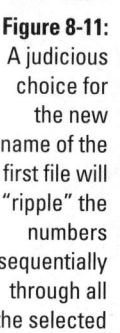

Figure 8-11:
A judicious
choice for
the new
name of the
first file will
"ripple" the
numbers
sequentially
through all
the selected
files.

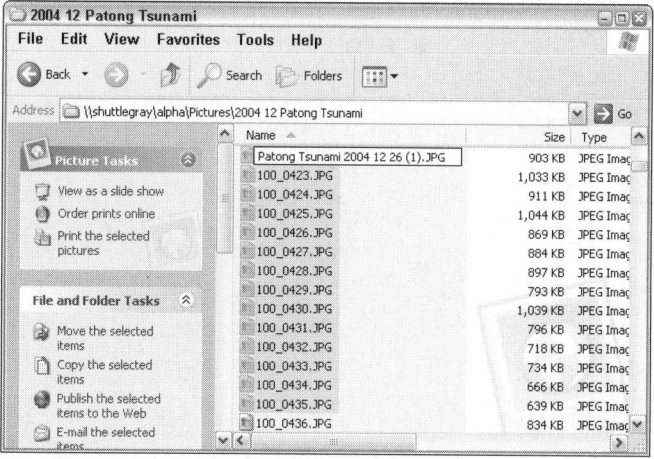

- You needn't select contiguous files — you can rename any files. Use Ctrl+click to choose any files you like.

- Don't forget to type the filename extension.

5. **Press Enter.**

Windows renames all of the files, appending a number in parenthesis to the end of the filenames (see Figure 8-12).

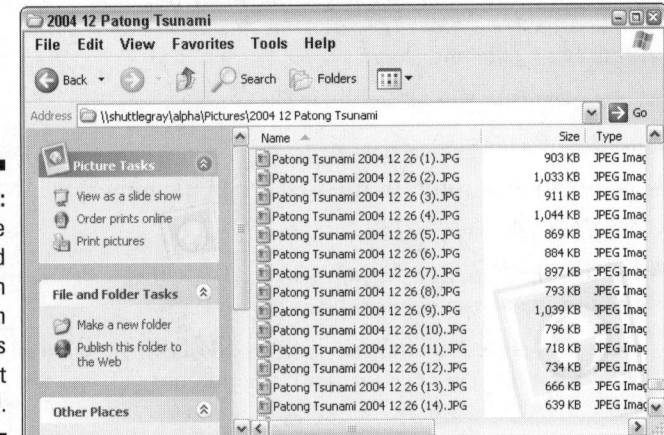

Figure 8-12: Files are renamed with numbers in parentheses appended at the end.

Chapter 9

Cool Keyboard Hacks and Menu Mods

Hard to believe that Microsoft spent all that money building Windows XP and didn't even include the ability to list all the files in a folder. WinXP's task panes make it easy to copy and move files, but why do you have to hunt all over the screen to do it?

Windows lacks a few key features, but it isn't that hard to build 'em yourself, in the finest hacking tradition.

Listing Files in a Folder

Barry Simon and I first published this hybrid Windows/DOS hack in 1993. More than a dozen years later, Microsoft still hasn't fixed the problem. Maybe they never will.

It all boils down to this: How do you create a list of all the files in a folder? It should be easy — say, right-click a folder and choose List Files, or some such. Unfortunately, you can't do that in Windows Explorer. Microsoft's "solution" (http://support.microsoft.com/kb/196628) involves making multiple screen shots and printing the screen as many times as it takes. Ouch.

There's a much easier way to see a list of all the files in a folder, but it involves (don't choke now) writing and running an old-fashioned DOS program. You may have heard that Windows XP doesn't use DOS anymore. To some extent, that's true. But when push comes to shove, you can get a lot of mileage out of a few lines of DOS. This is a great example.

You need to create a couple of .bat files, and if you don't have Windows fixed to show you filename extensions, you could run into all sorts of problems. If you haven't already, follow the steps in Chapter 8 to force Windows to show you filename extensions.

This hack actually consists of two hacks in one. I show you how to create a text list of all the files in a folder by right-clicking the folder and choosing List Files in Folder. Then, with a nip here and a tuck there, I show you how to create a Print List of Files in Folder command:

1. **Choose Start⇨All Programs⇨Accessories⇨Notepad to start Notepad.**

   Writing programs in Notepad is a bit like scratching out a corporate report with a stylus and papyrus. But what the heck; it works.

2. **Type the following program into Notepad:**

   ```
   dir %1 /-p /o:gn > "%temp%\List of Files.txt"
   start notepad "%temp%\List of Files.txt"
   ```

   You don't need to understand the program in order to make it work, but if you're curious, the commands go something like this. The dir %1 command generates a list of all the files in the current folder. /-p tells Windows not to pause when it hits a screenful of files in the list. /o:gn tells Windows to sort the list alphabetically, with folder names first. Then > "%temp%\List of Files.txt" tells Windows to put the list of files in the system's temporary folder, in a file called List of Files.txt.

   The start notepad command starts Notepad, feeding it the file called List of Files.txt from the system's temporary folder.

3. **Choose File⇨Save. On the left, click My Computer and then navigate to c:\Program Files. In the File Name box, type List Files.bat (make sure that you get the .bat part, as shown in Figure 9-1) and then click Save.**

   Your new List Files.bat program appears in Notepad like Figure 9-2.

   The second program looks a lot like the first one (which you've already saved in your Program Files folder, as shown in Figure 9-1).

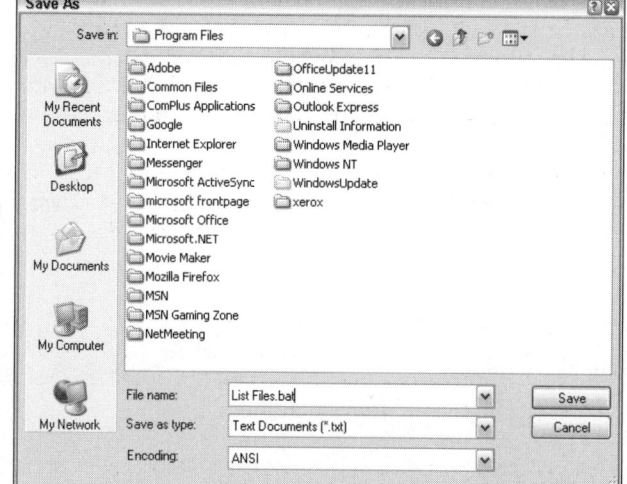

Figure 9-1:
Save the
program
in `c:\`
`Program`
`Files`; you
can find it
easily.

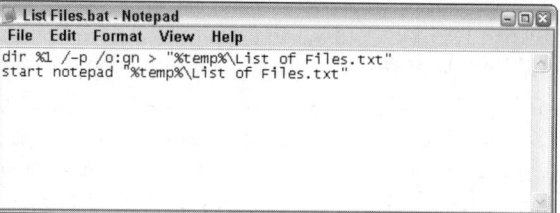

Figure 9-2:
The `List`
`Files.`
`bat` DOS
program.

4. **Go in and change the program you have on the screen so it looks like this:**

   ```
   dir %1 /-p /o:gn > "%temp%\List of Files.txt"
   start /w notepad /p "%temp%\List of Files.txt"
   ```

   This program has two changes: The `/w` tells Windows to wait until the `dir` is finished before starting Notepad. The `/p` tells Notepad that you want it to print the file that's being fed to it and then exit.

5. **Choose File⇨Save As and save this file as, oh, `Print Files.bat` in the `c:\Program Files` folder.**

6. **Choose File⇨Exit to get out of Notepad.**

7. **Bring up Windows Explorer by clicking Start⇨My Documents or Start⇨My Computer, or by using whichever method you prefer. Then click Tools⇨Folder Options⇨File Types.**

   Windows Explorer shows you the list of registered file types in Figure 9-3. (I talk about registered file types in Chapter 8.)

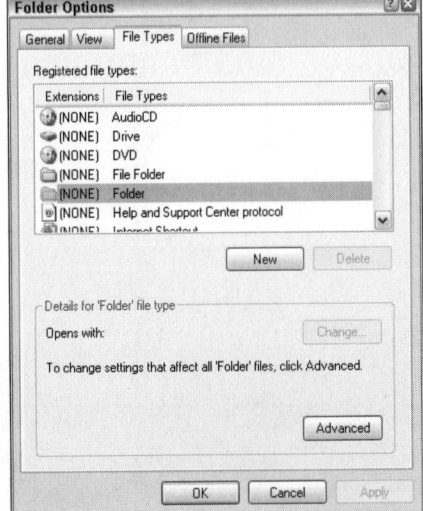

Figure 9-3:
Your
computer's
registered
file types.

8. **In the Registered File Types list, click on (NONE) Folder and then click the Advanced button at the bottom of the dialog box.**

   Explorer brings up the Edit File Type dialog box for Folders, as shown in Figure 9-4. From this dialog box, you can change the options that appear on the context menu that appears when you right-click on a folder.

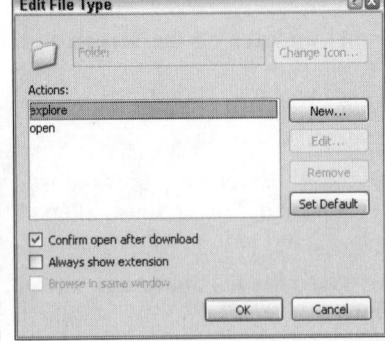

Figure 9-4:
Change the
right-click
context
menu for
folders.

9. **Click New to display the New Action dialog box.**

10. **In the Action box, type** List All Files in Folder. **Then click Browse, navigate to** c:\Program Files\List Files.bat, **and click Open.**

    The New Action dialog box looks like Figure 9-5.

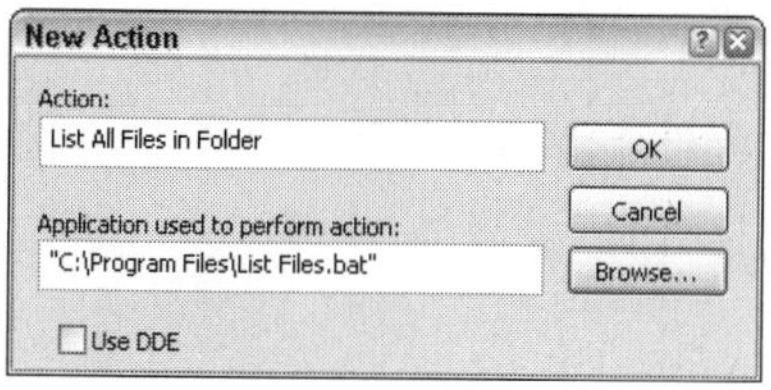

Figure 9-5:
Text you
type in the
Action box
appears in
the right-
click
context
menu.

11. **Click OK.**

    That adds a new action called List All Files in Folder for every folder on
    your computer.

12. **Click New again. In the New Action dialog box's Action box, type** Print
    List of All Files in Folder. **Click Browse, navigate to** c:\Program Files\
    Print Files.bat, **and then click Open. When you're back in the New
    Action dialog box, click OK.**

    The finished Edit File Type dialog box looks like Figure 9-6.

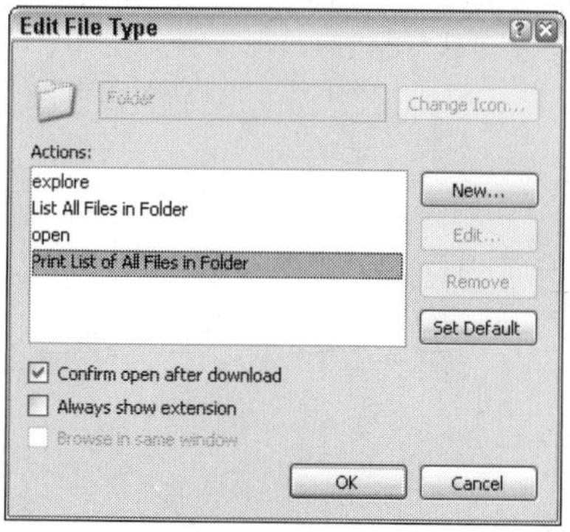

Figure 9-6:
Final Edit
File Type
settings.

13. **Click OK to get out of the Edit File Type dialog box and then click
    Close to get out of the Folder Options dialog box. Choose File⇨Close
    to get out of Windows Explorer.**

    You're done. Right-click any folder and choose either List All Files in
    Folder to see a list of the files in Notepad or Print List of All Files in
    Folder to have the list delivered to your printer.

    You can even look at all the files in folders on the Start menu. For exam-
    ple, it's easy to click Start, right-click My Documents, and choose Print
    List of All Files in Folder.

Unfortunately, Windows makes it deucedly difficult to delete entries in the context menu for folders. If you want to get rid of an entry, follow the instructions in Chapter 24 to go into the Registry. Search for the Action text (such as List All Files in Folder), and delete the corresponding entry under `HKCR\ Folder\shell`. If you go the manual route, be sure that you don't delete the *explore* or *open* key.

Copy to Folder and Move to Folder

Yes, it's possible to put Copy to Folder and Move to Folder on the Windows Explorer context menu that appears when you right-click. If you twiddle the right bits in the Registry, following the detailed instructions in many Windows books and Windows tip Web sites, you'll be able to right-click a file, choose Copy to Folder, and have Windows bring up the Copy Items dialog box, shown in Figure 9-7.

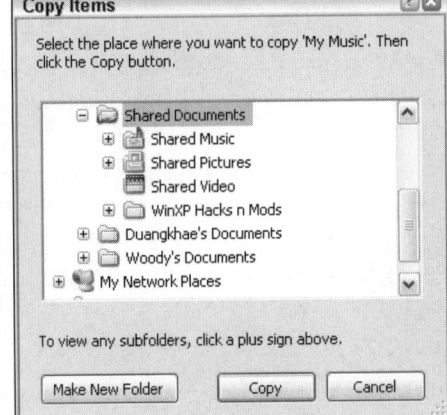

Figure 9-7: The Copy Items dialog box used by the Explorer Task pane.

Here's the rub: If you put Copy To/Move To on the context menu, every time you double-click an attachment in Outlook, Copy To/Move To jumps up and offers to copy or move the attachment. Unfortunately, the program can't copy or move the attachment. So you end up with a menu choice in Outlook that doesn't work right. Windows' designers don't call this a bug. They call it a *design restriction*. But you get what I mean.

So if you bump into that "hack," forget about it. In its place, though, you can put Copy to Folder and Move to Folder on the Windows Explorer standard button bar, where it won't do any harm — and may actually prove useful. Here's how:

1. **Start Windows Explorer by, for example, choosing Start⇨My Documents.**

2. **Right-click an empty spot on the standard button bar — the one that starts with Back. Choose Customize.**

   Windows Explorer brings up the Customize Toolbar dialog box, shown in Figure 9-8.

Figure 9-8:
The
Windows
Explorer
toolbar is
quite
custom-
izable.

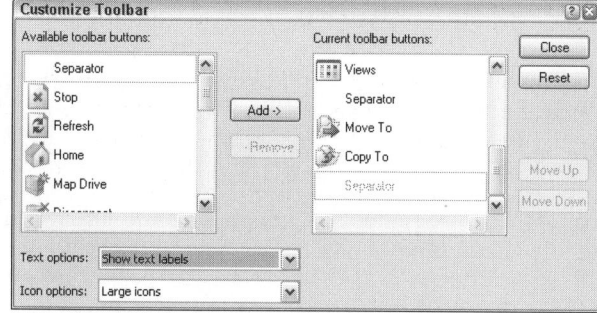

3. **On the left, under Available Toolbar Buttons, click Move To and then click Add (in the middle of the dialog box). Similarly, click Copy To and then click Add.**

   You might even want to put a separator on the standard button bar. Click Separator (at the top of the list on the left), click Add, and then click Move Up or Move Down to get it located properly.

   I'm also partial to showing text on the buttons. If you like to get a little written cue, in the Text Options box, choose Show Text Labels.

4. **When you're done, click Close.**

   Windows Explorer takes on the new buttons you specified, as shown in Figure 9-9.

Figure 9-9:
My
customized
toolbar, with
Move To,
Copy To,
and text on
the buttons.

Creating Custom Keyboard Shortcuts

Most people don't realize that Windows XP, right out of the box, lets you set up *hotkeys* — key combinations you pick that will launch programs, open documents, create new documents based on templates, run out to specific Internet sites, or tie your shoes while singing "Louie Louie" and defragmenting your hard drive. In reverse.

Okay, maybe I'm exaggerating a little bit.

In this chapter, I touch the surface, showing you how to set up a hotkey combination that opens a Word document for editing. If you want the whole story (which is quite complex!), check out Technique 19 in my other book, *Windows XP Timesaving Techniques For Dummies,* 2nd Edition.

Let's say you have a Word document called, oh, `Status Report.doc`, which you open and edit a zillion times a day. Here's how to tell Windows to launch Word and open `Status Report.doc` every time you press the key combination Ctrl+Alt+S (that is, hold down the Ctrl and Alt keys simultaneously and then press S):

1. **Navigate to the file you want to open with a magic key combination.**

    In this case, you might choose Start⇨My Documents, dig down a folder or two, and find `Status Report.doc`.

2. **Right-click the document and choose Send To⇨Desktop (Create Shortcut).**

    A new shortcut appears on your desktop.

3. **Right-click the new shortcut and choose Properties⇨Shortcut.**

    Windows Explorer brings up the Properties dialog box for that shortcut, as shown in Figure 9-10.

4. **Click inside the box marked Shortcut key and then hold down the key combination you want to use to open that document.**

    See Table 9-1 for a list of the key combinations that you can safely use. In Figure 9-10, I choose Ctrl+Alt+S.

5. **Click OK.**

    You're done. The next time you hold down the key combination, Word will start with the specified document loaded.

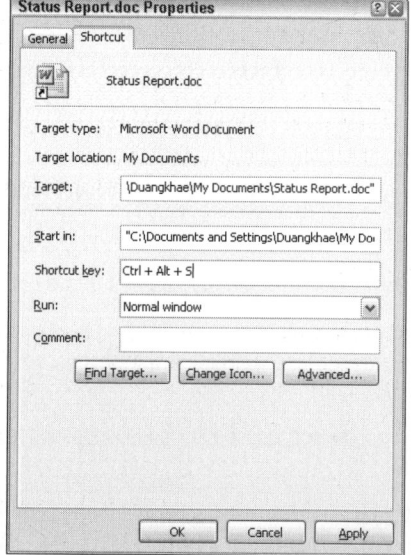

Figure 9-10:
Assign a
hotkey
in the
shortcut's
Properties
dialog box.

Table 9-1	Valid Windows XP Hotkey Combinations	
Use This	*Plus*	*Example*
Ctrl+Alt	Any letter or number	Ctrl+Alt+S
Ctrl+Shift	Any letter or number	Ctrl+Shift+A
Alt+Shift	Any letter or number	Alt+Shift+2
Shift	Any function key	Shift+F7
Ctrl	Any function key	Ctrl+F1
Alt	Any function key	Alt+F10

Key Combinations You Need to Know

I'm not a big fan of bizarre key combinations. If you tell me that pressing Ctrl+Alt+Tab+F42 will end world hunger and simultaneously divulge the secret to life, the universe, and everything, I might be interested. Other than that, though, I have better things to do with my time than memorize a bunch of keyboard shortcuts that somebody in Redmond dreamed up on a rainy day.

With a few exceptions.

There are, in fact, a small number of key combinations that every Windows XP user needs to know. If you don't already have them tattooed to the inside of your eyelids, you should consider making a copy of Table 9-2 and taping it to your monitor. Seriously.

Table 9-2	Really, Truly Crucial Key Combinations
Press This . . .	*. . . And This Happens*
Ctrl+C	Everything that's selected gets copied to the Clipboard
Ctrl+X	Everything that's selected gets "cut" to the Clipboard (that is, it's copied to the Clipboard and then deleted from its original location)
Ctrl+V	Everything on the Clipboard gets pasted at the current location of the cursor
Ctrl+A	Selects everything (for example, all the files showing or all the text in a document)
Ctrl+Z	Undoes the last action, whether you did it or the computer did it
Ctrl+click	Selects items one by one
Shift+click	Selects a bunch of items (click the first one, hold down Shift, click the last one)
Alt+F and then X	Closes most applications (via File⇨Exit), even if the power's off and you can't see the screen
Alt+Tab	Cycles through all running programs
Ctrl+Alt+Del	Brings up the Windows Task Manager, so you can shut down your machine
F1	Help
F5	Refresh — go back and retrieve the list of files, the Web page, or whatever has changed to make sure the most current information is displayed

If you have a keyboard with customizable keys (say, a key that's supposed to start Windows Calculator, or another that forwards e-mail) and you can't get the %$#@! keys to work, try cranking up TweakUI to see if it can get the keyboard mapped. Follow the steps in Chapter 4 to download and install TweakUI. Choose Start⇨All Programs⇨Powertoys for Windows XP⇨TweakUI. Then, on the left, double-click Explorer⇨Command Keys. Sometimes TweakUI can get recalcitrant keyboards back on track.

Chapter 10

Searching on the Desktop

I think it's wonderful when four multibillion-dollar tech companies (Microsoft, Google, Yahoo!, and AOL) battle one another to give away useful, sophisticated software. It's even nicer when every tech company in the book decides to join the fray.

The Lowdown on Searching

If you haven't yet installed a desktop search product, you really need one. Trust me. Your life will change.

Personally, I run Google Desktop Search and recommend that you do, too. Why? Because it's as good as all the others — possibly better in some respects — but most of all, it integrates nicely with Google on the Web, and it behaves much like the Web version. I use Google on the Web all the time. Better the devil ye ken, eh?

Google Desktop Search, straight out of the box, indexes the contents of:

▶ Word documents, Excel spreadsheets, PowerPoint presentations, text files, PDF files

▶ E-mail from Outlook, Outlook Express, Netscape Mail, Mozilla Mail, and Thunderbird

▶ The "meta tags" (typically title, artist name, and the like) on MP3 and other audio files, JPGs, and video files

▶ The contents of chats with AOL Instant Messenger

▶ Web pages that you've viewed

Desktop searching, now and then

In mid-2004, searching for stuff inside your computer was about as easy as looking for a neutrino in your back yard. Microsoft offered a handful of tools, none of which worked properly, all of which ran like slugs and tested the patience of even the most dedicated hacker. The Windows indexer was loaded with bugs, some of which Microsoft hadn't fixed in nearly a decade. There were a couple of good desktop search engines available from other software companies, but they were expensive and not widely used.

A year later, everybody and his brother offered a desktop search package — Microsoft, Google, Yahoo! (using the X1 search engine), AOL (using the Copernic engine), Ask Jeeves (Tukaroo), blinkx, Filehand, HotBot, and more. With few exceptions, they were reliable, not overly intrusive, and most of all free.

The reason for the sudden onslaught of free programs? Money. Each of the search vendors, in its own way, sought to gain some control over your Windows desktop and use the leverage to sell you things.

Any particular version of any of the desktop search packages can claim superiority in a number of areas. That's what marketing departments are for. One-upsmanship in the desktop search features arena proceeds on Internet time: Wait a few weeks, and a must-have feature in one package appear in the others, give or take a few twists.

It even stores snapshots — caches — of Web pages that you've accessed, so you can see the results even if you aren't online (see Figure 10-1).

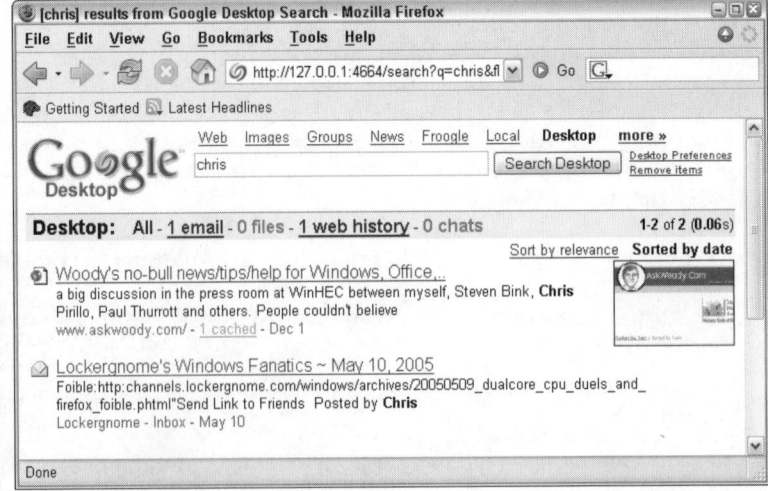

Figure 10-1: Google Desktop Search displays results graphically.

Installing Google Desktop Search

Installing Google Desktop Search (GDS) takes only a few minutes, but you have to let it scan and create an index for all the files on your computer — which can take three or four hours or more, depending on how much data you have and how fast your computer works.

I installed GDS on a portable with a hard drive that had been having intermittent problems — occasional Blue Screens of Death, a few corrupted files, and so on. The hard drive really took a thrashing when GDS went through and created its index. Ultimately, the hard drive died in the middle of the indexing, and I couldn't recover anything from it. For that reason, I suggest you back up everything on your hard drive (see Chapter 1) before installing GDS.

Here's how to get Google Desktop Search going on your PC:

1. **Allow yourself ten or fifteen minutes to install GDS, and then three or four hours (possibly overnight) for GDS to build its initial index.**

   While it's possible to get some work done while GDS is building its first index, both you and GDS will feel better if you don't try. Best to wait until you're ready to turn in for the night, or go out for a verrrrry long ball game or, oh, 81 holes of golf.

2. **Fire up your Web browser and head to http://desktop.google.com (see Figure 10-2).**

Figure 10-2:
Google
Desktop
Search
download
goes very
quickly.

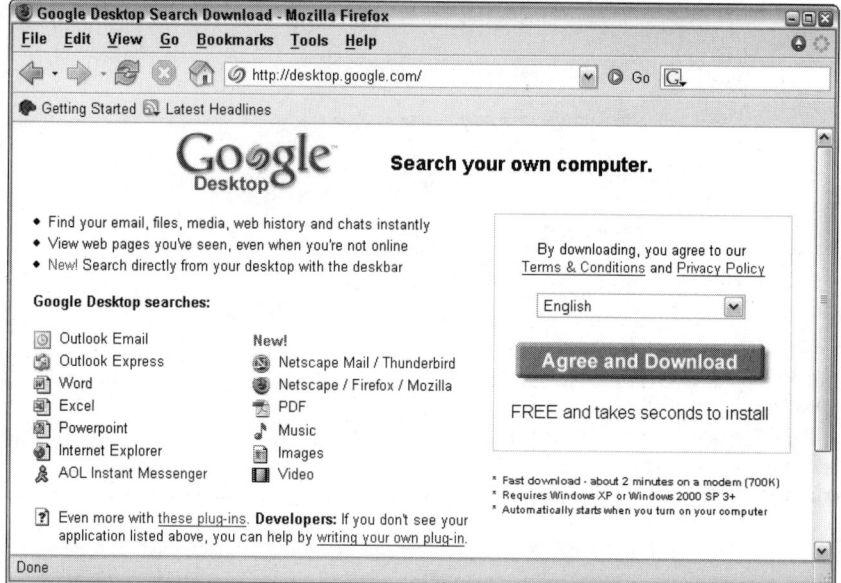

3. **Click Agree and Download on the Web page.**

   You download a file called `GoogleDesktopSearchSetup.exe`.

4. **Run `GoogleDesktopSearchSetup.exe`.**

   The setup program may require you to close Internet Explorer or Firefox and various Office programs. When it's almost complete, you see the Initial Preferences Web page, shown in Figure 10-3.

5. **Uncheck the box marked Enable Search Over Secure Web Pages (HTTPS).**

   Few people need to search for the contents of secure Web pages. Having GDS index those pages — including usernames and passwords — only exposes you to yet another possible security problem.

6. **Consider whether you want to Display a Search Box and set your preference accordingly.**

   Personally, I don't need to have a search box on my desktop — whenever I need GDS, I can click the icon in the System Tray, next to the clock. The box takes up a fair amount of room in the Windows taskbar (or it floats on the screen), so you may find it more intrusive than helpful.

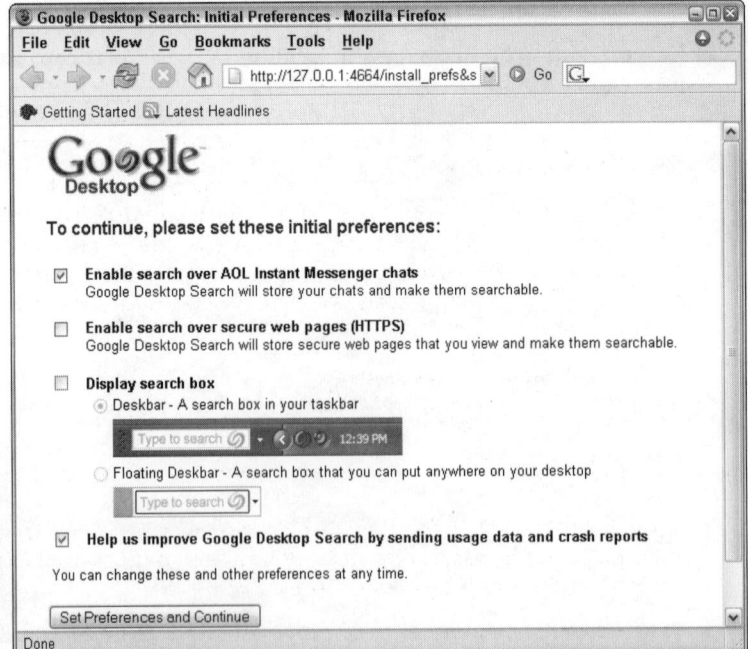

Figure 10-3:
Set your
GDS
preferences.

7. When you have the settings right, click Set Preferences and Continue.

GDS builds its initial index — a process that can take two hours, even on PCs with a modest amount of data (see Figure 10-4). On my main production machine, which is stuffed with more data than most people accumulate in 10 lifetimes, it took almost 24 hours.

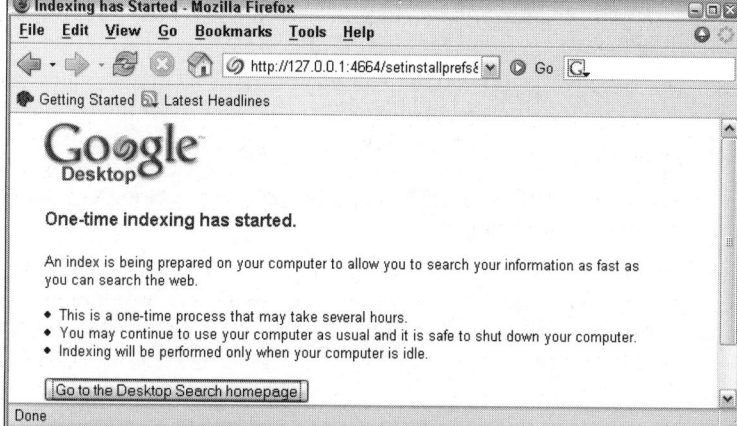

Figure 10-4:
When GDS starts taking over your computer, it issues this warning.

8. Oddly, GDS doesn't tell you when it's finished building the initial index. When your hard drive light stops flashing like a firefly in heat, you can start using your computer again without fear of stepping on the GDS indexer's toes.

Google's indexer generally waits until you aren't doing anything and then runs in quickly and indexes anything you've changed since the last update. In practice, the indexer gets in the way sometimes and slows things down when you first go back to work, but the annoyance is brief.

Running Google Desktop Search

You can run Google Desktop Search in so many ways that it's hard to miss:

✔ **Run a regular, old, everyday Google search.** If you have GDS installed, the first result in the Google list will be a link to display all the matches on your computer (see Figure 10-5).

No, Google didn't send all your personal information to Google Headquarters so that it could be regurgitated in a search result pane. Instead, GDS running on your machine intercepts the results from Google in the Sky, adds the local information to it, and presents you with the combined results.

✔ **Double-click the Google Desktop Search icon** on the desktop or the Google Desktop Search icon in the System Tray, near the clock.

✔ **Choose Start⇨All Programs⇨Google Desktop Search⇨Google Desktop Search.**

✔ **Use the Deskbar.** I don't like the Deskbar because it takes up too much room on my double-height Windows taskbar, but you may feel differently.

To bring up the Deskbar, right-click the Google Desktop Search icon in the System Tray and choose More⇨Deskbar (see Figure 10-6).

✔ **Use the Floating Deskbar.** You position this toolbar on your desktop, where it floats on top of all of your windows. That means it can get in the way, and you may find yourself spending a lot of time moving it around. To bring up the Floating Deskbar, right-click the Google Desktop Search icon in the System Tray and then choose More⇨Floating Deskbar. Figure 10-7 shows the Floating Deskbar.

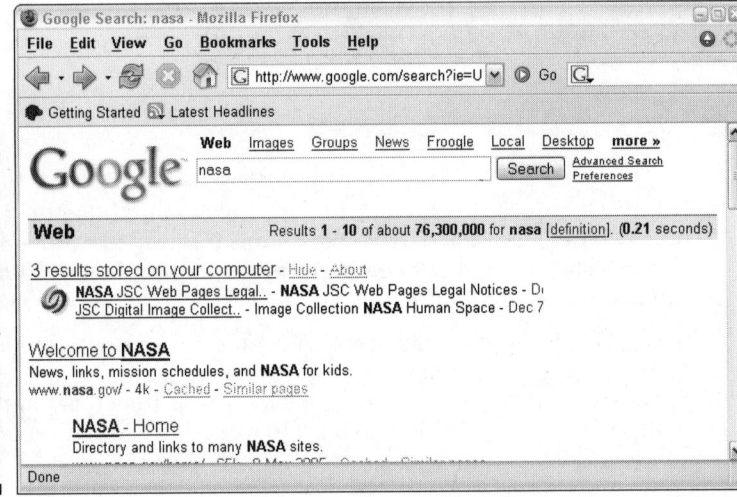

Figure 10-5:
Want to search your desktop? Run a regular Google search and click the first link.

Figure 10-6:
The Google Desktop Search Deskbar.

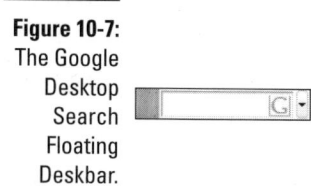

Figure 10-7:
The Google
Desktop
Search
Floating
Deskbar.

Both the Deskbar and the Floating Deskbar run regular Google searches —
although you install them with Google Desktop Search, the Deskbars go out
to Google itself to find the results you seek. Of course, if you have GDS running on your computer, the first result back from Google contains matches
from your computer (see Figure 10-5), so both of the Deskbars give you
results from your PC, too — along with every hit Google has to offer.

Google Desktop Search Mods

The minute you have Google Desktop Search installed, you should make sure
that it leaves its mitts off your private data. Why? Because some cretin, somewhere, someday, will find a way to break into GDS index files. Besides, the
index you build is accessible to anyone who uses your computer. Why leave
private stuff floating around?

Preventing GDS from indexing specific files

Here's how to ensure GDS keeps its eyes off the family jewels:

1. **Right-click the Google Desktop Search icon in the System Tray. Choose More⇨Preferences.**

   GDS responds with the Preferences page, shown in Figure 10-8.

2. **Be sure to uncheck the boxes marked Password-Protected Office Documents (Word, Excel) and Secure Pages (HTTPS) in Web History.**

   GDS isn't smart enough to crack passwords on Word and Excel documents all by itself. Instead, it waits until you open the document and
   then indexes the document while you have it open. As far as I'm concerned, any document that's sensitive enough to protect with a password is sensitive enough to keep away from GDS's prying spiders.

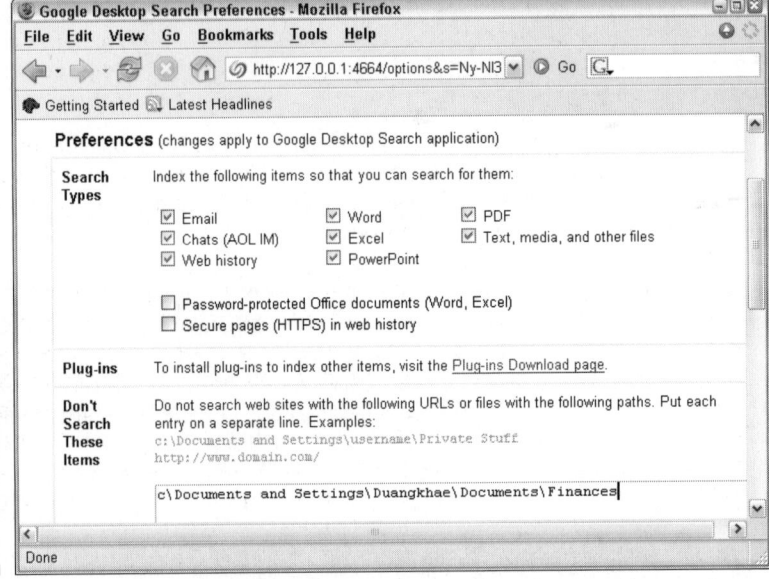

Figure 10-8:
Get GDS's
privacy
settings
right.

Secure Web pages (ones that start with `https://`) can have all sorts of private information. Unless you tell it to refrain from indexing secure pages, GDS not only scans and indexes the contents of the page, but also stores a cache copy of the page. All the more reason to uncheck the box.

3. **If you have any folders (or Web site viewing results) that you don't want indexed, add them to the Don't Search These Items box.**

   Note that "My Documents" has to be entered in the form `c:\Documents and Settings\<username>\ Documents`, where *<username>* is your username. (See Figure 10-8 for an example.)

4. **When you're comfortable with the changes, click Save Preferences at the bottom of the page.**

   Your changes take effect immediately.

Removing files from the index

GDS diligently watches over your shoulder, indexing everything in sight (except password-protected files and `https://` secure Web sites, if you follow the suggestions in the preceding section). So what if you surf to a Web site or receive a piece of e-mail that you don't particularly want to appear in response to a search?

Google Desktop Search makes it easy to remove an individual item from its index and an individual Web page snapshot from its cache. But you need to keep two things in mind:

 ✔ Removing the item from the index/cache doesn't remove the item from your computer. If GDS indexed a piece of hate mail from a co-worker, and you remove it from the index, the hate mail is still there in Outlook. If you look at the message again, it'll go back in the cache.

 ✔ Contrariwise, if you delete the hate mail from Outlook — even if you go to great pains to make sure it's permanently deleted — *it's still in the index.* If you want to delete the mail and the entry in the index, you have to perform each operation separately.

To completely remove a file from your computer, you need to delete the file (for example, by pressing Shift+Delete to "permanently" remove it) *and* you need to take the file out of GDS's cache. The two-step process applies to documents, spreadsheets — any file on your computer. For example, if you delete a Word document on your computer, the document either goes to the Recycle Bin or it's "permanently" deleted (Shift+Delete). Even though the document's deleted, GDS may still have a stored snapshot of the document hanging around. That's good news and bad news: If you hit an emergency and you need to bring a copy of the document back, you can run a GDS search and look at a cached copy (see the steps below). But if you thought that deleting the file would completely wipe it off your computer and keep it from prying eyes or wayward legal motions, well, you're in for a big surprise.

Follow these steps to remove a specific item from the index and cache:

 1. **Run a Google Desktop Search.**

    In Figure 10-9, I run a search for the term *security*.

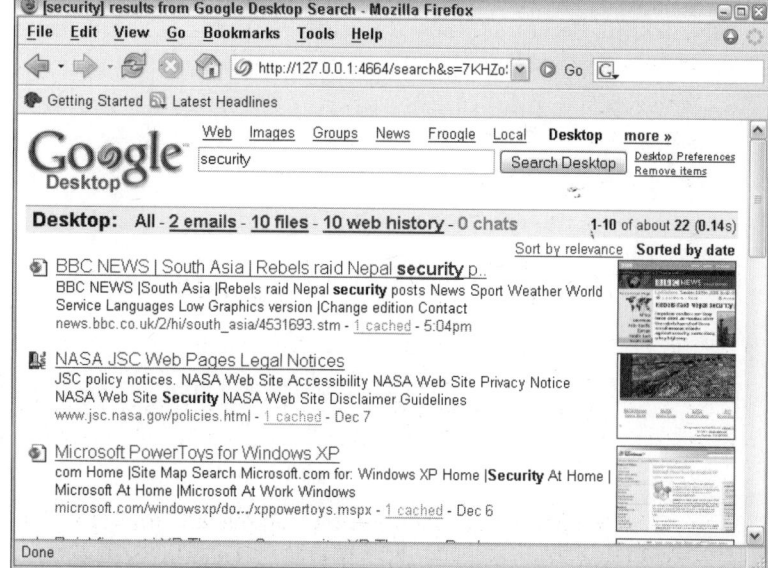

Figure 10-9: Searching for *security* returns a page I don't want to have in the index.

2. **Click the Remove Items link to the right of the Search Desktop button.**

   GDS shows you the Remove Specific Items page (see Figure 10-10).

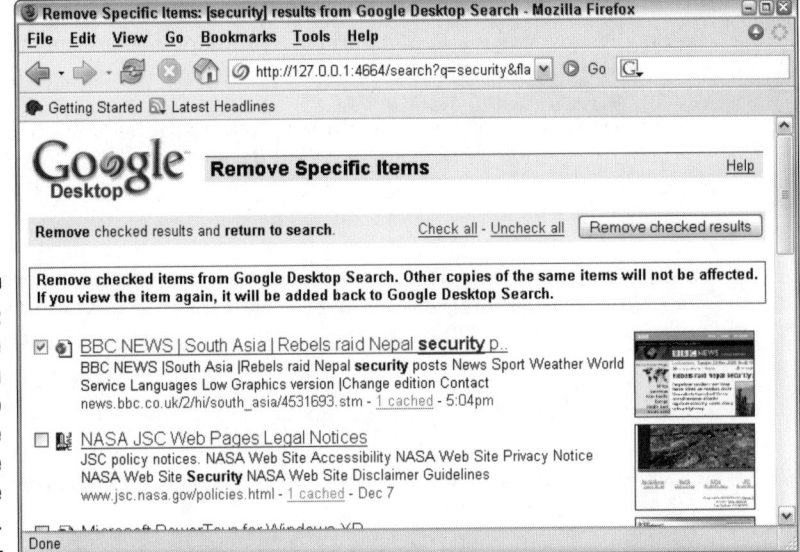

Figure 10-10:
Choose the
item(s) you
wish to
remove
from the
index/cache
here.

3. **Check the box to the left of the item(s) that you want to delete from the index and (in the case of viewed Web pages) remove from the cache.**

   To speed things up, you can click the text Check All or Uncheck All.

4. **Click the Remove Checked Results button.**

   GDS responds with a message saying how many items have been removed.

5. **Click OK.**

   You go back to the original search page, now modified to exclude the items that you removed.

Moving GDS's index file

As we went to press, one of the most persistent complaints about GDS was the fact that you couldn't tell GDS where to put its index and cache files. That's a big problem. The GDS index file draws gobs of activity. If you have a second, fast hard drive, it makes a lot of sense to move the index/cache files off of your battered, beleaguered c: drive.

Because Google is moving on Internet time, the Googlies may have fixed the problem by the time you read this. (Follow the instructions in the section "Preventing GDS from indexing specific files," earlier in this chapter, to bring up the Preferences page and see if the feature has been added.)

If you need to move the index/cache files manually, it's pretty easy — although you do need to make a trip into the Registry:

1. **Right-click the Google Desktop Search icon in the System Tray and click Exit. When GDS asks if you really want to exit, click Yes.**

    It's important that GDS not try to update its index while you're monkeying around with its files.

2. **Click Start⇨My Computer and double-click to navigate to `c:\Documents and Settings\<username>\Local Settings\Application Data\ Google`.**

    `<username>` is your username. Note that `\Local Settings` is a hidden folder, so if you haven't yet told Windows to show you hidden files and folders, run to Chapter 8 and straighten things out.

3. **Click the Google Desktop Search folder once and then, on the left, click Move This Folder.**

    Windows Explorer presents you with the standard Move Items dialog box.

4. **Navigate to where you want to put the index/cache files and click Move.**

    Windows Explorer moves the entire folder. It's important that you get the whole folder. Make sure that you jot down *precisely* where the folder went.

5. **Follow the instructions in Chapter 24 to start Regedit (choose Start⇨ Run, type `regedit`, press Enter).**

    If you've never fiddled with Registry bits before, take a moment to read through Chapter 24 and follow its nostrums.

6. **On the left side of Regedit, double-click to navigate to `HKEY_CURRENT_ USER\Software\Google\Google Desktop`.**

    Regedit looks like Figure 10-11.

7. **On the right, double-click `data_dir`.**

    Regedit presents you with its Edit String dialog box.

8. **Change the value data so it points to the new location of Google Desktop Search.**

    For example, if you moved Google Desktop Search in Step 4 to the location `E:\Utility`, change the value data to `E:\Utility\Google Desktop Search`.

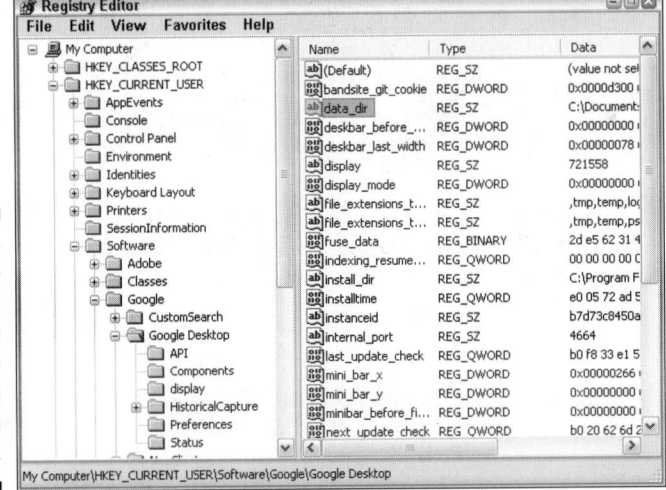

Figure 10-11:
The Registry
key you
need to
change to
tell GDS
where you
put its files.

9. **Choose File⇨Exit to get out of Regedit.**

10. **Choose Start⇨All Programs⇨Google Desktop Search⇨Google Desktop Search to restart GDS.**

GDS should spring to life with its original index and cache intact.

Smart searching with GDS

Give GDS a few tries, and I bet you never use Windows Search again. To get the most out of your GDS experience, keep these simple Google Desktop Search rules in mind:

✔ **To search for a specific kind of file (which is to say, a particular filename extension), use** filetype:. If you want to look for all Word documents (.doc files) with *jumping* in the title or in the body of the document, have GDS look for **jumping filetype:doc**.

✔ **To search for either of two words, use OR.** For example, looking for **hot or spicy** returns files that contain either or both words.

If you don't use OR, Google Desktop Search assumes you mean AND. So searching for

hot spicy matches files with both of the words *hot* and *spicy*.

✔ **To search for one word but not another, use–.** If you search for **hot –spicy**, you get files that contain the word *hot,* but only if they don't contain the word *spicy*.

✔ **To search for an exact phrase, put it in quotes.** For example, **"jumping frog"** matches only files with the precise phrase *jumping frog.*

Google Desktop Search's syntax is evolving rapidly, as are a myriad of options. To get the latest, see `http://.google.com/support`.

Chapter 11

Switching to Better Online Software

Microsoft's two big online packages leave much to be desired. Internet Explorer languished for years without a major overhaul, until Blake Ross (then a teenage Stanford student) and Ben Goodger (a twentysomething Kiwi), along with hundreds of volunteers, shook the browsing world with Firefox. Microsoft's still playing catch-up.

Then there's MSN Messenger. Oy. If you like funny icons and silly stuff, MSN Messenger works fine — as long as none of your friends uses AOL Instant Messenger or Yahoo! Messenger. While Microsoft is trying to make a version of MSN Messenger that reliably talks with other messaging programs, Trillian's been doing the polyglot shtick for years.

In this chapter, I show you how to give Internet Explorer and MSN Messenger the heave-ho. Good riddance, as far as I'm concerned.

Surfing with the Fox

Microsoft brass swore, under oath, that Internet Explorer (IE) couldn't be removed from Windows XP. In a literal sense that may be true, to some extent — Internet Explorer has its hooks in all sorts of Windows nooks and crannies. But from a practical point of view, you can install Firefox and ignore

Internet Explorer almost entirely. (I say "almost" because you still need to patch IE so that you don't get clobbered when it works under the covers with, say, Outlook.)

The Firefox-versus-IE debate rages. There's no question that Firefox is smaller and faster than Internet Explorer. After all, this isn't a level playing field: Microsoft has been patching and flogging the old IE workhorse for a decade. Whether the interface works better in Internet Explorer or Firefox is largely a personal decision. Features in one show up in the other, sooner or later.

The big open question? Security. Fred Langa, in an *Information Week* article called "The Pros and Cons of Firefox" (`www.informationweek.com/story/showArticle.jhtml?articleID=160900911`), makes the case that Internet Explorer is more secure than Firefox. I agree with Fred on many topics, but in this case I think he's all wet.

Although it's hard to debate how many bugs may or may not exist in a particular piece of software, the absolute number of gaping security holes isn't the problem. The real differentiating factor is how quickly (and thoroughly) the holes get patched. On that score, Microsoft doesn't even come close to the Firefox team. IE holes routinely go unpatched for months, sometimes a year or more, and after the patches arrive, they're frequently re-patched and re-re-patched. The Mozilla folks fix Firefox in days.

I've been recommending Firefox from the day it shipped, for three reasons:

- ✔ The features in Firefox are as good as Internet Explorer in almost every respect — and better than IE in some ways.
- ✔ As a new product, it's easier to fix when the inevitable security holes appear.
- ✔ *It ain't Microsoft.*

You owe it to yourself to download, install, and use Firefox for a couple of days. You don't need to uninstall or stunt Internet Explorer — the two coexist quite peacefully. If you don't like Firefox, simply uninstall it (choose Start➪ Control Panel➪Add or Remove Programs).

Installing Firefox

It only takes a couple of minutes to download and install Firefox. Here's how:

1. **Start Internet Explorer and go to `www.mozilla.org`.**

   Firefox is a product of the Mozilla project, the most popular open-source software developer on the planet. (*Open-source* software is not only free, but also, the source code for the software is free and readily available to anyone interested in looking at it.)

2. Click Free Download.

IE presents you a Security Warning (see Figure 11-1).

Figure 11-1:
A standard
Internet
Explorer
security
warning.
Don't worry.

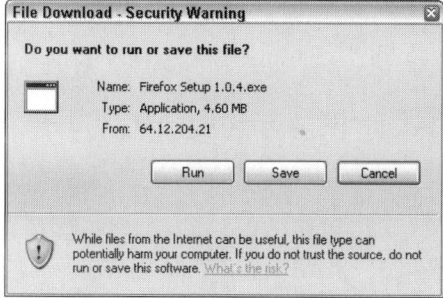

Figure 11-1: A standard Internet Explorer security warning. Don't worry.

3. Click Run.

Firefox downloads the installation file. Internet Explorer sticks you with another Security Warning.

4. Click Run.

The Firefox Setup wizard appears (see Figure 11-2).

Figure 11-2: The wizard takes you through the whole process.

5. Close any running programs, including Internet Explorer (just click "X" in the upper-right corner). When you have zero programs running, click Next.

6. Follow the wizard and take all the defaults.

7. **When you get to the Install Complete window, click Finish.**

   Firefox asks if you want to import your Internet Explorer favorites and then the browser starts automatically.

Firefox automatically checks for updates and fixes every time it's started. If a patch is available, you receive notification.

The Windows Update site, `windowsupdate.microsoft.com`, works only with Internet Explorer — Microsoft won't let Firefox get at the site (see Figure 11-3). For many of us, the only reason left to use IE is to check Windows Update.

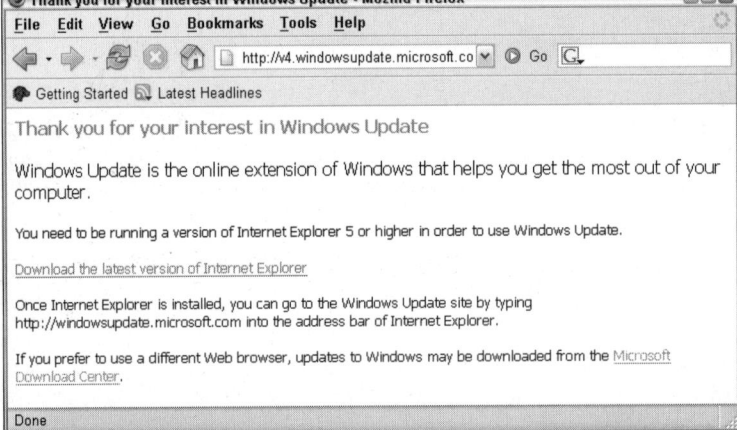

Figure 11-3:
Microsoft
will not
allow you
to use
Windows
Update with
Firefox.

Working with tabs

Most Internet Explorer users catch on to Firefox in a nonce. But if you've never used tabs, it may take a few minutes to get into the swing of things.

Try this:

1. **Start Firefox and navigate to a favorite site.**

   In Figure 11-4, I go to `www.Dummies.com`.

2. **Press Ctrl+T.**

   Firefox opens a new tab.

3. **Type the address of a second site.**

   In Figure 11-5, I type `www.AskWoody.com`. Firefox now has two tabs: one for `Dummies.com`, one for `AskWoody.com`.

Figure 11-4:
To experiment with tabs, start by bringing up a familiar Web site.

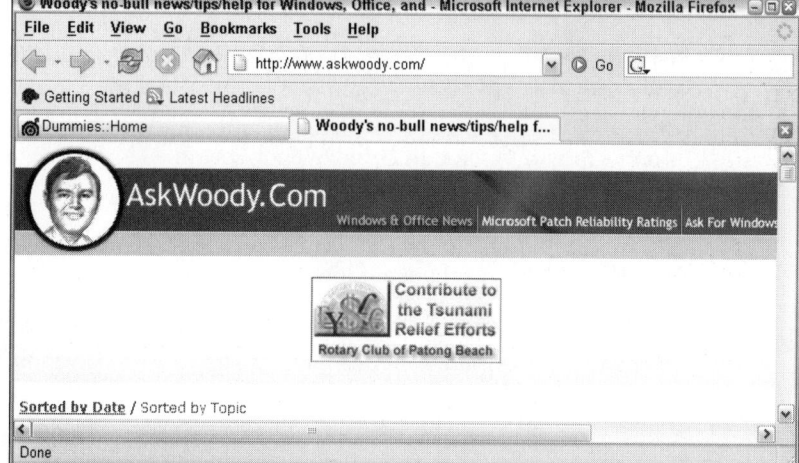

Figure 11-5:
Put a second site on the second tab.

4. **Click on each tab, or press Ctrl+Tab, to switch from one site to the other.**

   On the surface, tabbed browsing looks about as interesting as dried mud. The power of tabs lies slightly below the surface. Firefox lets you book-mark a tabbed window. When you bring up the bookmarked window, all the tabs appear. So if you commonly look at, say, five stock market tip sites, you need only set up one tabbed window to hold all the stock market sites. Bookmark the window and when you refer to it again, all five sites appear, each on its own tab. Try it.

5. **Click Bookmarks⇨Bookmark This Page.**

Firefox shows you the Add Bookmark dialog box (see Figure 11-6).

Figure 11-6:
The power of tabs lies in the ability to bookmark all of the tabs in a window.

6. **Check the box marked Bookmark All Tabs in a Folder and then click OK.**

Firefox creates a new folder in the Bookmarks list that contains entries for each of the tabs.

7. **Navigate to some other page. Then click Bookmarks and scroll to the bookmark you just created.**

Firefox lets you open each tabbed site individually, or you can choose Open in Tabs to open one Firefox window with each of the sites occupying its own tab.

8. **Choose Open in Tabs.**

Your bookmarked tabbed window appears.

You can also set up a tabbed window for Firefox's start page. Use Ctrl+T to set up as many tabs as you want and then choose Tools⇨Options⇨General, click Use Current Pages, and click OK. Your custom tabbed start page will appear every time you start Firefox.

Installing extensions

The people who designed Firefox showed an extraordinary degree of ingenuity. Their crowning achievement was devising a simple way to hook new programs into Firefox, so hundreds — thousands — of programmers could create new and exciting extensions to the product that act like they're part of Firefox itself.

Extensions aren't supported by Mozilla or the Firefox team. They're created (and sometimes supported) by individuals, almost always as a community service. Extensions that you download from the Firefox site (using the method that follows) will be "safe" and usable — but there are no guarantees.

Here's how to install a great extension:

1. **Start Firefox and click Tools➪Extensions.**

   An empty Extensions dialog box appears, as shown in Figure 11-7.

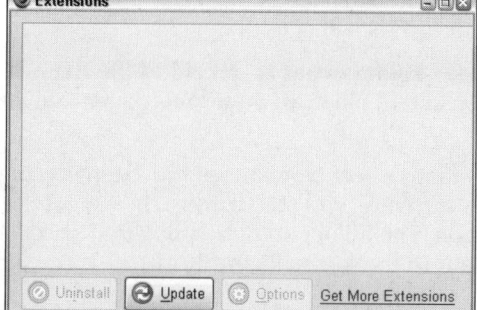

Figure 11-7:
Get more
extensions
here.

2. **In the lower-right corner, click Get More Extensions.**

   Firefox takes you to the Mozilla Update Extensions page, shown in Figure 11-8. You can scroll through the list of most popular and most recent extensions, or you can search directly.

Figure 11-8:
Search for
extensions.

In Figure 11-8, I type the keyword **forecast**, select Extensions from the drop-down list, and press Enter.

3. **When you find an extension you like, click Install Now.**

   In Figure 11-9, I choose an extension called ForecastFox, which displays current weather and forecasts from weather.com on the Firefox status bar.

   Firefox shows you a Software Installation warning box, advising you that you're about to install a program.

4. **Click Install Now.**

   Firefox returns to the Extensions dialog box, showing you the status of your new extension. Each extension is different, but most require you to restart Firefox in order to take effect.

5. **Click "X" in the upper-right corner to get rid of the Extensions dialog box. Then, if so instructed, close all your Web pages and start Firefox again.**

   Your new extension takes effect. Sometimes the extension puts you through a setup routine when you start Firefox. In the case of the ForecastFox extension, you fill out an option box that specifies which city or cities you want to track (see Figure 11-10).

Figure 11-9:
One of my favorite extensions, which shows current weather conditions and forecasts for many cities around the world.

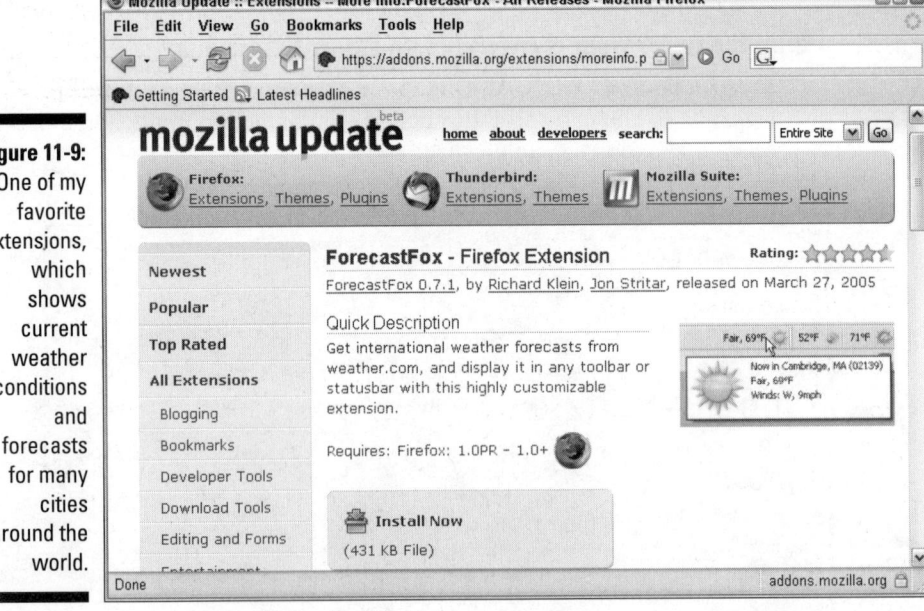

Must-have Firefox extensions

Here are some Firefox extensions I can't live without:

ForecastFox, the weather forecaster that sits at the bottom of the screen. I describe how to install it in the "Installing extensions" part of this chapter.

 Diggler, a small addition to the toolbar that lets you move "up" one level in an address. For example, if Firefox is sitting at AskWoody.com/viewpatch, and I click this button, Firefox moves "up" to AskWoody.com.

DictionarySearch looks up a word that you select in TheFreeDictionary.com, an online dictionary. Select the word, right-click, and choose Search Dictionary.

TinyURLCreator makes it one-click simple to convert horrendously long Web addresses into short addresses (such as, oh, `tinyurl.com/coltz`), using the services of tinyurl.com. Just click on the TinyURL icon. The extension goes to tinyurl.com, establishes a tiny URL, and copies it onto the Windows Clipboard.

CountdownClock gives you a countdown timer on Firefox's status bar, in the lower-right corner of the screen. You can tell the clock to put a message on the status bar or show a message on the screen when the timer goes off.

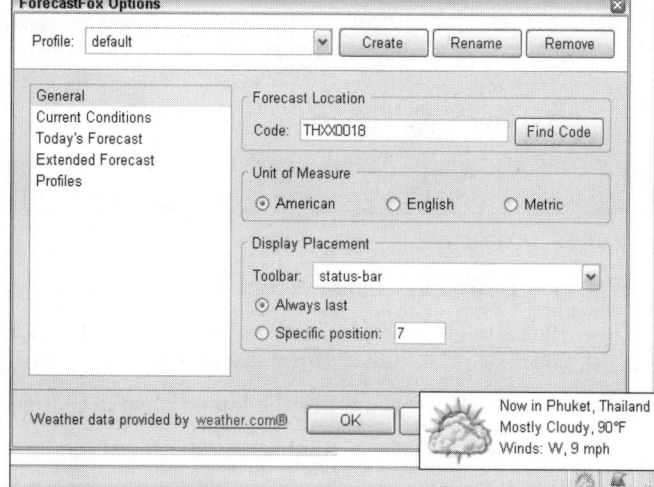

Figure 11-10: Tell ForecastFox which weather forecast you'd like.

Hacking and modding Firefox

In the follow sections, you find key hacks and mods for Firefox. Start with the essential changes and work through the steps for changing toolbar buttons, ridding yourself of blinking text, and more to your heart's content.

Essential changes every user should make

Most of Firefox's default settings work well, but I suggest you consider changing a couple of readily accessible options:

1. **Start Firefox. Choose Tools➪Options➪Advanced.**

   Firefox shows you its Advanced options (see Figure 11-11).

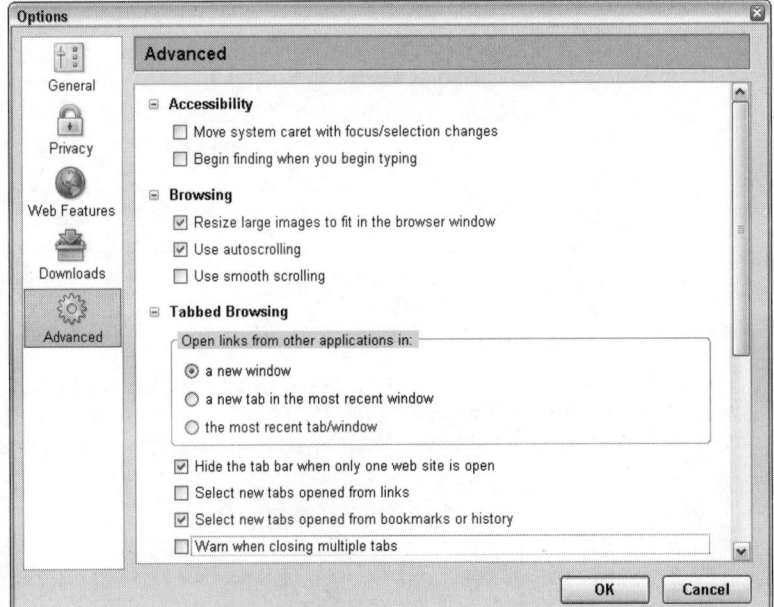

Figure 11-11:
Firefox's
Advanced
options.

2. **Under Tabbed Browsing, choose A New Window.**

   When you click a link in another application (say, a hot link in an e-mail message), Firefox can do one of three things:

   • Create a new window and put the linked page in that window

   • Create a new tab in the current window and put the page on the tab

- Replace the current window (or tab in the window, if the window is tabbed)

The default behavior is to replace the most recent window or tab. I find that annoying, and I bet you do, too. Far better, in my opinion, to force Firefox to open a new window and leave the current windows intact.

3. Uncheck the box marked Warn When Closing Multiple Tabs.

If you click "X" in the upper-right corner of a Firefox window, you want the window to go away, right? Unfortunately, Firefox's designers decided to put a dialog box on the screen if you attempt to close a tabbed window (see Figure 11-12). I say get rid of the dialog box.

Figure 11-12:
The annoying Confirm Close dialog box.

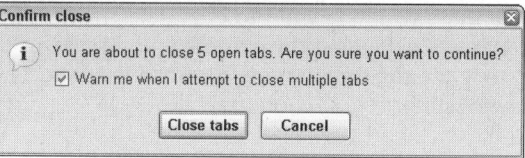

4. Click OK.

Your changes take effect immediately.

Changing toolbar buttons

Changing toolbar buttons in Firefox couldn't be simpler: Right-click any empty spot on the toolbar and choose Customize. Many extensions come with their own toolbar buttons, which you can drag onto the toolbar using this approach.

Nixing blinking text

Some Web pages have text that blinks, and I for one hate the distraction. If you want to eliminate blinking text once and for all:

1. Type about:config **in the address bar and press Enter.**

The Configuration window appears (see Figure 11-13).

2. Double-click the line called `browser.blink_allowed`**.**

The value for `browser.blink_allowed` changes to `false`, and blinking text now appears solid.

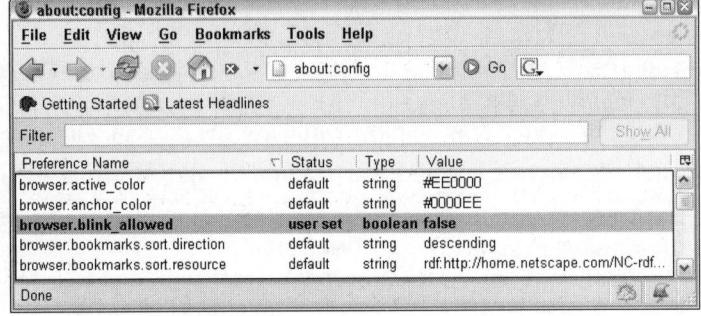

Figure 11-13:
Many
behind-the-
scenes
settings
lurk in this
odd file.

Speeding up Firefox

If you have a fast machine, you may want to eliminate the quarter-second delay before Firefox draws a page on the screen. If you have a slow machine, you probably want to leave the delay there, because the total time to draw the page on the screen will probably increase.

Here's how:

1. **Open the Configuration window by typing** about:config **in the address bar and pressing Enter.**

2. **Right-click any blank place in the Configuration window and choose New⇨Integer.**

   Firefox comes up with a New Integer Value dialog box (see Figure 11-14).

Figure 11-14:
The easy
way to
add new
settings to
Firefox.

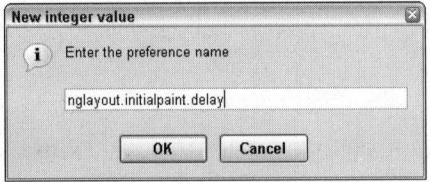

3. **Type** nglayout.initialpaint.delay **in the box and click OK.**

   Firefox asks for an integer value.

4. **Type** 0 **(that's the number zero) and then click OK.**

   The Configuration window shows a new Preference Name called `nglayout.initialpaint.delay`, with a value of `0`.

5. **Close all the copies of Firefox that are running.**

   The next time you start Firefox, your setting takes effect. Hold onto your hat. That quarter-second can be almost perceptible.

Delving deeper into Firefox

You can edit four different files that Firefox uses — `user.js`, `prefs.js`, `userChrome.css`, and `userContent.css` — but the point of diminishing returns looms nigh. If you're curious and want to play around a bit, look at Edward Heinrich's site, `http://the-edmeister.` `home.comcast.net/html/description_of_the_4_user_prefs_files.html`, for a comprehensive treatment. There's also an extensive list of hacks and mods for Firefox at `www.techspot.com/tweaks/firefox`.

You can find lots of opinions on the Internet about how to speed up Firefox by using the settings in the Configuration window. Personally, I'm skeptical. Unless the Mozilla people recommend a performance tweak, I wouldn't bother with it.

Keyboard shortcuts for Firefox and IE

Chapter 9 lists several keyboard shortcuts that work with both Firefox and Internet Explorer — and every semisentient Windows program. Ctrl+A (select all), Ctrl+C (copy), Ctrl+X (cut), Ctrl+V (paste) should be part of every Windows user's repertoire.

A handful of additional key combinations can speed up your use of either Firefox or IE, and they are well worth memorizing:

- ✔ **Ctrl+Enter** completes a `.com` address. For example, if you type `Dummies` in the address bar and press Ctrl+Enter, your browser searches for the full address `http://www.Dummies.com`.

- ✔ **Ctrl+H** brings up the History pane, which lists all the sites you've visited.

- ✔ **Ctrl+F** lets you "find on this page" — search for text on the current page. In Firefox, simply typing / accomplishes the same thing. Pressing **F3** repeats the find.

- ✔ If you want to force Firefox or IE to open a new window when it follows a link, hold down the **Shift** key when you click on the link.

- ✔ **Ctrl+F5** reloads the current page, all the way from the Web site, over-riding any copies that may be stored along the way. It's a true refresh.

- ✔ **Esc** should make the browser stop doing whatever it's trying to do. At least, that's what the designers say.

Printing a page in Firefox and IE

I hear this question over and over again: How do you print the important part of a Web page, without all that other garbage?

Here's the way I do it. Look at the top and the bottom of the page you want to print. If you see a button that says Print This Page or Printer Friendly Version, you're in luck. You can follow these easy steps:

1. **Click the Print This Page or Printer Friendly Version button and follow the instructions on the screen.**

2. **If there is no Print This Page or Printer Friendly Version button, try to drag your mouse pointer over the part of the Web page that you want to print. If you can select the stuff you want to print — and *only* the stuff you want to print — choose File⇨Print.**

3. **In the Print Range box (shown in Figure 11-15), click the button marked Selection and then click OK.**

   Don't use your Web browser's Print icon.

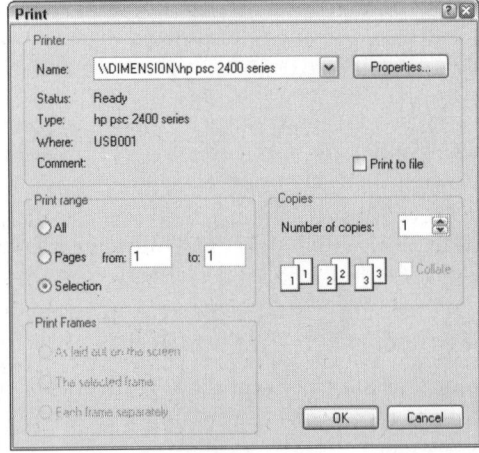

Figure 11-15: To print a selected range, choose Selection.

If you can't select the stuff you want to print — you get an extra picture, or a table, or junk off to the side — follow these steps:

1. **Select whatever you want to print, plus whatever junk comes along for the ride. Press Ctrl+C.**

   Everything goes onto the Windows Clipboard.

2. **Start Word (or your favorite word processor) and press Ctrl+V.**

   What you originally selected is pasted into a Word document.

3. **Go through the document. Click the parts you don't want and press Delete.**

You can get rid of an entire table by hovering your mouse in the upper-left corner of the table, waiting for it to turn into a four-headed arrow, and then clicking to select the whole table. If you manage to select the table, press Delete to delete it. Frequently, graphics on Web pages appear in tables, so getting rid of the table usually gets rid of the graphic.

4. **When you've pruned the document, click the Print icon to print it.**

5. **Choose File⇨Exit to close your word processor. No, you don't want to save changes.**

IMing with Trillian

All gall is divided into three parts. At least, the antics of the three big Instant Messaging companies seem galling.

For years, MSN Messenger (and its dowdy stepsister Windows Messenger), AOL Instant Messenger (AIM), and Yahoo! Messenger have dominated the IM scene. For years, they've fought tooth and nail to keep their three worlds separate — if you used AIM, you couldn't talk to someone with MSN Mess, and heaven help you if you worked with Yahoo!.

Lately we've seen a bit of détente, but we're still a long, long way from peaceful coexistence among the warring tribes.

If you have a choice, I recommend that you use a small, unobtrusive, positively genteel program called Trillian. With Trillian, you can talk with anyone using AIM, MSN Messenger, Windows Messenger, or Yahoo! Messenger. You don't need to sign up for all of the services or get separate accounts for AIM, Messenger, and Yahoo!: Your friends will find you just fine. You have just one program to learn, you can store all your contacts in one place, and you won't be bombarded with annoying advertisements every time you turn around. Most of all, *it ain't Microsoft.* Trillian Basic is free. Trillian Pro costs $25. No ads. No scumware. No problems.

That said, realize that you may not have a choice about which IM program to use. Some options in Microsoft Office 2003, for example, and some Windows/Exchange Server features require MSN Messenger and/or Windows Messenger. The situation's confusing, but if you are IMing at work, and your admin tells you that you have to run a specific version of Windows Messenger or MSN Messenger, well, you're stuck.

Installing Trillian

I find the polyglot (free!) Trillian a joy to install and use. Here's how:

1. **Start your browser and go to www.ceruleanstudios.com.**

2. **Click the button marked Download Trillian Basic 3.**

   Trillian Basic is the free version. The Pro version costs $25.

3. **Follow the instructions to download the installation file and then run the installer.**

4. **Take all the defaults. The installer finishes after a minute. When the installer finishes, click Launch.**

   You may be asked if you want to install QuickTime, to support Trillian's videoconferencing. If you think you will want to run videoconferences over your Webcam, go ahead and download it. But if your needs run to the more pedestrian, click No.

5. **Trillian steps you through its First Time Wizard. Take all the defaults.**

6. **When asked, provide your current usernames and passwords for Yahoo!, AOL, ICQ, and MSN Messengers. If you don't have usernames or passwords, don't worry — just click Next. You'll have a chance to add new services later.**

   Trillian comes up for the first time (see Figure 11-16).

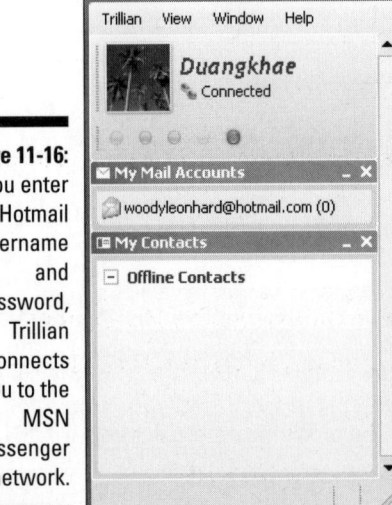

Figure 11-16:
If you enter your Hotmail username and password, Trillian connects you to the MSN Messenger network.

Adding contacts with Trillian

After Trillian is working, you should start adding Contacts:

1. **With Trillian running, click Trillian⇨Add Contact or Group.**

   Trillian responds with its Add Contacts Wizard.

2. **If you already have a list of Contacts, choose Import Contacts. Otherwise, choose Add Contacts or Groups and click Next, and Trillian shows you the Add Contact or Group dialog box, shown in Figure 11-17.**

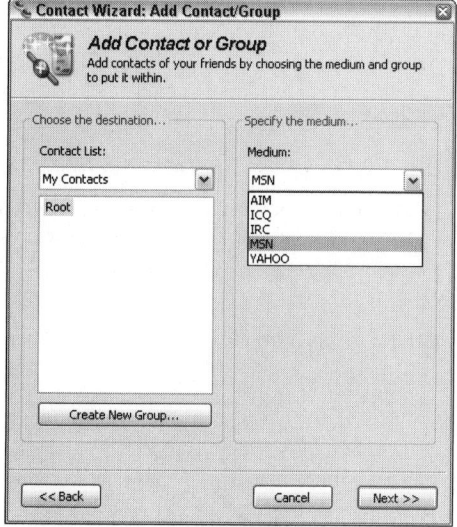

Figure 11-17: Contacts are grouped according to the network they use.

3. **In the drop-down box marked Medium, choose the network that this group of Contacts communicates over.**

   In Figure 11-17, I choose MSN.

4. **Click Next.**

   Trillian invites you to add contacts to this contact list (see Figure 11-18).

5. **Type the e-mail address for each contact, one by one, in the Name box, and click Add.**

6. **When you finish, click Done.**

   Trillian returns to its main window (see Figure 11-19).

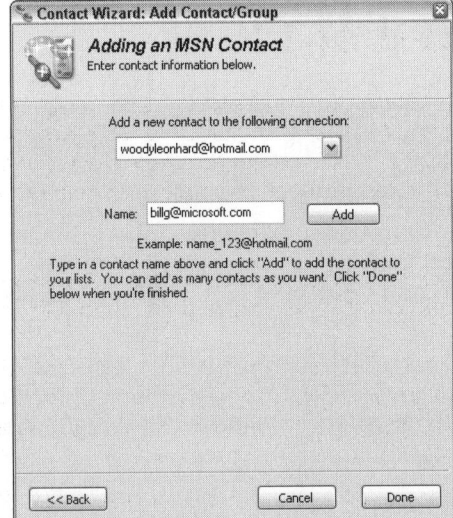

Figure 11-18:
Type e-mail
addresses
one by one.

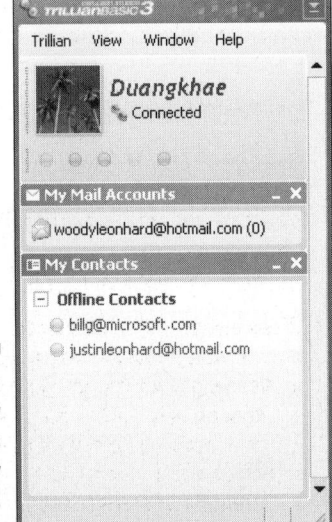

Figure 11-19:
New
contacts
are now
available.

For the latest Trillian hacks, mods, and news, see Jeff Hester's great Web site, `www.bigblueball.com/im/trillian`. Jeff will confirm that Trillian was eaten by the Bugblatter Beast of Traal, as you suspected all along, eh?

Disabling MSN Messenger

Wish I had a nickel for every time someone asked me how to zap MSN Messenger. Some folks make the mistake of associating their Windows logon name with a .NET Passport name, and for them the game's over; every time they start Windows, the MSN Doughboy pops up and logs them onto Messenger. Most annoying.

When it comes to cutting off MSN Messenger and Windows Messenger, there are four distinct levels of annihilation, some more polite than others:

✔ You can *break the connection* between your Windows ID and MSN Messenger, so you aren't automatically logged on to Microsoft's giant Messenger borg every time you start Windows. Messenger still starts automatically, but it doesn't reach out and connect.

✔ You can *keep MSN Messenger from starting* when you start Windows. That way, if you decide to manually start Doughboy, it'll still have the smarts to log you in automatically.

✔ You can *uninstall MSN and Windows Messenger,* and as long as Windows plays nicely, that should be the end of the problem. I give detailed steps for uninstalling the Messengers in Chapter 3.

✔ You can *cut the Messengers off at the knees,* so no wayward program on your computer can find either of them.

Windows Messenger vs. MSN Messenger

What's the difference between Windows Messenger and MSN Messenger? I could say that it's all cosmetic, but that isn't the whole story.

Windows Messenger ships with Windows: If you have Windows, you have Windows Messenger, even if you never use it. MSN Messenger may have come with your PC when you bought it, but unless your hardware vendor "helped" by preinstalling it, you have to download and install MSN Messenger to get it to work.

Windows Messenger is old, unsexy, and stable. MSN Messenger is young — there are updates several times a year — it's hot, it's cool, and it's not nearly as stable. MSN Messenger and Windows Messenger can both run on the same machine, although they can't both be running with the same account simultaneously: You have to log off one before starting the other or use two different Passport accounts.

If you care about fancy emoticons, telling everyone which song you're listening to at that very moment, and putting a picture of a Sith next to your name, MSN Messenger is for you. If your age exceeds, oh, one-tenth of your IQ, you can live with Windows Messenger — but Trillian works better than both.

If you intend to use Trillian, you don't need either of the Messengers (unless you're hooked on an MSN Messenger–specific service, such as MSN's online telephone or the Messenger-based method for starting Remote Assistance, as described in Chapter 15).

Shutting down MSN Messenger the polite way

If you want to be able to use MSN Messenger occasionally, at your specific request, it's best to break the connection and/or stop MSN Messenger from running automatically. Here's how:

1. **Start MSN Messenger if it hasn't started itself already, or double-click the Doughboy icon in the status bar.**

   The MSN Messenger window appears.

2. **Choose Tools⇨Options⇨General.**

   MSN Messenger shows you the Options dialog box (see Figure 11-20).

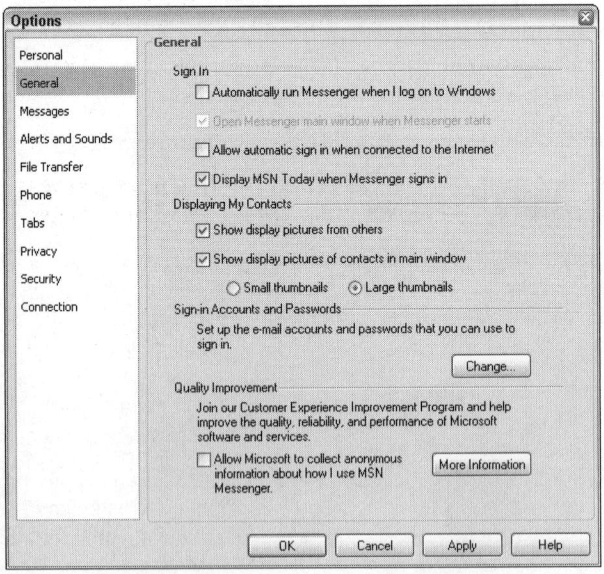

Figure 11-20: MSN Messenger options.

3. **To break the connection, preventing MSN Messenger from automatically logging on to Microsoft's network every time it starts, uncheck the box marked Allow Automatic Sign In When Connected to the Internet.**

4. **To keep MSN Messenger from starting itself when you start Windows, uncheck the box marked Automatically Run Messenger When I Log on to Windows.**

5. **Click OK and then choose File⇨Sign Out to log yourself off Microsoft's network.**

   You may want to restart your computer to confirm that MSN doesn't automatically start itself again.

Shutting down MSN Messenger the IMpolite way

If you never want to use MSN Messenger or Windows Messenger, follow the steps in Chapter 3 to uninstall both.

If Messenger refuses to uninstall itself, or if you encounter a situation in which it reinstalls itself, there's a simple way to cut both off at the knees:

1. **Choose Start⇨My Computer⇨c:\⇨Program Files.**

2. **Right-click the folder called Messenger, if it exists. Choose Rename, and rename it to** OldMessenger **(or something slightly less flattering).**

3. **Right-click the folder called MSN Messenger, if it exists. Choose Rename, and rename it to** HappySmileyFaces.

4. **Click "X" in the upper-right corner to get out of Windows Explorer.**

   There should be no way on heaven or earth that any program, including Windows, can find Windows Messenger or MSN Messenger.

Chapter 12

Pulling Off Pictures

1'll never forget the first time I tried to move pictures from my digital camera to my computer. Like a good boy, I read the manual, installed the manufacturer's software, followed the instructions, and . . . nothing. I clicked and clicked and clicked in Windows and nothing happened. Ends up that the software that came bundled with the camera didn't work worth beans.

I uninstalled the manufacturer's software and tried using the native picture support built into Windows XP. It worked flawlessly. No, I couldn't get Windows to do any fancy stuff with the camera — I had to futz with the camera itself to make exposure adjustments and the like. But I found that Windows, all by itself, makes it mighty easy to take pictures off the camera and put them on the computer.

This chapter takes you through those basics and much more.

Removing Problematic Camera Software

If you've been having problems with the software on your computer that controls your camera, man, you ain't alone. I've spent days and days struggling with lousy software from all of the major camera manufacturers.

On the other hand, if the software you have right now works great — you can transfer pictures from your camera to your PC without any hitches, or your webcam software rings your chimes — skip down to the section "Undeleting Images on a Camera." You live a charmed life. Remember the Windows XP Prime Directive: Ain't broke, don't fix.

To get rid of buggy camera software:

1. **Unplug your camera from your PC.**

2. **Choose Start⇨Control Panel⇨Add or Remove Programs.**

   You should be able to find the faulty program in the list of installed programs (see Figure 12-1).

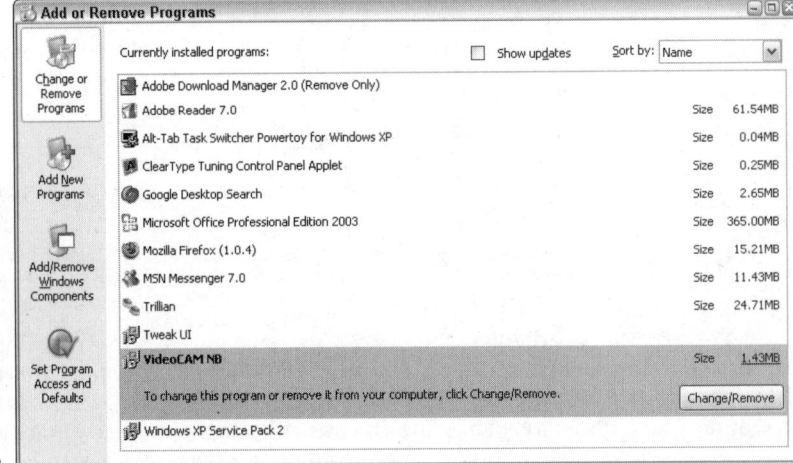

Figure 12-1:
Don't be afraid to remove software that's causing you fits.

3. **Click the program you want to remove and then click the Change/Remove button.**

   Depending on the software, you may be guided through a very simple uninstall wizard — or you may just sit there and stare at your screen for a minute or two while the program self-immolates.

4. **Restart your computer.**

   Sometimes the software is smart enough to do it for you. If it isn't, choose Start⇨Turn Off Computer⇨Restart. You want to get a clean start.

5. **Plug in your camera. And wait.**

   Sometimes Windows finds the driver and tells you that your camera is ready to use. Many times Windows doesn't need a driver — it already has everything it needs to work with your camera.

6. **If Windows doesn't automatically find your camera, choose Start⇨ Control Panel⇨Add New Hardware and follow the Add New Hardware Wizard.**

   Again, depending on the type of hardware, you may need to go to the manufacturer's Web site and download the latest driver. It's always better to download a new driver than to use the one on the CD that came with the camera. Always.

Transferring Pictures from a Camera

Nine times out of ten, Windows XP simply recognizes a camera when it's plugged into a PC. In my experience, the Windows-provided Scanner and Camera Wizard (combined with a couple of tricks that I show you in this section) works well enough for most people.

Here's how to use the Scanner and Camera Wizard:

1. **Plug your camera into your PC (usually through a USB cable) and then turn on your camera.**

   Most cameras have a specific mode for transferring pictures, one that's different from the mode for taking pictures.

   Windows stutters and mumbles about finding new hardware and then almost always responds with a message saying your new hardware is ready to use. Shortly after, you get a Camera Connected message like the one shown in Figure 12-2.

Figure 12-2: Almost always when you plug a camera into a Windows XP PC, you automatically get a message like this one.

If you don't get a message saying that your hardware is ready to use, you have two choices. First, you can simply pull the memory card out of the camera and use a multifunction card reader to make Windows look at the memory card just like any other hard drive. I talk about that option in the next section. Second, as Clint Eastwood put it so well, "You've got to ask yourself one question: Do I feel lucky? Well, do ya, punk?" If you're feeling lucky, you can follow your camera manufacturer's instructions and install the company's software. An *Ave Maria* might help.

If Windows tells you that your new hardware is ready to use, but you don't get an AutoPlay message like the one in Figure 12-2, download and run Microsoft's AutoPlay Repair Wizard. Start at www.tinyurl.com/stus.

2. **In the Camera Connected message, click Microsoft Scanner and Camera Wizard and then click OK.**

   The wizard starts with a do-nothing first page.

3. **Click Next.**

   The Scanner and Camera Wizard shows you all the pictures on the camera (see Figure 12-3).

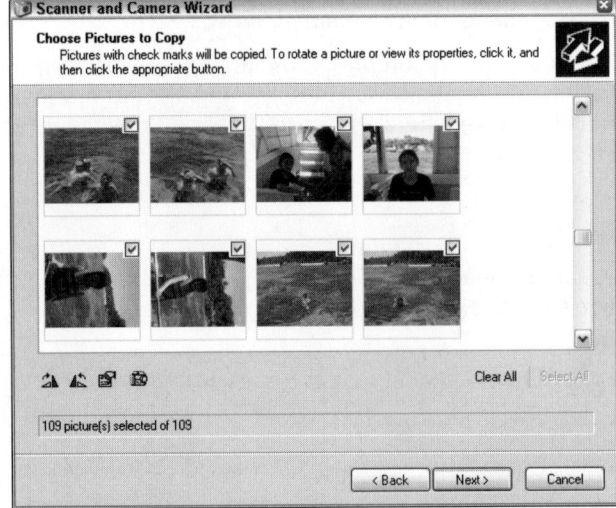

Figure 12-3: Choose the pictures you want to transfer from the camera to the PC.

4. **Unless you have a very, very good reason for keeping a picture on your camera, leave all of the pictures selected and click Next.**

   The wizard has you choose where to put the pictures and what to call them, as shown in Figure 12-4.

5. **Give the entire series of pictures a "root" name in the top box.**

   You can choose a name from the drop-down list, if you like. (If that list gets unwieldy and you want to clear the list, see the sidebar "Clearing the wizard's most-recently-used list.") The pictures are numbered sequentially — for example, Walla Walla 001.jpg, Walla Walla 002.jpg, Walla Walla 003.jpg.

6. **Click the Browse button and navigate to where you'd like to store the pictures.**

7. **Unless you want to repeat all this work again, check the box marked Delete Pictures from My Device After Copying Them.**

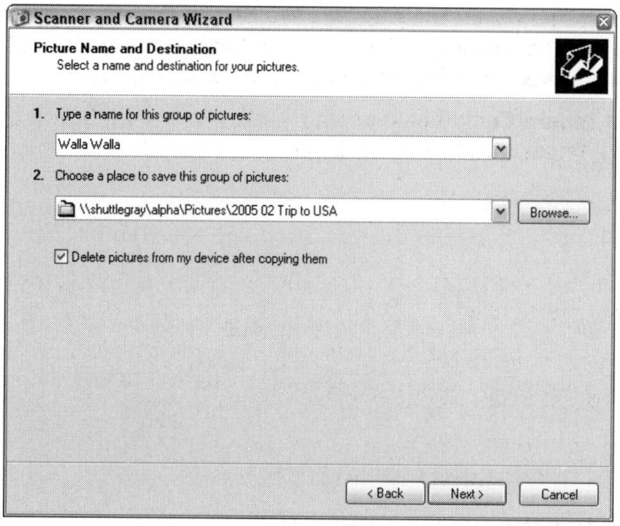

Figure 12-4:
Naming and
locating the
pictures.

8. Click Next.

The pictures leave your camera and enter your PC, one at a time
(Figure 12-5). Depending on how many pictures you have, it may be a
good time to grab a latte.

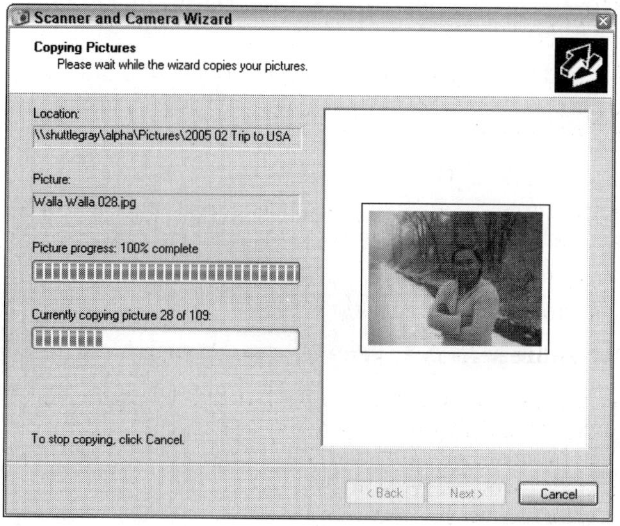

Figure 12-5:
Windows
shows you
each picture
as it gets
transferred.

The wizard returns with an Other Options pane whose express purpose
is to sell you space on Microsoft's Web servers or to make it easy to
order prints for which Microsoft draws a commission.

9. **Make sure you click the button marked Nothing, I'm Finished Working with These Pictures and I Don't Want to Give Even More Money to Microsoft (or something like that). Then click Next.**

   You see a do-nothing final wizard pane.

10. **Click Finish.**

    I suggest you immediately look over your pictures, following the suggestions in the section "Rummaging Through New Photos" later in this chapter.

 If you feel supremely confident in your ability to work with the Scanner and Camera Wizard, you can set it up to run on autopilot. That way, as soon as you connect your camera to your computer, the wizard kicks in and downloads all your pictures — no intervention required. Here's how to do it:

1. **Start the Scanner and Camera Wizard.**

   The easiest way is to plug in your camera and turn it on and then choose the Scanner and Camera Wizard from the Camera Connected dialog box (refer to Figure 12-2).

2. **On the first pane of the wizard, click the text *Advanced Users Only*.**

   This choice really isn't just for advanced users. If you take the card out of your camera and use a card reader, you go through the same choices (see the next section).

3. **On the left, under Camera Tasks, click Show Camera Properties and then click the Events tab.**

   You see the Events tab of the Camera Connected dialog box, shown in Figure 12-6.

4. **With Camera Connected in the Select an Event drop-down box, click the button marked Save All Pictures to This Folder.**

5. **Click Browse and choose a folder to save the pictures to.**

Clearing the wizard's most-recently-used list

The Scanner and Camera Wizard's drop-down lists of names and locations can be handy, but far too often the list gets clogged with utterly useless (and sometimes embarrassing!) filenames and locations.

It's easy to clear the lists, if you don't mind jumping into the Registry. Follow the steps in Chapter 24 to open RegEdit and go to

`HKEY_CURRENT_USER\Software\Microsoft\Windows\CurrentVersion\WIA\WiaAcquisitionManager`. To get rid of the list of filenames, delete the key value `RootFileNameMru`. To blank out the list of locations, delete the key value `DirectoryNameMru`. That way, you can start all over again.

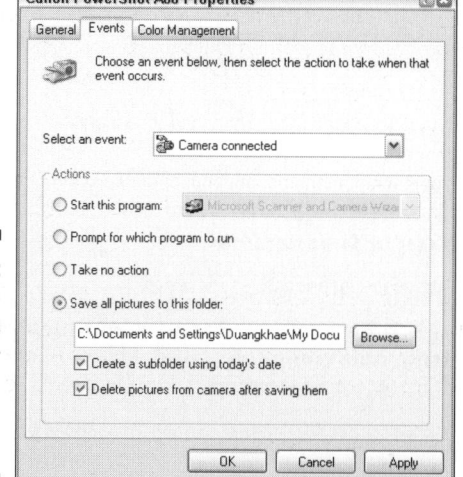

Figure 12-6:
Make
Windows
unload your
camera
automatic-
ally.

6. **Check the box marked Create a Subfolder Using Today's Date.**

   If you take a lot of pictures, putting them in separate folders each time you transfer the pictures can keep you from going blind. Or crazy. Or both. The folder name is of the form year-month-day, such as 2005-12-26. The individual files retain the weird names that they had inside the camera (for example, IMG_1557.jpg or DSCN01903.jpg).

7. **Check the box marked Delete Pictures from Camera After Saving Them.**

   Otherwise, you have to go back in and manually delete all of them.

8. **Click OK and then click "X" to exit the camera's Explorer window. Click Cancel on the first page of the wizard.**

   From that point on, every time you plug your camera into your PC, the wizard kicks in automatically. After transferring all the pictures, Windows politely asks if you are sure that you want to delete all the pictures on the camera. If you click Yes, they're all gone. (Well, sorta. See the section "Undeleting Images on a Camera," later in this chapter, if you make a mistake.)

Copying from a Camera Memory Card

Many people prefer to work directly with their camera's memory card. If you have a memory card reader (which costs, oh, about ten bucks at your friendly local computer shoppe), you have two options:

✔ Use the Scanner and Camera Wizard.

✔ Just do it — copy, move, or delete the files with Windows Explorer, just like any other files.

You can transfer pictures this way even if your camera's batteries are dead.

Here's how to dig into the card itself:

1. **Pull the memory card out of your camera.**

   Yeah, you should turn off the camera first. Sheeesh.

2. **Stick the memory card in a memory card reader and then plug the memory card reader into your computer.**

   Windows scratches its head for a minute or two, recognizes the memory card, and then responds with an AutoPlay dialog box like the one shown in Figure 12-7.

Figure 12-7: Windows' response to a memory card reader.

3. **If you want to play with the files directly, click Open Folder to View Files and then click OK.**

   Some cameras get a little touchy if you create folders or files with specific, reserved names, but as long as you don't do anything incredibly bizarre, Windows Explorer works fine: Click and drag, copy, move, delete to your heart's content.

4. **If you want to use the Scanner and Camera Wizard, click Copy Pictures to a Folder on My Computer Using Microsoft Scanner and Camera Wizard and then click OK.**

   The Scanner and Camera Wizard kicks in, precisely as described in the preceding section.

Rummaging Through New Photos

The minute you finish transferring photos to your computer, it's a very good idea to go through the pictures, verify that you got all of them, delete the ones you don't want, rotate any that need rotating, and then rename (and possibly move) the pictures so that the names bear some relationship to the pictures themselves.

Here's how I do it, in one fell swoop:

1. **Click the folder that contains the new pictures. Then click View▷ Filmstrip.**

   If Filmstrip is not available on the View menu, Windows made a big mistake. You need to tell Windows that this particular folder contains pictures. See Chapter 8.

2. **One by one, go through the pictures.**

   I find it easiest to use the right arrow on the keyboard.

3. **If an important photo is missing, immediately consult the "Undeleting Images on a Camera" section, later in this chapter.**

   Your chances of recovering a deleted photo on your camera increase greatly if you don't do anything to the camera until you read the next section.

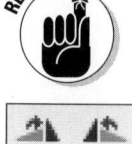
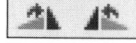

4. **Rotate pictures clockwise or counterclockwise by clicking the Rotate icons (see Figure 12-8).**

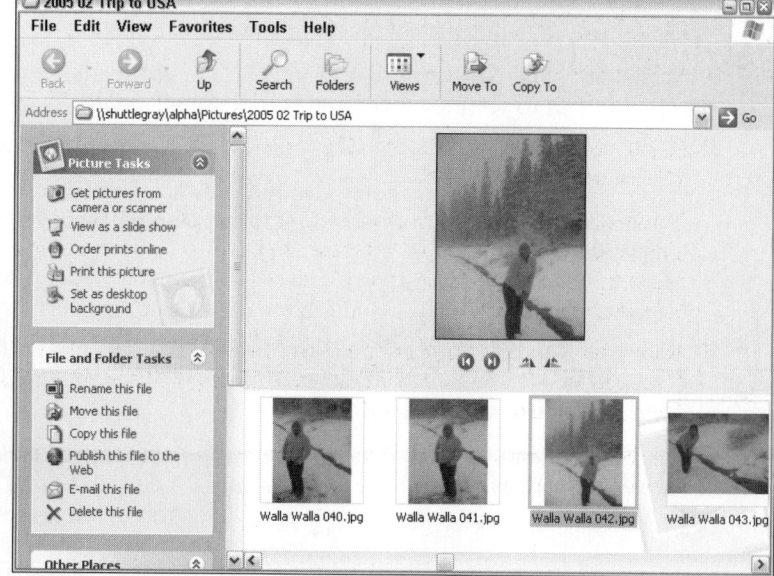

Figure 12-8: Rotate pictures with the Rotate icons so they're all upright.

If you get a warning saying that the quality of the pictures will be changed, don't get overly worried about it. In my experience, rotated photos look just like their unrotated kin. If you're the paranoid type, make a copy of a picture before rotating it.

5. **If you don't want to keep a picture, press Delete.**

6. **When you finish going through the pictures one by one, choose View⇨Thumbnails.**

7. **If there's a group of files that should be renamed (and there almost always is), use the renaming method described in Chapter 8.**

8. **Create new folders, if they'll help you organize things, and move the files around to where they make the most sense.**

If you do it now, while the events are still fresh in your mind, it'll be much, much easier than trying to remember two months from now.

Undeleting Images on a Camera

A remarkable free program called Restoration, from Brian Kato, can "undelete" pictures on your camera. It doesn't matter if you deleted the photos with the Scanner and Camera Wizard, or if your exceptionally bright but klutzy uncle just hit the wrong button when he was playing with the camera. Restoration doesn't cost a cent, and it has worked on every file I've thrown at it.

Two tricks:

✔ Anything you do with your camera can make it harder to restore deleted pictures. The moment you think that you might need to undelete a photo, turn off your camera and follow the advice in this section.

✔ It's easiest to use Restoration with a memory card reader. If you don't have one, run to your local computer outlet mall and get one. Well worth the investment.

Restoration scans an entire memory card but only lets you restore one file at a time, so if you've deleted hundreds of pictures, plan on spending a while retrieving them.

If you've never played around with undelete utilities, it may surprise you to know that "deleted" files aren't really deleted — even Windows files that have been permanently deleted, or ones that went away when you emptied the Recycle Bin.

Cameras are no different. Most cameras use an ancient method called a File Allocation Table (FAT) to keep track of their data. (A certain Gates, Bill, was intimately involved in the early days of FAT.) When you delete a file on a FAT disk, the data doesn't go away. The computer just changes a couple of pointers and doesn't bother to erase the deleted data. When the computer needs more room on the disk, though, it takes areas that were marked "deleted" and overwrites the data at that point. So if you're lucky, your old data — your old pictures — are still on the camera.

Here's how to restore most deleted photos:

1. **Turn off your camera and remove the memory card.**

   Anything you do with the camera can potentially overwrite the information that's still sitting on your memory card.

2. **Go to `www.snapfiles.com/get/restoration.html` and download the program Restoration.**

   As we went to press, the filename was `REST2514.exe`.

3. **Create a new folder to hold the final Restoration program.**

   This is a bit odd, but Restoration doesn't include the ability to create a new folder to hold the program. Personally, I choose Start⇨My Computer⇨C:⇨Program Files, right-click an empty spot in the folder, choose New⇨Folder, and create a folder called `c:\Program Files\Restoration`.

4. **Run the downloaded program.**

   It's a very rudimentary unzipper — not a real installer. You see a dialog box similar to the one in Figure 12-9.

Figure 12-9: Restoration is looking for a folder to unzip into.

> Restoration Version 2.5.14
>
> Extract to
>
> `C:\Documents and Settings\Duangkhae\`   Reference...
>
> Ok   Cancel

5. **Click the Reference button and navigate to the folder that you created in Step 3. Click OK.**

   Restoration returns to the installation dialog box shown in Figure 12-9.

6. **Click OK.**

   Restoration unzips its files and puts them in the folder you chose.

   There's a reason why Restoration doesn't install itself. It's trying not to disturb your hard drive, so if you're trying to recover deleted files on your hard drive, it isn't muddying the waters.

7. **Put your camera's memory card in the card reader. Connect the card reader to your computer (if it isn't already connected). Wait for Windows to recognize that the card is in the computer.**

   You may want to choose Start➪My Computer and make sure that Windows "sees" the camera's memory card.

8. **Navigate to Restoration.exe and double-click it to run it.**

   In this case, I choose Start➪My Computer➪C:➪Program Files➪ Restoration➪REST2514, and then double-click Restoration.exe.

   Restoration starts (see Figure 12-10).

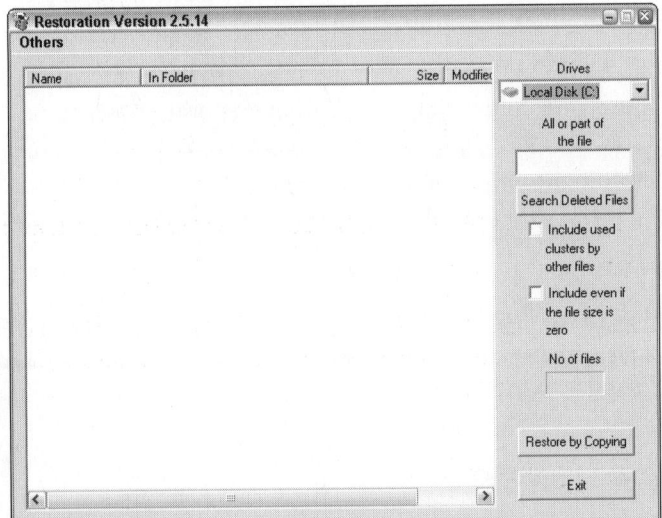

Figure 12-10:
Restoration
is ready to
scan.

9. **In the Drives drop-down list, choose the drive letter for the camera's memory card. Then click Search Deleted Files.**

   Restoration asks if you want to scan vacant clusters.

10. **Click Yes.**

    Restoration scans every nook and cranny of your camera's memory card. That can take a long time. When it's done, you see a list like the one in Figure 12-11.

11. **One by one, click a file you would like to restore and then click the Restore by Copying button.**

    In most cases it's very hard to tell which particular filename belongs to a specific picture (is IMG_1248 the shot of Aunt Gertrude standing on her head?). You may find it easiest to undelete all of the files, although it could take half an hour or longer.

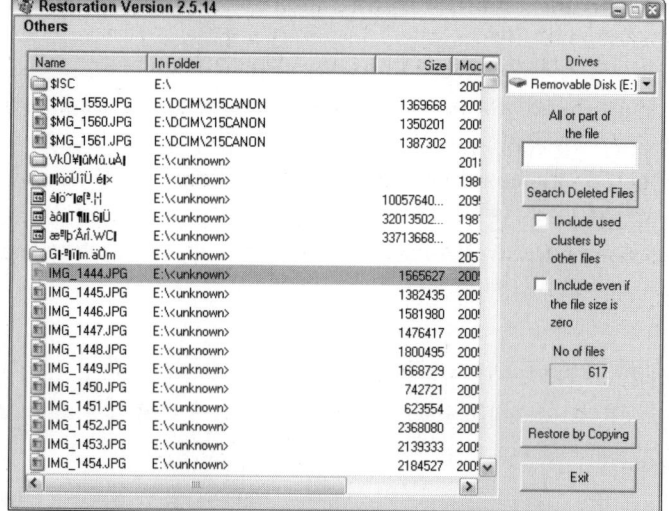

Figure 12-11:
Restoration comes up with a list of pictures that it can probably recover.

12. **Navigate to the place you would like to put the file and then click Save.**

Restoration puts the restored file in the location you specify.

If you're willing to spend $39.95, a product called File Rescue Plus will undelete masses of files, unattended. Details at www.softwareshelf.com.

Resizing Pictures

If you have a moderately well-endowed digital camera, chances are good that each and every picture you take occupies at least 1MB of space. A 1MB file produces downright decent prints at, oh, 8 x 10 inches. But storing, manipulating, and especially e-mailing more than a small handful of 1MB pictures puts the "slug" back in the word "sluggish."

Most of the time you don't need big pictures, and most of the time it's a waste to work with big files. Sending a 1MB close-up of your smiling face may cheer up your ailing great-aunt. Send her ten pictures that size, and she'll turn back into an old grump. For good reason.

Microsoft has a great, free image resizer called, uh, *Image Resizer,* that makes it incredibly easy to turn a high-resolution 1MB artistic masterpiece into a somewhat grainy but infinitely more manageable file, at one-tenth (or even one-hundredth) the size. Here's how to get it:

1. **Start your favorite Web browser and go to** `http://tinyurl.com/` `2meyw`**.**

   If you want to type the "real" address, it's `www.microsoft.com/` `windowsxp/downloads/powertoys/xppowertoys.mspx`.

2. **On the right side of the page, look for the Image Resizer. Click the text that says** `ImageResizer.exe` **and download the file** `ImageResizerPowertoySetup.exe`**.**

   No, I don't know why Microsoft puts one name on the Web page and uses a different name for the file itself.

3. **Run** `ImageResizerPowertoySetup.exe`**.**

   You go through a very brief installation wizard.

4. **Take all the defaults in the wizard and click Finish when it's done.**

   No need to restart your computer.

5. **To use the Image Resizer Powertoy, start with Windows Explorer and navigate to a big picture file (or files) and click to select it (or them).**

   For example, you might click Start⇨My Pictures and go from there. You can choose more than one file by using Ctrl+click or Shift+click or by lassoing them.

6. **Right-click the picture file (or one of the selected files) and choose Resize Pictures.**

   Resize Pictures (see Figure 12-12) is a new option installed by the Image Resizer Powertoy on the pop-up menu for picture files.

   The Image Resizer responds with the Resize Pictures dialog box, shown in Figure 12-13.

7. **Pick the size you want for the resized copy of the picture:**

   - **640 x 480** typically produces files much smaller than 100 kilobytes (K) in size.

   - **800 x 600** makes a copy that's under 200K.

   - **1024 x 768** goes up to 400K.

   - **Custom** is ideal for thumbnail pictures to post on the Web, which typically run 100 x 100 to 200 x 200 pixels.

   Do *not* check the box marked Resize the Original Pictures (Don't Create Copies). If you choose that box, Image Resizer throws away the original file and overwrites it with this smaller file. There's no Undo. You'll never be able to get the original file back again.

8. **Click OK.**

   Image Resizer resizes the image and places the resized copy in the same folder as the original, giving it the original file's name, plus a name that corresponds to the size: (Small), (Medium), (Large), or (Custom).

For example, I resize the file in Figure 12-12 called IMG_0788.JPG and choose Small (800 x 600) for the size. The result (shown in Figure 12-14) is a picture called IMG_0788 (Small).JPG.

The resized file is a picture just like any other picture — it's just smaller and has a lower resolution than the original. For example, the original picture in Figure 12-12 is 1MB, and it looks good when printed as an 8 x 10 glossy. The resized (Small) picture in Figure 12-14 runs 63K, or less than one-fifteenth the size of the original. The little guy's fine for posting on the Web or for e-mailing to friends, but you wouldn't want to print it.

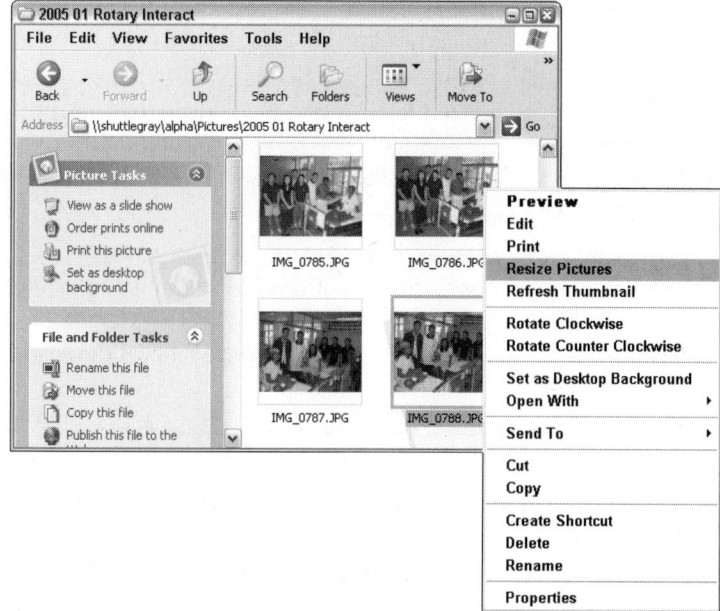

Figure 12-12: To resize, right-click a picture or pictures.

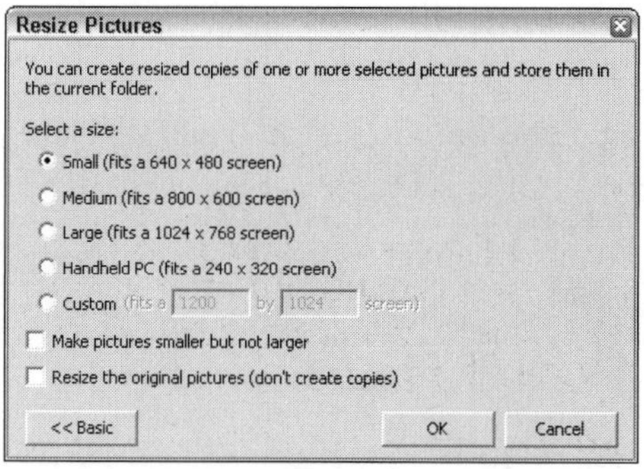

Figure 12-13: Specify the number of pixels in the resized picture.

Figure 12-14:
The resized
image gets
a name
similar to
the original.

Image Resizer doesn't change the type of picture file — if you start out with a Windows Bitmap, the resized file is a Windows Bitmap. Because some file formats are inherently more efficient than others, storing better-quality pictures in less space, the lack of a file type translation capability puts a big crimp on Image Resizer.

If you have a Windows Bitmap, TIFF, or GIF file, and you want to shrink it significantly, try converting the file to a JPG before running Image Resizer. See the next section for details on how to perform the conversion.

Converting Picture File Formats

Picture files come in many different flavors. You may have heard of them: JPEG (.jpg files), TIFFs (.tif), and GIFs (.gif) are the most widespread. Native Windows Bitmap (.bmp) files can be huge, but they contain all the color information in the original. There are many more.

The fundamental trade-off in any picture storage scheme is size versus picture quality. Some formats (such as JPEG) allow you to specify, to some extent, how much you're willing to sacrifice in quality in order to make a smaller file.

Long the 98-pound weakling of the Windows team, Windows Paint now sports a few worthwhile features. With Windows Paint, you can open or save files in JPEG, GIF, TIFF, PNG, or Windows Bitmap formats. Two problems: It isn't smart enough to let you specify compression levels for JPEGs, and it won't let you store in compressed TIF format.

Changing file formats with Paint

Changing file formats within those rather narrow limits is quite easy:

1. **Choose Start➪All Programs➪Accessories➪Paint.**

   Windows Paint appears.

2. **Open the file you want to convert.**

3. **Click Files➪Save As.**

4. **In the Save As Type drop-down list, choose the format you want to convert to and then type a name for the file and click Save.**

   Paint performs the conversion.

If you have something more than Paint can handle — particularly if you want to compress your JPEG files or if you need to work with multipage TIFs (which are commonly seen in fax programs and scanners with Automatic Document Feeders) — you need a far more capable program. I use the free IrfanView, from Irfan Skiljan (`www.irfanview.com`). Downloading and installing IrfanView is a breeze. Be sure to get the free Plugins and AddOns while you're at it.

Saving the contents of the Clipboard as a picture file

Sometimes you want to save the contents of the Clipboard as a picture file in JPEG, TIF, GIF, or BMP format. Doing so isn't as simple as pasting the contents of the Clipboard into a blank Paint picture, because Paint insists on drawing a white "canvas" that can extend beyond the bottom or the right edge of the picture you paste.

There's a trick. To save the contents of the Clipboard as a picture file:

1. **Choose Start➪All Programs➪Accessories➪Paint.**

   Windows Paint starts.

2. **Click Image➪Attributes.**

   Paint shows you the Attributes dialog box (see Figure 12-15).

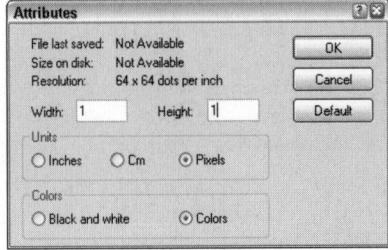

Figure 12-15:
Give Paint a
very, very
tiny canvas.

3. **In the box marked Width, type 1. In the box marked Height, type 1. Click OK.**

   You go back to Paint — but now the "canvas" is 1 pixel high and 1 pixel wide.

4. **Click Edit⇨Paste. Your picture gets pasted into the document, with no white edge at the bottom or on the right.**

   From that point, you can use the picture in any way you like — cut, copy, paste, save — the whole nine yards.

 Windows Paint stores the size of the current canvas and uses it when you start Paint again. So if you always want to start with a 1-by-1 pixel canvas, repeat the preceding steps, and at the end of Step 3, choose File⇨Exit. No need to Save Changes to the (blank) picture. The next time you start Paint, it'll have a tiny canvas.

Part IV
Modding to Monitor and Manage

The 5th Wave   By Rich Tennant

"I'm not say I belive in anything. All I know is, since it's been there, Windows XP has been running 50% faster."

In this part . . .

Somebody has to be in charge, right?

Hey, I've got a crazy idea. Why don't *you* take charge of your computer? Watch how your system performs. Keep on top of your disks. Zap out the programs that sneak into your computer every time you boot.

And if you run into trouble, do you have a friend who can lend a hand? If you and your friend are online at the same time, you can set things up so she can take over your computer, remotely, securely, and show you how to solve your problems.

Chapter 13

Seeing What's Happening

....

In This Chapter

▶ Looking behind the scenes with Windows Event Viewer

▶ Dealing with hellacious hardware hassles

▶ Getting a bird's-eye view of running programs

▶ Zapping wayward startup programs

▶ Dropping back ten yards 'n' punting in Safe Mode

....

Admit it. You know that demons lurk within Windows. Big, snarly, voracious demons that delight in driving you nuts. This chapter introduces you to several big sticks that may help you keep the demons at bay.

Or maybe not.

Windows hides a few tools away from the everyday punter. Most of the time you don't need them — in fact, if you change things willy-nilly, these tools can help you screw up your system royally. But when you need a big stick, they can become your best allies.

Using Windows Event Viewer

Windows keeps track of events: when it starts, how it connects to other computers, whether a hard drive is having trouble, when the system clock gets updated, how often your daughter's Little League team came in first. That sort of thing.

To be more precise, Windows keeps three event logs — one each for the system itself; for security-related events; and for applications running on your computer (although the "applications" involved are frequently part of Windows).

Opening the event logs from the Start menu

Every Windows user (at least, every user who has the good sense not to go ballistic when he sees an innocuous error message) should scan the event logs from time to time. I describe how to put the Windows Event Viewer on the Start menu in Chapter 5, but here's the fast way:

1. **Right-click the Start button and choose Properties.**

   Windows shows you the Taskbar and Start Menu Properties dialog box.

2. **Click Customize⇨Advanced.**

   You see the Customize Start Menu dialog box, shown in Figure 13-1.

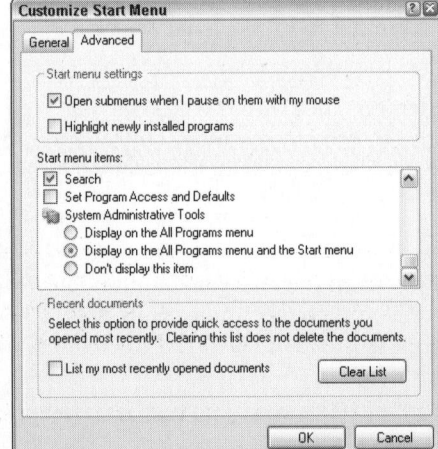

Figure 13-1:
Making it easy to see the event logs from the Start menu.

3. **At the very bottom of the Start Menu Items list, click the button in front of `Display on the All Programs Menu and the Start menu`.**

   If you don't expect to look at the event log very often, you can just put it on the All Programs menu, but I find it most useful to stick it on Start, too. There's usually extra room on the right side of the Start menu anyway.

4. **Click OK twice.**

   A new Administrative Tools item appears on the right side of the Start menu.

Poking around Windows Event Viewer

Once you have the Administrative Tools line on your Start menu (or at least in All Programs), it's easy to start playing with Windows Event Viewer:

1. **Choose Start➪Administrative Tools➪Event Viewer.**

   Windows Event Viewer appears (see Figure 13-2).

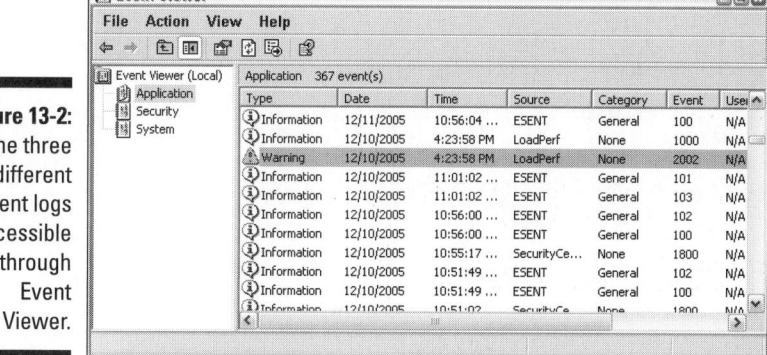

Figure 13-2: The three different event logs accessible through Event Viewer.

Does Event Viewer look a bit familiar? You may have seen something like it before. In fact, Windows Event Viewer is a snap-in program for Microsoft Management Console. The MMC appears in many different places within Windows, but you see it only if you're digging deep inside the belly of the beast.

2. **On the left, double-click Application so you can see the application event log.**

3. **If you bump into an entry that looks interesting, double-click it for details.**

   Most of the entries abound with dense gobbledygook. In Figure 13-3, I double-click the Warning entry shown in Figure 13-2.

4. **DON'T PANIC. If you look at enough Application event logs, you ultimately discover that they overflow with warnings and errors that require absolutely no action on your part. When you're done looking at the Event Properties details, click Cancel and go back to Event Viewer.**

   For example, the warning shown in Figure 13-3 was triggered by Outlook not being activated on this particular computer. You can "Contact the vendor of this service for additional information," as the warning message suggests, but if you do, the vendor — Microsoft — is likely to respond with a resounding yawn.

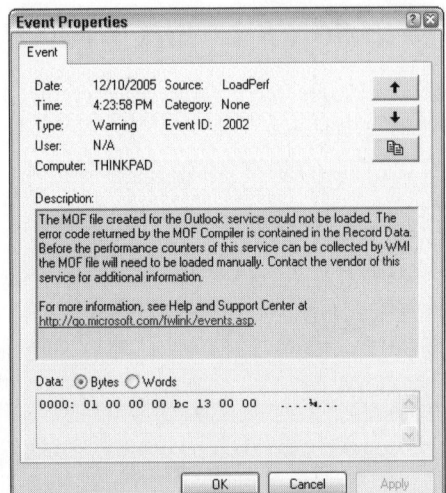

Figure 13-3:
The warning
shown in
Figure 13-2.

5. Double-click the Security line on the left.

It's unusual to have an entry in the Security log. If you see one, you should take it seriously. The Security log tells you if someone attempted to log on to your computer but didn't have the right password or if someone tried to open a folder that isn't being shared.

6. Double-click the System line on the left.

Again, you see many entries, and probably more than a few are marked Warning or Error. Those are worth perusing.

7. As curiosity and time allow, double-click warning and error entries.

Most of the entries aren't very interesting. For example, Figure 13-4 shows a W32Time warning. You might be momentarily alarmed with this kind of message, but it would behoove you to do the math. In this case, the clock hadn't been synchronized in 13 hours because the Internet connection was down. I figure the clock might've lost a tenth of a millisecond in the interim. Unsynchronized? Well, yes. Sorta.

On the other hand, some entries can help you pinpoint problems before they spread. For example, the error message shown in Figure 13-5 pointed me to a CD with a bad block.

8. If you find a warning or error entry that alarms you, click the link to go to Help and Support Center.

Windows Event Viewer tells you what information it intends to send to Microsoft.

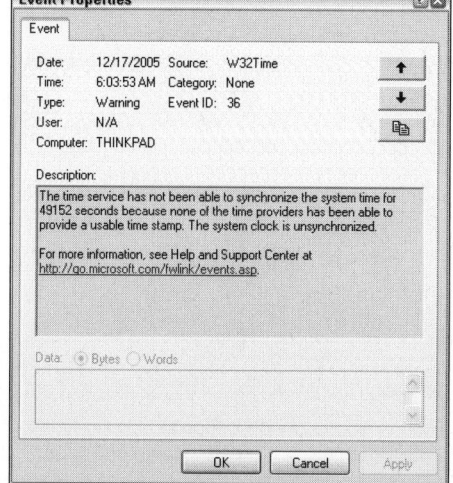

Figure 13-4:
The clock
hasn't been
updated in,
what, 13
hours?

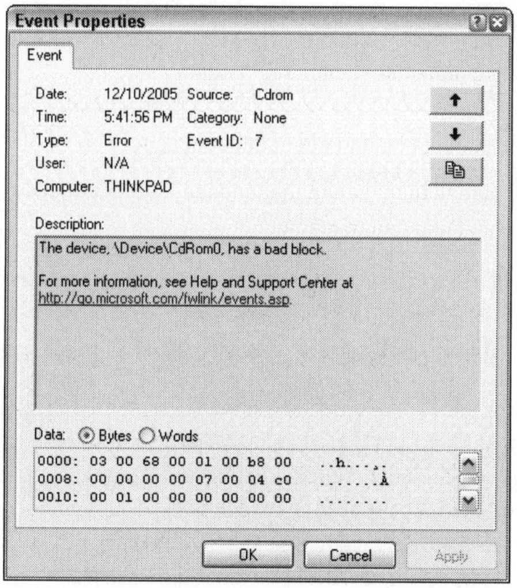

Figure 13-5:
Behind-the-
scenes info:
a bad block
on a CD.

9. **If you feel that the info isn't very sensitive (hint: it never is), click OK.**

Windows Event Viewer transports you to a Web site at www.microsoft.com, but all you see is a Help and Support Center entry for this specific problem, as shown in Figure 13-6.

In this case, I find that a CD has a bad sector. Fortunately, I could copy all of it to a hard drive and reburn the CD.

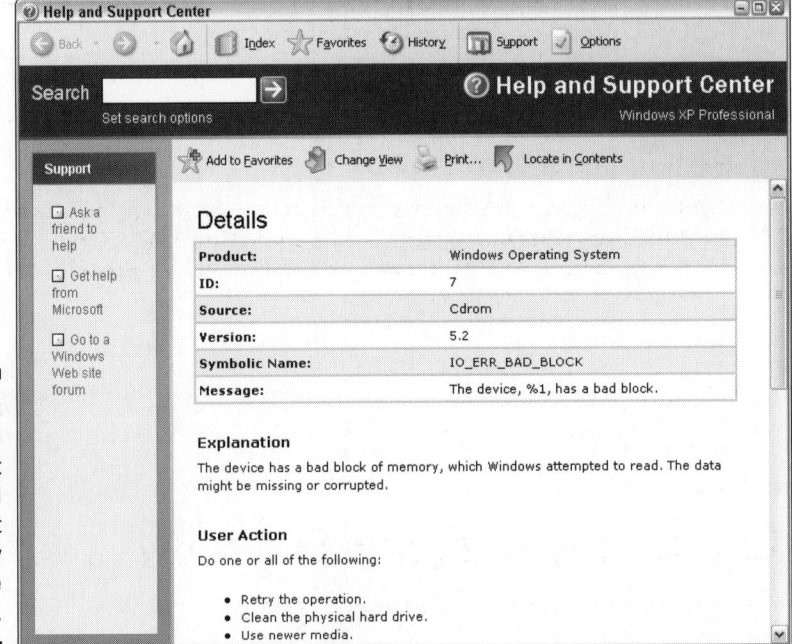

Figure 13-6:
The
Microsoft
Help and
Support
Center entry
for the
problem.

10. **Click "X" to get out of Help and Support Center and then click OK to dismiss the Event Properties dialog box.**

11. **When you finish with Event Viewer, click File⇨Exit to get out.**

In addition to checking the official Microsoft report on the error code via Help and Support Center (Step 8 of the preceding list), you can glean much insight from a Web site devoted exclusively to Windows Event Viewer shenanigans: EventID.net asks you to type in the event ID (in Figure 13-5, that's 7), and produces lots of details, comments, and links to related articles.

If you get a repeated error, or if a hardware or software manufacturer asks you to send them a copy of your event log, there's a specific procedure you must follow.

Don't bother copying any of the three event files with Windows Explorer. If you copy and then restore any .evt file, Windows Event Viewer claims it's corrupt.

Saving a log file

To save a log file:

1. **Start Windows Event Viewer (for example, by choosing Start⇨ Administrative Tools⇨Event Viewer).**

2. **Click one of the three event logs: Application, Security, or System.**

   You can't save all three at once.

3. **Choose Action⇨Save Log File As.**

4. **Choose native `.evt` format (which can be read only by Windows Event Viewer or a third-party tool that understands such things) or a tab- or comma-delimited text file (which can be read by almost anything — even Excel).**

5. **Click Save.**

   Event Viewer saves a backup copy.

6. **Click File⇨Exit to get out of Windows Event Viewer.**

Hardware Troubleshooting with Windows Device Manager

Back in the early days of Windows, nearly every hardware hiccup dictated an immediate trip to Windows Device Manager. Not so anymore. Thank your lucky stars that twiddling IRQs and I/O addresses and other worse-than-senseless things have gone the way of the dodo. At least, to a first approximation.

These days, Windows Device Manager primarily comes into play when a driver isn't working. Tracing down aberrant drivers, updating them, and rolling back when the "new" driver is (invariably) worse than the "old" driver is a complex subject, which I cover in Technique 58 of *Windows XP Timesaving Techniques For Dummies* (also published by Wiley).

There are several hacks and mods for Device Manager that go beyond the usual call of duty, as I describe in the following sections.

Making it easy to start Device Manager

Most people hunt and peck through many levels of Control Panel before they finally figure out how to start it. If you follow the instructions in the preceding section and put Administrative Tools on your Start menu, launching Device Manager is as simple as clicking Start⇨Administrative Tools⇨ Computer Management and then clicking Device Manager on the left (see Figure 13-7).

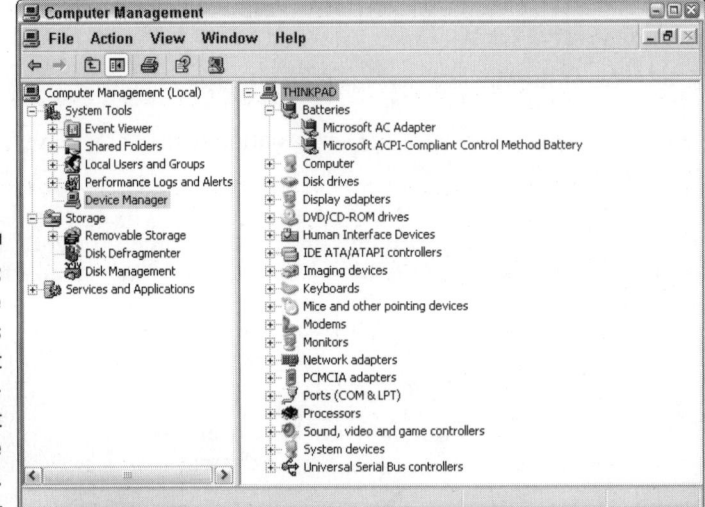

Figure 13-7:
Device
Manager as
a Microsoft
Manage-
ment
Console
plug-in.

Taking full advantage of Device Manager views

If you click View⇨Resources by Connection, Device Manager shows you an extensive list of memory locations, IRQ lines, and the like — all the stuff that's assigned automatically by Plug 'n' Play. That can help trace down problems with older (pre-Plug 'n' Play, which is to say, ancient) hardware.

Looking up Device Manager error codes

If any device appears in the Device Manager list with a yellow exclamation point (!), Windows had trouble getting the device to work. Double-click the exclamation point, and an error code appears in the Device Status box. You can look up the error and see what Microsoft recommends to fix it by using the (free!) *Windows Resource Kit* available online at www.microsoft.com/resources/documentation/Windows/XP/all/reskit/en-us/prjk_dec_lgsc.asp.

Check for "ghosted" hardware

Sometimes Windows gets confused with hardware that was once installed and no longer exists. At times, Windows "knows" that a device is there — using specific system resources, possibly tromping on other hardware — but doesn't show you any details in Device Manager. If you think you may be having problems with ghosts, try this procedure and see if you can scare up the dearly departed device:

1. **Choose Start➪All Programs➪Accessories➪Command Prompt.**

   Windows shows you the current incarnation of the DOS command line.

2. **Type** set devmgr_show_nonpresent_devices=1 **and press Enter.**

   Windows hesitates for a split second and then comes back. Your command just set something called an "environment variable," which communicates with Device Manager.

3. **Type** devmgmt.msc **and press Enter.**

   You see Device Manager.

4. **Choose View➪Show Hidden Devices.**

   Device Manager shows you all of the hardware that it was hiding (see Figure 13-8).

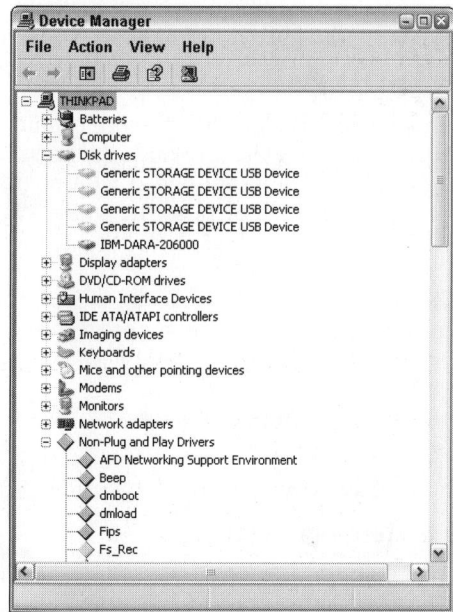

Figure 13-8:
Ghosted devices are grayed out.

Ghosted devices appear with a gray icon. In Figure 13-8, for example, you can see a bunch of disk drives that Windows reserved for USB disks that currently aren't plugged into the computer.

5. **If you see a piece of ghosted hardware that might be causing a conflict, right-click it and choose Uninstall.**

Windows asks you to confirm the removal. Click OK and all vestiges of the ghosted device disappear.

6. **Click File➪Exit to get out of Device Manager. If you deleted a ghosted device, restart your PC just to make sure the ghoul is gone.**

Controlling Applications with Task Manager

Many people don't realize that you can adjust Windows' priorities to make a program you choose run faster than it normally would. That's just one of Task Manager's many tricks.

When you see some of the inner workings of your computer, you may be alarmed. Don't be. As long as you promise that you won't shave your head, put on sackcloth and ashes, and start some sort of exorcism when you see how many `svchost.exe` programs are running, I promise to show you how to use Task Manager to speed up individual programs at the expense of others. Fair deal?

As I explain in Chapter 2, Windows programs, when they're running, act like amoebae in the Windows Primordial Ooze. One of Windows' most important jobs involves acting like the guy with the microphone at an Amoeba Karaoke Bar: Windows has to let each amoeba run, in turn, so the whole system keeps working.

Windows plays by *Animal Farm* rules: Some amoebae are more equal than others. Here's how to manually nudge your favorite amoeba so it gets preferential treatment:

1. **Hold down the Ctrl and Alt keys and press Delete.**

   Windows Task Manager appears. (Alternatively, you can right-click any empty part of the Windows taskbar and choose Task Manager.)

2. **Click the Applications tab (see Figure 13-9).**

   Task Manager shows you which programs are running. In Figure 13-9, I want to goose Microsoft Access so it gets a higher priority and thus runs faster than it normally would.

3. **Right-click the program you want to have a higher priority and then choose Go to Process.**

   Task Manager takes you to the process — the actual program — that's associated with the application. In Figure 13-10, I go to MSACCESS.EXE, which is the program . . . er, process running Access.

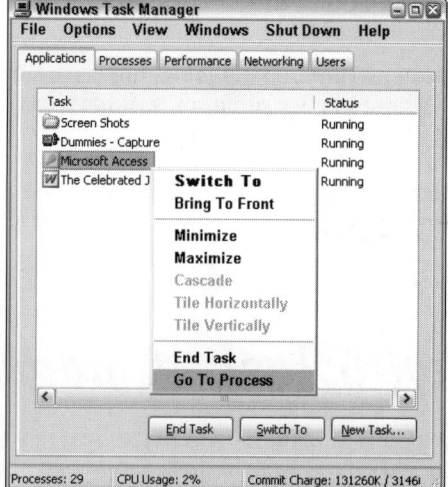

Figure 13-9:
Making
Access run
faster than it
normally
would.

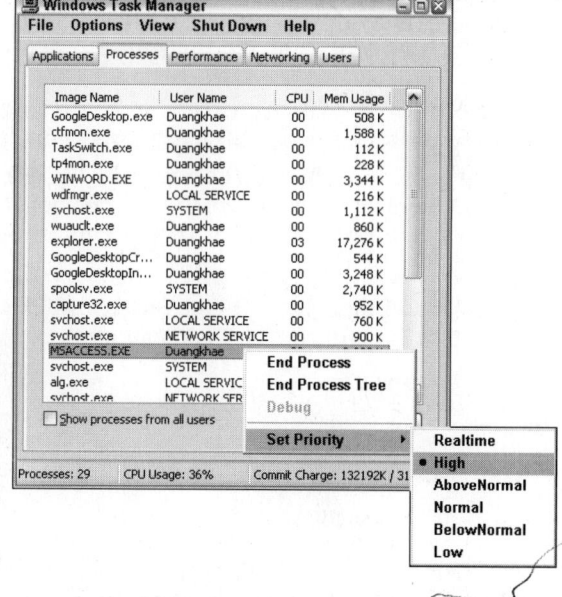

Figure 13-10:
Manually
setting
priorities
in Task
Manager.

4. **Right-click the process and choose Set Priority➪High.**

Do *not* use Realtime. Windows has a disconcerting habit of crashing and burning when one of its applications runs at the damn-the-torpedoes rating called Realtime.

Windows warns you that *Changing the priority class of this process may cause undesired results, including halitosis, incongruence, and an outbreak of psoriasis.*

5. Click Yes to clear the warning box and then choose File⇨Exit Task Manager to get out of Task Manager.

As long as the program keeps running, it has the highest priority of all application programs. (If you exit the program, you have to go through this process all over again.)

The program you set at high priority should run noticeably faster, although all the other programs on your computer will run slower. Think of it as amoeba *quid pro quo.*

Tracking Memory with Task Manager

If your computer gets bogged down *paging* — which is to say, moving data from *physical* memory (fast RAM chips) to slow *virtual* memory (on hard drives) — adding memory can boost your computer's performance more than any ten bit-twiddling tricks you'll ever encounter. Of course, that begs the question: How do you know when your computer gets bogged down paging?

Windows already has all the tools you need, but there are several tricks:

1. Wait until you're doing real work.

The best time to check on your system's memory demand is when you're in the middle of doing something that you normally do. For example, if you frequently leave Outlook and a couple of utilities running, and you use Photoshop with big pictures, wait until you start Photoshop and open a big picture.

2. Hold down Ctrl and Alt and then press Delete (or right-click any empty part of the Windows taskbar and choose Task Manager).

Windows Task Manager appears.

3. Click the Performance tab.

Windows shows you its performance monitor, which tracks memory usage (see Figure 13-11).

The *Total Commit Charge* tracks how much total memory the computer uses, both physical memory (the fast chips) and virtual memory (slow hard drives). *Peak Commit Charge* shows you the maximum value of the Total Commit Charge — it's the high water mark since the last time you logged on.

The *PF Usage* bar just tracks the Total Commit Charge. The *Page File Usage History* line seems to show the history of the PF Usage bar, but Microsoft doesn't document the graph — much less provide a description of the vertical axis — so it's hard to tell for sure what the graph shows.

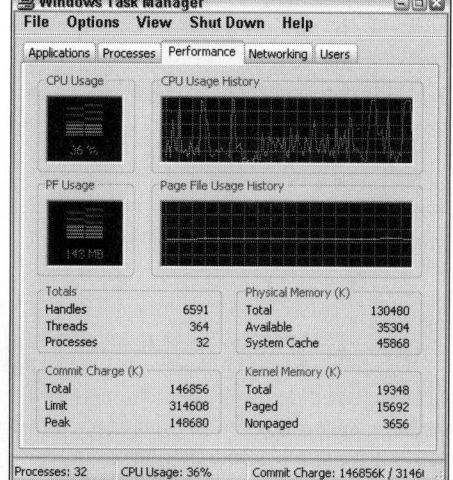

Figure 13-11:
Task
Manager's
Performance
tab keeps
track of
memory
usage.

4. **Check for these problem signs:**

  • If the Total Commit Charge commonly exceeds the Total Physical Memory, you may be able to speed up your computer significantly by buying more (or larger) memory chips.

  • In my experience, systems that need more memory usually show a Page File Usage History line that consistently goes above the halfway point. Unfortunately, the official documentation is so bad, it's hard to tell where to draw the line between "OK" and "too much."

  • If the Peak Commit Charge is close to the Limit Commit Charge, you're running out of room for virtual memory. Don't be alarmed — Windows allocates more space if it needs the room — but if it happens regularly and you have a lot of hard drive space, you should consider increasing the size of your page file. See the upcoming sidebar, "Beefing up your swap file."

In Figure 13-11, Total and Peak Commit Charges run 146MB to 148MB. The computer has 130MB. (Actually it has 128MB; the difference is due to the translation of 1,024K = 1MB.) The Page File Usage History line teeters around the halfway point. This computer running this workload could probably benefit from more memory, but the results wouldn't be very dramatic.

5. **If you're looking for a quick fix — you don't have the time or the money to add more memory — click the Processes tab in Windows Task Manager (refer to Figure 13-10) and then click the Mem Usage column header twice.**

Windows shows you a list of all the running processes, with the biggest memory hogs listed first.

Beefing up your swap file

So much has been written about hacking the Windows paging file that it's a wonder half the PCs in the universe don't crash. Here's the hard, cold truth: Changing Windows XP's virtual memory settings rarely produces any benefit whatsoever, and eliminating the paging file runs right up there with diving headfirst into a pond to gauge its depth.

Sometimes you have to change your swap file settings. For example, if you're running out of room on your C: drive and you want Windows to use your fast, new, empty D: drive, changing the swap file over makes sense. If Windows constantly bumps up against the maximum swap file size, making the swap file bigger makes sense. But hacking the Registry to tweak a virtual memory setting? Gimme a break.

If you need to make changes to the way Windows handles virtual memory, choose Start, right-click My Computer, choose Properties, click Advanced, and then in the Performance box click Settings. In the Performance Options dialog box, click Advanced, and then in the Virtual Memory box, click Change. Have at it, but don't say I didn't warn ya.

6. **For a quick fix, shut down any programs that appear high on the Memory Usage list. Then choose File⇨Exit to get out of Windows Task Manager.**

Memory shortage tends to be a chronic problem with only one solution: Buy more memory.

Tracking CPU Usage with Task Manager

Have you ever wondered why your computer went out to lunch? You click something, and the monitor just sits there and stares at you for 10 or 20 or 30 seconds (or 30 *hours,* for that matter) before anything worthwhile happens?

Most of the time, intermittent freezes happen while Windows waits for something — a slow Internet connection; a dozen programs trying to get at the hard drive at the same time; or an antivirus, spyware, or search scanning program that kicks in at an inopportune moment. But some of the time, Windows locks up because a program grabs the processor and only sporadically and briefly lets go.

That's called *red-lining* — a program comes in, takes over, and won't let go. Microsoft has drawn the ire of more than a few customers by releasing patches to Windows that cause common programs to red-line. The clincher? Usually you can't tell if a program has taken over or if Windows is merely sitting there, fat dumb and happy, waiting for the Internet to respond.

Once again, Windows Task Manager can help:

1. **If you think a program may be red-lining your computer, hold down Ctrl and Alt and press Delete. Or you can right-click any empty part of the Windows taskbar and choose Task Manager.**

   Sometimes you can get Windows to react to pressing the keys; sometimes it's easier to click.

2. **Click Performance.**

   Windows brings up the performance monitor shown in Figure 13-11.

3. **Double-click anywhere near one of the four graphs.**

   Task Manager shows you a detailed graph of your current processor usage and the recent history. Figure 13-12 shows repeated journeys into the red-line zone, where CPU usage hit 100%.

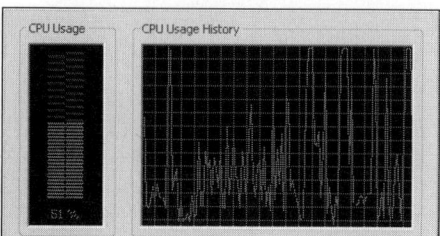

Figure 13-12: When CPU Usage hits 100%, Windows can appear to freeze.

4. **Double-click anywhere near one of the CPU Usage graphs.**

   Task Manager goes back to normal.

5. **Click the Processes tab and then click the CPU column heading twice.**

   Task Manager shows you a list of processes, in order by the amount of CPU time they're using.

6. **Shut down any offending processes, if you can. I generally proceed in this sequence:**

   • Try to shut down a red-lining program "normally" by going to the program and choosing File➪Exit (or something similar).

- If that doesn't work, right-click the program in the Windows taskbar and choose Close.

- If that doesn't work, try killing the program on the Applications tab in the Task Manager.

- If that doesn't work, right-click the process on the Processes tab in Task Manager and choose End Process.

7. Get out of Task Manager by choosing File⇨Exit.

It's always a good idea to restart your computer (or at least log out and log back on) after you manually kill a running process.

 You can tell Windows to leave the CPU monitor running in the System Tray, next to the clock, by clicking the Minimize button in the Task Manager, located in the upper-right corner of the window.

Chapter 14

Decoding IDs, Accounts, and Passwords

*S*omeday computers will recognize you by the sound of your voice, your fingerprint, or the wrinkles in the bags under your eyes. No doubt that when the time comes, Microsoft will maintain the largest eye-bag-wrinkle database in the world, and your personal copy of Windows will work only if you avoid blinking at inopportune moments.

This chapter covers the way people identify themselves to Windows — for the purpose of proving to Microsoft that it has extracted the proper pound of flesh and for keeping multiple users on a particular computer from stepping all over one another.

Activating and Reactivating Windows

Microsoft can wrap a million marketing weasel words around it, but the Windows Genuine Advantage program means just one thing to most Windows users: If you don't have a bought-and-paid-for copy of Windows XP running on your machine, you're going to get hung out to dry. You won't be able to apply updates to your copy of Windows — even patch major security holes.

Microsoft has published reams of information about Windows XP Product Activation — and all of their claims about privacy and minimal gathering of information about a particular computer appear to be accurate. (Although you can take the claims about minimal impact on legitimate customers with a grain of salt; see later in this section.) If you want to go through the details, start at `www.microsoft.com/piracy/activation_how.mspx` and follow the list of FAQs and Myths on the right.

The proverbial bottom line: When you activate Windows, you tie one specific copy of the software to one specific PC. There are three ways to acquire Windows XP, each with its own activation idiosyncrasies:

- ✓ **Buy a shrink-wrapped copy of Windows XP** and install it on your machine, either as an upgrade to an older version of Windows or as a brand-spanking-new operating system.

- ✓ **Buy a new PC with Windows XP preinstalled.** Usually the hardware manufacturer activates Windows for you. But therein lies the rub. Several rubs, in fact, particularly if you need to reinstall Windows and don't have the tools or magic incantations to re-activate it.

- ✓ **Buy a license for multiple copies of Windows XP.** Microsoft's volume licensing arrangement can cover as few as five copies of Windows.

Activating shrink-wrapped Windows

If you bought Windows XP from a store, the CD came with a yellow sticker that contains a 25-character product key, such as T9TRD-9CTTR-V8X7W-R8888-6TPYR. You install Windows XP, go through activation, and all is well with the world.

Even if your C: drive dies, as long as you use the same product key that you originally used to install Windows, and you install from the same CD, activation goes through without a hitch. And *that's* the problem. You have to use the same product key and the same CD. If you have four different Windows XP CDs hanging around and you don't know which one was used on which computer — or if you lost the jewel case/cardboard folder for the CD that you need to rescue — life gets real difficult, real fast.

Fortunately, a little program called Magical Jelly Bean Keyfinder from Aleks Ozolins can tell you what product key was used to install Windows XP on your PC. Here's how to get it:

1. **Fire up your favorite Web browser and head to** `www.magicaljellybean.com/keyfinder.shtml`.

2. **Click one of the download buttons and save the `.zip` file.**

   As of this writing, the latest version is `kf141.zip`.

3. **Double-click the `.zip` file and then double-click the `keyfinder.exe` installer.**

   Keyfinder runs and shows you the product key that was used to install Windows on this machine (see Figure 14-1).

4. **Write down the key. Now. While you're thinking about it. Then click File⇨Exit to leave Keyfinder.**

Figure 14-1:
Magical
Jelly Bean
Keyfinder
retrieves
Windows
XP product
keys.

Armed with the correct CD and the correct product key, you can reinstall Windows XP as many times as you like, and activation poses no problem at all.

Have an activation problem? *Call Microsoft.* The telephone number for your locale appears whenever an activation attempt fails. In my experience, if you have an explanation that doesn't involve little green men dancing the booga-loo on your keyboard, the 'Softies will get you a new key in no time flat. You can even tell them the truth — say, that the PC you originally used to activate Windows self-immolated — and they'll probably believe you.

At least in theory, the license for a shrink-wrapped copy of Windows XP is transferable if your old PC bites the dust. Although there's no set procedure to "deactivate" an activated copy of Windows XP, you should have few problems dealing with legitimately expired hardware. Get on the phone and ask.

Dealing with preinstalled Windows

If you buy a new PC with Windows XP preinstalled, all the rules change. First and foremost, the license for Windows XP that comes with the PC holds only for that PC: If the computer goes swimming with the dolphins at Sea World, you can't transfer the Windows license to a different PC.

With rare exceptions, the copy of Windows that comes with a new PC is pre-registered — inextricably associated with your computer's BIOS — so you don't need to deal with activation, product keys, or any of that folderol.

Or do you?

Here's the problem. PC manufacturers are cheap. So cheap they squeak. When you buy a new PC, you not only get lots of useless software (see Chapter 3), but you frequently also get a hidden partition on a hard drive crammed full of the same junk — occupying space you paid for — and there's no Windows XP recovery CD in sight.

Without a Windows XP CD, you have no way to perform a clean install of Windows. At best, if your system goes belly-up, the system manufacturer tells you to use the hidden partition to wipe out everything on your hard drive and reinstall the same junk you started with. Not a good solution. Sure, your copy of Windows gets reactivated automatically, but all that junk comes back to haunt you again.

An increasing number of manufacturers (now including DELL and Sony) prompt you to create a Windows XP installation CD as soon as you start your PC: Click a few buttons, stick a CD in the drive, and in a few minutes you have a preactivated backup copy of Windows XP on the CD that'll only install on that specific PC.

Far too often, though, you're left high and dry, particularly if your C: drive gives up. I recently had that problem with a Toshiba laptop. Here's how I navigated the activation gauntlet:

1. **My C: drive came to an abrupt, grinding halt. No chance to retrieve any data or programs before its untimely demise. I took the PC to my local Best Buy and had them install a new C: drive.**

2. **I took a handy Windows XP CD, which had already been activated on another PC, and installed it on the fresh new hard drive.**

3. **At the end of the installation routine Windows asked if I wanted to activate. I responded No, Not Yet.**

   That bought 30 days — the period of time you can run Windows without activating it — and the clock started ticking.

4. **I contacted the store that sold me the laptop. They were out of business. I contacted Toshiba and asked for a recovery CD. No luck. I begged, pleaded, and cajoled. Zip.**

   There's no reason to even try to activate Windows XP using the product key on the sticker attached to the bottom of the computer. Why? That product key only works with the right CD — and Toshiba didn't send it to me.

Similarly, there's no reason to try to activate Windows XP using the product key on the CD. Why? It had already been activated, on an entirely different PC.

5. **The day before Windows' 30-day expiration came up, I followed the instructions to activate online, failed, and called the product activation number on the screen.**

   The clerk on the phone listened to my tale of woe, asked me to read her the product key for the CD that I used, and had me activated in about five minutes. No questions, no hassles.

Microsoft has problems with counterfeit copies of Windows, but individuals attempting to activate Windows on a PC that came with Windows preactivated should have no difficulties at all. Er, providing you have an extra Windows CD hanging around.

Using volume licenses

Volume licenses rate as a completely different kettle of fish.

When a company (or an individual, for that matter) orders a volume license, they receive a single copy of Windows XP and a product key that bypasses activation entirely. You can install and reinstall Windows *ad infinitum,* and never be asked to activate your copy.

That's why pirates love VL versions of Windows. If you, uh, acquire a pirate copy of Windows XP that never asks to be activated, you are probably using a purloined VL product key. And if your key starts out with FCKGW-RHQQ2-YXRKT-BTG6W-?????, congratulations — you have a bogus VL product key that's been used millions and millions of times.

If you have a pirate VL product key and you want to replace it with a good one — that is, if you've gone out and bought a volume license, and now have a legitimate VL product key — changing your computer over to the new VL key is easy:

1. **Install and run Magical Jelly Bean Keyfinder, as described earlier in this chapter in the "Activating shrink-wrapped Windows" section.**

2. **In Keyfinder, click Options⇨Change Windows Key.**

   Keyfinder shows you the dialog box in Figure 14-2.

3. **Enter the new, valid key in the five boxes and then click Close.**

   Keyfinder changes your key.

Figure 14-2:
Magical
Jelly Bean
Keyfinder
will even
change
Volume
License
product
keys.

> **Change Microsoft Windows XP Key** ☒
>
> [   ] [   ] [   ] [   ] [   ]
>
> [Change] [Close]
>
> The Keyfinder uses scripts provided by Microsoft to change the
> key. For more information, please see this article.

4. **Choose File⇨Exit to get out of Keyfinder and then restart your computer.**

   The new key is in effect.

Microsoft has detailed instructions for manually performing the same process, at support.microsoft.com/kb/328874. But Keyfinder is much simpler.

If you have a pirated copy of Windows with a bogus VL key (in other words, if you installed Windows from scratch but were never asked to activate Windows) and you want to switch from a pirated copy to a legit copy without completely wiping out your hard drive and starting all over, you have to perform an In-Place Upgrade of Windows.

Here's how:

1. **Buy a legitimate copy of Windows XP that matches the version of Windows you're using — Home or Professional.**

2. **Start the pirated copy of Windows.**

3. **Put the new Windows XP CD in the drive.**

   You see a window that says Welcome to Microsoft Windows XP / What do you want to do?

4. **Click Install Windows XP.**

   The installer gathers some information and then shows a Welcome to Windows Setup screen.

5. **Choose Upgrade (Recommended) in the Installation Type box and then click Next.**

   The installer shows a typical License Agreement page.

6. **Click the button marked I Accept this Agreement and then click Next.**

   The installer asks for your product key.

7. **Enter the new, good product key. Then click Next.**

   The installer asks if you want to reach out over the Internet to retrieve the latest setup files.

8. **Click Yes, Download the Updated Setup Files (Recommended) and then click Next.**

   Windows goes through a lengthy file copying process.

9. **Take all the defaults. If your computer restarts and you're invited to Press Any Key to Boot From CD, do *not* press any key.**

   Eventually, Windows reboots your computer and you are invited to activate Windows over the Internet.

Changing Registered User and Organization

Want to know who's the registered owner of your computer? Click Start, right-click My Computer, and choose Properties. There in the Registered To block (see Figure 14-3) sit the name of the person who supposedly owns the machine and his or her company.

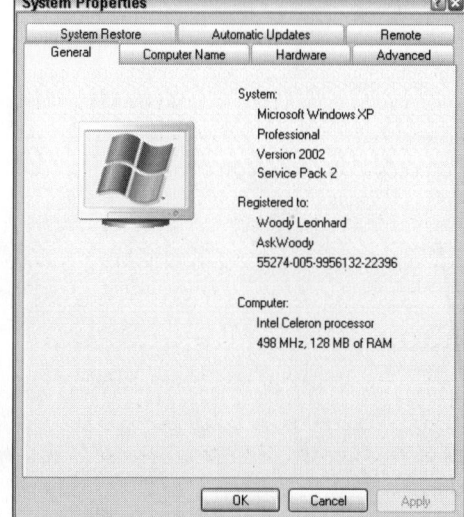

Figure 14-3:
The registered user and company may surprise you.

It always tickles me to find computers that are registered to "A Satisfied DELL User" or "Toshiba Customer" or "Duped Slave to Last Year's Technology."

The *Registered Owner* and *Registered Company* stored away in the Windows Registry have a strange habit of popping up in unusual places. Many programs adopt the names when they're installed, as if they had some bearing on reality.

If the registered names on your computer leave something to be desired, you can set them straight. (Or you can change them to *Weird Al Yankovic / Princeton Institute for Advanced Studies*, if you like.) Here's how:

1. **Follow the steps in Chapter 24 in this book to start the Registry editor.**

2. **On the left, double-click to navigate down to `HKEY_LOCAL_MACHINE\ SOFTWARE\Microsoft\Windows NT\CurrentVersion`.**

   Yes, you read that correctly. Windows NT.

3. **On the right, double-click RegisteredOrganization and change the Value Data to whatever text you would like to appear. Click OK.**

4. **On the right, double-click RegisteredOwner and change the Value Data to whatever text you would like to appear. Click OK.**

5. **Choose File⇨Exit to leave the Registry editor.**

   Your new settings take effect immediately (see Figure 14-4).

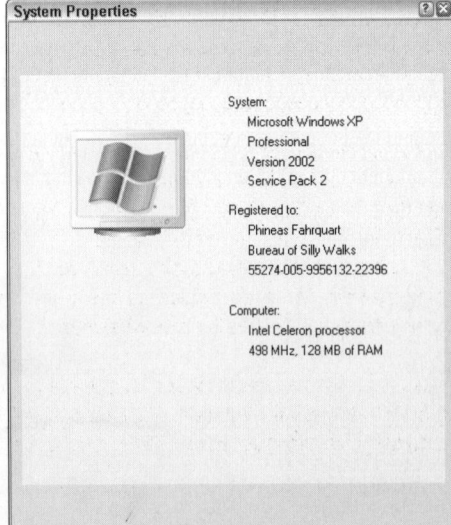

Figure 14-4:
It's easy to change the registered user and company.

Tweaking User Accounts

No doubt you realize that Windows XP, right out of the box, supports two different types of user accounts: *Administrator* accounts, which can do just about anything to or with the computer; and *Limited* accounts, which carry so many restrictions they're basically useless, except for novices. Microsoft's official description of Administrator and Limited accounts appears at tinyurl.com/c8jru.

You may *not* know that every Windows system — whether you installed it yourself or it came along with a new PC — contains a minimum of three user accounts:

- ✔ **Guest,** a limited account that's used internally by Windows. See the next section for details.

- ✔ **Administrator,** the ultraconfusing name for the Big Kahuna of all Administrator accounts. The account called Administrator comes into play if you start Windows Recovery Console: You have to provide the password for the account called Administrator in order to get into Recovery Console. (For a description of Recovery Console, see http://support.microsoft.com/kb/314058.) You can also put Administrator on the Windows Welcome screen. See the section "Showing/hiding accounts at logon," later in this chapter, for details.

If you use Windows XP Home Edition, the default password for the account called Administrator is blank. (If you're asked for a password, leave the box empty and click OK.) If you have Windows XP Pro, you probably typed in the password when you first set up the machine. To see if you remember the password, follow the steps in the section "Showing/hiding accounts at logon," later in this chapter.

- ✔ **Me** (actually, the third account probably has your name on it — *Woody* or *Phineas* or something similar). It's an Administrator account that you're expected to use day in and day out. You established the account when you installed Windows or when you first started Windows (or in rare instances, your PC manufacturer may have set it up for you). You can change the name on the account, but therein lies a story and a hack or two. See "Changing usernames," later in this chapter.

Your computer may have a zillion more users. You can create new ones with wild abandon by choosing Start➪Control Panel➪User Accounts➪Create a New Account and then following the instructions. Rocket science.

Working with Guest

Windows insists on saying that you "turn the Guest account on or off," but actually, you can never turn it off. The Guest account lurks behind the scenes whether you can see it on the Windows Welcome screen or not: Turning the Guest account "off" only removes it from the Welcome screen. If Guest appears on the Welcome screen, you can use it just like any other Limited account.

To make Guest appear on the Welcome screen:

1. **Choose Start⇨Control Panel⇨User Accounts⇨User Accounts.**

   Windows shows you a list of user accounts. Guest appears in the lower-right corner.

2. **Click the Guest account.**

   If the Guest account is off (that is, Guest is not one of the accounts on the Windows Welcome screen), you see the User Accounts dialog box, shown in Figure 14-5.

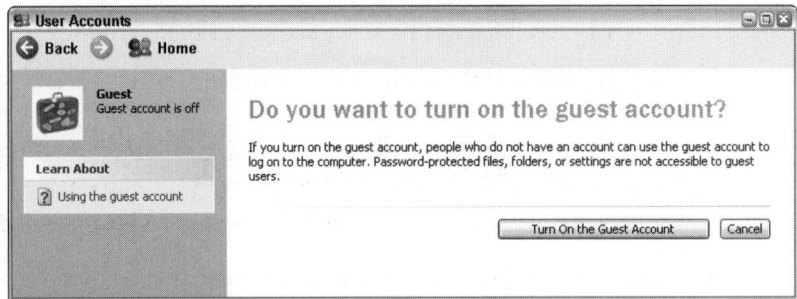

Figure 14-5: "Turn on" the Guest account here.

3. **To make the Guest account visible on the Windows Welcome screen, click Turn on the Guest Account.**

4. **Click "X" twice to get out of all the User Accounts dialog boxes.**

   The next time you bring up the Windows Welcome screen — say, when you log off or switch users — Guest appears as one of the available accounts.

I've seen some bizarre hacks posted on the Internet that attempt to remove the Guest account. Believe me, you don't want to. Windows XP uses the account called Guest to share files over a network, to share printers, and much more. Leave your Guest alone, OK?

Changing usernames

There's a reason why you're so confused about changing usernames. Windows XP doesn't have a single name for each user; it has two:

- ✔ **The internal name** (variously called the *username* or *user name*), which is the name Windows uses internally to establish the location of your files, grant access permissions to files and folders, and much more. This internal name identifies the user.

- ✔ **The display name** (called a *full name*) appears on the Windows Welcome screen, at the top of the Start menu, and in the Control Panel's User Accounts applet. The display name is only so much window dressing.

When you establish a new account in Windows XP — whether you do so when you install Windows, or by using the Control Panel's User Accounts applet — you type in only one name. Windows uses that name as both the internal name and the display name. The internal name is locked in concrete — you can't change it. The display name is easy to change:

1. **Choose Start⇨Control Panel⇨User Accounts⇨Change an Account.**

   Windows invites you to pick an account to change.

2. **Click the display name of the account you want to change and then click Change the Name.**

3. **Type a new name in the box provided, click Change Name, and then "X" out of both User Accounts dialog boxes.**

   The display name changes — but the internal name remains the same.

In particular, changing the display name doesn't change the location of his My Documents folder. If you create the account with the name Bob and then change the name to Robert, the My Documents folder remains `c:\Documents and Settings\Bob\Documents`, although Windows refers to the folder as Robert's Documents.

Showing/hiding accounts at logon

Every Windows XP system has at least three accounts. In the section "Working with Guest," earlier in this chapter, I show you how to make the Guest account appear on (or disappear from) the Windows Welcome screen.

You can do the same thing with any other user account — make it appear on, or disappear from, the Windows Welcome screen. In addition, if you have Windows XP Professional, even the account called Administrator (which is normally hidden) can appear, or not, at your discretion. (Microsoft decided to restrain Windows XP Home users.) Here's how:

1. **Follow the steps in Chapter 4 to download and install TweakUI.**

2. **Start TweakUI by choosing Start➪All Programs➪Powertoys for Windows XP➪TweakUI.**

3. **On the left, click Logon.**

   TweakUI shows you its Logon settings screen, as shown in Figure 14-6.

Figure 14-6:
Show or hide any user account (except Guest) from TweakUI.

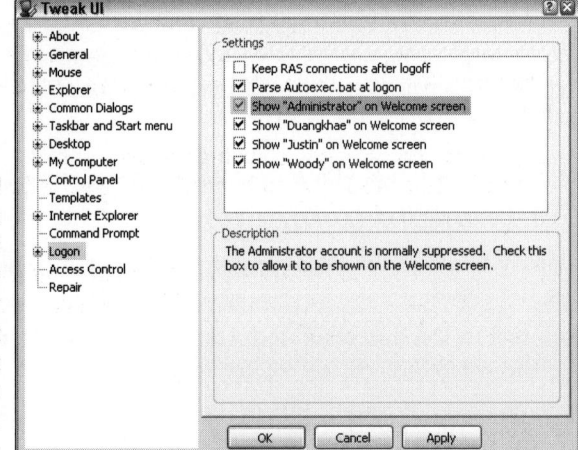

4. **Check the boxes next to the accounts you want to appear on the Windows Welcome screen and uncheck the boxes next to the ones you don't.**

5. **Click OK.**

   Your choices take effect immediately.

Ever wonder if you remembered the password for your computer's account called Administrator? If you have Windows XP Professional, follow the preceding steps to make the account called Administrator visible on the Windows Welcome screen and then:

1. **Choose Start➪Log Off and choose Switch Users.**

   You see the Windows Welcome screen.

2. **Click Administrator.**

   Windows prompts you for the password for the account called Administrator.

3. **Type the password for the account called Administrator and press Enter.**

   You can try as many times as it takes to get the password right.

   When (if!) you're successful, Windows starts, and you're suddenly using the account called Administrator.

4. **Kick around for a few minutes. You may be surprised to discover that the account called Administrator has a My Documents folder, and every other accoutrement of any garden-variety Administrator account. (Shared Documents is not the same as Administrator's Documents.)**

5. **When you're done, choose Start➪Log Off➪Log Off, switch back to the account you normally use, and (if you like) follow the preceding steps to take the account called Administrator off your Windows Welcome screen.**

   There's nothing inherently wrong with using the account called Administrator, but Windows XP grants it special privileges. Best to leave some things hidden, eh?

If you have Windows XP Home, chances are very, very good that the password for the account called Administrator is blank. Yes, you can change it. No, I won't tell you how. Life is too short.

Changing the picture

Are you tired of the picture that Windows assigned to your account? You know, the one that appears on the Windows Welcome screen and at the top of your Start menu? What, you don't want to be a blue butterfly or a rubber ducky?

Changing your picture — even by pulling a picture off a camera or scanning a picture with your scanner — is a piece of cake:

1. **Click Start and then click your picture.**

   No, I'm not crazy. It's that easy. Windows brings up the User Accounts dialog box for your account, ready to change the picture. If you have a camera or scanner attached to your computer, Windows also lists Get a Picture from a Camera or Scanner (see Figure 14-7).

2. **To use a picture that's already on your computer or network, click Browse for More Pictures, select the picture you want (*.bmp, *.gif, *.jpg, or *.png), and click Open.**

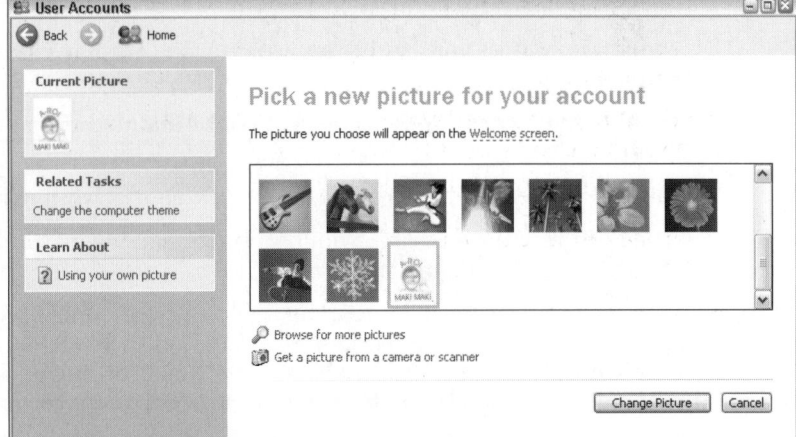

Figure 14-7:
Choosing a
new picture
may be the
simplest
cool mod in
all of
Windows.

3. **To use the Windows Scanner or Camera Wizard (see Chapter 12), click Get a Picture from a Camera or Scanner and follow the steps in the wizard. The wizard places your new picture at the end of the pictures in the dialog box (see Figure 14-7). Click the new picture and then click Change Picture.**

4. **Click "X" to get out of the User Accounts dialog box.**

   Your new picture appears on the Windows Welcome screen, at the top of your Start menu, and on your entry in the User Accounts dialog boxes.

Windows even resizes the picture so it fits in the space allotted. Slick, eh? Know why this works so well? Microsoft used this feature extensively when it demo'd Windows XP to its biggest customers. The folks who sign the checks at those big companies ate it up. All together now: "Ooooooooh! Aaaaaaahhhhh!"

Bypassing the Windows Welcome Screen

What, you're the only one who uses your computer? How quaint.

If you have only one user account, or if you almost always bring up the same user account, you don't have to go through the hassle of clicking your name — it's easy to ditch the Windows Welcome screen entirely (assuming you see a Windows Welcome screen; some people attached to Big Corporate Networks don't). Here's how to escape the surly bonds of Windows Welcome:

1. **Follow the steps in Chapter 4 to download and install TweakUI.**

2. **Log on to Windows using the account that you want to appear automatically.**

3. **Start TweakUI by choosing Start⇨All Programs⇨Powertoys for Windows XP⇨TweakUI.**

4. **On the left, double-click Logon and then click Autologon.**

   TweakUI comes up with the Autologon screen, as shown in Figure 14-8.

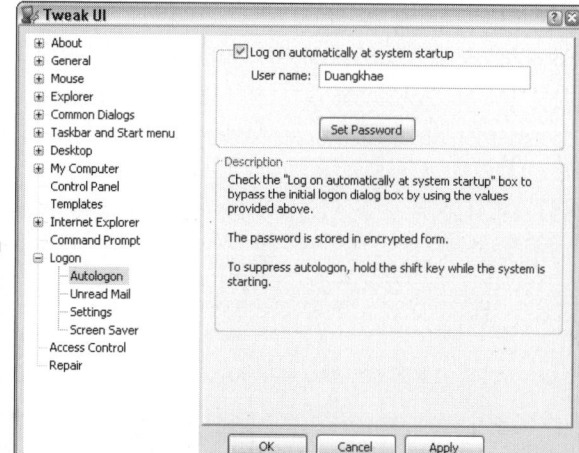

Figure 14-8:
Bypass the
Windows
Welcome
screen
entirely.

5. **Check the box marked Log on Automatically at System Startup.**

   TweakUI automatically fills in the name of the current user.

6. **If this account has a password, click the button marked Set Password, type the password (and the confirmation), and then click OK.**

7. **Click OK.**

   Restart Windows. You bypass the Windows Welcome screen completely and go straight to the user chosen in Step 2.

Chapter 15

Using Remote Assistance

*H*ow many times has this happened to you? The phone rings. It's your hapless, hopeless uncle, with a computer problem. "My Microsoft doesn't work." Huh? "Well, it says it doesn't work. I'm running Microsoft, you know, and I clicked that blue thing in the corner and it didn't do anything. Then I got a message saying that my Frumious Bandersnatch or something had to shut down."

Of course, your uncle lives on the other side of town, and he has to get this PowerPoint presentation done, like, yesterday, and would you be so kind as to get in your car, brave rush-hour traffic in a blinding snowstorm, and help him out, because you're such a good nephew and a really smart computer geek? Oh, and he'll take your son to the ballgame next weekend, maybe. Oy.

This chapter tells you how to guide your friend, co-worker, family member, lover, or tormentor (or any combination thereof), so that you can help them hack and mod *their* system with a minimum of fuss and bother.

Helping a Friend — Long Distance

Windows XP Remote Assistance rates right up there with *Star Wars,* TV remotes, dryer sheets, and blueberry bagels as one of the crowning achievements of humanity.

When it works, anyway.

In broad terms, here's how a Remote Assistance session works:

- ✔ Your friend contacts you and asks for help.

- ✔ You make sure that both you and your friend are running Windows XP, and make sure that both of you are connected to the Internet. If either of you uses a dial-up Internet connection, you have to stay connected through the whole process of setting up the session and then actually running Remote Assistance.

  It's possible to run a Remote Assistance session without being connected to the Internet, but both you and your friend have to be connected to the same local network, and your friend has to request the connection either by e-mail or by sending you a file. See details at the end of this section.

- ✔ You tell your friend to set up a couple of things and then step him through the process of starting a Remote Assistance session.

- ✔ You and your friend have to click the right buttons in the right sequence, and when you're done, you have control of his computer.

- ✔ Your friend watches his screen as you step through whatever you need to do. (Typically, you're either talking on the phone or both using Messenger simultaneously to chat with each other.) You make the hacks and mods necessary to get your friend back and working. Yes, you can even edit his Registry long distance.

- ✔ If your friend gets freaked out, he can always press Esc to end the Remote Assistance session immediately.

- ✔ When you're done, you disconnect, and your friend can get on with his so-called life.

Oh. I skipped a step. After it's all over, your friend showers you with praise and gifts, lets you drive his Ferrari, sets you up for a week at his timeshare in Whistler, and names his first-born daughter after you.

That's the theory. The reality can be a bit more . . . complex.

Asking for Help

So your friend needs help. You have three different ways to start a Remote Assistance session:

- ✔ **You and your friend can both crank up Windows Messenger or MSN Messenger.** Either of you can run just about any recent version of either Windows or MSN Messenger, but you must both be running Messenger. At least as of this writing, Trillian, AIM, and Yahoo! Messenger won't work.

✔ **Your friend can send you an e-mail invitation.** When you get the invitation, it will have a file attached. Double-click the file, and the Remote Assistance session starts.

If your friend has a dial-up Internet connection, he must stay connected until you're both done with your session.

✔ **Your friend can create a file, which he can send to you via a shared network folder, by e-mail, by schlepping the file to you on his cool key disk, or by tying a 3.5-inch floppy on the leg of a homing pigeon.** Again, if your friend has a dial-up connection, he has to stay connected.

Connecting via MSN or Windows Messenger

By far the easiest way to set up a Remote Assistance session involves both you and your friend using either Windows Messenger or MSN Messenger. If you don't use Windows Messenger or MSN Messenger, don't sweat it — just cruise on down to the next section, "Connecting via e-mail or by file."

Here's how to connect with Windows Messenger or MSN Messenger:

1. **Get on the phone with your friend.**

   There's no way you can step him through this without being on the phone. If your friend only has one phone line, and he's using it to dial in to the Internet, it's time for him to break out his cell phone.

2. **Have your friend fire up Windows Messenger or MSN Messenger (generally, choose Start➪Windows Messenger). Click the Sign In box.**

   Messenger asks for your friend's e-mail address and password. If your friend hasn't ever signed up for a Microsoft Passport, have him click Get a .NET Passport and fill out the application form to get a free Hotmail account. (Bonus points for signing up as Bill Gates or Phineas T. Farquahrt and leaving absolutely no personally identifiable information behind.)

3. **Have your friend enter his passport-approved e-mail address and password, and click OK.**

4. **You do the same.**

   Each of you sees the other as being Online.

5. **Double-click your friend's name to start a conversation.**

   A conversation box appears. Each version of MSN and Windows Messenger has a different format for the boxes; the conversation window for MSN Messenger 7.0 appears as in Figure 15-1.

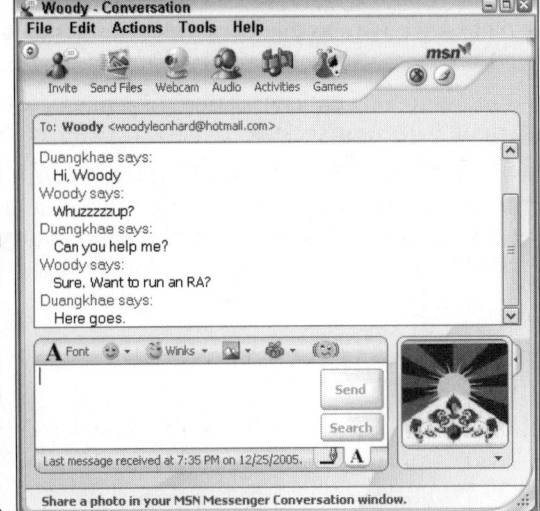

Figure 15-1:
To initiate a
Remote
Assistance
session,
start with a
conversa-
tion.

6. **The next step is confusing because it depends on which version of Windows or MSN Messenger your friend is running:**

   • If he has an older version of MSN Messenger, have him click Ask for Remote Assistance on the right side of the conversation window.

   • If he has MSN Messenger 7, tell him to click the Activities icon and then click Remote Assistance (see Figure 15-2).

Figure 15-2:
The method
for starting
a Remote
Assistance
session
varies
depending
on the
version of
Messenger.

- If he has Windows Messenger, have him click Actions⇨Ask for Remote Assistance, or he may be able to just click Ask For Remote Assistance on the right side of the window.

Your friend sees a message in the conversation window that says, "You have invited Phineas T. Farquahrt to start Remote Assistance. Please wait for a response or press Cancel (Alt+Q) the pending invitation."

At the same time, you see a message that says, "Bill Gates is inviting you to start using Remote Assistance. Do you want to Accept (Alt+T) or Decline (Alt+D) the invitation?"

7. You click Accept (or press Alt+T).

Your friend sees a message that says, "Phineas T. Farquahrt has accepted your invitation to start Remote Assistance."

You see a message that says, "You have accepted the invitation from Bill Gates to start Remote Assistance."

An eternity (in Internet time) passes while Remote Assistance gets its act together. Ultimately your friend sees the message in Figure 15-3.

Figure 15-3:
Your friend
has one last
chance to
bail out.

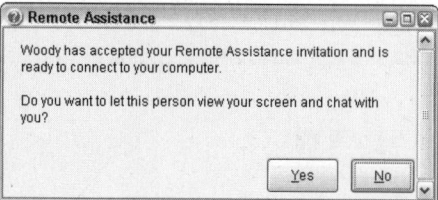

8. Have your friend click Yes.

Your friend's screen doesn't change, but you suddenly see a window that shows a control pane on the left and your friend's desktop on the right, as shown in Figure 15-4. ("Suddenly" being a relative term, completely dependent on the speed of your Internet connection.)

9. You can communicate with your friend by typing in the lower-left corner, where the pane says Message Entry. Schizophrenically, your friend's responses to your messages may appear in the Conversation window on the right.

10. If you want to take control of your friend's computer, click the Take Control icon in the upper-right corner of the Remote Assistance window.

Your friend sees the message shown in Figure 15-5.

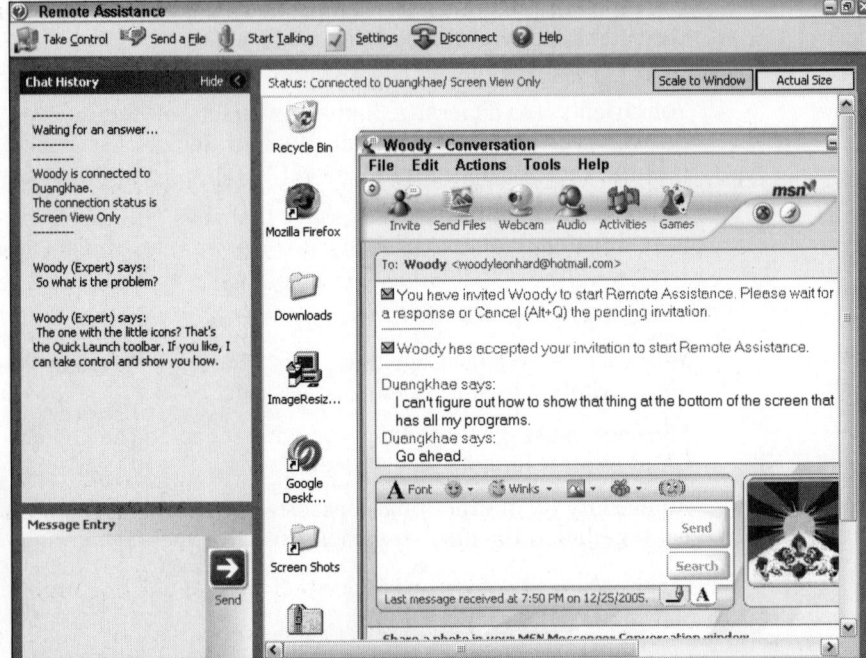

Figure 15-4:
You can see your friend's entire desktop.

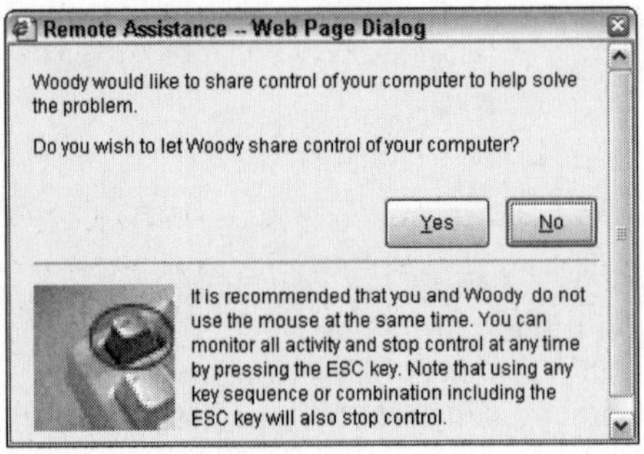

Figure 15-5:
One last chance to back down on handing over control.

11. **If your friend wants to let you take control of your computer, he should click Yes.**

Remote Assistance shows you a message saying that you are now sharing control of your friend's computer.

12. **You click OK.**

At that point, you have full control over your friend's computer. You can do anything that your friend can do except press Esc, because . . .

13. **Either you or your friend can end the Remote Assistance session at any point by pressing Esc.**

The connection is broken immediately.

Connecting via e-mail or by file

If you or your friend don't have Windows or MSN Messenger (which is to say, if either of you deleted the mangy mutt and doesn't want to put it back on the computer), it's still pretty easy to start a Remote Assistance session with a file. Your friend can send the file to you by e-mail, or he can tie it to the tail of a spur-thighed tortoise and send it your way.

Here's how:

1. **Have your friend choose Start⇨Help and Support. Under Ask For Assistance, have him click Invite a Friend to Connect to Your Computer with Remote Assistance.**

2. **On the right, have him click Invite Someone to Help You.**

   Help and Support Center offers three alternatives: Use Windows Messenger, e-mail, or save the invitation as a file. The latter option is marked *(Advanced)* but it really isn't that advanced.

3. **Have your friend type your e-mail address in the box provided and then click Invite This Person, or have him click Save Invitation as a File (Advanced).**

   Either option works about the same way.

4. **Your friend should type his name in the box provided. He should tell the Remote Assistance program how long the invitation should last. Most important, he should provide a password and somehow communicate the password to you.**

   The maximum expiration time, by default, is 30 days, although you can increase that on Windows XP Professional machines to 99 days by using the hack at the end of this chapter.

5. **Have your friend click Send Invitation (if he chose to send you a message) or Save Invitation (if he chose to save a file).**

   Your friend will undoubtedly see a warning from Outlook saying that a program is attempting to send a message, and it could be a virus. It isn't. Tell him to click OK or Send (depending on which version of Outlook he uses) and get on with it.

   In the end, your friend will either have an e-mail message with an attached file called RcBuddy.MsRcIncident (see Figure 15-6) or a file called RAInvitation.msrcincident. Have your friend send you the message or give you the file — and be sure that you get the password while you're at it.

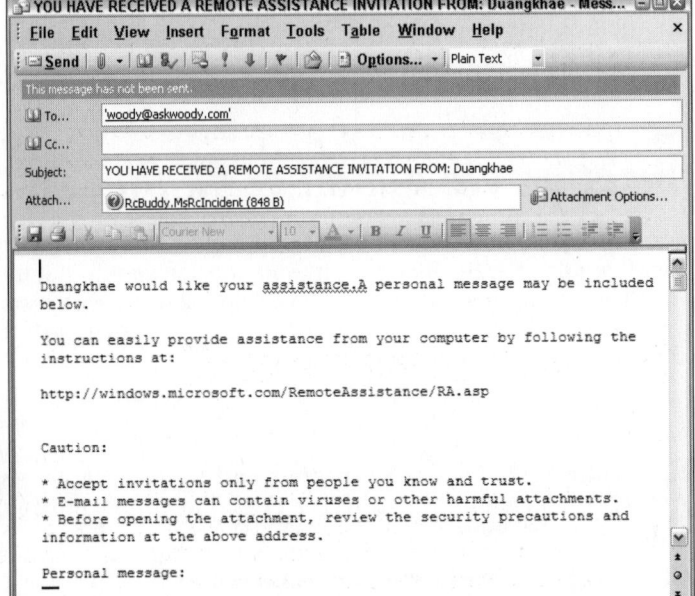

Figure 15-6:
An e-mail
invitation to
assist
remotely.

6. **When you receive the file (either via e-mail or on the leg of a carrier pigeon), double-click the file to open it.**

Remote Assistance shows you your formal, engraved invitation, as in Figure 15-7.

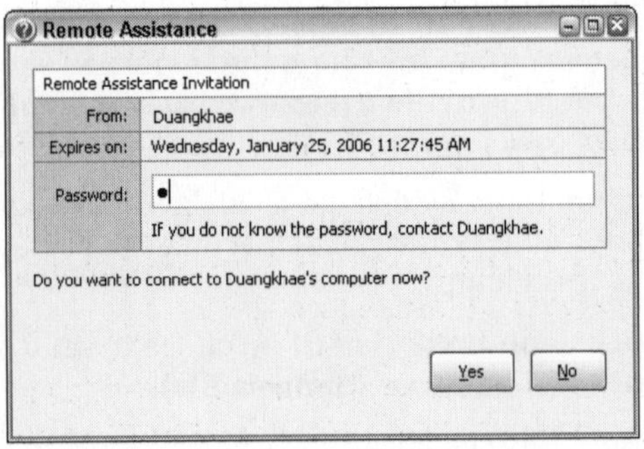

Figure 15-7:
An opened
invitation.

7. Type the password and click Yes.

Your friend sees the message in Figure 15-3, and you both may get the session going by starting at Step 8 in the preceding section.

Microsoft's documentation, in many places, says that you must be connected to the Internet in order to get a Remote Assistance session going. Baloney. As long as you're both connected to the same network and you use a file (possibly via e-mail) for the invitation, Remote Assistance can bypass the Internet entirely. It's much faster that way, too.

Poking Through the Firewalls

So what can go wrong with Remote Assistance? Plenty.

The biggest problem seems to come from the way the two computers attach to the Internet. Dial-up connections generally work fine. (At least RA will start, but it'll be horribly slow.) Problems arise when either or both computers are on networks. Three things to watch out for:

- ✔ **If either network is running Internet Connection Sharing on Windows 98 SE or Windows 2000, Remote Assistance can't get through.** ICS is a method for routing all Internet traffic through one computer on a network. If you have a cable modem or ADSL modem that uses a USB port, you probably run ICS on the computer that's connected to the modem. If that computer has Windows 98 SE or 2000, you're probably out of luck. If that computer runs Windows ME or XP, though, it'll probably work.

- ✔ **If either network goes through an older router or cable/DSL modem, RA may not work.** If the router or modem that dishes out IP addresses doesn't support UPnP (Universal Plug 'n' Play), RA probably won't work.

- ✔ **If either or both of you use a firewall other than Windows Firewall.**

When you issue a Remote Assistance invitation, or when you respond to one, Windows Firewall is smart enough to poke a hole through that allows the program `sessmgr.exe` to receive data (see Figure 15-8).

If either of you uses a firewall other than Windows Firewall (most notably including ZoneAlarm), you must manually allow the program `sessmgr.exe` to send and receive data. Alternatively, and less securely, you can open up port 3389, which is the port that Remote Assistance uses.

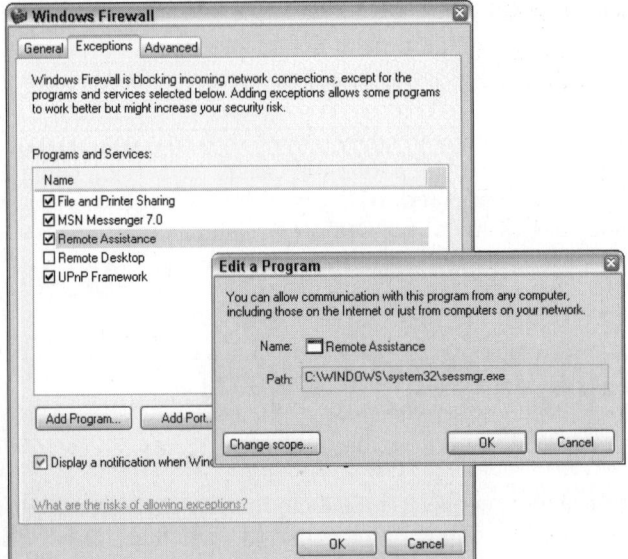

Figure 15-8:
Sessmgr.
exe has to
get through
the firewall.

Setting Up RA So That You Can Always Use It

If you create an RA invitation either as a file or as an attachment to an e-mail message, the Remote Assistance "wizard" includes an option to make the invitation valid for 99 days. If your friend sends you such an invitation, you can use it over and over again for more than three months.

If your friend has Windows XP Professional, it's relatively easy to set the maximum expiration at 99 days. Here's how:

1. **Run the Group Policy Editor by choosing Start⇨Run, typing** gpedit.msc, **and pressing Enter.**

   Windows brings up the Group Policy Editor.

2. **On the left, double-click to navigate to** Local Computer Policy\ Computer Configuration\Administrative Templates. **Then on the right, double-click to navigate to** System\Remote Assistance\ Solicited Remote Assistance.

   The Group Policy Editor shows you the Solicited Remote Assistance Properties dialog box, shown in Figure 15-9.

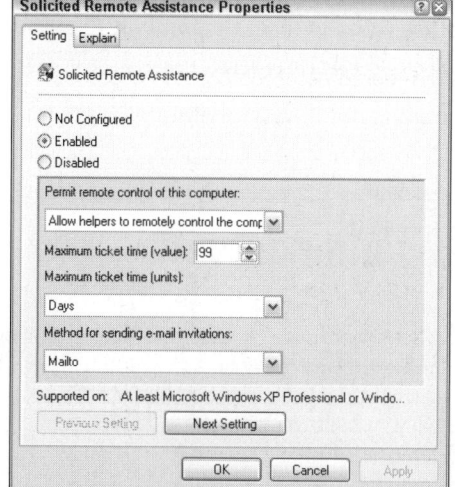

Figure 15-9:
Boost the
expiration
maximum
here.

3. **Click the button marked Enabled. Roll the Maximum Ticket Time (Value) box up to 99 and, in the Maximum Ticket Time (Units) box, choose Hours.**

4. **Click OK and then "X" out of the Group Policy Editor.**

The change takes effect immediately. Your friend can start sending out 99-day Remote Assistance invitations at any point.

Here's a mind-boggler. You can perform all of the preceding steps when you have control of your friend's computer using Remote Assistance. So if your uncle has a nasty habit of asking for help all the time, you can take a few extra minutes at the end of your next Remote Assistance session to set the maximum expiration date to 99, create a file invitation, and then e-mail it to yourself!

This hack works only with the Group Policy Editor and thus only with Windows XP Professional (XP Home doesn't have a Group Policy Editor). You can do the same thing in Windows XP Home, but you have to edit the Registry directly:

1. **Follow the instructions in Chapter 24 to get the Registry Editor going.**

2. **Double-click to navigate to HKEY_LOCAL_MACHINE\System\ CurrentControlSet\Control\TerminalServer.**

3. **Choose Edit⇨New⇨DWORD Value and create a new value called** MaxExpiryUnits. **Give it a value of** 2.

See Chapter 24 for details on creating new values and assigning data to them.

4. **Choose Edit⇨New⇨DWORD Value and create a new value called**
   MaxTicketExpiry. **Give it a value of** 99 **in decimal (or** 63 **in hexadecimal).**

5. **Choose File⇨Exit to get out of the Registry Editor.**

   Your friend can start sending out 99-day invitations immediately.

PC-sharing alternatives

Remote Assistance isn't the only game in town. Microsoft has a more powerful program called *Remote Desktop* that lets you log on to another machine, even when nobody's around to start the conversation. (Remote Assistance actually uses many of the programs in Remote Desktop.) For more information on Remote Desktop, see http://tinyurl.com/3as2s.

Laplink and pcAnywhere pioneered the remote control software genre, but two products in particular have lately overshadowed those progenitors. They both use Web browsers on the controlling machine, thus dispensing with firewall problems and all sorts of additional headaches. You download and run a program on the "controlled" machine, set a password, and leave it attached to the network. When you're ready to take over the machine, you fire up a Web browser, provide the password, and you're in.

If you can afford to spend $20 per month for a slick, amazingly easy-to-use remote program, look at GoToMyPC (www.gotomypc.com). There's also a great free alternative, LogMeIn Basic (www.logmein.com). LogMeIn Basic won't transfer files between the PCs, and it won't print files from one computer on the other, but it's much easier to use than Remote Desktop.

Chapter 16

Retooling Disks

Someday in the not-too-distant future, most hard drives will be solid state — no moving parts, just like your USB drive. I, for one, will mourn the passing of the noisy, cantankerous, power-sucking spinning platters of today's hard drives for about, oh, ten seconds.

If you've ever lost a hard drive, you know what I mean. If you haven't lost a hard drive, believe me, you will. You just haven't been trying hard enough.

Until we all reach the stage of solid-state enlightenment, care and feeding of the spinning platters rates as a high priority.

Installing a Second Hard Drive

In theory, when you buy a second hard drive, you follow the manufacturer's instructions, crack open the case, futz around with four (or more) screws, attach a couple of cables, put the case back together, run the manufacturer's software, and you're done.

In practice, life rarely conforms to expectations.

Several times, I've had new hard drives that simply failed to appear — I go through all of the docs, do everything precisely as instructed, reboot the computer, and . . . nothing. No drive D:. Windows sits there and stares at me like I'm looking for a Coke at Starbucks.

Should that ever happen to you, a Windows program might bring your new D: drive to life:

1. **Choose Start⇨Run, type** diskmgmt.msc, **and press Enter.**

   Windows brings up the Disk Management *snap-in* (see Figure 16-1). (A *snap-in* is a geeky term for a program that runs inside Microsoft Management Console. MMC provides the interface, the buttons, and the pretty pictures. The snap-in does the work.)

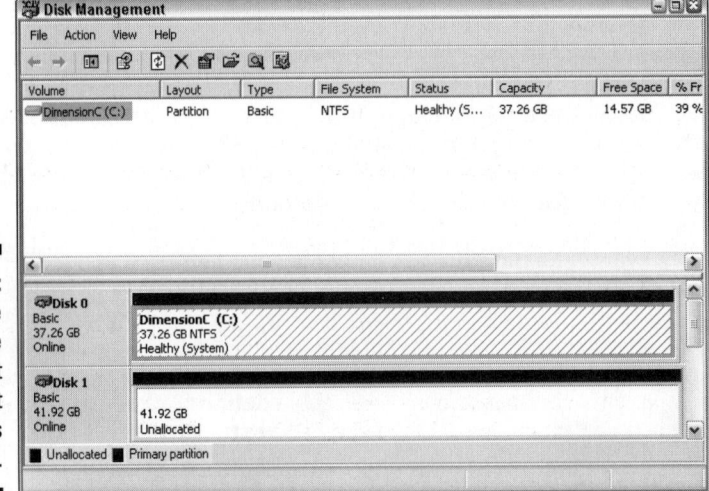

Figure 16-1: If you have a new drive that doesn't work, it appears as Unallocated.

This is a very odd situation. Windows itself doesn't recognize the D: drive — you can't get to it with Windows Explorer, for example, and it doesn't show up when you choose Start⇨My Computer. On the other hand, the Disk Management snap-in has no problem at all recognizing the drive, *even if it's been properly formatted.*

2. **At the bottom of the snap-in window, click the drive that hasn't been recognized.**

   The Initialize and Convert Disk Wizard usually appears. If it doesn't, go to Step 6.

3. **If the Initialize and Convert Disk Wizard appears, click Next.**

   The wizard asks you to select a disk to be initialized.

4. **Make sure that the disk you want to use is checked (usually Disk 1) and then click Next.**

   The wizard asks if you want to "convert" any disks. (*Convert* in this case means that you want to use multiple disks in advanced ways.)

5. **Make sure that no boxes are checked and then click Next and Finish.**

   Windows initializes the disk. You are ready to partition the drive, if it hasn't been partitioned already. Some drives are partitioned before they're shipped; if this is the case with your drive, skip to Step 8.

6. **If the Initialize and Convert Disk Wizard does not appear in Step 2, right-click the drive and choose Initialize.**

   The wizard starts and asks you to select a disk to be initialized.

7. **Make sure that the disk you want to use is checked (usually Disk 1) and then click Next.**

   Windows initializes the disk.

8. **To partition an Unallocated drive, right-click it and choose New Partition.**

   The New Partition Wizard appears.

9. **Click Next.**

   The wizard gives you the option of creating weird kinds of partitions.

10. **Unless you're going to put more than four partitions on a single hard drive (which is madness — see the sidebar "About partitions . . ."), choose Primary Partition and click Next.**

    The wizard wants to know how big to make the partition.

11. **If you insist on putting two partitions on a single drive, adjust the partition size. Otherwise, take the default and click Next.**

    The wizard wants to know which drive letter to assign.

12. **Most of the time, you want to use the next available letter — which is the default. Take all the rest of the defaults by clicking Next twice and then click Finish.**

    The wizard partitions and formats the drive. Your new D: drive is ready to go — no reboot necessary — and Windows Explorer sees it immediately (see Figure 16-2).

About partitions . . .

Some learned sages insist that any sufficiently large hard drive should be divided into two or three partitions.

I say balderdash. Having a single hard drive broken up into a C: drive, a D: drive, and an E: drive only makes life more difficult. It doesn't improve performance, doesn't make things more secure, doesn't do anything but make it harder for you to find and manage your data. Sooner or later, one of the partitions will fill up, and then you'll have to monkey with Partition Magic (which I don't recommend) or a less-expensive alternative such as BootIt NG (www.bootitng.com) to get your broken-up drive redistributed.

Yes, there are exceptions. If you set up a computer to multiboot into different operating systems, you want a partition for each operating system, and you may need to set up different kinds of partitions depending on which OS you're using. But if you're serious about multi-booting, you're better off installing virtual machines using a product such as VMware (www.vmware.com) anyway. Partitioning for the sheer delight of it doesn't make any sense.

Find out how to use folders. Buy a second hard drive if you want a D: drive. But don't carve up a drive thinking that it will buy you something. It won't. How did U2 put it? "One world. One life. One drive. One letter." Something like that.

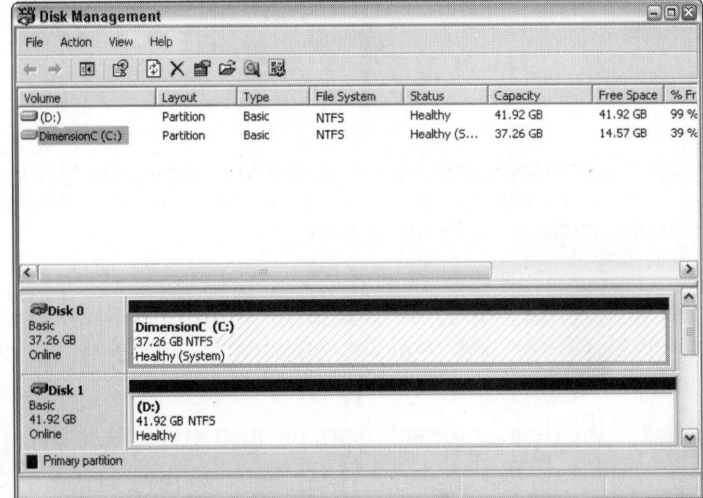

Figure 16-2:
Your new D: drive is ready to go.

Reassigning Drive Letters

Has this ever happened to you?

You install a new drive — maybe a hard drive, maybe a CD or DVD drive — get it going, and then a day or a month or a year later decide to remove a drive. All of a sudden, Windows gets mixed up. The drive that used to be E: is now F:, or vice versa. Programs that "know" what drive to look for (including the Windows and Office installers) get confused.

The example I use in this section shows another reason why many people want to change drive letters. I have an aging computer with a small hard drive known affectionately as C: (see Figure 16-3). Windows has assigned my CD drive the letter D:. I know that I'm going to install a new hard drive sooner or later, and I'd rather have my CD drive known as F:.

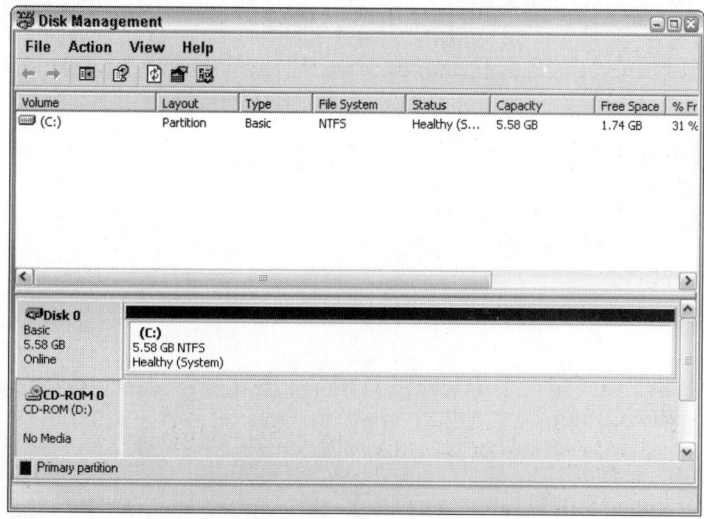

Figure 16-3: I want to change the D: to an F:.

Why? Because many installers, some games, and all sorts of other software run more smoothly if the programs "know" which drive holds the CD. If I install a game from the D: drive, the game "knows" to look on D: for its files. If I then add a new hard drive, that drive becomes D:, and the CD becomes E:. At that point, my game will go looking for love in all the wrong places. You know what I mean?

Because I know I'll be installing a new hard drive, I may as well give the CD drive a new letter. In this example, I give it an F:, just because I never liked the drive in the first place.

There are a dozen different ways for drive letters to get screwed up in Windows XP, but only one way to unscrew them. Here's how:

1. **Choose File➪Run, type** diskmgmt.msc, **and press Enter.**

   Windows shows you the Disk Management snap-in (refer to Figure 16-1).

2. **Right-click the disk you want to change and choose Change Drive Letter and Paths.**

   You can click on the disk anywhere it appears — on the top or on the bottom.

   Disk Manager shows you a dialog box entitled Change Drive Letter and Paths (see Figure 16-4).

Figure 16-4: Modify drive letters in this dialog box.

> **Change Drive Letter and Paths for D: ()**
>
> Allow access to this volume by using the following drive letter and paths:
>
> 🖴 D:
>
> [Add...] [Change...] [Remove]
>
> [OK] [Cancel]

3. **Click the drive you want to change (if it isn't selected already) and click Change.**

   Disk Manager asks you to choose a new drive letter.

4. **Choose a new letter and click OK.**

   Disk Manager warns you that changing the drive letter of a volume might cause programs to no longer run (which is certainly true if you have installed programs from that particular drive) and asks if you're sure.

5. **Click Yes.**

   The drive letter is changed immediately — no reboot necessary. In the future, the drive will always be known by that letter.

Converting a FAT Disk to NTFS

Something has to keep track of your files, and in the PC milieu that "something" is called a *file system*. Just as operating systems have evolved from DOS to Windows 3 to Windows XP, with a few interim hops, file systems have evolved as well. Windows XP supports three different file systems, begrudgingly:

- ✔ **FAT** (or FAT16), the 16-bit File Allocation Table file system, is still used for floppy drives and ZIP disks, but by and large it's ancient technology, with severe size limitations. (Some cameras use FAT16.) Bill Gates wrote most of the original FAT16 code himself.

- ✔ **FAT32,** the 32-bit File Allocation Table, was used in Windows 95, 98, SE, and ME. It was built to handle disks larger than the 2GB maximum for FAT16. It's considerably more efficient than FAT16 but susceptible to problems, especially when the power goes out.

- ✔ **NTFS,** the Windows NT File System, is the primary file system for Windows NT, 2000, and XP. If you bought a new computer with Windows XP preinstalled, chances are very good that your disk(s) are already set up to use NTFS. It's much more capable than FAT32 and more reliable.

If NTFS is so superior, why would anyone with a Windows XP computer use FAT32? Three reasons:

- ✔ If you set up your computer so that it will boot to Windows 98 or ME, you need a FAT32 drive. Those versions of Windows can't even see an NTFS drive.

- ✔ It's easy to get at data on a FAT32 drive. If your computer goes down in flames and you have to pull data off a drive, you can always use an old, old DOS boot disk and get to the drive.

- ✔ Some people still have custom utility programs that require FAT32 drives. If you haven't yet turned in your ancient copy of Norton Disk Doctor 1.0, though, you need a different kind of doctor.

Finding out what kind of drive you have

Wonder what kind of drive you have? It's easy to find out:

1. **Choose Start➪My Computer.**

2. **Right-click the drive in question and choose Properties.**

   Windows shows you a dialog box like the one in Figure 16-5.

3. **Look for the file system at the top of the dialog box. When you're done, click OK to exit the Properties dialog box.**

This drive uses FAT 32

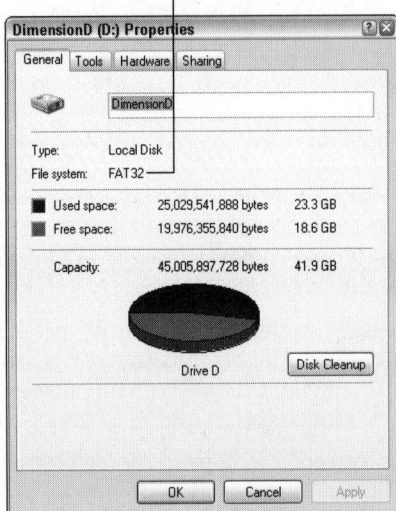

Figure 16-5:
The
Properties
dialog box
for a drive
tells you
what file
system it
uses.

Converting FAT32 to NTFS

Do you have an old FAT32 drive that you want to convert to NTFS? Good. You made the right choice. (Proselytizing can be so much fun.) Here's how to do it:

1. **Choose Start⇨All Programs⇨Accessories⇨Command Prompt.**

   You see the Windows command prompt.

2. **Type** convert *x*: /fs:ntfs /v, **where *x* is the drive you want to convert, and press Enter.**

   To convert your D: drive, for example, you type **convert d: /fs:ntfs /v**.

   Windows may tell you that it can't convert the volume because it is in use by another process . . . Would you like to force a dismount on this volume? (Y/N)

3. **Type** Y **and press Enter.**

   Windows may tell you that it cannot dismount the volume and ask if you would like to schedule it to be converted the next time the system restarts (Y/N)?

4. **Type** Y **and press Enter. Ponder whether the people who write these routines speak anything resembling normal English and ask yourself what it must be like to be forcibly dismounted. Ah well. I digress.**

5. **Choose Start⇨Turn Off Computer⇨Restart and go out for a sauna.**

   By the time you come back, if you're lucky, the drive may be converted.

Maintenance Hacks

No doubt you defragment your drives regularly. Defragging shuffles files around so they can be scooped off your drive faster. I have extensive advice on defragmenting, both manually and automatically, in *Windows XP Timesaving Techniques For Dummies* (Wiley Publishing).

You probably run Disk Cleanup from time to time, too, particularly when you start running out of disk space.

Here are a couple of tricks that go beyond the call of duty.

Stifling the disk cleanup warning

Enough is enough. I don't mind that Windows warns me once when I'm running low on disk space. (*You are running very low on disk space on* C:. *To free space on this drive by deleting old or unnecessary files, click here.*) But why does it have to keep harassing me like a pushy TV commercial?

Telling Windows to put a cork in it is easy — if you know where to look:

1. **Follow the steps in Chapter 4 to download and install TweakUI.**

2. **Choose Start⇨All Programs⇨Powertoys for Windows XP⇨TweakUI.**

   TweakUI appears in all its glory.

3. **On the left, double-click Taskbar and Start Menu.**

   For the life of me, I don't have the slightest idea why TweakUI puts this setting in with the Taskbar and Start Menu.

4. **Uncheck the box marked Warn When Low on Disk Space.**

5. **Click OK.**

   Windows will stop nagging you.

Forcing a defrag

Normally, Disk Defragmenter won't completely defrag a drive unless it has at least 15 percent available free space: Trying to defrag an almost-full drive is a slow, laborious task, and Defrag is loathe to try it. But if you have less than 15 percent available space, you can force Defrag to run anyway by using this trick:

1. **Choose Start⇨Run.**

2. **Type** defrag x: /f, **where x is the drive you want to defragment (for example,** defrag c: /f**).**

   Windows brings up a command window and runs the defrag.

3. **When the Defragmenter is done, click "X" to exit the command window.**

Sometimes Windows won't defrag a disk at all — no way, no how. You get the error message "Disk Defragmenter has detected that Chkdsk is scheduled to run on volume D:. Please run chkdsk /f." If that happens:

1. **Choose Start⇨Run.**

2. **Type** chkdsk x: /f, **where x is the drive you want to defragment (for example,** defrag c: /f**).**

   Windows brings up a command window and runs Chkdsk, which scans your hard drive and repairs any errors. (The /f tells Chkdsk to "fix" errors that it finds. Without the /f, Chkdsk only scans the disk and reports on errors.)

3. **When Chkdsk is done, run Disk Defragmenter again.**

Disk Defragmenter comes from a company called Executive Software. If you're interested in a beefed-up defragmenter (which can defrag the page file, defrag on boot, and run continuous defragments or scheduled defrags), look for a program called Diskeeper at www.executive.com/coverpage.asp.

Part V
Protecting Yourself (And Your PC)

In this part . . .

Did you hear the story about Microsoft's MS05-018 security patch? A few unlucky people walked into their offices one morning to find their computers had keeled over with a "blue screen of death." When they rebooted, the computers kept crashing with BSODs. The only solution? Reformat the hard drive and start from scratch.

You know what they did wrong? They allowed Microsoft to update their computers automatically. When these folks walked out of their offices at night, their computers worked fine. When they came back, automatic update had done its thing, and left their PCs in shambles.

Sometimes protecting yourself means protecting yourself from Microsoft.

Chapter 17

Changing (In)Security Settings

*W*indows XP Service Pack 2 represents a quantum leap in Windows' ability to protect against viruses, Trojans, spam, and much more.

That isn't saying much. The original version of Windows XP was so riddled with holes and hooks that hackers — the other kind of hackers — made hundreds of millions of dollars spying, cracking, spamming, and zombifying PCs that were "locked down" with the best technology at the time.

The moral of the story? You have to take control of your own PC. If you trust Microsoft to do it for you, well, look at its track record.

Don't Let Microsoft Muck with Your Computer

The folks at Microsoft get their zithers in a dither when I advise people to turn off automatic updating in Windows XP. From Microsoft's point of view, forcing the vast unwashed masses of Windows XP users to have their machines updated within days of a patch becoming available keeps pandemic infections from spreading.

I take a very contrary view. Yes, I turn on automatic updates for my dad because he doesn't want to deal with Microsoft's inanities. Statistically, that makes sense: Most of Microsoft's patches work right on, oh, 95% of all PCs.

Fact is, some of the patches don't do what they're supposed to do, and many of the patches introduce problems where there were no problems before. You may fool all the people some of the time, you can even fool some of the people all of the time, but you cannot fool a good hacker more than once or twice.

Patch Keystone Kops

No doubt you've heard about the Windows XP "critical updates" from Microsoft that get patched and re-patched and re-re-patched. Two of my favorites:

- **The GDI+ scanner debacle, known as Microsoft Security Bulletin MS 04-028.** Seems that a cretin can put a program inside a JPEG file — a picture. When you try to view the picture, boom, the program runs, supposedly taking over your computer. (At this writing, nobody has found a way to make the program do much except crash the computer.) Microsoft released the original patch on September 14, 2004. It didn't work, so Microsoft re-released it several times, finally spinning off separate patches for different programs (such as Visio and Project). Version 3.0 of the patch still doesn't catch all the vulnerable programs on a computer.

- **The Windows Media Player "poisoned" license circus.** Microsoft never issued a Security Bulletin for this gaping security hole, but you can see the tip of the iceberg at `http://support.microsoft.com/kb/892313`. Ed Bott has full details at `www.edbott.com/weblog/archives/000641.html`. A bad bug in WMP 9 and 10 could trick you into going to a malicious Web site if you try to play a media file that requires a license. Even if you uncheck the box that allows WMP to "Acquire licenses automatically for protected content," WMP may still go out, retrieve a Trojan, and ask you to install it under the guise of a song license. The Knowledge Base article currently stands at version 6.0. That's just the documentation. I don't think anybody has ever figured out how many different versions of this patch appeared and reappeared in different places under different guises.

I call Microsoft's adventures in this space the *Patch Keystone Kops*. I fully expect Laurel and Hardy to feature in one of the Security Bulletins.

What is a critical patch?

Microsoft has a formal severity rating system that describes each security patch as critical, important, moderate, or low. You can see the Party Line at `www.microsoft.com/technet/security/bulletin/rating.mspx`.

It all sounds grand — etched in granite, no less — but the simple fact is that severity ratings can, and do, change. If enough customers complain, Microsoft has been known to turn an "important" update into a "critical" one.

The Security Bulletin system adds to the confusion. Back when Microsoft started issuing Security Bulletins, we saw one bulletin for each security patch (or groups of patches that plugged the same hole). Lately, Microsoft has started bundling patches, so a single Security Bulletin — indeed, a single downloaded patch — plugs two or three completely unrelated security holes. Why? So the 'Softies can minimize the number of Security Bulletins: This year we only had 45 of 'em, but last year there were 50. Good job, eh?

To add to the confusion, Microsoft has released important security patches without issuing Security Bulletins. The Windows Media Player "poisoned" license patch, mentioned in the preceding section, is a good example.

The proverbial bottom line: Any reasonably proficient Windows user shouldn't — indeed, *can't* — rely on Microsoft to patch her computer.

Turning off automatic updating

As I see it, you have two choices:

- ✔ **Let Microsoft update your computer automatically.** On the plus side, that means you have the latest updates all the time. On the downside, if one of the updates gets screwed up, it can take out your machine: You could wake up one morning and your computer won't start — thanks to a wayward patch installed automatically overnight.

- ✔ **Have Microsoft advise you when updates are available, but install them manually.** On the plus side, you have a chance to see whether other people are having problems before you let the patch onto your machine. On the downside, it may take a week or a month for you to feel comfortable about a specific patch, and you'll be vulnerable for that length of time. In practice, very few dangerous exploits appear in the wild immediately after a patch is posted. Either the hole is well known for months before Microsoft finally fixes it; or it takes malware writers a while to figure out how to take advantage of the hole.

Recently, the most virulent attacks have centered around security holes that Microsoft patched months — even years — before the malware hit the fans. It's important that you apply important security patches eventually. But immediately? I think not.

Here's how to set your own Windows update destiny:

1. **Choose Start⇨Control Panel⇨Security Center.**

   Windows brings up Security Center.

2. **At the bottom of Security Center, under Manage Security Settings For, click Automatic Updates.**

Security Center shows you the Automatic Updates tab, shown in Figure 17-1.

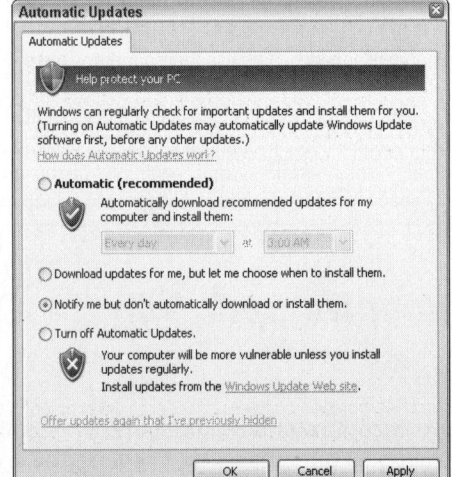

Figure 17-1: Choose the method of updating that makes sense for you.

3. **Choose among the settings based on the description in Table 17-1.**

4. **Click OK.**

Your choice takes effect immediately.

It's important to realize that only Windows itself gets updated this way. If you're using Office, for example, you have to jump through completely different hoops to keep it updated.

Table 17-1	Automatic Update Settings
Setting	*Means*
Automatic (Recommended)	Allows Microsoft to install Windows patches without your knowledge or consent. In particular, any Windows security patch rated as *critical* gets installed. You should choose this setting for any computer that isn't used regularly, or if you're setting up a system for a friend who doesn't want to be bothered with following the Patch Keystone Kops. If you fit the Hacks & Mods profile, though, and you don't trust Microsoft to keep your system working, avoid this setting.

Setting	Means
Download Updates for Me, Don't Install	This setting makes sense only if you have a slow Internet connection and it takes a while to download the (sometimes massive!) patches.
Notify, but Don't Download	My recommended setting, if you're willing to stay on top of the latest patch developments (see the next section).
Turn off Automatic Updates	The worst of all possible worlds. Avoid this setting like the plague.

Analyzing Updates

Look before you leap.

Microsoft posts Security Bulletins (`www.microsoft.com/security/default.mspx`) and Knowledge Base articles (referenced in the Security Bulletins) for each Windows security patch. Microsoft also issues Security Advisories (`www.microsoft.com/technet/security/advisory/default.mspx`) and runs a blog (`http://blogs.technet.com/msrc/default.aspx`) that air the Official Party Line. The detailed technical information in the Security Bulletins can be quite valuable. Other than that, with rare exceptions, I've found most of the information in those locations to be self-serving, misleading, and in some cases just plain wrong.

If you want to take an active interest in reviewing updates before you install them on your computer, I recommend four independent sources of information:

✔ My site, `AskWoody.com`, has a page devoted to the topic: Microsoft Patch Reliability Ratings covers Windows security patches, as well as other patches available from the folks in Redmond.

✔ Brian Livingston's Windows Secrets newsletter and Web site, `www.windowssecrets.com`, also commonly review patches and their sometimes deleterious side effects.

✔ It doesn't hurt to run a Google search on a security patch before installing it. For example, if you want details on Security Bulletin MS06-003, go to Google and search for **MS06-003**.

✔ By far, the most detailed information sits in the newsgroups. Go to `http://groups.google.com` and search for the Security Bulletin number and/or the Knowledge Base article number. Take the results critically, though: People have a habit of blaming Windows patches on all of their systems' ills.

Applying Updates

Microsoft changes the Windows Update Web site about as frequently as Bill changes socks, so detailed instructions for hacking and modding your way through Windows Update glitches are rather superfluous. Instead, permit me to step you through the general process and point out a few of the obstacles that confront the unwary:

1. **To start Windows Update, choose Start⇨All Programs⇨Windows Update. (You can also click the balloon that occasionally appears down in the notification area, next to the clock, which says Updates Are Ready for Your Computer/Click Here to Download These Updates.)**

   Windows fires up Internet Explorer (even if you use Firefox) and brings up the main Windows Update screen, which probably looks a little bit like Figure 17-2.

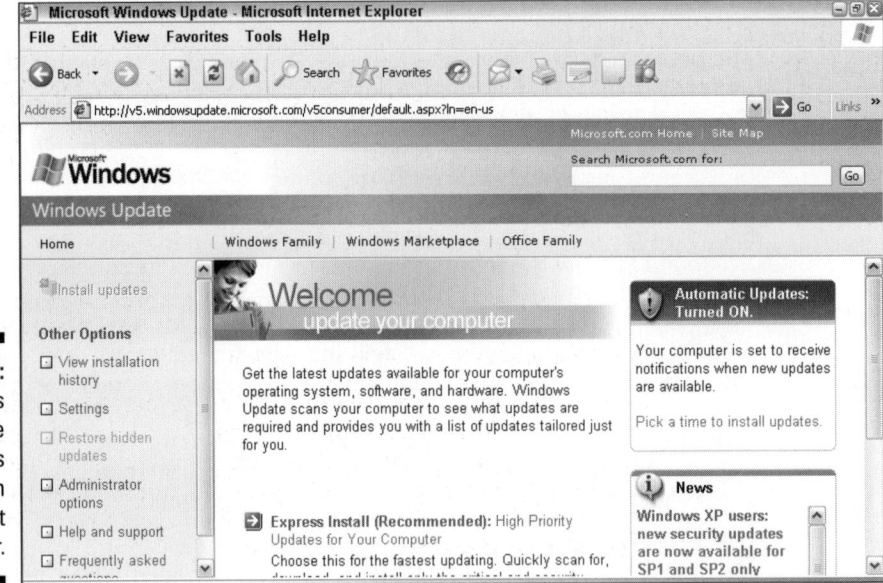

Figure 17-2:
Windows
Update
works
only with
Internet
Explorer.

2. **If Microsoft's servers are overloaded, or if its system has crashed (again), you may get a notice like the one shown in Figure 17-3. If you do, forget about following the links provided. Wait about ten minutes and try again.**

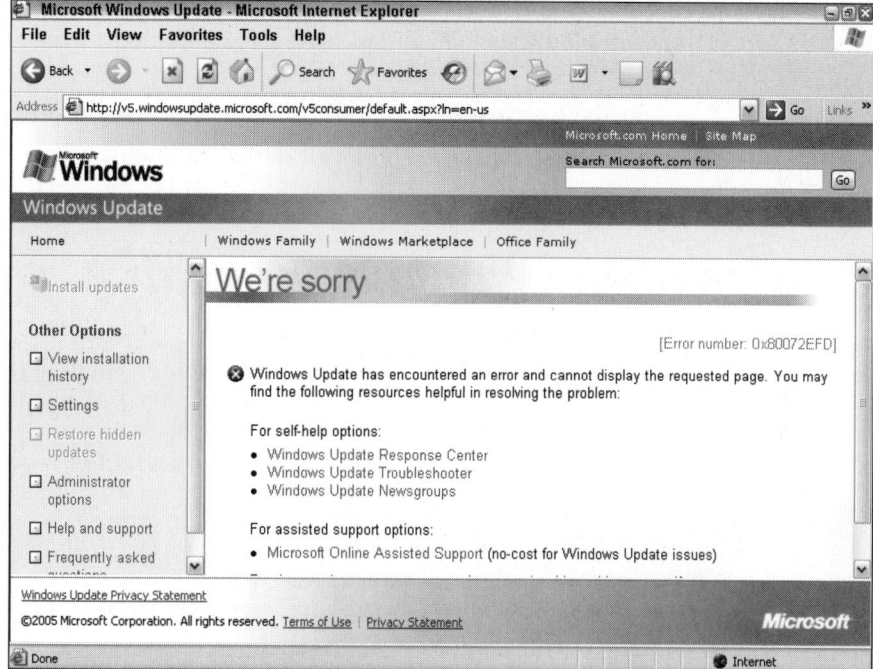

Figure 17-3:
You didn't
do anything
wrong.
Windows
Update died
again.

3. **Take what you read with a huge grain of salt.**

   For example, in Figure 17-2:

   - Windows Update says that Automatic Updates are turned ON. That's a crock. My systems are all set for notification only, just as I recommend in the preceding section.

   - If you click the line marked Pick a Time to Install Updates, the program lets you set the time for updating. Of course, the resulting dialog box doesn't make it clear that if you choose a time, your machine is reset for automatic updating. Worse, there's no Cancel button in the dialog box. You must click Set up Later to back out of this piece of deceptive advertising.

   - Microsoft may change the consequences of clicking Express Install (Recommended), but at one point, choosing Express Install set Windows up for automatic updating. Ever get the idea that Microsoft *really* wants you to enable automatic updates?

4. **Click Custom Install.**

   It takes Windows a bit longer to scan your machine for all available updates, so this option is a bit slower than choosing Express Install

(Recommended). But running Custom Install shows you everything that's available, including new drivers and patches to some ancillary programs.

5. **Follow the instructions to choose and install the updates you want.**

   Many updates require a reboot before they take effect.

Dealing with Windows Firewall

To a first approximation anyway, a *firewall* sits between your computer and the network, controlling the flow of information, helping to keep the bad guys out of your computer.

If your computer is connected directly to the Internet (not very common these days, except with a dial-up connection), your firewall stands as your only defense against a constant bombardment of programs trying to connect directly to your computer. If your computer connects to the Internet through an ADSL or cable modem, via satellite, or through a router (typically a wireless router), your computer's firewall provides a second level of defense, behind the firewall built into the connecting hardware.

Windows XP Service Pack 2 includes a tremendous half of a firewall called Windows Firewall.

Setting up Windows Firewall

Half of a firewall?

Yep, you read that correctly. Windows Firewall only works in one direction: It keeps probing programs out of your computer. It doesn't even try to prevent malicious outbound traffic. If you get infected by, oh, a Trojan attached to an e-mail message, and your computer turns into a zombie, your computer can send out hundreds of thousands of infected messages, and Windows Firewall won't even hiccup.

In spite of its manifest limitations, even if you have a firewall in your ADSL or cable modem, Windows Firewall nonetheless protects you against infection from other computers on your system, and it may (may!) catch creepy-crawlies that manage to get through your first-line firewall. I suggest that you enable it and keep a log of penetration attempts that it blocks.

The network you save may be your own. Here's how to get Windows Firewall set up in Hack & Mod mode:

1. **Choose Start⇨Control Panel⇨Security Center.**

   Windows shows you Security Center.

2. **At the bottom of Security Center, under Manage Security Settings For, click Windows Firewall.**

   Security Center shows you the Windows Firewall dialog box (see Figure 17-4).

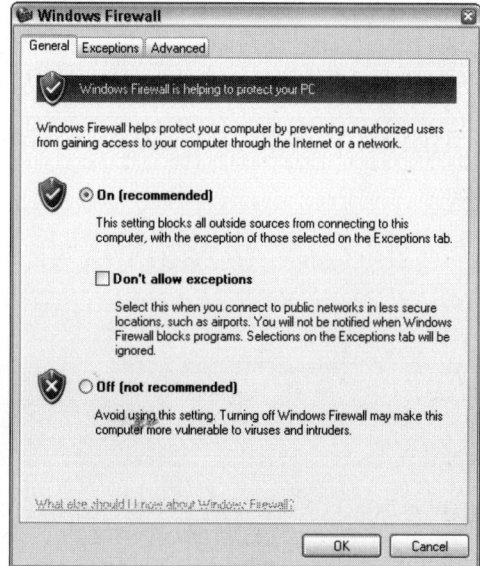

Figure 17-4:
Windows
Firewall
command
center.

3. **Make sure that the On button is checked and then click Advanced.**

4. **In the middle of the dialog box, where it says Security Logging, click the Settings button.**

   Windows Firewall shows you the Log Settings dialog box (see Figure 17-5).

Figure 17-5:
Tell
Windows
Firewall to
keep a log.

5. **Check the boxes marked Log Dropped Packets and Log Successful Connections. Then click the Save As button and choose a good place to put the Windows Firewall log.**

   In Figure 17-5, Duangkhae put the log on her desktop.

6. **Click OK twice.**

   Your changes kick in immediately, and the log appears wherever you put it.

The firewall log keeps track of all attempted connections to the computer, including allowed access to shared folders (see Figure 17-6), printers, and the like.

Figure 17-6:
Log of a
permitted
network
access to
a shared
folder.

```
Firewall log.log - Notepad
File   Edit   Format   View   Help
#Version: 1.5
#Software: Microsoft Windows Firewall
#Time Format: Local
#Fields: date time action protocol src-ip dst-ip src-port dst-port size tcpflags tcpsyn
tcpack tcpwin icmptype icmpcode info path

2005-12-29 12:38:05 OPEN UDP 192.168.3.105 192.168.3.101 137 137 - - - - - - - - - -
2005-12-29 12:38:05 OPEN-INBOUND TCP 192.168.3.101 192.168.3.105 1601 139 - - - - - - - - - -
2005-12-29 12:39:43 CLOSE UDP 192.168.3.105 192.168.3.101 137 137 - - - - - - - - - -
2005-12-29 12:40:08 OPEN TCP 192.168.3.105 192.168.3.101 1056 139 - - - - - - - - - -
2005-12-29 12:42:19 CLOSE TCP 192.168.3.105 192.168.3.101 1056 139 - - - - - - - - - -
2005-12-29 12:44:05 OPEN TCP 192.168.3.105 192.168.3.1 1057 5431 - - - - - - - - - -
2005-12-29 12:45:05 CLOSE TCP 192.168.3.105 192.168.3.1 1057 5431 - - - - - - - - - -
2005-12-29 12:52:15 OPEN UDP 192.168.3.105 192.168.1.1 1060 53 - - - - - - - - - -
2005-12-29 12:52:15 OPEN TCP 192.168.3.105 64.233.189.104 1061 80 - - - - - - - - - -
2005-12-29 12:52:15 OPEN UDP 192.168.3.105 192.168.1.1 1062 53 - - - - - - - - - -
2005-12-29 12:52:15 OPEN TCP 192.168.3.105 140.211.166.206 1063 80 - - - - - - - - - -
2005-12-29 12:52:15 OPEN TCP 192.168.3.105 64.233.189.104 1064 80 - - - - - - - - - -
2005-12-29 12:52:15 OPEN TCP 192.168.3.105 63.111.66.50 1065 80 - - - - - - - - - -
2005-12-29 12:52:16 OPEN TCP 192.168.3.105 212.58.240.43 1066 80 - - - - - - - - - -
2005-12-29 12:52:16 CLOSE TCP 192.168.3.105 140.211.166.206 1063 80 - - - - - - - - - -
2005-12-29 12:52:18 CLOSE TCP 192.168.3.105 212.58.240.43 1066 80 - - - - - - - - - -
2005-12-29 12:52:23 OPEN TCP 192.168.3.105 64.233.189.104 1067 80 - - - - - - - - - -
2005-12-29 12:52:32 OPEN TCP 192.168.3.105 204.1.226.226 1068 80 - - - - - - - - - -
2005-12-29 12:52:32 OPEN TCP 192.168.3.105 204.1.226.226 1069 80 - - - - - - - - - -
```

Testing your firewall

Every Windows XP user should hit Steve Gibson's ShieldsUP! site at least once, to make sure his firewall (or, in most cases, combination of firewalls, both hardware and software) works correctly. Although ShieldsUP! may not be the flashiest or most complete firewall tester in the universe, it's thorough

and easy to use. Steve's explanations stand as a model of clarity in this truly murky area. And, of course, it's free.

Here's how to run a ShieldsUP! test:

1. **Point your favorite Web browser at** `http://grc.com`, **Steve Gibson's home for SpinRite and ShieldsUP!. Scroll down (maybe way down) to the line marked ShieldsUP! and click it.**

   ShieldsUP! checks to see if your IP address has a Reverse DNS entry. Follow Steve's analysis of the situation if you do have an Internet Service Provider that supports this potentially invasive capability. (*Hint:* If you come up positive, change ISPs!)

2. **Click Proceed.**

   ShieldsUP! presents six services: File Sharing, Common Ports, All Service Ports, Messenger Spam, and Browser Headers.

3. **One by one, click each of the services and follow the recommendations in the generated reports (see Figure 17-7 for an example of a Common Ports run).**

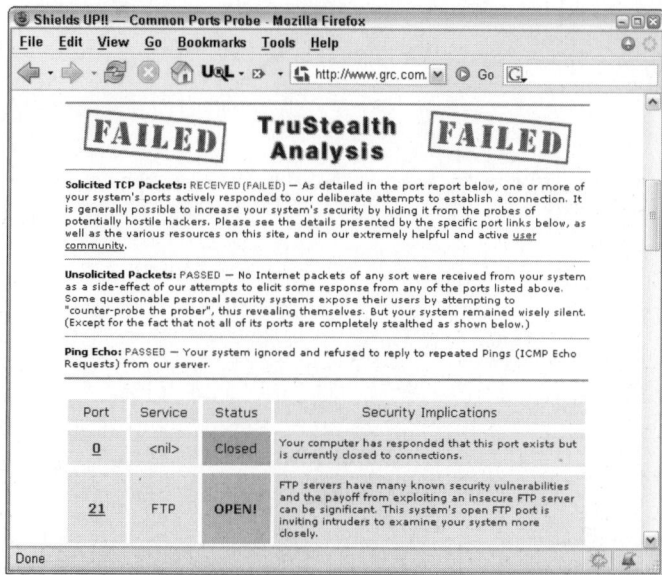

Figure 17-7:
Common
Ports
analysis
FAILED.

Steve's explanations and recommendations go to the heart of the matter. Ignore them at your own peril.

4. **Choose File⇨Exit to exit your Web browser.**

Bet you hit a few surprises, eh?

Chapter 18

Taking the "Mal" Out of Malware

· ·

In This Chapter

▶ Using full-featured, free antivirus software

▶ Paying Microsoft to fix its products

▶ The "two logs crossing" principle

▶ Taking advantage of other free alternatives

· ·

1 call it *scumware.*

Any program that changes my Internet home page; sticks a toolbar anywhere except where I put it; connects to a Web site without my explicit permission; tries to trick me into allowing it to update itself automatically; monitors my activities; or changes anything at all on my computer without warning me, in advance, what it'll change and how, is scum. It deserves to die.

That's what this chapter is all about. Scumbusting.

Catching Viruses Free

Are you tired of antivirus programs that keep plugging you to pay the piper? I have quite a few friends who work for antivirus companies, so I'm not going to throw brickbats at the working stiffs who keep us all one step ahead of viruses, Trojans, worms, and other malware. But while I have endless praise for the folks in the trenches, the people who run those antivirus companies realize they've hit a gold mine, and they're going to strip it for all it's worth.

The business model for most antivirus companies is just like the business model for a shaving company: Give away the razor and sell the blades. AV companies frequently give away their software — almost all new computers come with Norton or McAfee installed, and Microsoft's getting into the game, too — but after a week or a month, the AV company charges for the updates. No matter how you slice it, an AV program isn't much good if you don't update it frequently. So millions and millions of Windows users demand their AV updates, gladly shelling out shillings, shekels, and satang for stopgap solace that grows stale on a daily basis. It's an incredibly lucrative addiction.

One company marches to a different drummer. Grisoft, a privately held German company with offices in Europe and the United States, claims 20 million users of its AVG antivirus package worldwide. Its business model parallels the one used by some shareware companies: The company lets individuals use the product for free and sells low-cost licenses to companies, schools, and other institutions. Remarkably, folks who install the free version of AVG get all the protection that paying subscribers receive. Those who pay (about $35, total, for two years) get to download their updates from a faster server, and they qualify for technical support.

Installing AVG Free

If you're currently running an antivirus program, follow the steps in Chapter 3 to safely disable your current program while you install AVG Free.

Here's how to hook in to AVG Free for "private, non-commercial, single home computer use":

1. **Start your favorite Web browser and go to** `http://free.grisoft.com`.

   If you can't find `free.grisoft.com`, try `www.grisoft.com`. You may have to click around a bit, but both the AVG Products page and the Downloads page have links to AVG Free.

2. **Click Get AVG Free.**

3. **Scroll down the resulting page and look for a section marked AVG Free Edition Installation Files. Click the filename (probably** `avg7free_something.exe`**) and save it to disk.**

   It's a large file — more than 12MB — so the download may take a while.

4. **Double-click the downloaded file to start the installation wizard.**

5. **Take all the defaults for the Standard Installation.**

   If you get a notice about an expired installation package, go ahead and install anyway. You'll have a chance to update the virus signature file immediately after installing.

   The wizard installs AVG Free and then starts the AVG Free — First Run Setup Wizard (see Figure 18-1).

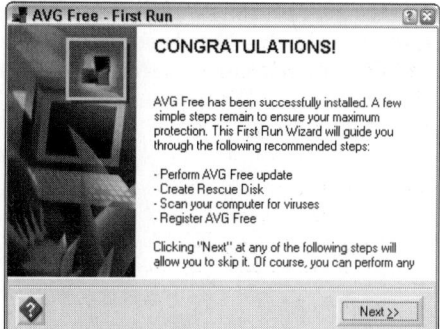

Figure 18-1:
AVG takes
you through
minimal
setup steps.

6. **Click Next and then, one by one, take the steps recommended by the First Run Setup Wizard. In particular, make sure that you click Check for Updates to get the virus signature database updated.**

   AVG updates itself automatically. In the final step of the wizard, you can run an immediate manual scan of your computer — an excellent idea if you have a spare hour or two.

   The First Run Setup Wizard ends with a message saying Your Computer Is Protected.

7. **Click Continue and then "X" out of the Test Center.**

   AVG Free is working, protecting your computer.

AVG Free has hooks into major applications (such as Word and Excel), so it scans files before you open them. It works with your e-mail program (in Outlook or Outlook Express) to scan attachments. It fetches updates automatically in the middle of the night, every night, and runs complete scans according to the schedule you set. When it finds a piece of malware, it lets you zap the bugger out or quarantine it (in case you change your mind later, you can bring the offending file back). In short, AVG Free has all of the features you'd expect from any full-priced product — and it doesn't have the temerity to ask you to feed the corporate coffers every time you turn around. I don't understand why any individual pays for antivirus protection anymore. And if your company spends more than $20 per seat per year for antivirus programs, support, and updates, it's paying too much!

Adjusting AVG Free settings

As soon as you install AVG Free, go into the program and make a couple of adjustments:

1. **Start the AVG Free Test Center by either double-clicking the shortcut on the desktop or by right-clicking the AVG Free icon in the System Tray (next to the clock) and choosing Launch AVG Free Test Center.**

2. **On the left, click Scheduler.**

    AVG Free shows you the list of Scheduled Tasks, as shown in Figure 18-2.

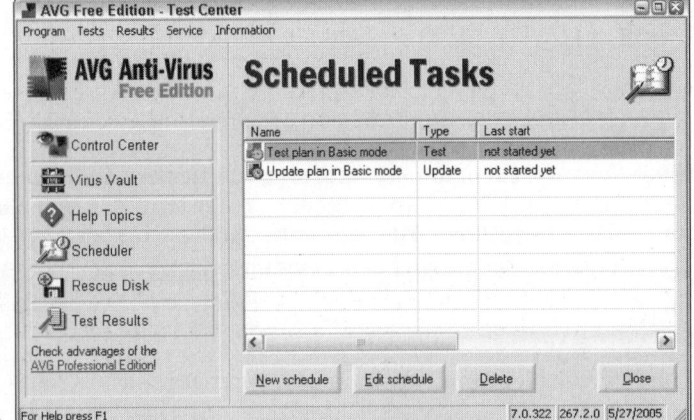

Figure 18-2: Control the timing of AVG Free updates and scans here.

3. **Double-click the first entry, Test Plan in Basic Mode.**

    AVG Free brings up a dialog box that allows you to set the start time for daily system scans.

4. **Pick a time for daily scans that's good for you, typically very early in the morning, and then click OK.**

5. **Double-click the second entry, Update Plan in Basic Mode.**

    AVG Free brings up a slightly different dialog box, where you can pick the time of day to update the virus signature database.

6. **Choose a time *earlier than* the time you set in Step 4 (so AVG updates the database before it runs a scan) and then click OK.**

7. **Click Close to close the Scheduler and then click "X" to get out of the Test Center.**

    AVG should give you years of hassle-free service.

Fighting Spyware

Spyware has rapidly become the top corporate IT concern. For good reason. Back in the not-so-good-old-days, we had to deal with virus and Trojan writers who, with some notable exceptions, had the intelligence of toothpaste.

That's changed. There's a lot of money to be made with spyware, and some very, very clever programmers have turned to the Dark Side of the Force.

Using Microsoft Antispyware

There used to be a tremendous antispyware program called GIANT. (Yeah, they spelled it with ALL CAPITALS.) Then this little company called Microsoft bought GIANT, and the program disappeared. Much to Microsoft's credit, the folks in Redmond released a free replacement for GIANT (dubbed the Microsoft Antispyware Beta) a couple of months later. All looked well in antispyware land until Microsoft decided it could make money selling software that protects people from the security holes in . . . Microsoft's software.

Imagine.

As we went to press, the details hadn't been ironed out, but given the GIANT pedigree, it appeared likely that Microsoft's antispyware product (which may be part of OneCare, the extra-cost service) will be a category killer.

Check AskWoody.com for the latest details.

Running CounterSpy

Back in 1943, a fellow by the name of Walter Edmonds published a book about John Haskell, a boy who goes trapping in upstate New York to support his family after his father died. John learns the tricks of the trade from an old Native American, who left John with some sound advice about traversing streams in the wilderness: "Remember this. Whatever you do when you travel, always use two logs crossing."

Of course, John went out trapping on his own, and of course, he gathered so many furs he could hardly carry them all. On his way back to town, he tried to cross a creek using a single log and (tell me if you've heard this one before) he fell in, losing all his furs. John skulked back into town, wet and half dead. His old mentor saw him, shook his head, and said, "You forgot to use two logs crossing."

CounterSpy is your second log. It's free for 15 days, after which registration costs $19.95, including a year of updates (subsequent years run $9.98). Here's how to get it:

1. **Log on to `www.sunbelt-software.com`. Click the CounterSpy ad (which probably takes up most of the page).**

2. **Scroll down to the bottom of the page and click Download, fill out the registration form, and click Download CounterSpy.**

TIP

The download page also offers to sign you up for the Sunbelt Software newsletter, WinXP News. Believe it or not, it's a very good e-mail newsletter — one of the few I recommend regularly. Don't hesitate to sign up, if you feel so inclined.

3. **Follow the instructions to download** `counterspy.exe`, **the installation file. Then run** `counterspy.exe`.

   The CounterSpy installation wizard kicks in.

4. **Take all the defaults and install CounterSpy. Click Finish, and CounterSpy reboots your computer.**

   When you reboot, CounterSpy updates itself with the latest spyware definitions and software.

5. **When the update finishes, double-click the CounterSpy icon on the desktop or in the System Tray, next to the clock.**

   CounterSpy takes you through a setup wizard. Take all the defaults. The last step of the setup wizard (shown in Figure 18-3) offers to let you run a scan now.

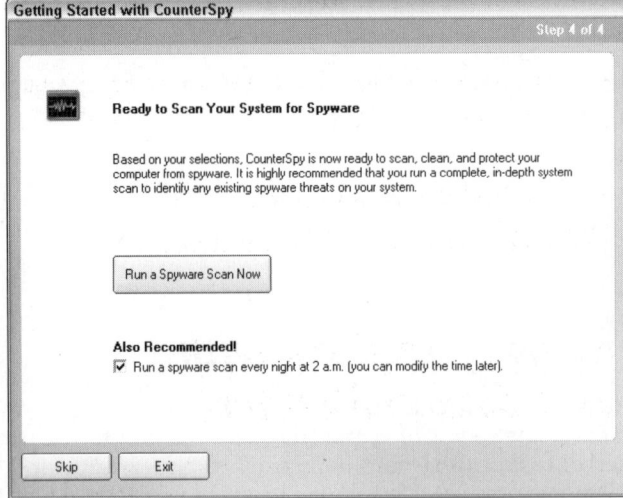

Figure 18-3:
Take advantage of the opportunity and scan your computer now.

6. **Click Run a Spyware Scan Now and then, in the CounterSpy main window, click Scan Now.**

   CounterSpy has the fastest scans in the business. Hold onto your hat. When CounterSpy finishes its initial scan you see a report like the one shown in Figure 18-4.

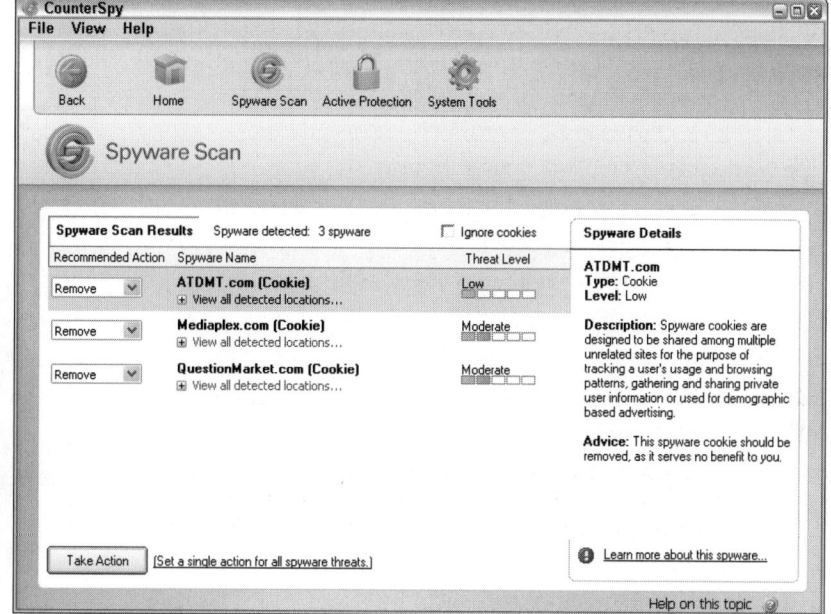

Figure 18-4:
Don't be
surprised if
CounterSpy
picks up
scumware
that other
programs
miss.

7. **To take the recommended actions, in the lower-left corner, click Take Action.**

   Off with their heads, sez I.

8. **Click "X" to dismiss the main window.**

   CounterSpy continues to work in the background.

Blocking your Registry with Mike Lin's StartupMonitor

A truly remarkable, tiny program from a guy who does great work, Mike Lin's StartupMonitor watches your Registry and warns you if a program tries to hook into the Registry, so it'll start whenever you start Windows.

Microsoft's Antispyware program catches most modifications to the Registry, but StartupMonitor gives you an extra layer of protection — and it doesn't let Microsoft's programs get away with installing themselves. Figure 18-5 shows StartupMonitor trapping an attempt by Office XP to reinstall its speech recognition software.

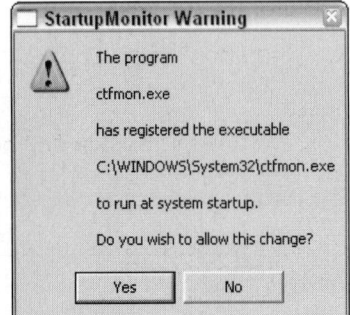

Figure 18-5:
Office XP's
speech
recognizer,
ctfmon, tries
to sneak
back in.

To install StartupMonitor:

1. **Go to `www.mlin.net/StartupMonitor.shtml` and click the line that says Download StartupMonitor. Save `StartupMonitor-1.zip` to disk.**

2. **Double-click `StartupMonitor-1.zip` and then double-click `StartupMonitor.msi`.**

   The installation wizard kicks in.

3. **Take all of the defaults and then click Close to exit the installer.**

   You have to reboot your machine for StartupMonitor to take effect.

Startup sleuthing

Most scumware manages to load itself every time you start Windows. You might think it would be easy to tell Windows, "Hey, don't start this program." It isn't. That's proved to be one of Windows' worst design faults.

Auto-starting programs can hide in a dozen different places. More than a dozen. If you get to the point where your favorite antispyware program can't find the auto-starting program that bedevils you (remember the "two logs crossing" principle), you may decide to take your Startup group into your own hands.

There are two ways to approach the pruning of your auto-starting programs: the right way and the wrong way. Permit me to describe the wrong way first. Windows has a program called the System Configuration Utility that lets you poke and prod at many of the settings that affect how Windows starts. To use the System Configuration Utility (remember, this is the wrong way):

1. **Choose Start➪Run, type** msconfig, **and press Enter.**

   Windows brings up the System Configuration Utility.

2. **Click the Startup tab.**

   The Startup tab (shown in Figure 18-6) shows you many (but not all!) of the programs that run on startup.

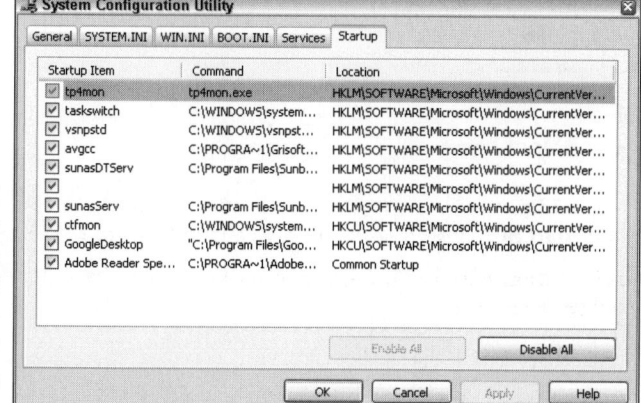

Figure 18-6:
The
Windows
System Con-
figuration
Utility.

3. **Stop. Don't do anything. There's a better way. Click Cancel to get out of the System Configuration Utility.**

Many books and Web sites recommend using msconfig to control auto-starting programs. Don't. It's a wretched startup utility for many reasons, including the fact that it doesn't find all auto-starters; there's no way to manage (or permanently delete) the programs that it finds; and it has a nasty habit of popping back up every time you restart Windows.

There's a much better, and free, alternative from the guy I mentioned in the preceding section, Mike Lin. Here's how to get it:

1. **Take your Web browser to** www.mlin.net/StartupCPL.shtml.

2. **Click the line that says Standalone EXE Version and save** StartupCPL_EXE.zip **to your disk.**

   Mike has two different versions, one of which sits in the Windows Control Panel, and the other is a plain ol' program. I like plain ol' programs. If you prefer the Control Panel version, go ahead and click Download Startup Control Panel.

3. **Double-click StartupCPL_EXE.zip and then click and drag the file Startup.exe to your Desktop.**

   You can right-click the icon and rename it Startup Control Panel.exe if you want.

4. **Double-click the new icon to run the program.**

   Startup Control Panel appears (see Figure 18-7).

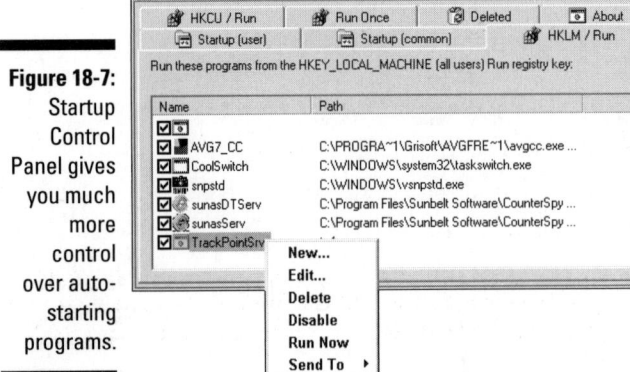

Figure 18-7:
Startup
Control
Panel gives
you much
more
control
over auto-
starting
programs.

5. **Click each tab to see what runs at startup. If you want to temporarily disable a program, uncheck the box in front of it and restart Windows. If you want to permanently disable an auto-starter, right-click it and choose Delete.**

   If you delete a program, Startup Control Panel doesn't really delete it. If you look on the Deleted tab, the wayward program appears; right-click it and you can restore it again.

6. **Click "X" to leave Startup Control Panel. Restart your computer for the new settings to take effect.**

   And don't forget to send Mike a tip — "50 cents, a dollar, whatever you see fit." Click the PayPal Donate box on any of his Web pages or the Tip Jar box on the program's About page.

Chapter 19

Keeping Your Privates Private

*A*dmit it. At least once, you've done something on your computer that you don't want other people to know about. Whether it's your kids, your boss, your nosy neighbor, the authorities, or your significant other(s), ain't nobody's business but your own.

Perhaps it's true, as Sun CEO Scott McNealy says, "You have no privacy. Get over it." I, for one, won't accept Scott's death sentence. Privacy stands as a fundamental freedom that every person should expect — demand, if need be.

Here's what I say: *Protect your privacy. Get with it.*

This chapter gives you a few tools to fight back.

Covering Your Tracks Online

Online privacy falls into two broad categories: working online without leaving your footprints in the sand and removing records of what you've done from your own computer.

Some people fret over sending anonymous e-mail: How can they send an e-mail message to, say, their boss, or a politician, without having it traced back to them? Nothing could be simpler. Go to any Web café or library with public computers. Log on to `hotmail.com` and sign up for a new account under the name William Gates III, One Microsoft Way, Redmond WA 98052-6399, phone 425-882-8080. Send the message. End of story. It's that easy.

Windows Media Player presents its own, truly astonishing threats to your privacy. (Imagine a program that's told not to retrieve a license from the Web but goes out to the Web and retrieves the license anyway.) I talk about Windows Media Player's flagrant indiscretions in Chapter 20.

Anonymous surfing

Every time you visit a Web site, you leave your footprint. Specifically, your browser sends the Web site the following information:

- ✔ Your Internet (IP) address, which uniquely identifies systems that have always-on connections, such as ADSL or cable modems
- ✔ The Web page you were looking at before you moved to the current Web page
- ✔ The name of the Web browser you're using
- ✔ Lots of miscellaneous information, including your language
- ✔ The contents of any cookies associated with this Web site

To see precisely what information your browser sends, drop by Steve Gibson's ShieldsUP! site:

1. **Start your browser and go to www.grc.com. Scroll down (way down) to the line that says ShieldsUP! and click it. Then click Proceed.**

   You see the ShieldsUP! main page.

2. **Look in the block marked ShieldsUP! Services. Click the button marked Browser Headers.**

   ShieldsUP! shows you a complete list of all the information passed to the Web site by your browser (see Figure 19-1).

   Note, in particular, that your IP address appears in the header information.

3. **Follow Steve's discussion about cookies and try his test to see how cookies get set and sent. When you're done, "X" out of your browser.**

   A real eye-opener, eh?

If you want to surf the Web without leaving your footprints behind for anyone to see, you need something called an *anonymizer* or *proxy server*. The basic idea is pretty simple: You go to the anonymizer's Web site and type the address of the Web page that you want to see; the anonymizer reaches out, grabs the page, and then returns it to you. That way, the only footprints left behind are ones for the anonymizer, not yours.

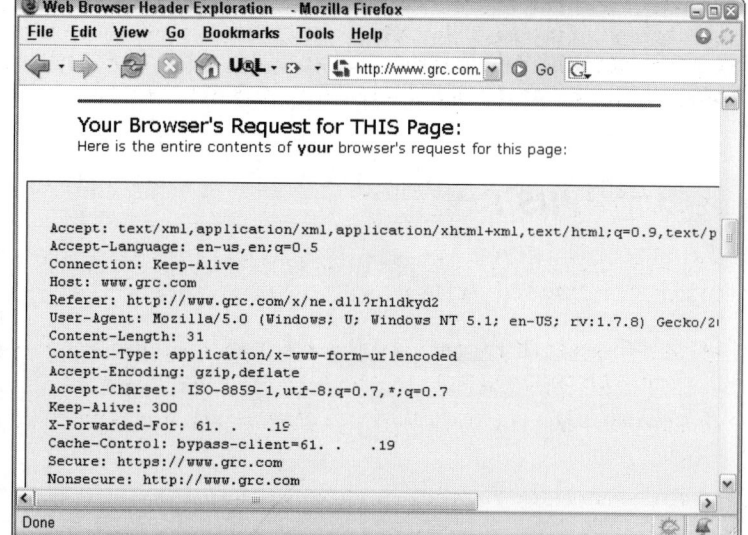

Figure 19-1:
The infor-
mation
Firefox
sends to
ShieldsUP!

My favorite free anonymizers:

✔ **The-Cloak** (`www.the-cloak.com/anonymous-surfing-home.html`)
limits the number of times you can use the service free from a specific IP
address, but it's quite reliable and very fast.

✔ **SurfShield** (`surfshield.net`) has no limits, but the service goes up
and down.

✔ **Anonymizer** (`www.anonymizer.com/index.shtml`), the granddaddy of
them all (shown in Figure 19-2), can be slow unless you subscribe to one
of the packages.

Browser amnesia

Both Firefox and Internet Explorer keep logs of what you've typed, where
you've been, and what you've seen.

To delete history information in Firefox:

1. **Start Firefox. Choose Tools⇨Options and, on the left, click the Privacy
   icon.**

   Firefox shows you the Privacy options shown in Figure 19-3. Some of the
   options are a bit hard to understand, so follow along here.

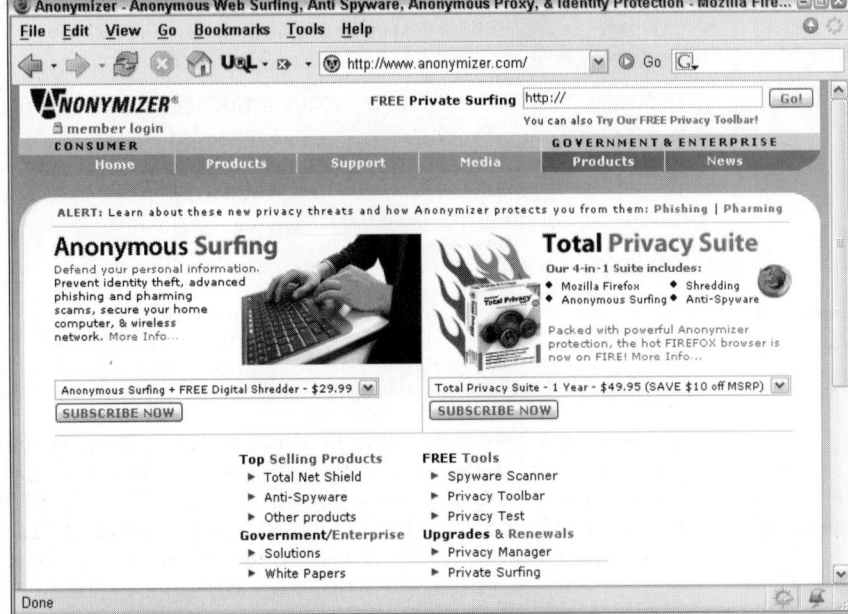

Figure 19-2:
Anonymizer
offers
excellent
anonymous
surfing —
for a price.

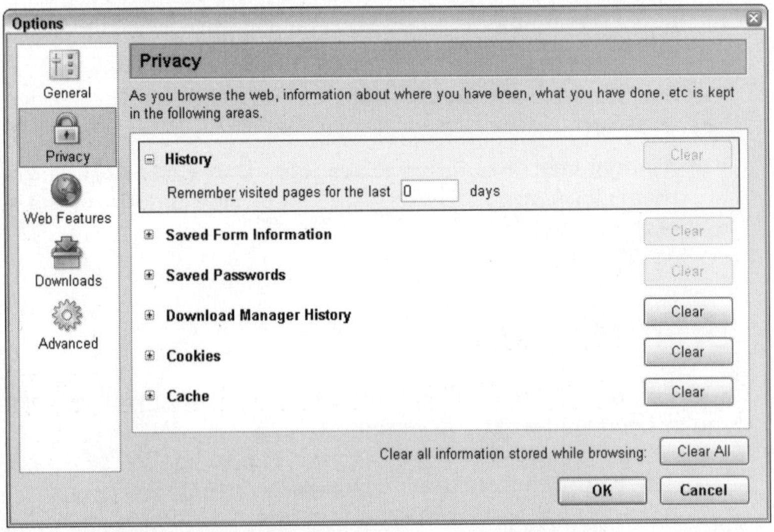

Figure 19-3:
Firefox
Privacy
options.

2. Click the + next to History.

The History entry not only controls the Firefox history pane — the list of all Web sites you visited, accessed by pressing Ctrl+H while in the main Firefox window — but also controls the drop-down list of typed addresses at the top of the main Firefox window.

3. **To clear the current history list, click Clear. To keep Firefox from maintaining a history list, set the Remember Visited Pages For the Last _ Days box to zero.**

   I don't know why — it may be a bug — but setting the box to zero does *not* keep Firefox from maintaining the drop-down list of typed addresses, temporarily. If you set the box to zero, the drop-down list only sticks around for the current session, until you close the Firefox window. But it's there if prying eyes want to look.

4. **Click the + next to Saved Form Information.**

   The Saved Form Information entry not only controls information that you type into forms that you encounter on the Internet, but also controls the list of items that you've typed into the Google Search box in the upper-right corner.

5. **To clear the Saved Form Information list, click Clear. To keep Firefox from maintaining information about what you've typed into forms and what you've typed in the Search box, click the + sign next to Saved Form Information and uncheck the box marked Save Information I Enter in Web Page Forms and the Search Bar.**

   I bet you wondered how to clear out the Search box.

6. **Similarly, review the options under Saved Passwords and Download Manager History. Clear or make changes as you see fit.**

7. **Click the + sign next to Cookies (see Figure 19-4).**

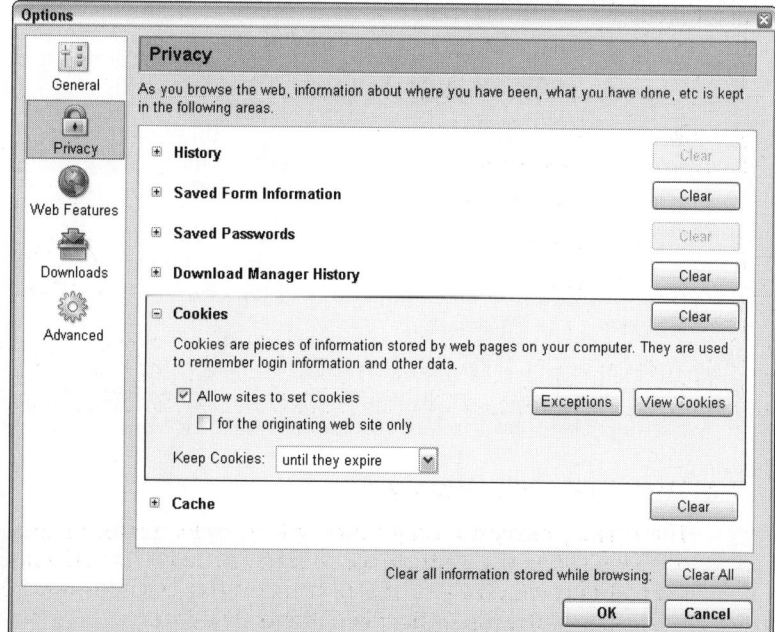

Figure 19-4: Click the + sign to see the Cookie options.

Be cautious in clearing the cookies on your PC: Most cookies are quite benevolent, even useful, and your antispyware program (see Chapter 18) should be able to catch the bad ones.

8. **Make any changes to cookies you think appropriate.**

   For a full discussion of cookies and how they can be used to spy on you, see *Windows XP Timesaving Techniques For Dummies.*

9. **Click the + sign next to Cache.**

   Firefox's cache contains pictures that you've recently viewed on the Web. Yes, the ads are right; you *do* have dirty pictures on your machine. Everybody does. Even if you accidentally brushed by a porn site, fleetingly, chances are good at least one of the pictures is still sitting in the cache.

10. **Make cache settings you can live with.**

    You're presented with a damned-if-you-do-damned-if-you-don't dilemma. If you clear the cache or set Use Up to _ KB of Disk Space For the Cache to zero (which permanently disables the cache), Firefox will run much slower. If you keep the cache, Firefox runs faster because it doesn't have to download pictures that are already sitting on your computer, but copies of all the pictures you've seen recently appear in the cache.

11. **Click OK.**

    Your changes take effect immediately.

Internet Explorer's privacy-related settings are scattered all over the program, and many of IE's settings don't do much. (Content Advisor and P3P come to mind.) With that in mind:

- To clear the History list and the typed address list, choose Tools➪ Internet Options➪General and look in the History box at the bottom.

- To clear the stored information IE uses to fill out forms, including passwords, choose Tools➪Internet Options➪Content, click the AutoComplete button, and click Clear Forms and/or Clear Passwords.

- Cookie settings in IE are quite extensive and rather confusing. The options are under Tools➪Internet Options➪Privacy. I have a full description of the settings and their implications in *Windows XP All-in-One Desk Reference For Dummies.*

- To delete or change the cache, choose Tools➪Internet Options➪General and under Temporary Internet Files, click Delete Files and/or click Settings to adjust the size (or permanently clobber) the cache.

Covering Your Tracks in Windows

Windows has an annoying habit of not respecting your privacy — but it's much harder to adjust Windows' behavior than it is to bend Firefox or Internet Explorer to your wishes.

Protecting from prying eyes

Keep in mind that, unless you take steps to protect your files, anybody who uses your computer can see anything on the computer. You can make things quite difficult by assigning passwords to all accounts and having each user mark his sensitive folders as Private, but a sufficiently determined cracker can get at the data anyway.

If you give yourself a password and mark any folder as Private, you better make a password reset disk. If you forget your password, the only (easy) way you can get at your data is with the password reset disk.

Making Windows moderately secure, to keep folks who share your computer out of your files, rates as a nontrivial task. I cover it extensively in *Windows XP Timesaving Techniques For Dummies*.

Well and truly deleting a file

When you delete a file in Windows XP, Windows just moves it to the Recycle Bin, right? Usually, anybody with a passing interest can get into the Recycle Bin and pull the file out.

You can go to the Recycle Bin and delete the file — just click the file and press Delete. That removes the file from the Recycle Bin, but it doesn't take the file off your computer. There are hundreds of free utilities on the Internet that will "undelete" files that have been removed from the Recycle Bin.

If you want to truly delete a file, you have to zap it with a program that overwrites the data in the file, preferably in truly clever and devious ways, so the original data can't be recovered — even if a determined cracker takes apart your hard drive and scans it with sophisticated equipment. Enter Heidi.

Heidi Computer's Eraser (free, from `www.heidi.ie/eraser`) erases files, erases its history of erasing files, erases all the free space on a drive, and — if you so desire — can completely wipe out a hard drive.

If you only have a few files that require protection, consider using the encryption feature (if any) in the program that created each file. All the Office programs have very strong encryption abilities. WinZIP (www.winzip.com) can zip a file and lock it with a password that's very hard to crack. Just remember to zap the original file (see the sidebar "Well and truly deleting a file").

Clobbering the MRU lists

Windows, and many programs, keep Most Recently Used lists in order to make it easier and faster to retrieve files you may want. Of course, the MRU lists also provide detailed information about which files you've recently opened, to a first approximation, anyway — the MRU facility in Windows XP is notorious for not remembering certain kinds of files or files opened in unusual ways.

You might think that turning off My Recent Documents on the Start menu (see Chapter 5) would convince Windows that it shouldn't keep track of the most recently used files. Nope. Even if you don't have My Recent Documents showing on the Start menu, Windows maintains a list — actually, a longer list than the one that appears on My Recent Documents — as a bunch of shortcuts in the folder C:\Documents and Settings\<username>\Recent, where <username> is your username. If you navigate to the folder in Windows Explorer, instead of Recent, you see My Recent Documents.

Figure 19-5 shows the Recent folder for Duangkhae — and she doesn't have My Recent Documents showing on her Start menu.

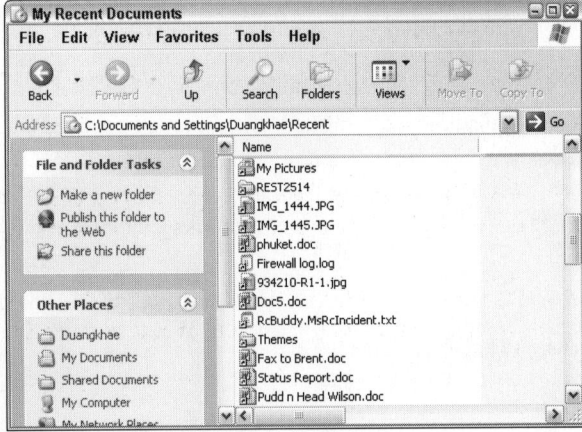

Figure 19-5:
Windows
keeps a list
of your
recently
accessed
documents.

It's easy to remove a single file from the My Recent Documents list on the Start menu: click Start⇨My Recent Documents, right-click the file you want to remove, and click Delete.

It's also easy to clear the entire My Recent Documents list:

1. **Right-click Start and choose Properties.**

2. **Click Customize and then click Advanced.**

3. **At the bottom of the window, where it says Recent Documents, click Clear List.**

   Note that the box marked List My Most Recently Opened Documents controls only where My Recent Documents appears on the Start menu. It doesn't clear the list, and it doesn't keep Windows from putting entries in the Recent folder.

It's possible to tell Windows to clear the list every time you log off Windows. See the steps following for details.

Clearing the list isn't the same thing as preventing Windows from maintaining the list in the first place. You can turn the feature off — you can tell Windows to stop tracking Most Recently Used files — but if you do, many programs won't be able to maintain *their* Most Recently Used lists. For example, all the Office programs (Word, Excel, PowerPoint, and Access, in particular) will lose the Most Recently Used file list at the bottom of the File menu.

If you want to get rid of the Windows My Recent Documents folder, *and it doesn't bother you that you'll also eliminate the MRU lists for many programs,* here's how to do it:

1. **Follow the instructions in Chapter 4 to download and install TweakUI.**

2. **Choose Start⇨All Programs⇨Powertoys for Windows XP⇨TweakUI.**

3. **When TweakUI appears, click Explorer (located on the left side of the window).**

4. **To make Windows clear its My Recent Documents folder every time you log off Windows, check the box marked Clear Document History on Exit.**

   If you choose this option, the Office applications (and others) will list only documents opened during the current Windows session at the bottom of the File menu.

5. **To make Windows completely "forget" to add files to the My Recent Documents folder, uncheck the box marked Maintain Document History.**

   If you choose this option, the Office programs (and others) won't show anything at the bottom of the File menu.

6. **Click OK to leave TweakUI.**

   Your choices go into effect immediately.

Keeping Windows from phoning home

Ever have a program tell you that it has encountered a problem and needs to close (see Figure 19-6)?

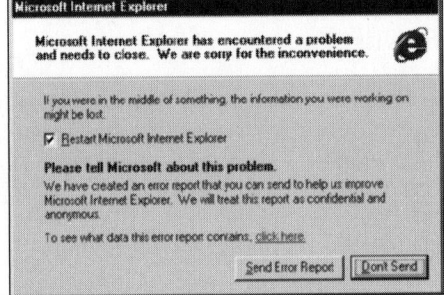

Figure 19-6:
Internet
Explorer
gets indi-
gestion.

Ever been tempted to send an error report to Microsoft?

Think about it. The U.S. Department of Energy's CIAC group says the error report for Office programs and Internet Explorer "includes a memory dump which may contain all or part of the document being viewed or edited. This debug message potentially could contain sensitive, private information." See www.ciac.org/ciac/bulletins/m-005.shtml.

Microsoft counters that it has made enormous improvements to Windows and all its applications because of this automatically collected information. They also claim that nobody — but nobody — sees information that they shouldn't. You can see the information being sent by clicking the appropriate spot on the dialog box.

I don't doubt that everything Microsoft says is true. But I still won't send Microsoft my crash reports. Would you?

Instead of relying on your mouse finger to do The Right Thing every time you encounter an offer to send an error report, you can turn off the "feature" once and for all:

1. **Choose Start, right-click My Computer, and choose Properties.**

   Windows shows you the System Properties dialog box.

2. **Click the Advanced tab. Then, at the bottom, click Error Reporting.**

   You see the Error Reporting dialog box, as shown in Figure 19-7.

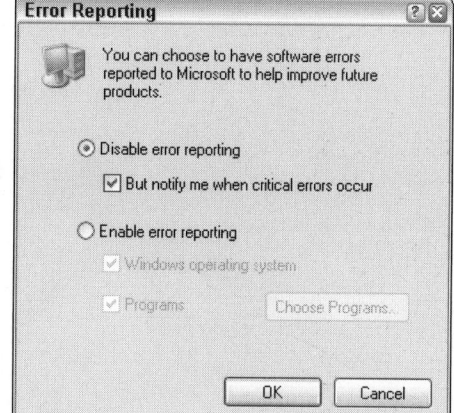

Figure 19-7:
Turn off the "Dr. Watson" error reporting here.

3. **Click the Disable Error Reporting button. (Or, if you're willing to wrestle with the devil, click the Choose Programs button and set up different rules for Microsoft and non-Microsoft programs.)**

4. **Click OK twice.**

   Windows won't ask anymore.

Part VI
Entertaining Yourself

The 5th Wave

By Rich Tennant

INTENSE BUT UNINFORMED AUDIOPHILE BILLY WIGGINS ENJOYS HIS CUSTOM BURNED CD COLLECTION OF DIAL UP MODEM WARBLES

In this part . . .

Man, I love my iPod. What a great machine. The only thing wrong with it? I have to put up with iTunes, its incessant pushy advertising, and its really clueless insistence on slapping "AAC" copy protection on all my music. I hate it when a computer takes a tune that I've bought, and keeps me from playing that tune on my computer, in my car, or on my precious iPod.

Until I figure out the right hacks, of course.

This part shows you how to take back control from the big software companies, so the music you buy can be used the way you want. It also presents some novel ideas for buying music and safely sharing files of all types.

Chapter 20

Making the Most of Media Player

*W*indows Media Player ain't the only game in town. In fact, if you own an iPod, I recommend (in the next chapter) that you shell out $15 and use Winamp Pro.

That said, there's a lot to like about Windows Media Player (WMP). It "feels" like a Windows program (which is much more than I can say for Apple's iTunes). It *rips* (copies songs from audio CDs onto the computer) and *burns* (copies music files onto audio CDs) well, if you know how to jigger the settings. It comes with a free MP3 ripper (as does iTunes). I, personally, use WMP frequently.

That said, WMP bugs the daylights out of me. It's a vintage Microsoft product, with advertising packed into every nook and cranny, relentlessly trying to sell, sell, sell. Earlier versions took extreme liberties with my personal information — even exposed me to viruses, in spite of my settings — and I'm still wary.

As long as you're willing to accept the fact that Microsoft is trying to sell you a bill of goods with WMP, it's not a half-bad program. But you need to stay on your toes and keep your credit card in your pocket. Literally and figuratively.

Knowing Your File Format$

Microsoft has grand designs to take over the world.

That shouldn't come as any great surprise.

In this particular case, the "world" is the world of music and movies. Microsoft introduced the WMA (Windows Media Audio) file format in December 2000, and the music business will never be the same. Designed to compete with, and ultimately displace, the 1992-vintage wide-open MP3 standard, WMA is owned lock, stock, and barrel by Microsoft Corp. If you want to distribute songs in WMA format, you need a license from Microsoft. If you want to build a WMA player, you need a license from Microsoft. See how that works?

There are a few undisputable facts about WMA:

✔ Technically, WMA runs rings around MP3. Depending on the amount of wax in your ears, WMA files occupy about one-half to one-third as much space as MP3 files of the same sound quality.

✔ Record companies love WMA and WMV (Windows Media Video file format). Why? Because they can lock up the files and make you pay to listen to them. MP3 files are distributable and can be played on anything, so you don't have to worry about the Digital Rights Management consequences of copying a file from your PC to your MP3 player.

✔ If a person blithely takes all the defaults in Windows Media Player and rips a song from a CD that she owns, she'll end up with a copy-protected WMA file that only plays on the computer that ripped the song.

Microsoft spent millions of dollars trying to convince people that WMA music, in various guises, "Plays for Sure." Not true. MP3 plays for sure. WMA has marketing money. There's a difference.

Installing the Latest Windows Media Player

It's important that you install the latest version of Windows Media Player because Microsoft has a nasty habit of releasing patches to WMP by simply changing the downloadable file. See `www.edbott.com/weblog/archives/000641.html` for a hair-raising example.

Here's how to get the latest:

1. **Point your Web browser at `www.microsoft.com/windows/windowsmedia/download`.**

2. **Choose the latest version of WMP and click Download Now.**

   Download the setup file to a convenient location on your disk.

3. **Double-click the downloaded file.**

   The WMP installer kicks in.

4. **Click Next a couple of times and sit back while the installer does its thing.**

   You may get a security warning about running Microsoft Music Assistant, which is a program that WMP uses to connect to the MSN Music Web site — in other words, it's there to sell you things. I searched high and low and couldn't find *any* documentation about Microsoft Music Assistant beyond the marketing pablum stage. It doesn't appear to hurt anything, so you might as well click Run to let it start.

   When the installer comes up for air, it shows a do-nothing screen.

5. **Click Next.**

   The WMP installer shows you the Privacy Options page (see Figure 20-1).

Figure 20-1:
Time to
make some
important
decisions.

6. **Use the descriptions in Table 20-1 to see whether you need any of the "services" on offer, but keep in mind that if you let Windows Media Player connect to the Internet at any time, Microsoft gathers every scrap of information about you — including your Internet (IP) address, which can identify your computer uniquely if you have an always-on Internet connection (such as ADSL or cable modem).**

   Personally, I uncheck everything and then override the choices when I want to gather album information while ripping a CD.

7. Click Next.

WMP offers to take control of all the major audio file types. If you have another audio player that you like better (iTunes, WinAMP, or MusicMatch), uncheck all the boxes.

8. Click Finish.

Windows Media Player is ready — but you aren't. Follow the steps in the next section before you start grooving.

Table 20-1	What the Privacy Options Really Mean
This Setting . . .	*. . . Really Means*
Display Media Info from the Internet	Whenever you play a CD or DVD, WMP goes to the online store (probably `music.msn.com`), retrieves information about the CD or DVD . . . and then offers to sell it to you. Go figger.
Update Music Files by Retrieving Additional Media Info from the Internet	When you rip a CD or add items to the Library, WMP goes to the Internet, retrieves the titles of the tracks and a picture of the album cover, and updates the album info accordingly.
Acquire Licenses Automatically for Protected Content	HA! If you check this box, WMP automatically goes out to the record company's site and asks for a license (read: $$$) if it encounters a file that requires a license. Yes, it'll go out and try to get money from you for a freshly ripped song while the CD you bought is still in the drive. Microsoft got caught ignoring this setting in a big security flap. See `http://securitytracker.com/id?1013945`.
Send Unique Player ID to Content Providers	WMP sends a number that uniquely identifies your computer to people trying to sell you things. Yeah, right. Microsoft lost a court case over this one; they can't check the box by default, so they try to convince you to do it.
I Want to Help Make Microsoft Software and Services Better by HA! HA! HA!	Sorry, I can't even bring myself to repeat this garbage. Somebody help me off the floor, please.
Save File and URL History in the Player	So WMP can send Microsoft a complete list of everything you've played, from time to time. HA! HA! HA!

Setting Up WMP

Before you do anything with Windows Media Player, take a few minutes and get the settings right:

1. **Start WMP. Right-click the top line, next to where it says Windows Media Player, and choose Tools⇨Options⇨Rip Music (see Figure 20-2).**

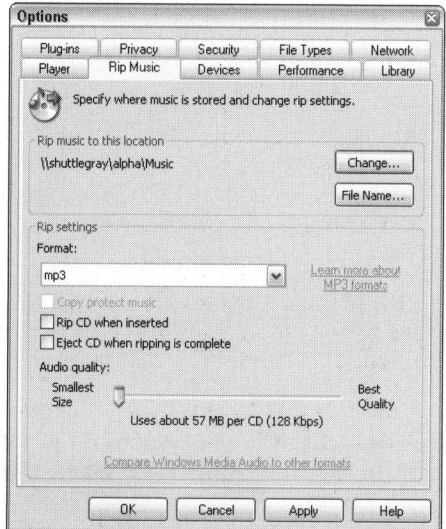

Figure 20-2: Make WMP rip to MP3 format files.

2. **In the Rip Settings Format drop-down box, choose MP3.**

   Do your part to keep Microsoft's hands off our music. Oh. Didja notice? The check box marked Copy Protect Music turned gray. How about that.

   You can slide the Audio Quality bar to the right, if you like, particularly if you're going to be listening to the music on a super cool sound system. But for everyday use, 128 Kbps works just fine.

3. **In the Rip Music to This Location area, click the Change button, navigate to the Shared Music folder, and click OK to get out of the Browse for Folder dialog box.**

   It's always smartest to put your music in a shared folder. In Figure 20-2, Duangkhae rips music directly to a systemwide shared hard drive.

4. **Click the Devices tab.**

   WMP shows you a list of your CD drive(s), monitors, speakers, and more.

5. **Click any CD drive you use for ripping music and then click Properties.**

WMP brings up the Properties dialog box for that drive (see Figure 20-3).

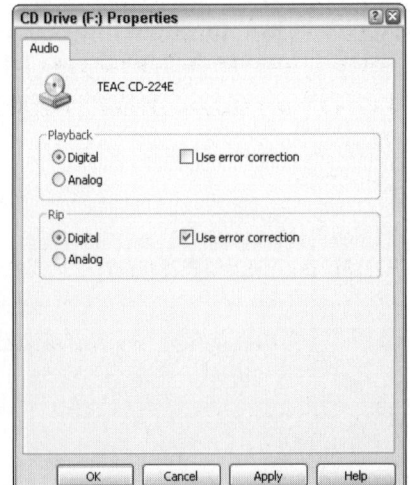

6. **In the Rip area, at the bottom, check the box marked Use Error Correction. Then click OK to clear the Properties dialog box.**

With Error Correction set, Windows Media Player tries its darnedest to retrieve audio files from a scratchy CD. I've used this setting to rip ancient, damaged CDs and have the ripped songs come out good as new.

7. **Click the Privacy tab.**

Double-check to make sure that all of the boxes are unchecked, with the possible exception of Update Music Files by Retrieving Media Info from the Internet. (Oh, and it's OK to Set Clock on Devices Automatically.)

8. **Click OK.**

WMP is ready to go.

Using TweakMP

Some people swear by TweakMP, the Media Player–tweaking utility from Microsoft, putting it in the same league as TweakUI (see Chapter 4). I don't buy it. Microsoft may update TweakMP one of these days, but as of this writing, only one feature is worth the effort of downloading TweakMP.

If you want to give it a try, here's how:

1. **Go to http://wmplugins.com and use the search box to find TweakMP. You are presented with one choice after the search. Click the picture to the left of the entry to get to the TweakMP download page.**

2. **Click the line marked Download from Microsoft and download the setup file to your hard drive.**

3. **Double-click the setup file to run it.**

   It's a very simple installer — not even a wizard.

4. **When the installer finishes, choose Tools⊅Plug-Ins⊅TweakMP. Then click the CD tab.**

   TweakMP shows you the CD Options dialog box, shown in Figure 20-4.

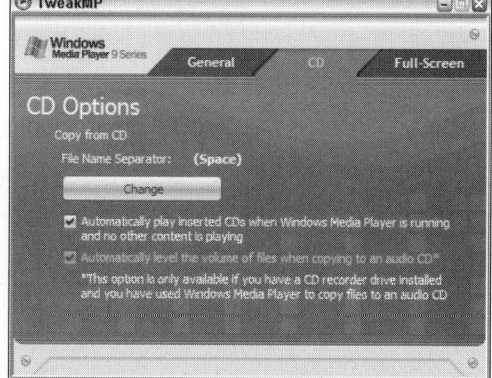

Figure 20-4:
The volume-
leveling
feature in
TweakMP.

5. **Check the box marked Automatically Level the Volume of Files When Copying to an Audio CD.**

   If you have a bunch of audio files that were ripped at different volume levels, checking this box ensures that when you burn them to a CD, they're all at more or less the same volume.

6. **Click "X" to get out of TweakMP.**

   The change takes effect immediately.

Chapter 21

Buying Music and Videos

· ·

In This Chapter

▶ Understanding the limitations for music you buy online

▶ Choosing an online music (and video) store

▶ Getting around the limitations, by hook or by crook

▶ What every iPod owner needs to know

· ·

So you plunked down $400 for a flashy new iPod, and you hooked up iTunes so you could fill your iPod with the latest music from Apple's iTunes Music Store. Then you did the math. Lesseeee . . . at 99 cents per song, the iPod will hold 10,000 songs (enough for 25 days of continuous play!), so that's . . . uh . . . no, that can't be right. $400 for the iPod and $9,900 for the music to go in it?

That's ridiculous. I must've slipped a decimal point there somewhere. Hey, 400 clams for a little MP3 player is stretching things, but for a cool accessory, I guess it could be worse. Then thousands of dollars for the music to go in it?

Guess I'd better go out and get one of those Plays for Sure machines. Oh. Wait a sec. Lemme see if I understand this. I pay for the Plays for Sure music, and I can't play that music on my iPod? I get Napster to Go — Napster plays for sure, doesn't it? — and my To Go songs won't play on a Rio Carbon or Zen Micro? WUH?

This chapter gives you some insight — and maybe a few answers.

Music Restrictions

It's a jungle out there. Apple got the drop on Microsoft by creating a player that everybody wants and an online music store to go along with the iPod. Microsoft fought back by enlisting every hardware manufacturer from here to Hainan to build music players, launching its own online music store, and branding it all with the infamous "Plays for Sure" doublespeak.

Here's what you need to know. For sure:

✔ Almost every music player will play MP3 files. (That's why they're called MP3 players, eh?) But most online music stores don't carry MP3 files because they can't be locked down, and the record companies won't distribute MP3s.

✔ Apple, the iPod, the iTunes software, and the iTunes online music store all prefer AAC format music (using something called the FairPlay protection scheme). An iPod plays MP3 files, but if you buy your music from iTunes, you get AAC.

✔ Microsoft, its hardware cronies, Windows Media Player, and the MSN Music Store all prefer WMA music, which is a Microsoft-proprietary format. (I talk about WMA in Chapter 20.) The Plays for Sure machines play MP3 files, but if you buy your music from MSN or almost every online music store other than iTunes, you get WMA, and the WMA files are "locked" — their use restricted — compliments of Microsoft's Digital Rights Management software.

Digital Rights Management doesn't refer to your rights. It refers to the music company's rights.

✔ Whether you use Windows Media Player or iTunes, you can and should rip your current audio CD collection into MP3 format. (I explain how to do that in *Windows XP Timesaving Techniques For Dummies* and in *Windows XP All-in-One Desk Reference For Dummies*.)

✔ iTunes makes it easy to convert an unprotected WMA file to AAC format. Essentially all the WMA music available online is protected, so the only real benefit here is if you made the mistake of ripping your CDs to WMA format. It's more or less impossible to convert AAC to WMA directly, but you can do it indirectly by using the trick I describe in "Bypassing Restrictions," later in this chapter.

✔ Some record labels are actively sabotaging Apple and iTunes. Sony BMG, in particular, uses SunnComm technology (www.sunncomm.com/support/sonybmg) on some of its CDs, and iTunes can't rip those CDs. Those same CDs might not even play on your computer unless it has an active Internet connection. Hey, I love the Dave Matthews Band, but this is too much.

✔ Everything changes. Every week. I doubt that you'll ever see Bill Gates dance the Funky Chicken with Steve Jobs, but if it'll sell a few more songs, ya never know.

What rights do you, as a consumer, have if an online music store sells you something and then the company's outrageous licensing policies bite you in the back? Not much, it turns out. Mostly, you can take your money somewhere else.

Rent or Buy?

Let's say you can buy a song for 99 cents (at any of dozens of online music stores), or you can rent a huge library of songs for $10 per month (at, say, Napster to Go, Rhapsody to Go, or Virgin). Which is better?

The answer: It depends. And money is only part of the equation.

If you're going to rush out and buy 500 songs, it'll cost you $500, and for that amount of money you could rent all the songs in an entire library for four years. It's a fair bet that you might want one or two more songs in the next four years, so renting makes a lot of sense, yes?

Well, no. Few people sit down at their computers and buy 500 songs at a crack. Most people have sizable CD collections already, and they can rip the CDs for their hot new machines. (Just make sure you rip to MP3, right?) Almost everyone tires of rifling through online music catalogs after a month or two. In the end, you may spend less money — and get more of the music you want — by buying.

There's another factor. Rented songs are inevitably "tethered" to a specific computer, a specific audio player, or both. Usually that isn't a Real Big Deal, but some online music stores make your life unnecessarily, unnaturally difficult. Complaints about To Go songs not playing abound. Besides, what happens when you're grooving on a trail at the bottom of the Grand Canyon when suddenly your 30 days run out?

Which Online Music Store Is Best?

Tough question.

As I see it, the online music world is currently divided into the following categories:

- ✔ **MP3 shops.** Some stores sell MP3 files, the kind that aren't copy protected and work in just about every audio player. *eMusic* (www.emusic.com) has a limited catalog, but at $10 per month for 40 downloaded songs, it's a bargain. *AllOfMP3* (www.allofmp3.com) takes an, uh, imaginative approach: It's based in Russia, where copyright law isn't quite as restrictive as in the United States. Fairly extensive catalog, with lots of rock oldies. At 2 cents per megabyte, you can choose your format and recording rate/quality. But you should realize that the artists (and their labels) probably aren't getting a dime . . . er, ruble. Other free or nearly-free MP3 sites crop up all the time, such as `www.mp3miracle.com` (from Bulgaria?). To find them, Google "mp3 free download" and prepare to wade through a lot of chaff.

✔ **iTunes Music Store.** The first (arguably) and still the largest online music store, Apple's iTunes (`www.itunes.com`) boasts an enormous collection of songs of every imaginable type. At 99 cents a pop, or $9.95 an album, you can burn individual songs onto an unlimited number of CDs for your personal use, listen to the songs on an unlimited number of iPods, and play songs on up to five computers. The *RealPlayer* music store (`www.real.com`) also offers iPod (AAC) songs.

✔ **WMA shops.** The "Plays for Sure" posse includes *MSN Music* (`http://music.msn.com`), of course; *Wal-Mart* (`http://walmart.com/music`); *Napster* (`www.napster.com`); Yahoo's *Musicmatch* (`www.musicmatch.com`); *Rhapsody* (`www.listen.com`, from RealPlayer); in the United Kingdom, *Virgin* (`www.virgindigital.com`) and *Tesco* (which now sells iPods that can't play music from its own music store, `www.tescodownloads.com`); and Uncle Billy Bob's Backyard Super Secure Server Sweatshop, which differentiates itself by selling songs for 86 cents each, 2 cents less than Wal-Mart. (Just kidding.)

Sony, again, is the odd man out, running its own proprietary format — and, at least in the early days, not very well. If you bought a Sony music player, a PSP, Sony's Connect online music store is the only game in town.

If you decide to get an audio player other than the iPod, you should take your time and not rush out and buy all the music you see. Consider subscribing to one of the To Go services, scarfing up all the music you can handle.

But be aware of the fact that many, many people — including some well-known computer book authors, who are pretty good at this stuff — have had no end of problems getting To Go packages to work with audio players, in particular. If you can't get To Go to, uh, go on your MP3 player, don't lose any sleep over it. Try a different company. Better yet, start collecting MP3s. They'll play for sure.

I, personally, love my iPod, and I accumulate all the MP3s I can get. But there's a trick. See the section "Windows and the iPod," later in this chapter.

The market has fragmented tremendously, and some of the companies in business today won't be around in a year or two. Keep that in mind before you commit to any long-term contracts.

Bypassing Restrictions

So you can't do this and you can't do that . . . what *can* you do?

There's an old trick for converting copy-protected files into free MP3s. It doesn't work all the time, but if you can burn your copy-protected music files onto a CD (which is the case for songs purchased from most online stores), it's easy to rip them back as MP3s. The quality drops off in the conversion, but if you start with a very-high-quality song, you get back one of decent quality.

I've modified the old trick here to help you get back song information that's lost in the burning process. As far as I know, this approach has never been documented anywhere before. Here are the crux of the problem and its (partial) solution:

- ✔ Almost always, you can burn your "restricted" music files to an audio CD. Once burned, twice shy — er, sorry . . . once burned, you can rip the songs into MP3 format.

- ✔ Unfortunately, all the information about the songs — names of the songs, artist, genre, album art — all of that is stripped away when you burn the file. So the songs you get back have such interesting names as Track 1, Track 2, and the like.

- ✔ If you burn an entire album onto a single CD and then rip it, you can use Windows Media Player (or any other player, including iTunes) to retrieve the song information from the Internet. That's the same process you use to identify the songs on store-bought CDs.

- ✔ Surprisingly, you can put an album and a some extra songs on a CD and trick Windows Media Player into retrieving the information for all of the songs in the album. You still have to enter the information for the extra songs by hand, though.

There are lots of gray areas in the digital rights management sphere, but this isn't one of them: You can make copies of legit copyrighted material for your own personal use. So if you paid a buck for a song from a big-name online store, you can change it to MP3 format, no problem. The problem arises when you share the song with 100 million of your closest friends.

Here's how to un-Digital-Rights-Manage the songs you bought by using Windows Media Player 10:

1. **Start Windows Media Player. If you want to keep all the song information (names of individual songs, artists, album art, and the like), select**

an entire album. If the song info doesn't matter much to you, or you don't mind typing it in again, select any individual songs that you want to convert to MP3.

You can select by clicking, Shift+clicking, Ctrl+clicking, choosing a playlist using Ctrl+A, or any other way you like.

2. Right-click one of the selected songs and choose Add To⇨Burn List.

WMP shows you the list of songs that it will burn on the right side of the screen.

3. If you want to add more songs or change the order of the songs, click and drag the songs to the Burn List on the right side of the screen (see Figure 21-1).

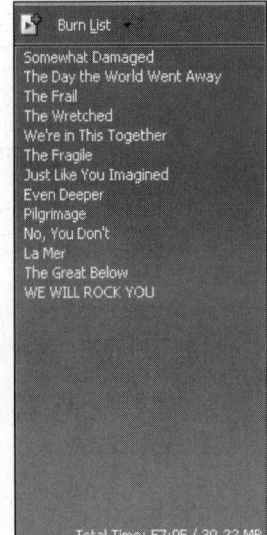

Burn List

Somewhat Damaged
The Day the World Went Away
The Frail
The Wretched
We're in This Together
The Fragile
Just Like You Imagined
Even Deeper
Pilgrimage
No, You Don't
La Mer
The Great Below
WE WILL ROCK YOU

Total Time: 57:05 / 30.22 MB

Figure 21-1:
The list of songs that will be burned.

Note that adding songs to the *end* of an album won't get in the way of WMP identifying the album when you rip the songs back. So if you're careful to stick additional songs at the end of the Burn Playlist, WMP will still grab song names, album art, and the like when you rip. Weird, but true.

The total size of all the files waiting to be burned appears at the bottom of the burn list. You need to keep the total size less than the size of the media (CD or DVD).

4. Click the Burn button at the top of WMP, put a blank CD or DVD in your drive, and click Start Burn.

It may take a long time, but eventually WMP burns the CD and ejects it.

5. **Push the CD back into the drive. If Windows asks what you want to do, click Play Songs with Windows Media Player.**

   Now it's time to rip the music back into your computer. This time you want unprotected, un-DRMd, gloriously hassle-free MP3s.

   When you play the CD, you see that there is no album information (see Figure 21-2). That's normal.

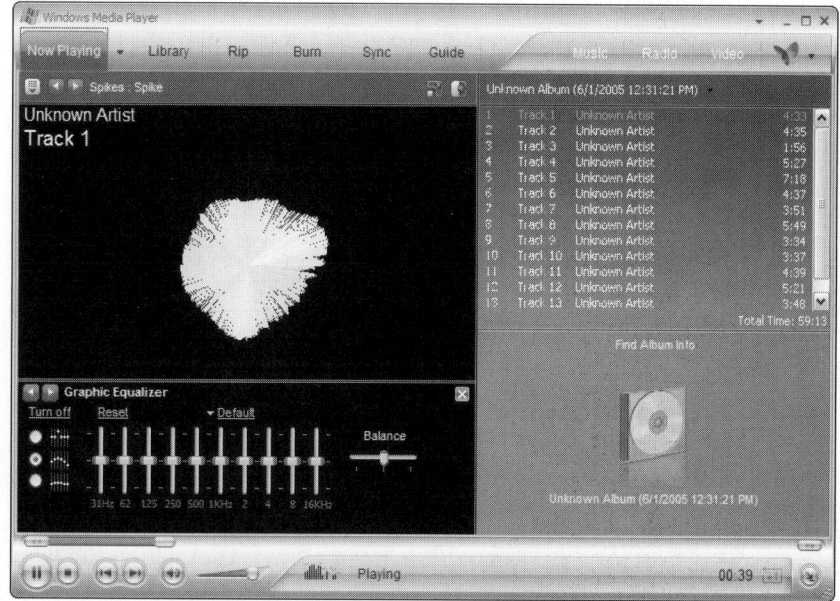

Figure 21-2: All the song information has been stripped from the album.

6. **Right-click the top line of WMP — next to where it says Windows Media Player — and choose Tools⇨Options⇨Rip Music. Verify in the Rip Settings box that WMP knows you want to rip to MP3 format.**

   If MP3 doesn't appear as an option, you don't have the latest version of Windows Media Player. See Chapter 20 and get your free update.

7. **Click the Privacy tab and check the box that says Display Media Information from the Internet. Click OK.**

   You can uncheck the box after you're done ripping.

8. **Click the Rip button at the top of WMP and then click the button on the top right that says Find Album Info.**

   WMP goes out to the Internet and tries to find the song information for your burned CD. If you burned an entire album, chances are very good that WMP will find all the information, and you can proceed to Step 11. If you added songs to the end of an album, WMP presents you with the Search for Album Information page, shown in Figure 21-3.

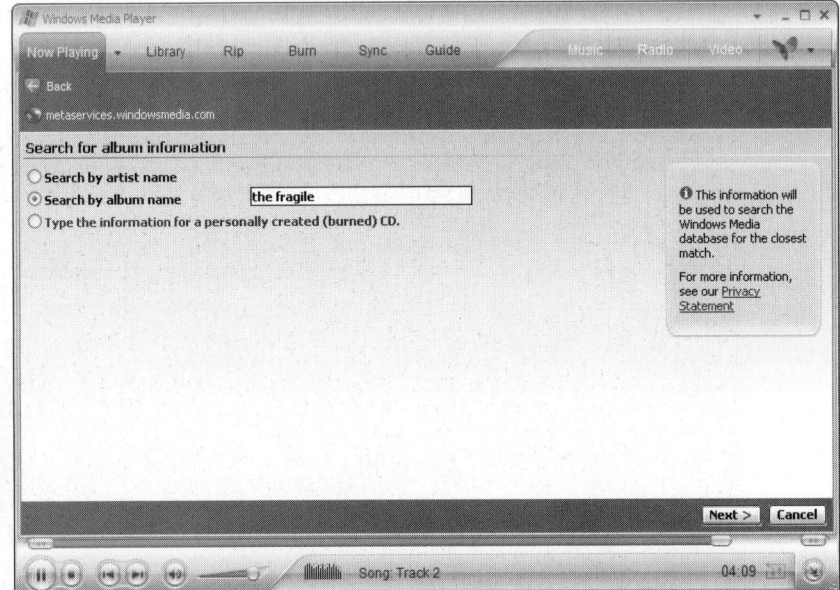

Figure 21-3:
Take WMP
by the hand
if it can't
find your
song info.

9. **Type the first part of the album name and then click Next.**

It's important that you match the name of the album quite precisely. In Figure 21-3, I type **The Fragile** so WMP can find the Nine Inch Nails album. If I had typed **Fragile**, WMP never would've found it.

10. **WMP presents you with a list of albums that match the name you typed. Click the correct album and then click Finish.**

When WMP comes back up for air, it fills in all the missing information for the album (see Figure 21-4). If you have an extra track at the bottom of the list (as is the case in Figure 21-4), WMP leaves it "Track n."

11. **Click the Rip Music button, in the upper right.**

Microsoft attempts to lure you to the Dark Side of the Force, asking if you want to rip to Microsoft's WMA format. Ignore it, Luke.

12. **Click the button marked Keep Your Lousy Fingers off My Settings, I Want My MP3! (or Keep My Current Format Settings, if you can't read the subliminal message) and then click OK.**

WMP rips your files to MP3 format. No Digital Rights Management. No screwy limitations.

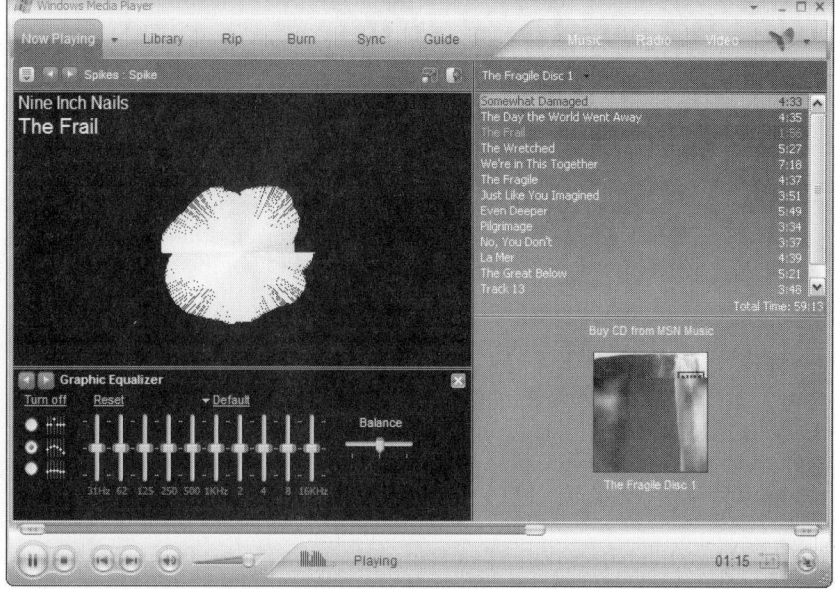

Figure 21-4:
WMP
retrieves
all the
information
for the
album at the
begging of
the CD.

This same process can be used to convert almost any song file format into any other, providing you can burn the songs to an audio CD (and most songs you buy online can be burned).

Some extra-cost products will save song information before you burn the CD and then restore it as you rip. The method for using the programs can be a bit, uh, tedious, but if you don't want to burn and then rip whole albums, buying an add-on will definitely save you hassles in restoring song information. See, for example, www.zittware.com/Products/CDMaster32/ Tutorials/CopyProtected_WMA_to_MP3.html for instructions on using CDMaster to save and restore song information.

There's a completely different approach to creating MP3 files that's roughly analogous to hooking up a tape recorder to your stereo speaker cords. Products such as the Alive MP3 Recorder from Alive Media ($29.95, www.alivemedia. net/guide_convert_copy_protected_wma.htm) plug themselves into the output stream from Windows Media Player, recording the output in MP3 format. Basically, if you can play a file with WMP, you can record it with Alive. Very slick and very good quality.

Windows and the iPod

Do you have an iPod? Yeah, I love mine, too.

But man, I hate some of its idiosyncrasies:

- Your iPod gets married to the computer that feeds it songs. There's no way to add more songs to an iPod from a different PC. You can download a *different* set of songs from a new PC, wiping out the original ones, but that's a pain in the neck.

- If you accidentally erase a song from your computer, you can't retrieve it from the iPod. If you want to play that erased song on your PC or burn it on a CD, you have to go back to the iTunes store and *buy* it again. That's a pain.

- And tell the truth now, don't you get a little bit tired of all the advertising on iTunes?

There's a better way. Meet Winamp, a small, versatile media player that doesn't bug you with a lot of advertising and extraneous garbage. Winamp lets you move your iPod from machine to machine. Winamp lets you copy music from your iPod to your PC. The trick lies in the bridge between Winamp and the iPod called `ml_ipod`. Designed by Justin Frankel, the same guy who originally wrote Winamp, `ml_ipod` rates as the ultimate iPod hacker's tool, whether Apple likes it or not.

To get your iPod to talk to Winamp and give iTunes the heave-ho:

1. **Go to `www.winamp.com`, download and install the latest free version of Winamp. Take all the defaults except the option that allows Winamp to gather usage statistics.**

   You need the full version.

2. **Go to `www.mlipod.com`, click the Downloads button, and download the latest version of `ml_ipod`. Double-click the `downloaded.exe` file, run it, and then click Install to install `ml_iPod`.**

   When the installer finishes, it invites you to start Winamp. Do so.

3. **Plug in your iPod.**

   Windows should recognize it. If Windows doesn't, consult the iPod documentation.

4. **Winamp puts an entry on the left side of the Media Library, identifying the iPod (see Figure 21-5).**

Figure 21-5:
The iPod
appears on
the left side
of the Media
Library.

If Winamp doesn't "see" your iPod, follow the instructions at `http://forums.winamp.com/showthread.php?threadid=215342` to trace down the problem.

5. **Right-click the iPod line, choose iPod Configuration, and then click the Transfer Settings tab.**

   `ml_iPod`'s Transfer Settings Preferences page appears (see Figure 21-6).

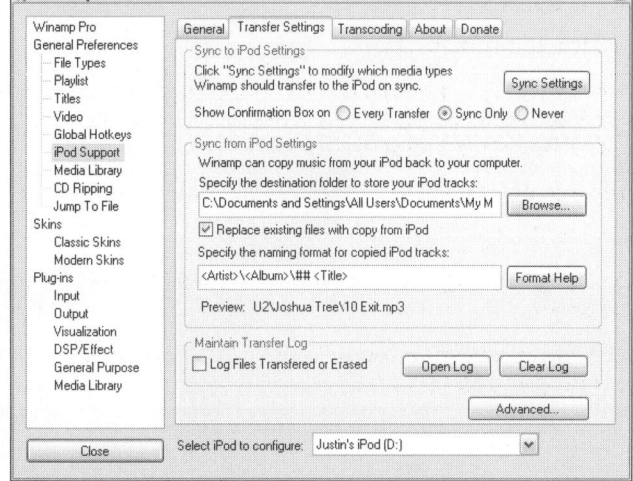

Figure 21-6:
Tell Winamp
where to
put music
that it
transfers
from the
iPod.

6. **In the Sync from iPod Settings box, click Browse, navigate to a location where you'd like songs copied from the iPod to go, click OK, and then click Close to return to Winamp.**

7. **Back in Winamp (refer to Figure 21-5), right-click the iPod and choose iPod Tools⇨Copy to Hard Drive All Songs Not in ML.**

   You see a Reverse Sync Progress bar that apprises you of the progress. You are permitted to say, "Ooooooh! Aaaaaaah!"

8. **That's just the beginning. Take the tour at `www.mlipod.com/?page=documentation` and marvel at the clever ways you can use your iPod now.**

   Someday, all hacked MP3 players will work this well.

Chapter 22

Trading Music and Videos

· ·

In This Chapter

▶ The legalities of sharing files

▶ Choosing a P2P network

▶ Using BitTorrent, my favorite P2P program

▶ Looking for files in other places

· ·

*I*f you have a file (song, movie, photo, whatever) and you make that file available for other people to download, you run the risk of getting sued by the people who hold the copyright for the material in the file, or their representatives. Why? Because what you're doing is against the law. It's really that simple.

There are exceptions. Many files contain content — usually old stuff — in the public domain. Any live recording of the Grateful Dead or Phish can be traded freely: The bands encourage it. (The Dead have encouraged free exchange of recordings since the 1960s.) Bruce Hornsby, Los Lobos, Bela Fleck & The Flecktones, Little Feat, Dave Matthews Band, Blues Traveler, Pearl Jam, Widespread Panic, and many other famous bands and individuals have allowed specific recordings, or kinds of recordings (such as live shows), to be exchanged, as long as nobody collects any money.

P2P (Peer-to-Peer) file sharing, pioneered by Napster, demonized by the Recording Industry Association of America and restricted in university campuses all over the world, hasn't yet reached the level of social respectability of, say, picking your nose. But everybody does it. Or wants to.

2P or Not 2P?

Many people who look at file sharing get turned off by stories of spyware-ridden programs, infected shared files, grandmothers who get sued because their grandsons left the computer on, and really poor-quality music and videos.

In some cases, the reality is worse than the rumor:

✔ Many — if not most — of the file-sharing programs available these days come with loads of scumware. If you're concerned about a specific program, look at www.spywareinfo.com/articles/p2p for the latest scum-busting advice.

✔ A sizable percentage of all the files available over file-sharing networks is infected. Although the number is nowhere near what the recording industry would have you believe, infected files do exist in droves. You should always scan a downloaded file with your antivirus software before opening it.

✔ Trading copyrighted material is illegal unless the copyright holder specifically waives his rights. But the number of people sued for downloading files is orders of magnitude smaller than the number of people sued for making files available. If you live on a university campus, that may be a moot point — some schools have gone to extraordinary lengths to keep their networks from melting down — so make sure you understand the real rules before you P2P.

✔ The quality of audio, and especially video, recording runs the gamut. If you download the latest episode of *Star Wars* the day before it officially opens, you can expect to get a copy created with a handheld digital camcorder and a pencil-eraser microphone, with lots of shots of the backs of heads and background chatter in a language you don't understand.

You can keep up with the latest news and rumors in the P2P world at the Slyck News site, www.slyck.com. It's a big, fast-moving topic.

If you decide to try file sharing just a little bit, make sure that you follow the advice in this chapter (or from some other reputable source, such as Slyck News) to keep from getting zapped. No, you can't trust the manufacturer's Web site to tell the whole story.

Choosing a P2P Network

Peer-to-peer file sharing gets its weird name from the way connected computers talk to each other. Instead of one computer holding all the files and other computers downloading files from the central computer, peer-to-peer networks rely on computers connected to the Internet to hand files to each other. Each computer that wants to join a P2P network has to rely on some coordination, at the very least to find one other computer on the network. (Some networks have more advanced coordination.) After an initial connection is established, computers can connect to each other automatically, and files can flow without any intervention by a central authority.

Each P2P network runs inside the Internet: At any given moment, on the most popular networks, more than 5 million computers are talking to each other, sharing a billion files. Five networks carry the bulk of the traffic. You need to choose a P2P program that interacts with the network you want to use:

✔ The **BitTorrent** network specializes in large files — movies, TV shows, and the like. BitTorrent (`www.bittorrent.com`) software breaks up large files into small pieces, each of which can be located on a different machine. Very fast, very popular.

✔ The **eDonkey** network also handles large files well but offers a much greater diversity of files, with eDonkey2000 (`www.edonkey2000.com`) and eMule (`www.emule-project.net`) being the most popular programs.

✔ A small but highly regarded — and fast — network called **WPNP3** is the sole provenance of WinMX (`www.winmx.com`).

✔ The **FastTrack** network links computers running KaZaA (`www.kazaa.com`), long a target of scumbusting software. FastTrack has been eclipsed by eDonkey and BitTorrent. Similar but incompatible networks run Grokster (`www.grokster.com`) and iMesh (`www.imesh.com`), both of which have had their share of scum, too.

✔ The **Gnutella** (and **Gnutella2**) network, created by the same people who made the original Winamp media player, works with many of the best-known P2P programs, including BearShare (`www.bearshare.com`, watch for scum alerts), LimeWire (`www.limewire.com`; older versions had scumware problems, but recent ones are much better), and other programs you don't want to deal with.

Shareaza (`www.shareaza.com`) and MLDonkey (`www.mldonkey.org`), both excellent programs, connect to the Gnutella2, BitTorrent, and eDonkey networks.

It's important that you download these programs *only* from their respective sites. Some unscrupulous scum manufacturers build a wrapper around the more popular P2P programs and offer their own versions, hoping you'll install their scum.

You can safely choose from any of these programs. Personally, I use both BitTorrent and WinMX (when I can't find what I want on BitTorrent). But that's just me.

Downloading and Installing BitTorrent

BitTorrent contains a built-in bias to carrying the latest, most popular files. It's almost a congenital defect: Less-popular files disappear from the network quickly.

On the flip side, BitTorrent rates as the fastest (and most popular) peer-to-peer network for large files. It was designed from the ground up to share big, big files. Currently, BitTorrent carries the lion's share of peer-to-peer traffic on the Internet.

Downloading and installing BitTorrent is a piece of cake:

1. **Point your favorite browser at `www.BitTorrent.com` and click the appropriate button to download the Windows "client."**

2. **Run the downloaded `.exe` file.**

   BitTorrent has a very rudimentary installer, which requires no interaction. When the installer's done, it presents you with the message: "BitTorrent has been successfully installed! To use BitTorrent, visit a Web site which uses it and click on a link."

   You are transported to BitTorrent's home page, where you are asked to make a donation. Leave the page open for a bit. You may be most impressed.

   Unlike most other P2P programs, BitTorrent doesn't maintain a list of files that you can download. Instead, you have to go out and find them yourself. You can use a Web search engine like Google to find BitTorrent files that interest you, or you can rely on one of thousands of sites that list files.

3. **Run the query bittorrent grateful dead through Google and then click one of the Google links. Alternatively, you can start with the list of completely "legit" files at `http://bt.etree.org` (see Figure 22-1) or go looking for lists of sites at places like `http://Link2u.tk`.**

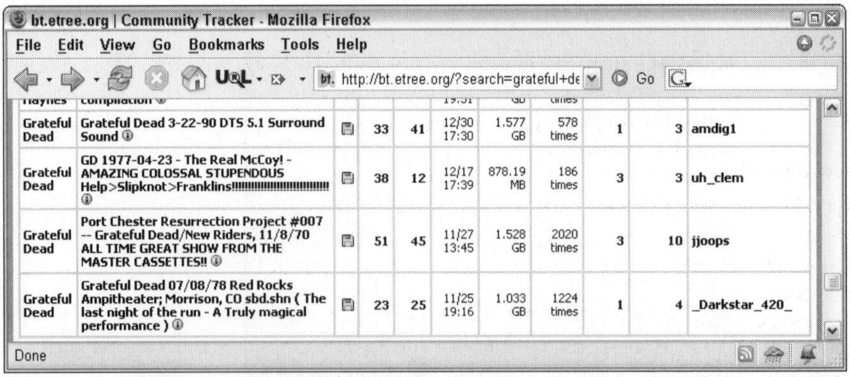

Figure 22-1: bt.etree.org is a good place to start because all of its files are "legit."

You see lots and lots of hits on Google. The list sites actually point to other sites which, in turn, have the files. There's a huge world of BitTorrent files out there.

4. When you find a file you want to download, click the file's name or (depending on the site) click the Download button next to the file's name.

Windows Firewall pops up a security alert like the one shown in Figure 22-2.

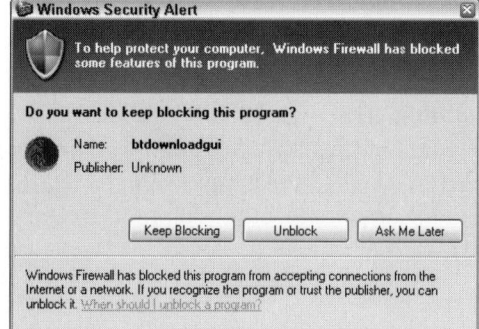

Figure 22-2: BitTorrent wants to listen for incoming files.

5. Click Unblock to let BitTorrent accept messages that are directed to it over the Internet.

Windows Firewall allows one specific program — btdownloadgui.exe — to accept incoming messages.

Your Web browser asks if it's OK to let BitTorrent open the .torrent file you clicked (see Figure 22-3). The .torrent file doesn't contain the music or the movie. Instead, it contains something like a pointer to the music or the movie. BitTorrent knows how to sort it all out.

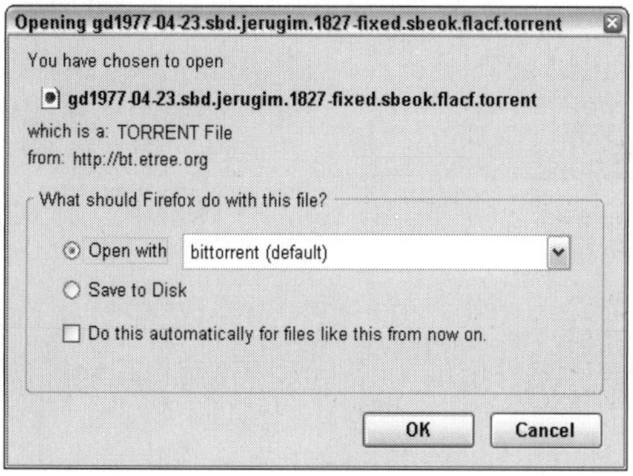

Figure 22-3: Make sure that the browser connects BitTorrent with the file.

6. **Make sure that the browser knows that it should use BitTorrent to open the file and then click OK.**

BitTorrent begins downloading the file.

If nothing happens, you may have to "unstick" a firewall port. Look at `http://PortForward.com` for help. Or, if you want to try a different approach, check out `www.winmx.com` for a P2P program that manages to coexist with Windows Firewall.

7. **When BitTorrent finishes downloading your file, there's a message that says, "Done, share ratio: X%, will seed indefinitely."**

8. **Leave BitTorrent running.**

The longer you can leave BitTorrent running, the higher your rating, and the faster your future downloads. What goes around comes around, eh? Unless there's a major security gaffe, other computers can only download BitTorrent files.

Finding Files in All the Wrong Places

This chapter scratches only the surface of all the ways to find, download, and possibly share, files. Your other options:

✔ **Newsgroups:** Anything you can find with P2P, you can find on an Internet newsgroup. Unfortunately, reconstructing files from newsgroup postings is a nontrivial exercise, requiring special software (much of which is free) and a little bit of time (but maybe not as much as searching eDonkey). On the bright side, the RIAA can't monitor your IP address while you're downloading, and there's no moral obligation to stay connected to add to the community bandwidth. For a comprehensive introduction to downloading files from the newsgroups, see `www.slyck.com/ng.php`.

✔ **MP3 search engines:** I talk about two cheap MP3 Web sites in Chapter 20. Many, many more sites offer less comprehensive collections. Yes, you can use Google to search for MP3 files and sites (just click the line that says Advanced Search). But no, Google doesn't go out intentionally looking for MP3s. Some sites do. My favorite: WinMP3 Locator (`www.winmp3locator.com`).

✔ **Google:** Looking for a specific kind of picture? Google has a great picture finder, Google Images. (No, you won't find music or video here, but images are files, too.) Tell Google to turn off its filters. From the main image page (`images.google.com`), click the line on the right that says Advanced Image Search. Under Safe Search, click the button that says No Filtering. Then give image search a try. *Now* you know why they needed a filter, eh?

Chapter 23

Getting Games to Work

. . . .

In This Chapter

▶ Wreaking the most havoc from your PC

▶ Knowing which Hacks and mods to avoid

▶ Getting around Windows Firewall

▶ Troubleshooting the troublesome DirectX

▶ Getting your hardware in gear

. . . .

*Y*ou might think that giant AutoCAD drawings, engineering simulations, and massive number-crunching applications would demand the most from a PC.

You'd be right. Running games on a PC doesn't take the same amount of resources as, say, designing a nuclear reactor. But games come close.

How much is enough? Well, how long is a string? I take a look at both questions, metaphorically at least, in this chapter.

The Gamer's Conundrum

You know you need the fastest, greatest, bestest hardware to run those new computer games, right? Well, maybe yes and maybe no. Fact is, games vary greatly both in the minimum amount of oomph that's necessary to get the game going and in the kind of horsepower you really need to get into it.

There's a Web site that'll usually tell you, at least theoretically, if your hardware will run a specific game. You need to understand from the get-go that this site is a Microsoft marketing tool. Although the games offered for sale come from many different companies, and the site itself sits on the Futuremark domain (Futuremark is best known for its PCMark and 3DMark benchmarking tools), the Windows XP Game Advisor is a bona-fide member of Windows Marketplace. Game manufacturers pay Microsoft to have their products listed on the site, as do hardware manufacturers trying to peddle their latest wares and retail outlets trying to sell the games themselves.

Here's how to use the Windows XP Game Advisor:

1. Start Internet Explorer.

Firefox won't work. This is Microsoft land, even if the Web address may lead you to think otherwise.

2. Go to `http://ccon.futuremark.com/gameadvisor/service/advisor.jsp`.

The Game Advisor lets you choose among many popular games.

3. Pick a game and click Will It Run on My Computer?

Follow the instructions to install an ActiveX control and then let the Advisor examine your system. If it doesn't crash (see Figure 23-1), you see a report like the one shown in Figure 23-2.

Figure 23-1:
Windows XP Game Advisor has more than its fair share of problems.

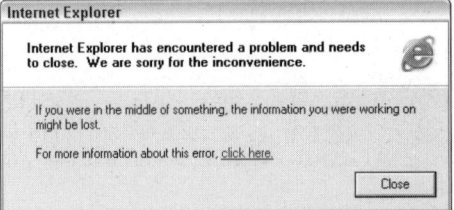

Figure 23-2:
The verdict — complete with extensive advertisements.

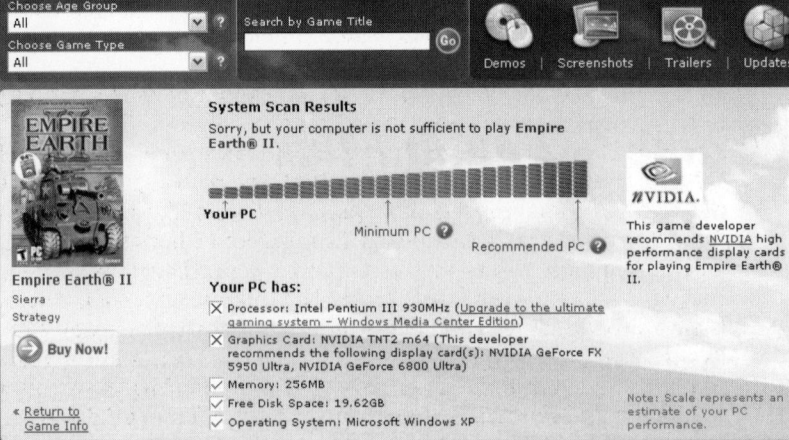

4. **Take the results with a grain of salt.**

   Sometimes the recommendation makes no sense at all (see Figure 23-3), but usually any glaring deficiencies in graphics hardware or memory get highlighted. Look for X's in the boxes. Don't worry about the color slider at the top.

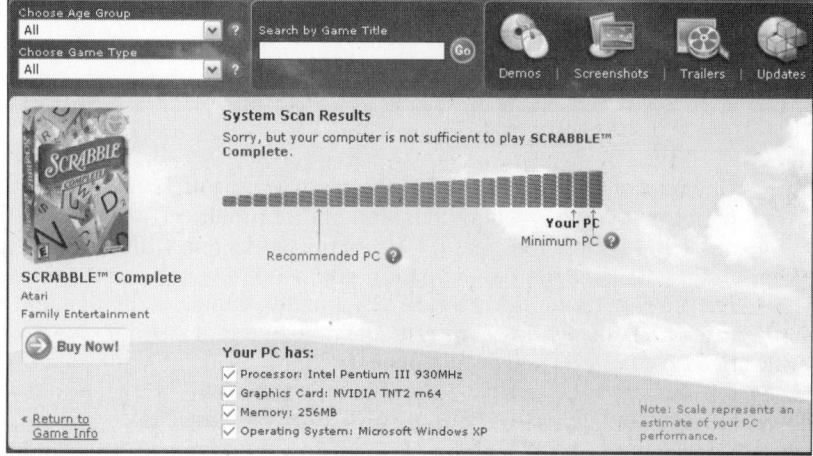

Figure 23-3:
Take the results with a grain of salt.

5. **If your computer isn't up to snuff, make the recommended changes to your hardware and run the Advisor again *before* buying the game.**

   Sometimes it's hard to tell if a new graphics card, in particular, meets the manufacturer's minimum requirements.

A personal tale of woe. If you buy a game and it doesn't work on your computer, *you* may be the loser. I bought a copy of Doom 3 the day it hit the stands, thinking that it would work on my late-model fancy Toshiba Satellite. When it wouldn't run, I contacted Activision tech support. They took me through a laborious series of steps, over several days, before concluding that my video card wasn't up to snuff. I took Doom 3 back to the retailer and asked for a refund. No luck; no refunds on open boxes. I asked Activision if they would give me a refund. Nope. The folks at Activision acknowledged that their hardware requirements list on the box starts by saying "3D Hardware Accelerator Card Required" — no problem for my system — but then pointed to the fine print at the bottom, which says Doom 3 will only run on certain ATI Radeon and nVidia GeForce video chips. ATI and nVidia manufacture the lion's share of high-performance video chips these days, but my Satellite didn't make the grade.

Zapping Windows services

I keep reading online and in various books that serious gamers should go into Windows and disable certain programs — services — that run when Windows starts up.

Sorry, but I don't buy it. There may be one or two services that a gamer doesn't need, but the amount of overhead consumed by a service doesn't put a fraction of a dent in the performance of your computer. Monkeying around with services is a sure way to make Windows less stable. Don't do it.

One part of your machine that the tests won't touch: the refresh rate on your monitor. If you have an old-fashioned CRT monitor (the bulky kind) that was made in the past five years, it probably works fine with all the new games. But if you use a flat-panel display, you need to watch out for the screen refresh rate (pixel refresh rate). Fast action games really demand a refresh rate of 8 milliseconds (or better, if you can find it). Otherwise those blasted demons' innards smear *and* pixelate. Not a pleasant sight.

Given a choice, use DVI connectors, both on your video card and on the monitor. They really are faster and do make a difference in "the gaming experience" (oh, how I hate that phrase!). If either your video card or your monitor has only analog connectors, don't worry about it.

For the retro audience: If you're trying to get an old DOS game to run on that fancy Windows XP computer of yours, take heart — others have stepped in it, too. If you have problems, start with DOSBox (`http://dosbox.sourceforge.net`), an open-source, free solution to many a VOGONS (Very Old Games on New Systems) curse.

Getting Ahead in Games

So you're on the seventeenth level of Doom 6, and you can't figure out how to release the Raster Blaster from the Handsome Hand of Hannibal without getting swarmed by Inky Incubus Intestines?

Hey, that's what Google is for.

Want the easiest, fastest way to crack through a tough spot in a game? Forget shelling out $20 for the official game guide. Go to Google, type the name of the game, and then type:

✔ **walkthrough** to see sites with descriptions of every nook and cranny in the game (see Figure 23-4). Good walkthroughs get updated frequently as players learn about more hidden secrets.

✔ **cheats** or **codes** to get sites that list codes you can type into the game to give you unlimited lives; add money to your stash; allow you to walk through walls; or (best) hop into god mode, where you're invincible.

✔ **news** to get the lowdown on the latest patches and hacks.

Figure 23-4:
Fan sites include every conceivable detail about the games.

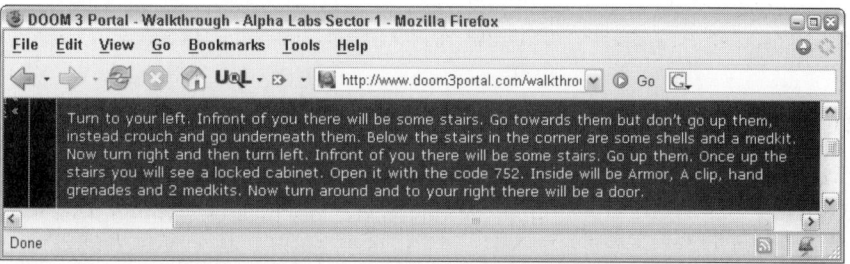

Things change fast in the PC game industry, and rumors fly like banshees in the night. The best ongoing source of the latest reliable gaming information is Neowin's gamer's news, at `http://neowin.net/index.php?category= gamers`.

Sometimes the manufacturer's Web site includes worthwhile tips, but Justin (my son, who's an expert on such things) swears he'd Google first and hit the official sites last.

Troubleshooting Hardware Problems

In my experience, something like 80 percent of all game problems turn out to be video driver problems (see the next section). And most of the remaining 20 percent can be blamed on audio drivers.

What's a hacker to do? First and foremost, you need to make sure you have the latest video and audio drivers. Although general-purpose Windows users shouldn't change a video driver unless it's absolutely necessary, gamers need to stay on the bleeding edge — even if it means their spreadsheets smear as they scroll. Some things are more important than numbers, right?

When in doubt, check your driver. Table 23-1 lists the major video chip manu-facturers, their boards, and where to find the latest drivers.

Table 23-1	Video Driver Locations	
Video Chip	*Board Manufacturers*	*Driver Site*
ATI	All-In-Wonder; Radeon; Rage	`http://support.ati.com/ics/support/default.asp?deptID=894`
nVIDIA	GeForce; nForce; Quadro; RIVA	`www.nvidia.com/content/drivers/drivers.asp`
Intel	Standard on many new machines	`http://downloadfinder.intel.com`
XGI	Volari	`www.xgitech.com/sd/sd_download.asp`

Sound drivers are hard to nail down simply because there are so many manufacturers and so many audio cards. The best general approach goes like this:

1. **Click Start, right-click My Computer, click Properties, click the Hardware tab and, at the top, click the Device Manager button.**

   Windows brings up Device Manager, which I talk about in Chapter 13.

2. **Double-click Sound, Video and Game Recorders.**

   Rummage around in the list and you should be able to make out the name or model of your sound card and the manufacturer's name.

3. **Click OK twice to get out of Device Manager.**

4. **Run a Google search on the manufacturer and model.**

   You should be able to find the latest driver there.

Surviving the DirectX Experience

When a video card doesn't work, the problem almost always lies with Microsoft's fast video-rendering program, DirectX. Not that DirectX is at fault, mind you — video card driver programmers are notorious for pushing DirectX beyond the limits.

Fortunately, Microsoft has a program that you can run to test your system's compliance with DirectX. It's hidden a bit, but you can run it this way:

1. **Choose Start⇨Run, type** dxdiag, **and press Enter.**

   The DirectX Diagnostic Tool asks if it's okay to connect to Microsoft and download the latest database of officially certified hardware drivers.

2. Click Yes.

You see the DirectX Diagnostic Tool main screen, as shown in Figure 23-5.

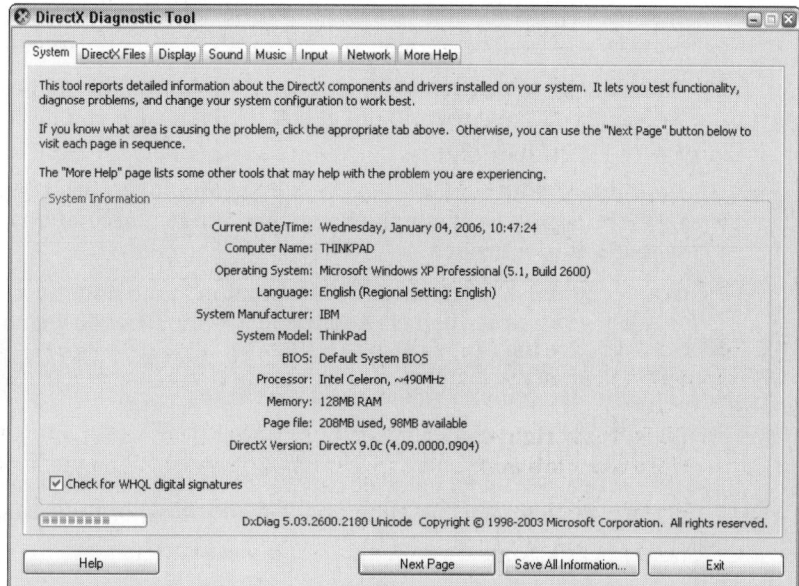

Figure 23-5:
The
information
page of the
DirectX
Diagnostic
Tool.

3. Check the DirectX version number, near the bottom of the System Information box.

Many games require specific versions of DirectX. DirectX 9.0b rates as the most common low-water mark, but some games require DirectX 9.0c, and others aren't nearly as picky. In Figure 23-5, Duangkhae's computer runs DirectX 9.0c. At least in theory, that should suffice for games that require DirectX 9.0, DirectX 9.0b, or DirectX 9.0c.

4. At the bottom, click Next Page.

In fact, the DirectX Diagnostic Tool doesn't go on to the next page; it just "clicks" the next tab. Never mind.

5. At the bottom, in the box marked Notes, see if the DirectX Diagnostic Tool found any problems with the internal DirectX files. If so, you should download the latest version of DirectX and install it directly.

Usually DirectX updates come along for the ride when you update your video driver, but in some cases that isn't good enough. Microsoft keeps the latest version of DirectX at www.microsoft.com/windows/directx/default.aspx.

6. **Click Next Page again.**

   You see the Display tab.

7. **Click the Test DirectDraw button.**

   The DirectX Diagnostic Tool takes you through a series of tests. You need to tell the tool whether the proper designs appeared on the screen.

8. **Make a note of any problems listed at the bottom in the box marked Notes. If you have a problem, check to make sure you have the latest video driver installed.**

9. **Continue in this vein — click Next Page and then click the Test button (if there is one) to check the hardware. Make a note of any problems listed in the Notes box.**

10. **When you finish, click Save All Information at the bottom, save the diagnostic text file, and then click Exit to leave the DirectXDiagnostic Tool.**

    If you have problems with DirectX, a tech support person at your video or audio card company may need that file.

If you get any weird error messages in a game, copy down the precise message (yes, use a pen and a piece of paper). Then run a Google search on the text of the message, enclosing it in quotes. For example, if you run this through Google:

```
doom "The current video card driver combination does not
          support the necessary features"
```

you can go to many different sites that describe the precise problem and how to solve it.

Part VII
The Part of Tens

"Now, when someone rings my doorbell, the current goes to a scanner that digitizes the audio impulses and sends the image to my PC where it's converted to a Pict file. The image is then automated, compressed, and sent via high-speed modem to an automated phone service that sends me an e-mail message back to tell me someone was at my door 40 minutes ago."

In this part . . .

Yes, you *can* fiddle with your Registry. It isn't that hard. You won't crash your machine, make Windows flop around like a glob of gelatin on your kitchen floor, or increase the national debt. Just follow a few simple rules, and you'll be fine. I show you how.

Once you feel comfortable with the Registry, I have ten really cool hacks that I saved for the end of the book. Some of them may actually speed up your computer. Really.

Chapter 24

Ten Steps to Mastering the Registry

In This Chapter

▶ Understanding how the Registry hangs together

▶ Backing up all of the Registry

▶ Backing up the part that you're about to hopelessly screw up

▶ Making changes safely

▶ Fixing the stuff you hopelessly screw up

*T*he Registry is a deep, dark, scary place loaded with secret settings that can make your computer turn on a dime — run at least *twice* as fast as it does now — but if you make one wrong move, you'll tie up Windows so badly it'll never run again.

Okay. I'm pulling your leg.

The Registry is a cesspool of inconsistent, poorly documented (and in many cases completely nonsensical) settings that you can occasionally change to some benefit. You shouldn't make random changes to the Registry just to see what happens, but if you exercise even a modicum of care, you shouldn't have any problems at all.

The most inscrutable part of the Registry? The incredibly stupid terminology. Only the Registry could have a "value" that's really a variable (or a "key" in Registry parlance) and "value data" that's really just a value. But I digress.

In this chapter, I break down all the basics you need to know to modify the Registry into ten steps, each as simple as they can be. Steps 1 through 3 walk you through a few concepts you need to understand before you fiddle with the settings. After you're familiar with those, you can skip to Steps 4 through 10, which you can use to tweak any Registry value.

Understanding the Registry's Anatomy

The Windows Registry has been around for a long, long time, and nobody's tried to maintain any consistency. As a result, it looks like my son's bedroom, with so much stuff scattered hither and yon, it makes you wonder what "hither" and "yon" really mean.

You may have heard that the Registry's a big database full of Windows and program settings, but that isn't the whole story. The Registry gets assembled from a bunch of different places, with some pieces pulled in from your hardware, other pieces built on the fly, some drawn in from hidden system files, and still others updated constantly by timers and counters. You can go in and change some of the Registry settings, but part of the Registry just can't be changed (or if you do change it, Windows just changes it back).

Before you start working with the Registry, it helps to understand the main ways in which its somewhat twisted mind works. The following sections help untangle that mess for you.

Step 1: Understand how the Registry is like Windows Explorer

The Registry stores settings in *keys,* much like Windows stores data in folders that you can navigate using Windows Explorer. Here are the main ways in which the Registry is like Windows Explorer:

- Keys may have other keys and settings inside, just as folders may have other folders and files inside. It's a very simple and effective storage system.

- *Regedit,* the Registry Editor, helps you move down and down through the keys, finally arriving at the key or setting you need, just like Windows Explorer helps you move down through folders until you get to the folder or file that you need.

- You can add or delete keys in Regedit; you can add or delete folders in Windows Explorer.

- When you delete a key in Regedit, you delete all the keys and settings underneath the key. Ditto for deleted folders, subfolders, and files in Windows Explorer.

It isn't a perfect analogy, though — Regedit and Windows Explorer are different in some very fundamental ways. For example, when you delete a key in Regedit, it's gone for good; no fairy godmother or Recycle Bin stands ready to help if you mess up. You can move a folder in Windows Explorer, but you can't move a key in Regedit. And so on.

Step 2: Know the five high-level keys

The Registry has five *high-level keys* (shown in Figure 24-1), which, in turn, hold all the lower-level keys. (Microsoft occasionally calls the high-level keys *root keys* or *predefined keys*.) The five keys have long names, but everybody uses the common abbreviations shown in Table 24-1.

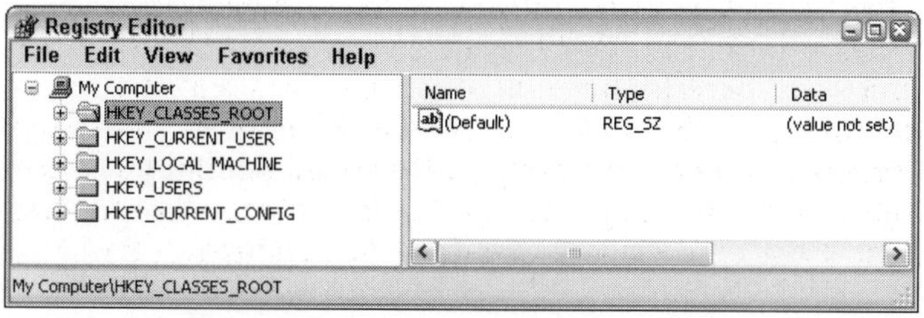

Figure 24-1:
The
Registry's
five high-
level keys.

Table 24-1	Abbreviations for the Five High-Level Keys
Abbreviation	*The "Real" Name*
HKCR	HKEY_CLASSES_ROOT
HKCU	HKEY_CURRENT_USER
HKLM	HKEY_LOCAL_MACHINE
HKU	HKEY_USERS
HKCC	HKEY_CURRENT_CONFIG

Step 3: Recognize the different data types

When you go spelunking in the Registry, you invariably want to change a value, whether it's adding a new value, or changing or deleting an existing one. Occasionally, you want to add a new key, but you almost always deal with values.

Every value in the Registry has a *name* and *data*. (I hate the terminology, and I bet you find it confusing, too. But it's the "official" jargon, so I use it here.) For example, in Figure 24-2, the second Google Desktop Search value has a *name* of `bandsite_git_cookie` and *data* of `0x0000d300` (which is a hexadecimal number equal to 54,016 in decimal). You can also tell from Figure 24-2 that the number is a DWORD data type, which is programmer's lingo for a 32-bit number.

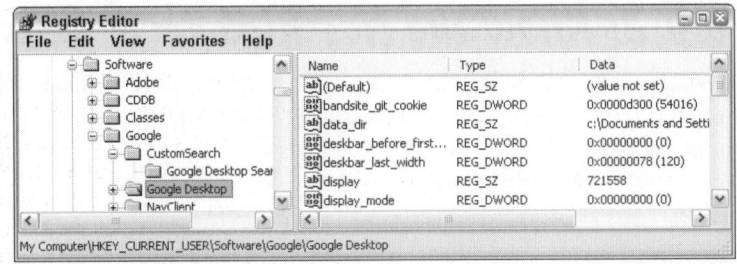

Figure 24-2:
Several
Google
Desktop
Search
values.

When you change a value or add a new value, you have to be careful to get the right data type. Table 24-2 lists the kinds of data that commonly appear in the Registry.

It's important to realize that the programmers who built Windows (and other programs that store data in the Registry) chose the data types that they wanted to use when they created their programs. When you change something in the Registry, be careful not to change the data type. If you do, the program will probably stop working. If you find a hack that requires you to add a new key to the Registry, make sure you follow the instructions precisely and use the data type that Windows expects.

Table 24-2	Common Registry Data Types	
Data Type	**Official Name**	**This Data Type . . .**
Strings	REG_SZ	Can contain letters, numbers, odd characters, just about anything. The length of a string can change at any time. Programmers love to work with strings in the Registry because they're hard to mess up.
Double Word	REG_DWORD	Is a 2-word (= 4-byte = 32-bit) integer between 0 and 4,294,967,295 in decimal or 00 00 00 00 and FF FF FF FF in hexadecimal. When programmers want to work with a number that isn't going to get huge, they usually choose a DWORD. Regedit lets you work with DWORDs in decimal, so you don't need to translate into hex. Thank goodness.

Data Type	Official Name	This Data Type ...
Binary	REG_BINARY	Is a lot like a DWORD except the binary number can be of any length. Many programmers store strings as Binary fields. Why? Because they think that way. Bizarre. You have to be very careful when working with Binary values so you don't change the length of the value. If you change the length, Windows (or the program) may not know how to interpret whatever you changed.

Running an Example

In this chapter, to show you how to make a simple change in the Registry, I go through the steps necessary to tell Windows Explorer to sort things alphabetically. That may sound a bit weird, but it isn't.

Windows XP uses a very strange method for sorting filenames. For example, if you have five files with the names `Pic22.jpg`, `Pic3456.jpg`, `Pic5.jpg`, `Pic56.jpg`, and `Pic7.jpg`, most programs sort the files and present them to you in this sequence:

```
Pic22.jpg
Pic3456.jpg
Pic5.jpg
Pic56.jpg
Pic7.jpg
```

That's a typical alphabetical sorting, and it's what most computer users expect. Starting with Windows XP, though, Windows Explorer shows the files in this order:

```
Pic5.jpg
Pic7.jpg
Pic22.jpg
Pic56.jpg
Pic3456.jpg
```

Some people find the new behavior helpful. I, for one, find it maddening. You can change it. If you follow the example in this chapter, you force Windows Explorer to revert to its old, more alphabetic ways.

Step 4: Create a Restore Point

Some people suggest that you back up the Registry before you start making changes. I think it's smarter to set an entire Windows Restore Point. Why? It's easier to undo your changes by rolling back to the Restore Point — and if your system crashes, you can bring back the old Registry settings by using the "Last Known Good" option when you boot (see "Step 10: Recover if things go bump," later in this chapter).

To create a Restore Point:

1. **Choose Start⇨All Programs⇨Accessories⇨System Tools⇨System Restore.**

   The System Restore Wizard appears.

2. **Select the Create a Restore Point radio button and then click Next.**

   The wizard asks for a name for the Restore Point so you can get back to the right point if you need to (see Figure 24-3).

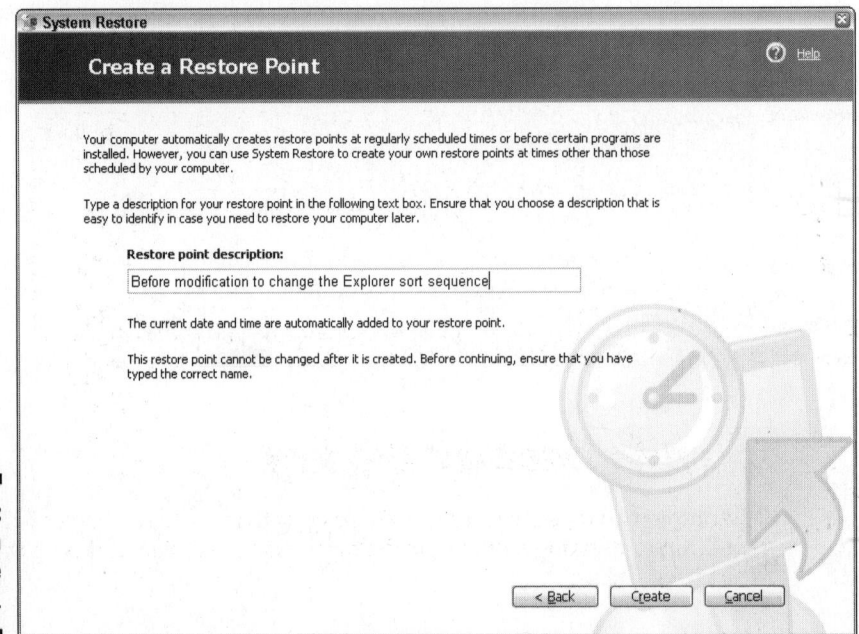

Figure 24-3:
Pick a descriptive name.

3. **Give the Restore Point a name you'll remember and then click Create.**

   The System Restore Wizard can take an eternity, but when it's done, it says, "Restore Point Created" and gives you the date and time.

4. **Click Close.**

   You now have a fully functional System Restore Point.

Windows XP saves Restore Points for 90 days or until it runs out of room.

Step 5: Find the key

So you've decided that you want to change a Registry key or value. You trust that the person who suggested the change knows what she's talking about, and you're ready to take the plunge. Fair enough.

Start by finding the key:

1. **Choose Start➪Run, type** regedit, **and press Enter.**

   The Registry Editor starts.

2. **On the left side, double-click down the tree until you get to the key you want.**

   In the example for this chapter, I double-click down to `HKEY_CURRENT_USER\Software\Microsoft\Windows\CurrentVersion\Policies\Explorer` (see Figure 24-4).

Figure 24-4:
The key that controls Windows Explorer's sort sequence.

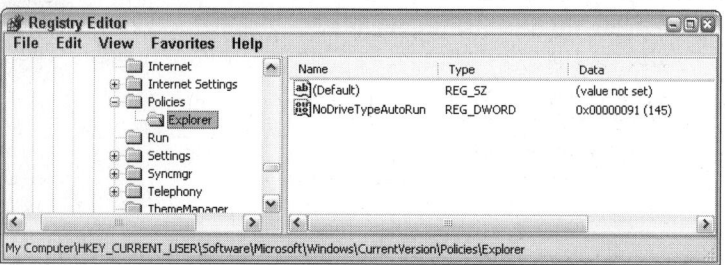

Step 6: Back up the key

Before you change a key, I strongly suggest that you back it up. (This is in addition to creating a full Restore Point, which I explain earlier in this chapter.) Here's how:

1. **Click once on the key you want to back up.**

   In this case, I click the key Explorer on the left.

2. **Click File⇨Export.**

   Regedit brings up the Export Registry File dialog box and asks you to give the Registration (*.reg) file a name.

3. **Choose a location for the backup file, type a name you will remember, such as, oh,** Original Explorer Settings Before Changing Sort Order, **and click Save.**

   Regedit puts all the current Registry entries under the key you have chosen in a text file and stores it in the location you specify.

Step 7: Change, add, or delete a value

When you go to change the data, you can change an existing value, add a new value, or delete a value.

The example in this chapter requires a new value, rather than changing an old one. So if you're following the example, just jump to "Adding a new value (or key)," later in this section. To be thorough, I show you how to change and delete values, too.

Changing an existing value

I show you how to change values by working with an existing value, called NoDriveTypeAutoRun. Here's how:

1. **To bring up an existing value so you can change it, double-click the value name. For example, in Figure 24-4, double-click NoDriveTypeAutoRun.**

   Because NoDriveTypeAutoRun is a DWORD value, Regedit brings up the Edit DWORD Value dialog box, shown in Figure 24-5.

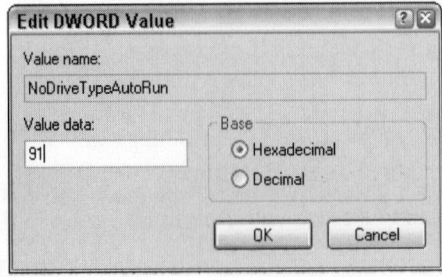

Figure 24-5: Edit DWORD value data.

You can view DWORD value data in either hexadecimal or decimal by clicking the corresponding button in the Base box. *Decimal,* or base 10, is the number system we humans use all the time. *Hexadecimal* (usually called *hex*), or base 16, resembles the way numbers are stored inside the computer. Most people find decimal much less vexing than hex. Say you want to change a Registry setting for the number of minutes Windows should wait between attempts to synchronize its clock. If you click decimal and type 120, Windows knows to wait two hours between sync attempts. But if you work in hex, you enter the number 78 — which is the hexadecimal equivalent of 120. Avoid confusion: Use decimal.

2. Make any changes you want to make to the value data and then click OK.

In the example in this chapter, you don't want to make any changes, so click Cancel and the Registry escapes unscathed.

Binary data values (see Figure 24-6) — which is to say, Registry values in the binary data type — have to be adjusted very, very carefully. You can delete or type new data either on the left (in hex) or on the right (which shows the ASCII value of the hex). Watch closely and make sure that you don't make the new value data longer or shorter than the original. For details on identifying the different types of data types, see "Step 3: Recognize the different data types," earlier in this chapter.

Figure 24-6:
Make sure
you don't
make Binary
Value Data
longer or
shorter.

Edit Binary Value	
Value name:	
fuse_data	
Value data:	

```
0000  2D E5 62 31 41 E3 2E BF   -åb1Aã.¿
0008  BD 1D 3A 37 0E 77 9E 06   ½.:7.w..
0010  38 2A 86 82 B7 4C A1 1D   8*...Lí.
0018  0E 5C 2B AF 43 DF 4E 0B   .\+¯CßN.
0020  87 92 72 93 40 84 A6 37   ..r.@.¦7
0028  C8 87 B0 B1 86 4A 30 BF   È.°±.J0¿
0030  EF A1 1E B3 34 64 77 1B   ï¡.³4dw.
0038  DB 84 19 ED 63 18 CE 1E   Û..íc.Î.
0040
```

[OK] [Cancel]

Deleting a value

To delete a value:

1. Click the value name in the Registry Editor.

2. Right-click the value name and choose Delete.

Rocket science.

Adding a new value (or key)

If you need to add a new value, as opposed to changing an existing one, the process is quite simple (And if you're following my example to make Windows XP list files alphabetically, these are the steps you need):

1. **Right-click the key that will hold the new value, click New, and then select the type of value you need (String, Binary, DWORD, Multi-String, or Expandable String).**

   In this chapter's example, I need a new DWORD value under the Explorer key called NoStrCmpLogical. So, on the left in Figure 24-4, I right-click Explore and choose New⇨DWORD Value.

   Regedit creates a new value of the chosen type with a dummy name (see Figure 24-7) and puts it under the indicated key.

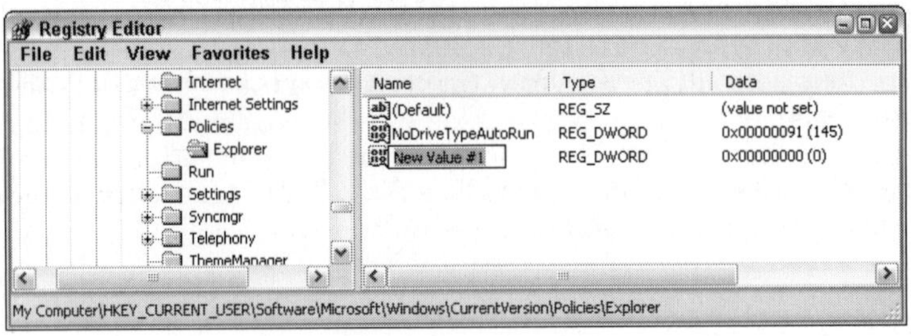

Figure 24-7:
A new
DWORD
value.

2. **Immediately type the new value name.**

   If you click someplace else before typing in the new name, Regedit sticks with the name New Value #1. To change the name, right-click New Value #1 and choose Rename.

   In this example, I type **NoStrCmpLogical**.

3. **Press Enter twice.**

   The first Enter changes the name. The second Enter brings up the edit dialog box for the value. In Figure 24-8, I bring up the Edit DWORD Value dialog box for NoStrCmpLogical.

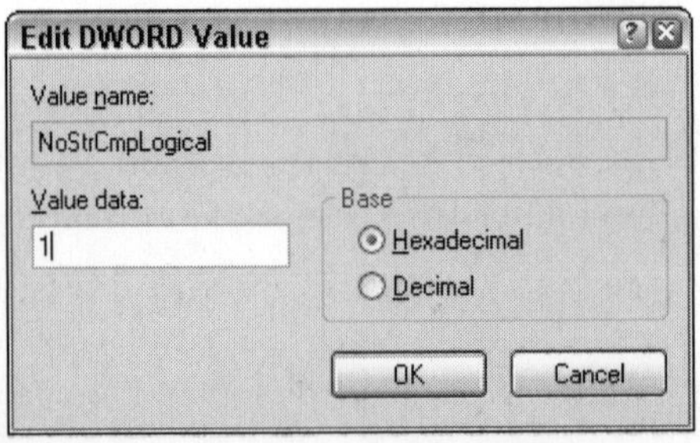

Figure 24-8:
New value
data of 1
(which is
the same in
hex and
decimal).

4. Enter the value data and click OK.

In this example, I set the value data to **1**.

Your new value is safely stored in the Registry.

Some Registry values don't really need value data: the mere fact that a certain value name (or even key name) exists is sufficient for the program to know what to do. In those cases, don't bother changing the default value data.

To add a new key, you follow a nearly identical procedure. Navigate to the key that will get the new key underneath it. Right-click the parent key and choose New➪Key. Give it a name, and you have a new key that's every bit as "legit" as any other key in the Registry.

Step 8: Get out of the Registry

The Registry's kind of like Hotel California. You can check out, but you can never leave.

To check out of Regedit, choose File➪Exit. Regedit fades away, but the Registry is still there, controlling your Windows destiny.

Step 9: Make Windows accept the change

Sometimes Windows "takes" Registry changes immediately. In the example in this chapter, if you simply start Windows Explorer after making the Registry change, you see files sorted in the "alphabetical" order, the way Mother Nature intended, as shown in Figure 24-9.

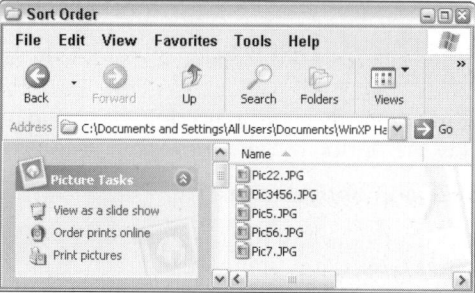

Figure 24-9:
Mirable dictu,
Windows
now sorts
properly.

Most of the time, though, you need to log off of Windows (Start➪Log Off➪ Log Off) and log back on.

Occasionally — rarely, in fact — you have to restart your computer for the Registry changes to kick in. You know the drill: Start➪Turn Off Computer➪ Restart.

Step 10: Recover if things go bump

After you make a change to the Registry, check to make sure that your change took effect, of course, but also keep your eyes open for weird side effects.

If the change didn't do what you wanted, you can get rid of it quickly by just double-clicking on the backup file you created (see "Step 6: Back up the key," earlier in this chapter). That pretty much restores the whole key to its original state. (I say "pretty much" because there can be some subtle changes that don't come unglued when you double-click the stored .reg file.) You may have to log off and log back on for the old key to take effect.

If the .reg file doesn't bring Windows back to its original state, try rolling Windows back to your manual Restore Point. Choose Start➪All Programs➪ Accessories➪System Tools➪System Restore and choose Restore My Computer to an Earlier Time. Running a System Restore rolls back the Registry to its earlier state in its entirety.

If Windows won't let you get at System Restore, or your system completely crashes and burns, DON'T PANIC! Here's how to recover:

1. **Turn off your computer completely. Pull the plug out of the wall or remove its still-beating heart . . . er, pull out its battery, if you have to.**

2. **Wait 30 seconds and turn it back on again.**

   Your computer starts running its low-level routines, lists the display driver, and probably starts counting memory.

3. ***Before* Windows comes up with its first screen, press F8.**

   It doesn't hurt to press F8 every couple of seconds after the memory countdown appears on screen.

   You may see a Windows Advanced Options menu or you may see a list of alternatives, including the option to boot into Safe Mode.

4. **Choose Last Known Good Configuration.**

   Windows automatically rolls back to the previous Restore Point and starts. Your change gets tossed out in the wash.

Chapter 25

Ten Speed-Up Hacks — Maybe

*I*n my experience, Registry hacks purporting to speed up your computer make great headlines, draw plenty of Web traffic, sell a lot of books and magazines — not to mention software — but in the end don't do much. Sound and fury, you know?

Everyone would like to believe that The Really Mean People at Microsoft have hobbled Windows XP, and if one or two bits get flipped in the right places, their machines will suddenly run 50 percent faster.

Ain't gonna happen. Not even 5 percent faster.

I have dozens of Registry hacks in this book that will speed up your computer — a little bit. TweakUI handles most of them, very easily.

This chapter contains my ten favorite speed-up hacks that aren't described elsewhere in this book. The first two don't involve monkeying directly with the Registry; the last eight require a dance with the devil Regedit. Some of them may work for you. Give the list a glance and tinker away....

Performance Versus Pizzazz

That gorgeous Windows XP interface — the pretty face you work with every day — consumes a considerable amount of processing power. If you're willing to work with a slightly, uh, ugly version of Windows, you can speed things up noticeably:

1. **Click Start, right-click on My Computer, choose Properties, click the Advanced tab, and at the top in the Performance box, click Settings.**

   Windows shows you the Performance Options dialog box, shown in Figure 25-1.

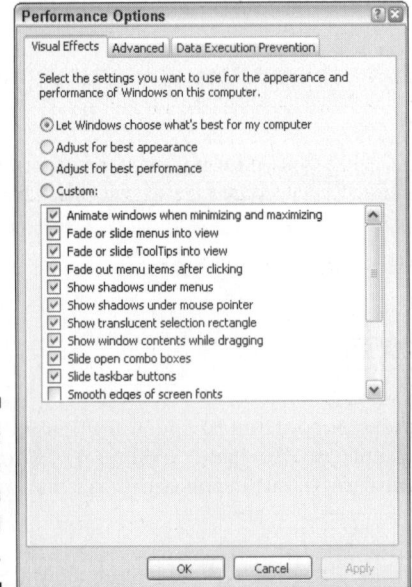

2. **Uncheck boxes next to the visual effects that you're willing to forgo in pursuit of speed.**

   The Windows default is to check all of the boxes except Smooth Edges of Screen Fonts.

3. **When you're happy with your selections, click OK twice to return to Windows.**

   Try your new settings for a while. With a few exceptions (documented in this Part of Tens!), I bet you'll hate them, and the speed boost won't be nearly as much as you expected. If you want to see Windows' pretty face again, go back to Step 1 and turn everything on.

Intel Application Accelerator

If you have an Intel processor, there's a truly outstanding utility from Intel that speeds up the way the processor talks to hard drives. It's called the Intel

Application Accelerator, and it's so good that there are only two questions you need to ask:

✔ **Do I already have it?** Windows XP Service Pack 2 is supposed to install IAA, but you should take a minute to check.

✔ **Can your Intel processor use it?** Unfortunately, IAA doesn't work for every processor.

Here's how to find out if you already have IAA installed. This only works with Intel processors. If you don't have "Intel inside" don't bother.

1. **Click Start, right-click My Computer, choose Properties, click the Hardware tab and, in the Device Manager box, click the Device Manager button.**

   Windows shows you Device Manager (see Figure 25-2).

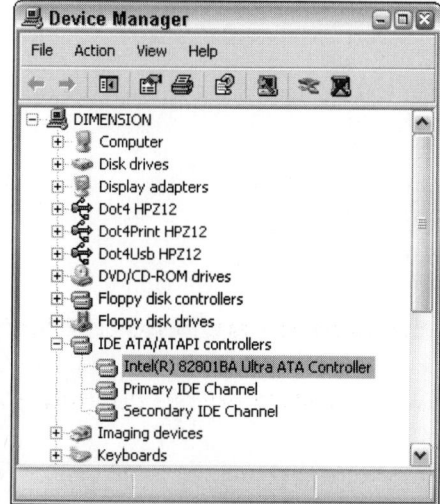

Figure 25-2:
Look for
your IDE
controller.

2. **Click the + sign next to IDE ATA/ATAPI Controllers and then look for an entry that says Intel(r) 82801xx Ultra ATA Controller. (xx can be AA, AB, BA, or CAM.)**

   If you don't have an 82801xx controller, you can't use IAA. Skip down to the next tweak.

3. **Double-click the Intel 82801xx Ultra ATA Controller and, in the resulting dialog box (which can take a while to appear), click the Driver tab and then the Driver Details button.**

4. **If you see IdeBusDr.sys listed (as in Figure 25-3), you already have IAA, and you can skip to the next tweak.**

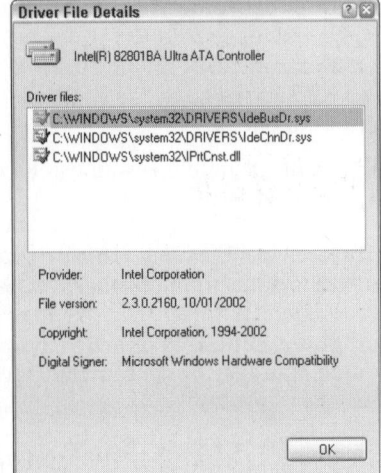

Figure 25-3:
This
computer
already
has IAA
installed.

If you don't have IAA, it's worth taking ten minutes right now to install it.

Next, you need to find out what Intel chipset is on your computer and whether that chipset can run IAA. Here's how:

1. **Go to** `www.intel.com/support/chipsets/inf/sb/CS-009266.htm` **and download** `ChipUtil.exe`, **the Intel Chipset Identification Utility.**

   You need to identify your operating system (Windows XP, of course) and accept a terms-of-use agreement before downloading.

2. **Double-click** `ChipUtil.exe` **to run it.**

   The Chipset Identification Utility shows you what kind of chip you're using (see Figure 25-4).

Figure 25-4:
Positive
identification
of the chip.

3. **Compare the chip number with the list of IAA-supported chips at** `www.intel.com/support/chipsets/iaa/sb/CS-009312.htm`.

   If your chip isn't on the list, you can't use IAA. Skip to the next tweak.

If you discover that you don't have IAA installed, but you do have a chip that can use IAA, head over to www.intel.com/support/chipsets/iaa and follow the instructions to download and install IAA.

Big Memory Virtual Speedup

If you have 1GB of memory or more, you should tell Windows to stop paging drivers and certain system programs out to disk. The speed gains won't be much, but changing things won't hurt: There's no need for Windows to put those programs out to pasture.

To tell Windows to keep those programs in memory:

1. **Follow the steps in Chapter 24 to back up the Registry and bring up Regedit.**

2. **Navigate to the key** HKLM\System\CurrentControlSet\Control\ Session Manager\Memory Management.

3. **On the right, double-click the value name DisablePagingExecutive and change the value data to 1. Click OK.**

4. **Choose File⇨Exit to get out of Regedit.**

   You need to restart your computer for the change to take effect.

Bypassing Zip Space-Saving Calculations on Cleanup

If you use Windows' Disk Cleanup routine much at all, you can save yourself a lot of time with this Registry tweak.

Disk Cleanup scans your hard drive to see where and how you can save space — delete temporary files, empty the Recycle Bin, and so on. Unfortunately, a Disk Cleanup scan can take forever because Disk Cleanup also looks at files that you haven't used recently and calculates how much space you could save if you zipped those files.

To see what I mean, run Disk Cleanup:

1. **Choose Start⇨My Computer, right-click a hard drive, and choose Properties.**

   Windows shows you the Properties dialog box for the hard drive.

2. **Click Disk Cleanup.**

   The cleanup routine picks up some of its information quickly but then runs — and runs and runs — while scanning all the older files on your drive (see Figure 25-5).

3. **When Disk Cleanup (finally!) finishes, click Cancel twice to leave without changing anything.**

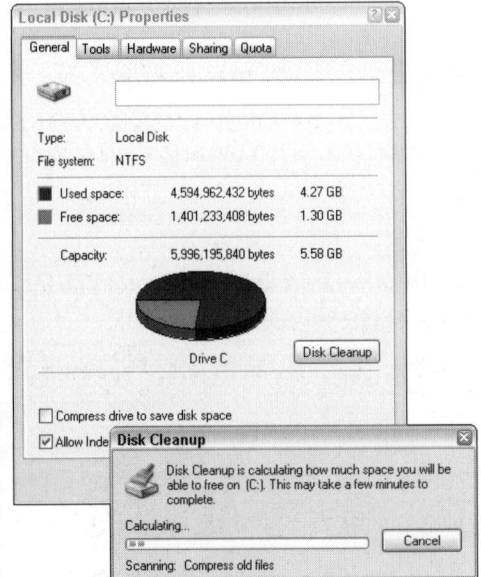

Figure 25-5:
The slow side of Disk Cleanup.

A simple Registry change tells Disk Cleanup to skip checking old files for their squishability. Here's how:

1. **Follow the steps in Chapter 24 to back up the Registry and start Regedit.**

2. **Navigate to the key HKLM\Software\Microsoft\Windows\Current Version\Explorer\VolumeCaches\Compress Old Files.**

   It's an odd key. See Figure 25-6.

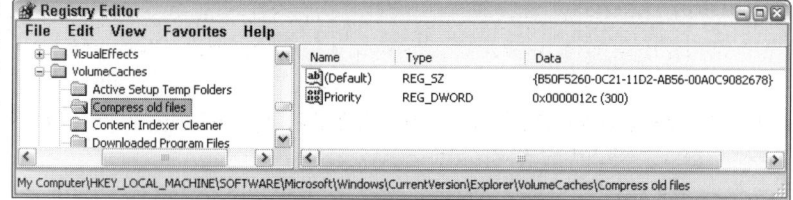

Figure 25-6:
The key that
controls
Disk
Cleanup's
squishing
scan.

3. **Follow the instructions in Chapter 24 to export the key.**

   That way, if you ever change your mind, you can restore Windows to its original behavior by double-clicking on the saved .reg file.

4. **On the right, double-click (Default).**

   Regedit shows you an Edit String dialog box.

5. **Delete everything in the Value Data box and then click OK.**

6. **Choose File⇨Exit to get out of Regedit.**

   You need to log off and then log back on to your computer for the change to take effect.

Forget Creating Old-Style Names for Folders

I don't like this hack, but you might find it useful. Back in the not-so-good old DOS days, every file had an "8.3" name, consisting of a maximum of eight characters, followed by a period, followed by a maximum of three characters. (Truth be told, even Windows 3.1 was similarly hobbled.)

Windows has maintained backward compatibility since the days of the pterodactyls, storing an 8.3 filename along with the "real" long filename on hard drives, just in case an older program needed the short name.

A Registry hack can prevent Windows from storing 8.3 filenames on NTFS disks. It's supposed to save a little bit in disk overhead. I can't recall the last time I used a program that required an 8.3 filename, but it's hard for me to imagine that the amount of time saved is worth the potential conflict.

Anyway, if you want to take the plunge:

1. **Follow the steps in Chapter 24 to back up the Registry and get Regedit going.**

2. **Navigate to the key `HKLM\System\CurrentControlSet\Control\FileSystem`.**

3. **On the right, double-click the value name NtfsDisable8dot3NameCreation and change the value data from 0 (the default) to 1. Click OK.**

4. **Choose File➪Exit to get out of Regedit.**

   Restart your computer for the change to take effect.

Stop "Sharing" Scheduled Tasks

I found this hack to have a very tiny effect on how quickly I could connect to shared folders and printers on other computers. Some people say it speeds up their network connections greatly. Your, uh, results may vary.

The story: When you connect to another computer on your network, Windows lets you get at shared folders, and you can also get at shared printers and the Scheduled Tasks folder. That way, at least in theory, you can change Scheduled Tasks on any computer from any other computer on the network. Supposedly, connecting to the Scheduled Tasks folder slows things down, so if you tell Windows that you don't want to share your Scheduled Tasks folder, network access to your computer should speed up.

That's the story. Here's how to turn off access to Scheduled Tasks:

1. **Follow the steps in Chapter 24 to back up the Registry and start Regedit.**

2. **Navigate to the key `HKLM\Software\Microsoft\Windows\CurrentVersion\Explorer\RemoteComputer\NameSpace`. Double-click NameSpace.**

3. **Right-click {D6277990-4C6A-11CF-8D87-00AA0060F5BF} and choose Delete.**

4. **Choose File➪Exit to get out of Regedit.**

   Restart your computer for the change to take effect.

Change Location of Event Logs

If you have two hard drives, this Registry tweak should speed things up a little bit, but mostly it'll give Windows enough room for its Event Log files so you can hold onto many days' worth of data without fear of losing anything important.

As I explain in Chapter 13, Windows maintains three Event Log files, one each for the system, security, and applications. By default, they're clipped at 512KB each: If your system generates more events than will fit in the allocated space, the oldest event gets the heave-ho.

To move the Event Logs to a different drive, and give them more room:

1. **Follow the steps in Chapter 24 to back up the Registry and start Regedit.**

2. **Navigate to the key** `HKLM\System\CurrentControlSet\Services\EventLog\System.`

3. **On the right, double-click the value name File.**

   Regedit brings up an Edit String dialog box for the value (see Figure 25-7).

Figure 25-7: Change the location of the System Event Log.

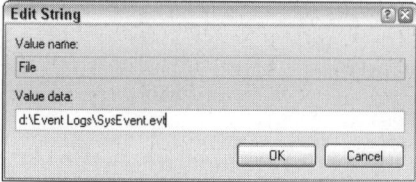

4. **Change the value data to the new location for the System Event Log file. Click OK.**

   For example, you might put the System Event Log in `d:\Event Logs\SysEvent.evt`, as in Figure 25-7.

5. **Repeat Steps 3 and 4 for** `HKLM\System\CurrentControlSet\Services\EventLog\Security.`

   That changes the location of the Security Events Log, `SecEvent.evt`.

6. **Repeat Steps 3 and 4 one last time for** `HKLM\System\CurrentControlSet\Services\EventLog\Application.`

   That changes the location of the Application Events Log, `AppEvent.evt`.

7. **To adjust the maximum size of any or all of the Event Log files, follow the steps at the beginning of Chapter 13 to put Administrative Tools on the Start menu and then click Start⇨Administrative Tools⇨Event Viewer.**

    Windows shows you the Event Viewer, as described in Chapter 13.

8. **Right-click Application and choose Properties.**

    You see the Application Properties dialog box, shown in Figure 25-8.

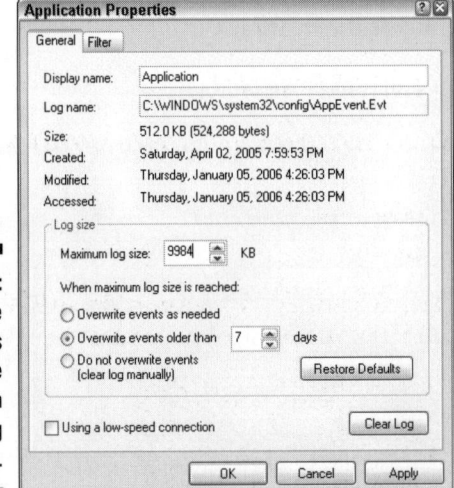

Figure 25-8: Change settings for the Application Event Log here.

9. **Adjust the size of the Application Event Log file in the Maximum Log Size box.**

    As a practical matter, keep each under 100MB.

10. **Repeat Steps 8 and 9 for the Security Event Log.**

11. **Repeat Steps 8 and 9 for the System Event Log.**

12. **Choose File⇨Exit to leave Event Viewer.**

    Restart your machine for the changes to take effect.

Tweaking Communication Settings

Windows fanatics love to debate the pros and cons of Registry tweaks. Communications fanatics love to debate the pros and cons of communications settings. Put the two together, and the air positively curdles with debates — and the jargon runs thicker than mud.

Fortunately, there's a program that goes into your machine, extracts the information it needs, asks you a couple of very simple questions, and then twiddles all of the appropriate Registry bits to optimize Internet access on your machine. It works on dial-up. It works on cable. It works on DSL. Best of all, TCP Optimizer from SpeedGuide.net is free.

For example, there's a key setting called Max MTU that needs to be adjusted so the packets you send out are as long as possible without getting chopped up into smaller packets by another program along the way. You can run a program that sends packets and tells you if they got chopped and then try to zero in on the maximum MTU. Or you can just let TCP Optimizer do the work for you.

Here's how to download and run TCP Optimizer:

1. **Go to `http://speedguide.net/downloads.php` and click to download TCP Optimizer.**

2. **Double-click `TCPOptimizer.exe`.**

   There is no installer. It just runs. Great!

   You see the TCP Optimizer main window, shown in Figure 25-9.

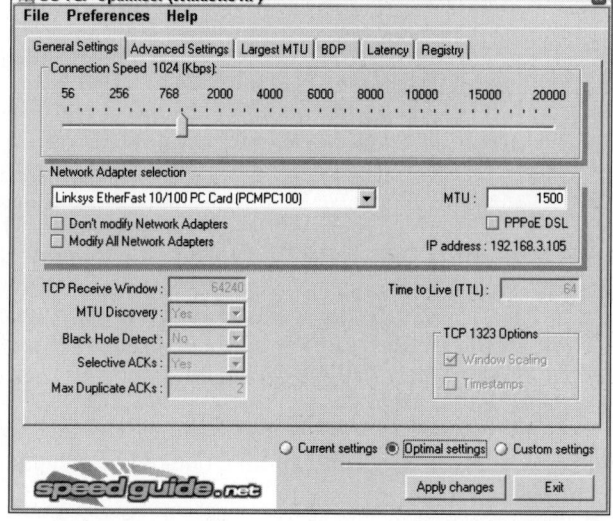

Figure 25-9:
TCP
Optimizer
changes a
slough of
Registry
settings in
one fell
swoop.

3. **At the bottom, click the Optimal Settings button.**

4. **At the top, adjust the slider to match your (real) Internet connection speed.**

5. **If you use DSL, you may or may not use PPPoE (which is a weird acronym for a common DSL connection). Check the documentation for your DSL modem. If you can confirm that you use PPPoE, check the box marked PPPoE DSL.**

6. **Click Apply Changes.**

   TCP Optimizer comes back with a dialog box that asks whether you want to apply the changes.

7. **Click OK and then click Yes to reboot your computer.**

   The changes take effect after you reboot.

Communications people talk funny. If you want to dig into TCP Optimizer — a tremendously powerful and interesting program — wade through the FAQ at www.speedguide.net/faq_in.php?category=100.

Removing Negative DNS Cache Entries

This tweak saved my butt once. It actually slows Windows down just a touch but makes sure that you get through to a Web site as soon as it's available. So in that respect, it speeds things up. Makes sense?

You probably know that the name you type into Firefox, like www.dummies.com, has to be translated into a weird set of four numbers, like 208.215.179.139, before Firefox can make a connection with the Web site. Translating addresses that you and I can read into numbers (called IP addresses) that make sense on the Internet is the job of a Domain Name Server.

Windows XP keeps a table, called a *DNS cache,* to help speed things up. The first time you type www.dummies.com, Windows XP retrieves the IP address from the Internet and stores both in the DNS cache. The second time you type www.dummies.com, Windows can bypass the lookup on the Internet and just go straight to 208.215.179.139. It's slick and effective. (If you've ever heard of the Windows HOSTS file, that's something different. The contents of HOSTS get loaded into this internal DNS cache, but you can't dig into or open up the cache, as you can HOSTS.)

When you type www.dummies.com into Firefox, one of two things happens:

✔ **Firefox finds the IP address for** www.dummies.com. In that case, the two addresses get stored in the DNS cache, and they're kept there for one day. That's called a *positive response*.

✔ **Firefox doesn't find the IP address for** www.dummies.com. In that case, the failure is noted in the DNS cache, too, and for the next 15 minutes, every time you type www.dummies.com, Windows simply says the address can't be found. It doesn't try to look for the address. It just gives up, without trying. That's called a *negative response*.

The problem arises when a Web site goes up and down, or if a Web site gets overloaded and it times out, just once. As long as the DNS cache has an entry saying "this site is out to lunch for the next 15 minutes," you can't get through, no way, no how. It isn't a question of, say, pressing F5 or Shift+F5 and forcing Firefox to go to the site and reread what's there. You can't even get to the site.

Fortunately, there's a way to tell Windows that you only want it to hold onto its negative DNS cache entries for a minute or — better — to not keep negative DNS cache entries at all. Here's how:

1. **Follow the steps in Chapter 24 to back up the Registry and start Regedit.**

2. **Navigate to the key** HKLM\ SYSTEM\CurrentControlSet\Services\ Dnscache\Parameters. **Click once on Parameters.**

3. **Choose Edit⇨New⇨DWORD Value.**

   Regedit comes up with a new value called, uh, New Value #1.

4. **Immediately type** MaxNegativeCacheTtl **to give the new value that bizarre name (see Figure 25-10).**

   If you forget and click somewhere else before you type in the new value name, right-click New Value #1 and choose Rename.

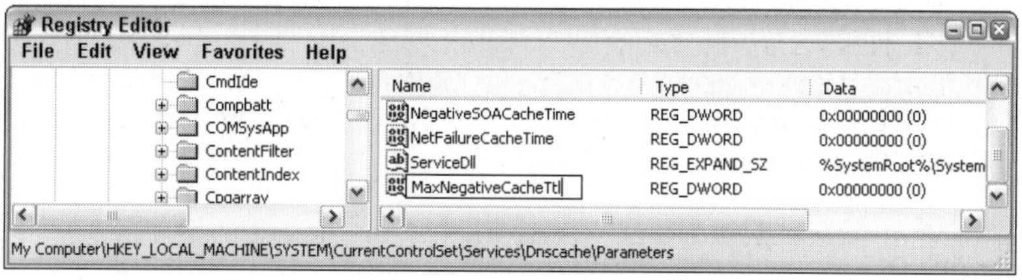

Figure 25-10:
Naming the new value.

5. **Press Enter twice and give MaxNegativeCacheTtl new value data. Click OK.**

   The number you type in the Value Data box is interpreted as seconds: type 60 to keep negative DNS cache entries for a minute or, better, leave it at zero to ensure Windows doesn't even store negative DNS cache entries.

6. **Choose File⇨Exit to get out of Regedit.**

   You need to reboot for your changes to take effect.

Really Speed Up Windows XP

Really want to speed things up?

- ✔ If you have less than 512MB of memory, buy more memory.
- ✔ If you have anything less than 2 Mbps Internet download speed, get a faster connection.

Those two improvements, unsexy though they may be, will do more to speed up Windows XP than all the tips in all the books, magazines, and Web sites.

Index

• G •

• H •

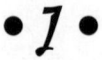

• *Z* •

BUSINESS, CAREERS & PERSONAL FINANCE

0-7645-5307-0

0-7645-5331-3 *†

Also available:

- Accounting For Dummies †
  0-7645-5314-3
- Business Plans Kit For Dummies †
  0-7645-5365-8
- Cover Letters For Dummies
  0-7645-5224-4
- Frugal Living For Dummies
  0-7645-5403-4
- Leadership For Dummies
  0-7645-5176-0
- Managing For Dummies
  0-7645-1771-6

- Marketing For Dummies
  0-7645-5600-2
- Personal Finance For Dummies *
  0-7645-2590-5
- Project Management For Dummies
  0-7645-5283-X
- Resumes For Dummies †
  0-7645-5471-9
- Selling For Dummies
  0-7645-5363-1
- Small Business Kit For Dummies *†
  0-7645-5093-4

HOME & BUSINESS COMPUTER BASICS

0-7645-4074-2

0-7645-3758-X

Also available:

- ACT! 6 For Dummies
  0-7645-2645-6
- iLife '04 All-in-One Desk Reference
  For Dummies
  0-7645-7347-0
- iPAQ For Dummies
  0-7645-6769-1
- Mac OS X Panther Timesaving
  Techniques For Dummies
  0-7645-5812-9
- Macs For Dummies
  0-7645-5656-8

- Microsoft Money 2004 For Dummies
  0-7645-4195-1
- Office 2003 All-in-One Desk Reference
  For Dummies
  0-7645-3883-7
- Outlook 2003 For Dummies
  0-7645-3759-8
- PCs For Dummies
  0-7645-4074-2
- TiVo For Dummies
  0-7645-6923-6
- Upgrading and Fixing PCs For Dummies
  0-7645-1665-5
- Windows XP Timesaving Techniques
  For Dummies
  0-7645-3748-2

FOOD, HOME, GARDEN, HOBBIES, MUSIC & PETS

0-7645-5295-3

0-7645-5232-5

Also available:

- Bass Guitar For Dummies
  0-7645-2487-9
- Diabetes Cookbook For Dummies
  0-7645-5230-9
- Gardening For Dummies *
  0-7645-5130-2
- Guitar For Dummies
  0-7645-5106-X
- Holiday Decorating For Dummies
  0-7645-2570-0
- Home Improvement All-in-One
  For Dummies
  0-7645-5680-0

- Knitting For Dummies
  0-7645-5395-X
- Piano For Dummies
  0-7645-5105-1
- Puppies For Dummies
  0-7645-5255-4
- Scrapbooking For Dummies
  0-7645-7208-3
- Senior Dogs For Dummies
  0-7645-5818-8
- Singing For Dummies
  0-7645-2475-5
- 30-Minute Meals For Dummies
  0-7645-2589-1

INTERNET & DIGITAL MEDIA

0-7645-1664-7

0-7645-6924-4

Also available:

- 2005 Online Shopping Directory
  For Dummies
  0-7645-7495-7
- CD & DVD Recording For Dummies
  0-7645-5956-7
- eBay For Dummies
  0-7645-5654-1
- Fighting Spam For Dummies
  0-7645-5965-6
- Genealogy Online For Dummies
  0-7645-5964-8
- Google For Dummies
  0-7645-4420-9

- Home Recording For Musicians
  For Dummies
  0-7645-1634-5
- The Internet For Dummies
  0-7645-4173-0
- iPod & iTunes For Dummies
  0-7645-7772-7
- Preventing Identity Theft For Dummies
  0-7645-7336-5
- Pro Tools All-in-One Desk Reference
  For Dummies
  0-7645-5714-9
- Roxio Easy Media Creator For Dummies
  0-7645-7131-1

* Separate Canadian edition also available
† Separate U.K. edition also available

Available wherever books are sold. For more information or to order direct: U.S. customers visit www.dummies.com or call 1-877-762-2974.
U.K. customers visit www.wileyeurope.com or call 0800 243407. Canadian customers visit www.wiley.ca or call 1-800-567-4797.

SPORTS, FITNESS, PARENTING, RELIGION & SPIRITUALITY

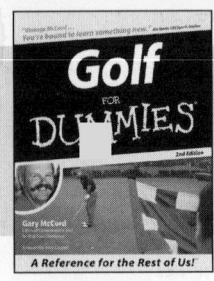

0-7645-5146-9

0-7645-5418-2

Also available:

- Adoption For Dummies
  0-7645-5488-3
- Basketball For Dummies
  0-7645-5248-1
- The Bible For Dummies
  0-7645-5296-1
- Buddhism For Dummies
  0-7645-5359-3
- Catholicism For Dummies
  0-7645-5391-7
- Hockey For Dummies
  0-7645-5228-7

- Judaism For Dummies
  0-7645-5299-6
- Martial Arts For Dummies
  0-7645-5358-5
- Pilates For Dummies
  0-7645-5397-6
- Religion For Dummies
  0-7645-5264-3
- Teaching Kids to Read For Dummies
  0-7645-4043-2
- Weight Training For Dummies
  0-7645-5168-X
- Yoga For Dummies
  0-7645-5117-5

TRAVEL

0-7645-5438-7

0-7645-5453-0

Also available:

- Alaska For Dummies
  0-7645-1761-9
- Arizona For Dummies
  0-7645-6938-4
- Cancún and the Yucatán For Dummies
  0-7645-2437-2
- Cruise Vacations For Dummies
  0-7645-6941-4
- Europe For Dummies
  0-7645-5456-5
- Ireland For Dummies
  0-7645-5455-7

- Las Vegas For Dummies
  0-7645-5448-4
- London For Dummies
  0-7645-4277-X
- New York City For Dummies
  0-7645-6945-7
- Paris For Dummies
  0-7645-5494-8
- RV Vacations For Dummies
  0-7645-5443-3
- Walt Disney World & Orlando For Dummies
  0-7645-6943-0

GRAPHICS, DESIGN & WEB DEVELOPMENT

0-7645-4345-8

0-7645-5589-8

Also available:

- Adobe Acrobat 6 PDF For Dummies
  0-7645-3760-1
- Building a Web Site For Dummies
  0-7645-7144-3
- Dreamweaver MX 2004 For Dummies
  0-7645-4342-3
- FrontPage 2003 For Dummies
  0-7645-3882-9
- HTML 4 For Dummies
  0-7645-1995-6
- Illustrator CS For Dummies
  0-7645-4084-X

- Macromedia Flash MX 2004 For Dummies
  0-7645-4358-X
- Photoshop 7 All-in-One Desk Reference For Dummies
  0-7645-1667-1
- Photoshop CS Timesaving Techniques For Dummies
  0-7645-6782-9
- PHP 5 For Dummies
  0-7645-4166-8
- PowerPoint 2003 For Dummies
  0-7645-3908-6
- QuarkXPress 6 For Dummies
  0-7645-2593-X

NETWORKING, SECURITY, PROGRAMMING & DATABASES

0-7645-6852-3

0-7645-5784-X

Also available:

- A+ Certification For Dummies
  0-7645-4187-0
- Access 2003 All-in-One Desk Reference For Dummies
  0-7645-3988-4
- Beginning Programming For Dummies
  0-7645-4997-9
- C For Dummies
  0-7645-7068-4
- Firewalls For Dummies
  0-7645-4048-3
- Home Networking For Dummies
  0-7645-42796

- Network Security For Dummies
  0-7645-1679-5
- Networking For Dummies
  0-7645-1677-9
- TCP/IP For Dummies
  0-7645-1760-0
- VBA For Dummies
  0-7645-3989-2
- Wireless All In-One Desk Reference For Dummies
  0-7645-7496-5
- Wireless Home Networking For Dummies
  0-7645-3910-8

0-7645-6820-5 *†

0-7645-2566-2

Also available:
- Alzheimer's For Dummies
  0-7645-3899-3
- Asthma For Dummies
  0-7645-4233-8
- Controlling Cholesterol For Dummies
  0-7645-5440-9
- Depression For Dummies
  0-7645-3900-0
- Dieting For Dummies
  0-7645-4149-8
- Fertility For Dummies
  0-7645-2549-2

- Fibromyalgia For Dummies
  0-7645-5441-7
- Improving Your Memory For Dummies
  0-7645-5435-2
- Pregnancy For Dummies †
  0-7645-4483-7
- Quitting Smoking For Dummies
  0-7645-2629-4
- Relationships For Dummies
  0-7645-5384-4
- Thyroid For Dummies
  0-7645-5385-2

DUCATION, HISTORY, REFERENCE & TEST PREPARATION

0-7645-5194-9

0-7645-4186-2

Also available:
- Algebra For Dummies
  0-7645-5325-9
- British History For Dummies
  0-7645-7021-8
- Calculus For Dummies
  0-7645-2498-4
- English Grammar For Dummies
  0-7645-5322-4
- Forensics For Dummies
  0-7645-5580-4
- The GMAT For Dummies
  0-7645-5251-1
- Inglés Para Dummies
  0-7645-5427-1

- Italian For Dummies
  0-7645-5196-5
- Latin For Dummies
  0-7645-5431-X
- Lewis & Clark For Dummies
  0-7645-2545-X
- Research Papers For Dummies
  0-7645-5426-3
- The SAT I For Dummies
  0-7645-7193-1
- Science Fair Projects For Dummies
  0-7645-5460-3
- U.S. History For Dummies
  0-7645-5249-X

Get smart @ dummies.com®

- **Find a full list of Dummies titles**
- **Look into loads of FREE on-site articles**
- **Sign up for FREE eTips e-mailed to you weekly**
- **See what other products carry the Dummies name**
- **Shop directly from the Dummies bookstore**
- **Enter to win new prizes every month!**

† eparate Canadian edition also available
eparate U.K. edition also available

ailable wherever books are sold. For more information or to order direct: U.S. customers visit www.dummies.com or call 1-877-762-2974.
. customers visit www.wileyeurope.com or call 0800 243407. Canadian customers visit www.wiley.ca or call 1-800-567-4797.